JUNGLE CAMPAIGN

JUNGLE CAMPAIGN

*A Memoir of National Service
in Malaya, 1949–51*

John Scurr

The Book Guild Ltd
Sussex, England

First published 1994 by Owl Press
This edition published by
The Book Guild Ltd.
25 High Street,
Lewes, Sussex

© John Scurr 1994, 1998

Set in Times
Typesetting by
SetSystems Ltd, Saffron Walden, Essex

Printed in Great Britain by
Antony Rowe Ltd, Chippenham, Wiltshire

A catalogue record for this book is
available from the British Library

ISBN 1 85776 343 2

CONTENTS

When I was a youngster gossips would say
When I grew older I'd be a soldier.
Rattles and toys I threw them away
Except a drum and a sabre.
When I was older, as up I grew,
I went to see a grand review.
Colours flying set me dying
To embark on a life so new.

Roll, my merry drums, march away.
Soldier's glory lives in story.
His laurels are green when his locks are grey,
Then hurrah for the life of a soldier!

'Hey for the Life of a Soldier', *T. S. Cooke*
(Song from the Crimean War, 1854–56)

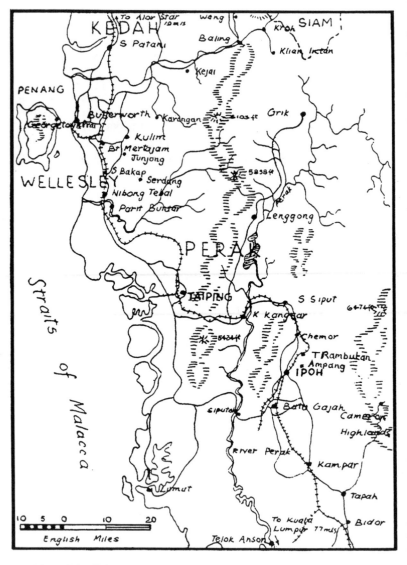

Map of the KOYLI's operational area in North Malaya, 1947–51.

viii

PREFACE TO SECOND EDITION

The first edition of this book was published by Owl Press in 1994 with a modest print of 500 copies. These were principally circulated to former members of my regiment. Some ex-servicemen from other units nonetheless managed to obtain copies and the enthusiastic tone of the letters that they wrote to me convinced me that my book deserved a far wider distribution. With 1998 being the fiftieth-anniversary year of the start of the Malayan Emergency, this would appear to be the ideal time to produce a new edition.

The State of Emergency in Malaya lasted from 16 June 1948 to 31 July 1960. During that period, the brunt of active operations was undoubtedly borne by the Federation of Malaya Police Force and the Brigade of Gurkhas, but the British Army played a conspicuous part in the conflict, while the Malay Regiment plus Australian, New Zealand, East African and Fijian Commonwealth forces also made valuable contributions.

Though the SAS, Marine Commandos and Guards regiments commendably maintained their tough reputations, it is interesting to note that with regard to eliminations of the Communist enemy, the top-scoring 'bandit-hunters' among all the British units were the men of an ordinary infantry regiment of the line – the 1st Battalion, Suffolk Regiment – nearly two-thirds of whose personnel were National Servicemen. The Suffolks in fact killed 181 terrorists for the loss of only 12 of their own men.

The Malayan Campaign was an infantryman's war in which actions were fought by small units, normally less than platoon strength and using only small arms against an enemy similarly armed. Most infantrymen, however, spent little time actually fighting the enemy and a great deal of time struggling through the jungle searching for him. In his most interesting book about the Brigade of Gurkhas, *The Happy Warriors* (The Blackmore Press, 1961), Brigadier A.E.C. Bredin, DSO, MC, rightly takes issue with Colonel F. Spencer Chapman's statement that *The Jungle is Neutral* (Chatto and Windus, 1949). The Malayan jungle was an implacable enemy to the security forces and, as Brigadier Bredin points out, decidedly favoured the Communist terrorists against the soldiers and policemen who sought them in some of the most difficult operational terrain in the world.

If Malaya was an infantryman's war, it is also fair to say that as far as the British Army was concerned, it was very much a National Serviceman's war. Although there are undoubtedly some individuals who are critical of their involvement in the campaign – who always seem to show up on TV documentaries about National Service – I am convinced by my contacts over the years that the majority of ex-NS men are proud of their service in Malaya, and rightly so. But even more worthy, in my opinion, are the regular soldiers who during a normal three-year tour had to tread the jungle paths for twice as long as National Servicemen did. Roy Nixon, a former regular corporal of the Somerset Light Infantry, wrote to me in January 1996: 'It was a long, hard slog. Looking back on those days of carrying 60/70 lbs through the jungle, I sometimes wonder how we survived it. I arrived back in the UK weighing 10 st 2 lbs. My parents hardly recognised me.' I am sure many Malaya veterans, whether regular or National Service, will readily identify with these remarks.

In addition to persons whose assistance is acknowledged in the preface to the first edition, I should also like to thank old comrades Redvers Battersby, Roy Caldecott, Sid Grant, Peter Griffiths, Bill Lyness, Alan Richardson, Ted Slade, Fred Sparkes and Gerry Sweeney for testimonies they have supplied which have enabled me to correct and amplify sections of the book describing actions in which they were participants. I also wish to thank Raymond Bays, Allan Trotter and George Williams for providing extra photographs and the Imperial War Museum for their kind permission to print photographs 2, 9, 21 and 32, plus the illustration on the front cover.

Finally, I would like to express the hope that my book might be regarded as a tribute to all armed forces personnel who served in the jungle campaign.

John Scurr, 16 June 1998,
on the fiftieth anniversary
of the start of the
Malayan Emergency

PREFACE TO FIRST EDITION

This book is based upon a journal that I wrote 40 years ago while serving with the King's Own Yorkshire Light Infantry in Malaya. At that time, the jungle campaign against the elusive, but nonetheless deadly, Communist terrorists was at its height.

Unfortunately, my journal does not adequately tell the whole story. The first entry is dated 25 January 1950, which was the day following my embarkation on a troopship bound for the Far East. Consequently, I have no written record of my first five months of National Service at the Light Infantry Brigade Training Centre in Bordon, Hampshire. Also, while my journal relates many incidents and conversations in considerable detail, lack of time or inclination decreed that other entries were comparatively brief and there were even occasions when I completely omitted events of some interest.

For these reasons I decided to present my story as a memoir, intermixing recorded descriptions with memories of happenings that were not noted down at the time. The early chapters, describing my recruit training, are entirely constructed from memory, but both here and in the greater period covered by my journal, no personal experience or conversation is included which I do not clearly remember. Within this flexible framework I have nonetheless endeavoured to relate most of my experiences in the original wording of my journal.

Any honest account of army life must include the imperfections and injustices as well as the nobler aspects. I hope, however, that former members of my regiment will take no offence from any critical reference and will appreciate – as I'm sure my text makes clear – that after a painful period of adjustment, the proudest and by far the best days of my life were spent in the King's Own Yorkshire Light Infantry.

There are some events described in this book in which I was not a participant. My accounts of these happenings are constructed from details that I heard and noted down at the time, supplemented by the brief reports published in the KOYLI Quarterly Journal, *The Bugle*, and by considerable information recently gleaned from old comrades. Especially helpful in supplying information or photographs were Colonel John Cowley, Regimental Secretary of the Light Infantry Office (Yorkshire), Mrs K. Magill of the Ministry of Defence Records Department, and old comrades John Crisp, Arthur Greenacre, Gordon Hill, Frank Keenan, John Kitchen, Tom Morgan and Jim Preston. I am greatly indebted to them all.

Although I have striven diligently to present the true facts in all cases, I am nonetheless very aware that some former KOYLI soldier may say of some described incident: 'This isn't right. It wasn't Jim Smith – it was Bill Robinson.' While I will naturally regret any such error, I can only give my assurance that I have done all that I can to attain maximum accuracy, checking statements of participants against available records.

In general format, my National Service experiences were no doubt similar to those of thousands of other young men of my generation who were called up into the army and drafted to Malaya, and indeed similar in many respects to the fortunes of soldiers throughout the ages. Yet, no matter how similar, all lived experience is surely unique, just as all human beings are unique. I certainly believe that the core of my story is 'different'.

Additional to a personal memoir of National Service and a concise history of the KOYLI in Malaya, I hope to have presented within these pages a human story of the dreams of youth clashing with harsh reality and struggling to achieve final reconciliation.

John Scurr, 31 August 1991,
on the fortieth anniversary
of my date of discharge
from the army

1

'When I Grew Older I'd be a Soldier'

The year 1949 dawned with me in eager anticipation. I had reached the age of 18 and was due to be called up. Whereas the majority of youths awaiting conscription into the armed forces during those post-war years viewed their pending fate with some dismay, my call-up heralded the fulfilment of my boyhood dreams.

I was born in Edinburgh on 19 January 1931, the youngest of a family of three children. My brother Bill was seven years my senior and my sister Thelma had preceded me by two years. My parents had previously lived in the environs of Newcastle-upon-Tyne, where their fathers had worked together in the shipyards. My father's family, in fact, originated from the Richmond area of the North Riding of Yorkshire and several relatives continued to live in Yorkshire and Tyneside. As a chemist, my father had risen to the position of a branch manager in Scotland's capital city. My mother had been a piano teacher prior to her marriage and remained an excellent pianist.

Of the stresses and strains of family relationships I do not wish to comment, other than to say that I was well into my teens before I had learned to replace anxiety and distress with a calmer, more stoic attitude. My mother was mild-mannered, gentle and consistently kind. She had infinite patience and always seemed intent on keeping the peace rather than fighting back. Yet she appeared to have an inner strength that always carried her through unpleasant or trying situations. I think that in some ways I took after my mother, although in my case inner strength did not manifest itself until after my childhood days.

1

From my earliest years I was fascinated by toy soldiers, model forts and all things military. My very first trip to the cinema with Thelma, at the age of six, to see Shirley Temple in the Hollywood version of Rudyard Kipling's *Wee Willie Winkie* confirmed my resolution to be a soldier when I grew up. Later that year, whilst on a family holiday at my grandparents' home in Neashem, County Durham, I marched across a field with the weight of a shotgun on my small shoulder as a rebuke to a farmworker who had jested that I wasn't big enough to be a soldier and carry a gun.

In all games that I played during my primary school years, either with friends or alone, I was regularly engaged in imaginary battles. The combative zeal of my games, however, was not matched in the real world. I was a rather small, perhaps even delicate, child and although I frequently participated in friendly playground rough-and-tumbles, I nonetheless always avoided situations which might lead to serious bouts of fisticuffs. Considering that I was not physically strong, this may have been very wise! I can still remember the personal and communal fear engendered by local bully-boys who took pleasure in beating up any lad that they found on his own.

On reaching the age of 12, I was the only boy in my class to achieve sufficiently high marks in the Qualifying Examination to merit a place at Boroughmuir Secondary School. Consequently, I was separated from the close friends that I had grown up with. Friendships formed at my new school were fairly superficial, so that during my teens, I tended to be a lone wolf outside school hours, going to the cinema on my own and playing games alone in the house or spending many hours sketching. The subjects of my games and sketches invariably involved either soldiers or pirates. There was never any sign of my developing what might be considered to be more mature interests.

I grew up, of course, during the years of the Second World War, when the national press, radio and cinema newsreels proclaimed in unison that the finest, noblest thing that any human being could do was to put on a uniform and go forth to kill or be killed 'for King and Country'. My generation was raised on patriotism and unquestioning reverence for men-at-arms.

My brother Bill rallied to the nation's call and volunteered for the army when he was 18 years old. A keen rugby player, tough and high-spirited, Bill was quite the opposite to me; yet we were very close. He nearly always treated me with kindness and affection and was generally protective towards me. His arm around my shoulder used to give me a feeling of being safe and secure, which was something that I badly needed during those formative years.

On 21 May 1942, Bill enlisted in the Royal Scots. Eleven months later, having attained the rank of lance corporal, he volunteered again; this time for the Indian Army. He arrived in India on 1 September 1943 and after seven months of instruction at the Officer Training School in Bangalore, he was commissioned into the 3rd Gurkha Rifles as a second lieutenant on 16 April 1944.

In a letter to my mother, Bill described how he led his first patrol into the jungle in Burma. The going was very hard, he said, but he declined the offer of his Gurkha soldiers to carry his pack. He then commented briefly: 'There were Jap patrols out too who we had to fight sometimes.' After that, he never again mentioned active operations in his letters.

On 28 August, he was posted to the 38th Gurkha Rifles, which I understand was a training regiment, and was promoted to first lieutenant on 16 January 1945. He was then re-posted to the 1/3rd Gurkha Rifles on 19 January – my birthday.

To wish me many happy returns of that fourteenth birthday, Bill wrote me a letter, dated 7 January 1945, in which he said: 'I am looking forward to the time I get back. We will have a damned good time. We will go out walking and when we have tramped for miles and miles and are just about exhausted and have worked up a hell of a thirst we will pop into the nearest pub and down gallons of beer. Or else if I have enough money and have a long enough leave

3

we might hire a boat and go sailing. At any rate we shall have to do something good to celebrate.'

I remember the night of 7 May when the telegram arrived. I was in bed reading. When the doorbell rang, I somehow knew that it was a telegram. I heard the telegraph-boy say: 'It's not very nice. Is there someone in there with you?'

My mother's voice quavered as she said to my father: 'It's a telegram. I can't read it. Is it Billy?'

My father replied: 'Now, now. It's probably nothing of the kind.' A few moments later, my father came into my bedroom and said: 'Well, John, poor Billy's dead.' I bit my lip but could not speak.

When I was once more alone, I lay in bed trembling for a considerable time. I did not weep. I loved my big brother but I can clearly remember that my feelings of sorrow were substantially tempered by the fact that I was so very proud of him. While I trembled, my sister paced endlessly around a table in the adjoining room. I suppose we were both in a state of shock. When I saw my mother the following morning, she was clearly grief-stricken, though facing up to the loss very bravely.

Bill had been killed on 28 April 1945 while leading his platoon in an attack upon a Japanese-held Burmese village situated to the north-east of Pegu. In a letter to my parents, his commanding officer wrote that Bill 'was shot by a sniper and died almost instantly. When the company took the village, they slaughtered fifty Japs. A poor consolation but a fine revenge!'

If my elder brother was a heroic inspiration to me, I was also greatly influenced by the cinema. High on my list of favourite films were those set in the far outposts of the British Empire – *The Four Feathers*, *The Drum*, *The Charge of the Light Brigade*, *The Lives of a Bengal Lancer* and *Northwest Passage*. I saw all of these films many times and always watched enthralled as Ralph Richardson, Roger Livesey, Errol Flynn, Gary Cooper and Spencer Tracy led their men across the burning deserts of the Sudan, over the rugged mountains of India's North-West Frontier or through the untamed American wilderness, vanquishing dervishes, tribesmen or Red Indians in death-or-glory battles.

My number one screen idol was undoubtedly Errol Flynn. Whether wielding a sword in *The Adventures of Robin Hood* or *The Sea Hawk* or portraying General Custer fighting with his regiment to the last man in *They Died With Their Boots On*, Errol was the principal inspiration of all my boyhood dreams. Most of all, I hoped one day to emulate his role as Major Geoffrey Vickers of the 27th Lancers in *The Charge of the Light Brigade*.

I used to break out in goose pimples every time I watched the final scenes which depicted the famous charge at Balaklava during the Crimean War. On the screen, squadrons of mounted lancers advanced in extended lines into 'the valley of death', gradually increasing their speed to the accompaniment of Max Steiner's stirring background music. 'Onward, men! Onward!' Errol urged his soldiers as they charged 'through shot and shell'. After having his horse shot from under him, Errol leapt upon another and was one of the first to reach the Russian gun emplacements. Then, fatally shot through the chest, he fell to the ground close to where a tattered Union Jack fluttered proudly over the dead standard-bearer. As Errol's eyes closed contentedly, there was a final flourish of bugles.

At this point I would be so bursting with emotion that my eyes would fill with tears. Afterwards, I would return home from the cinema, completely convinced that service in the British Army would be the only life for me and dreaming of performing feats of glory like the gallant Major Vickers.

From the age of 16 I cultivated an 'Errol Flynn' moustache. Otherwise, I bore little resemblance to my screen hero either in physique or temperament. I was always extremely shy and introverted and a poor performer on the school sports fields. Although I loved hockey, my playing ability was very erratic and normally below average. As for occasional forced participation in football, cricket or athletics, my efforts regularly drew good-humoured, though still hurtful, derision from my classmates.

During my teens, my closest friend was my cousin, John Kitchen, who was a few months younger than myself and who lived in Wallsend-on-Tyne (my mother's original home). We always spent summer and Easter holidays together and corresponded regularly in between. Our favourite game was 'pirates', which was played in authentic detail with charts of the Spanish Main and all voyages and battles recorded in my captain's logbook. The highlight of each holiday was always the day that our model galleons met in battle in the bath. After shooting it out with miniature cannons loaded with gunpowder and match-heads, one of the fairly expensive and painstakingly constructed vessels would eventually go up in flames and the explosion of the powder magazine would wreak the final destruction. The excitement that we derived made it all worthwhile, however, and the loser would shortly commence building another ship to be ready for the next holiday.

As for girls, I only had one girlfriend during my teens. When I was 15, I kissed Isobel while playing postman's knock at the Scouts and Guides Christmas party, and after that, went out with her regularly over a period of about four months. Isobel was a year older than me and a very attractive blonde. She had an ample bosom but when we sat together in the darkness of the cinema, the only thing I ever held was her hand! Then, one Saturday afternoon when I was on my way to meet her as usual, I suddenly decided that I'd prefer to go to the pictures by myself – so I did. When I think about it now it seems crazy, but that's what happened.

Two years later, when I was 17, I fell in love with a strikingly beautiful girl at school called Mary. However, I only loved her from afar and, in fact, never once spoke to her. Even so, my devoted and pure adoration continued for more than a year. I should hasten to add that the state of innocence described above was by no means uncommon among teenagers during the 1940s.

Despite my quiet and reserved manner, I did rather well in the two youth organisations of which I was a member. Six years in the Boy Scouts culminated in my achieving the rank of troop leader, while I was perhaps even more successful in the Army Cadet Force.

My three years' service – September 1946 to August 1949 – in No.1 Company, Edinburgh Cadet Battalion, Royal Scots, was a very happy time which I believed would suitably prepare me for my intended military career. Wearing my uniform, with the glengarry and badge of the Royal Scots, filled me with pride. I faithfully attended all of the twice weekly parades and every annual and weekend camp that was held. I could recite the infantry training manuals by heart and obtained War Certificate 'A' with high marks. Once I became an NCO, I displayed an unexpected ability to drill and instruct the lads of my company and had considerable success in bringing them up to Certificate 'A' pass standards. Eventually, I rose to the rank of company sergeant major.

The minimum age for enlistment in the regular army was 17½. As I approached that age, my headmaster informed me that my preliminary examination results indicated that it would be advisable for me to repeat my fifth year studies before sitting for my Higher Leaving Certificate. On receiving this news, I told my father that I wanted to leave school there and then, and join the army. However, my father insisted that I should stay on at school and obtain the Higher Certificate, which he assured me was essential for my future. I was able to console myself with the knowledge that possession of the certificate would no doubt assist me in fulfilling my most cherished dream of obtaining a place in Sandhurst Military Academy and becoming a regular army officer.

Following the end of the Second World War, the Labour Government had felt obliged to continue with compulsory conscription in order to meet the needs of national defence and overseas commitments. In accordance with the National Service Act of 1947 (amended in 1948), I duly registered at my local branch of the Ministry of Labour and National Service in the proximity of my eighteenth birthday in January 1949. Due to the fact that I was soon to sit for my school examination, I was granted six months' deferment of call-up.

In the spring of that year, I obtained my Scottish Higher Leaving Certificate in English, Art, History, French and Arithmetic. I could now see no reason why I should not immediately enlist in the regular army and intended to broach the subject again with my father. However, my mother pointed out to me that my National Service was fast approaching and strongly urged that I should sample army life before committing myself. Rather reluctantly, I accepted this suggestion, knowing that I would not have long to wait.

I finally reported for medical examination at Queensferry House, Edinburgh, in July 1949. To my delight and great relief, I was classified as Grade 1 fit – the absolute requirement for the infantry. Had I been reduced to serving in some non-combatant corps, it would have broken my heart.

My status as an army cadet with Certificate 'A' guaranteed me my choice of regiment. Being a Royal Scots Cadet whose brother had first enlisted in that regiment and who had long believed that the Royal Scots was indeed 'First of Foot, Right of the Line and Pride of the British Army', my choice of regiment would seem obvious. However, under the brigade training system of that time, one regiment from each brigade ceased to be active for a period of a year and became training battalion for recruits allocated to the brigade. In the Scottish Lowland Brigade at that particular time, this task was being undertaken by the Royal Scots. I also took into consideration that it would be nice to serve in the same unit as cousin John, who was due for his National Service in a few months' time. Also an army cadet, John intended to serve his time in the Durham Light Infantry. I therefore decided that I would also apply to join that regiment.

When I was finally interviewed by the recruiting officer, on completion of the medical examination and attendant documentation, I told him of my hopes of becoming a regular officer. Immediately, his face lit up and he tried to persuade me to sign on, there and then, for a full career.

'It's my mother, sir,' I explained. 'I promised her that I'd try National Service first to see what the army's like.'

'But you know what it's like,' the recruiting officer protested genially. 'You've been in the cadets. The army's just the same.'

'Oh yes, sir,' I replied. 'I know I'll like it but I've given my word.'

'Very well,' he conceded. 'I understand. Just give it a few weeks and you can sign on after that.' Then, as I stood up to leave, he said brightly: 'Well, good luck, Scurr – and I hope you get your commission!'

'Thank you, sir!' I left his office happily confident that in due course I would be wearing those officer's stars. (The recruiting officer must have been very persuasive, because another intended conscript came out of his office having signed on in the Scots Guards for 22 years!)

In August, my Enlistment Notice arrived, instructing me to report to the LIBTC in Bordon, Hampshire, between 9 a.m. and 4 p.m. on Thursday, 1 September 1949. Enclosed were a rail travel warrant and a postal order for four shillings (20p), being an advance of one day's pay.

At the army cadet force drill hall, I handed in my uniform and was given my Cadet Discharge Certificate. The character reference written by my company commander, Captain Fulde, was extremely complimentary. It stated: 'John Scurr has been one of the most outstanding Cadets who has served in this Battalion. Always clean and smartly turned out on parade, his promotion would have been more rapid had the Company establishment permitted, because of his ability as an instructor – patient, lucid and knew his subject. His exemplary character gained him the esteem of his officers. I trust he will do well in the career he has chosen.'

So now I was all set to go. I was extremely curious as to

9

which unit I had been assigned. There had been no mention in the Enlistment Notice of the Durham Light Infantry and I pondered in vain as to the meaning of 'LIBTC'. With mounting excitement tempered by some anxiety, I travelled down to London on Wednesday, 31 August. On the train with me was an American woman and her small son. I told her that I was on my way to join the army and how much I was looking forward to it, and she replied that she thought it would be a very good experience for a young man.

On arrival at King's Cross station that evening, I was met by cousin John, who was now working in London with the Inland Revenue. We went to see a film – Gene Kelly in *The Three Musketeers*. It was a really exciting and lavishly produced swashbuckler with a great background score by one of my favourite Hollywood composers, Herbert Stothart. But I can remember that although I enjoyed the film, I was constantly aware of a growing feeling of uneasiness about the following day.

I spent that night in the South Kensington hostel where John was a resident, sleeping on the floor. The following morning, 1 September, we took a boat out on the Serpentine in Hyde Park; rowing had always been one of our favourite pastimes. Suddenly, I laid down my oars and said to John despondently: 'I'm scared.'

'Why?' John asked.

'Because I don't know what might lie ahead of me.'

'A sort of fear of the unknown, you mean?'

'Yes, I suppose so.' I sighed. 'Oh, well, I guess it'll be OK once I get there.'

When I boarded the train at Waterloo early on that Thursday afternoon, I found myself in a compartment with four other 18-year-olds, all clutching brown-paper parcels like myself. 'Are you chaps by any chance conscripts?' I greeted them, trying to sound cheery. They confirmed that they were. I was then horrified to hear that all four of them were on their way to report to the Army Catering Corps. As I still had no idea what 'LIBTC' stood for, I now assumed that I must also be destined to become an army cook! When the train stopped at Aldershot, however, and my companions announced that they were all getting off, relief flooded over me like a man reprieved from the gallows. Then, as I journeyed on alone, my feeling of relief was soon replaced by those of isolation and anxiety.

My boyhood dream was about to become reality.

2

The Light Infantry Brigade Training Battalion – Bordon September–November 1949

Alighting on the platform at Bordon station, I was heartened to see a dozen other youths with brown-paper parcels descending from other compartments of the train. A waiting, stern-faced corporal, wearing the badge of the Somerset Light Infantry on his dark green beret, ordered us into the back of a 3-ton truck. Then a short drive along a country road brought us to Bordon Camp, depot of the LIBTC – Light Infantry Brigade Training Centre. Here, the Somerset Light Infantry, under the command of Lieutenant Colonel Howard, was fulfilling the role of Training Battalion for the Brigade. All recruits for the six Light Infantry regiments, whether National Service or regular army, reported to this centre for basic training.

Initial documentation by a headquarters clerk established that my Intake Group Number was 4917, my Army Number was 22176690, my Trade on Enlistment 'Student', my Religious Denomination 'Church of England' (actually I was baptised as a Scottish Episcopalian but the clerk insisted that I had to be registered as C of E), that I was enlisted at Bordon on 1 September 1949, my Date Due for Discharge was 28 February 1951, my height was 5 ft 7in., my weight 124 lb, my maximum chest measurement 31 in., my complexion fresh, my eyes grey-green, my hair fair, my distinctive marks were 'mole right jaw' and 'scar right outer leg' and my next of kin was my mother. All of these details were duly noted down on my service record by the clerk and recorded again in my Soldier's Service and Pay Book (AB 64 Part I). I then exchanged my ration book and sweet and clothing coupons (wartime restrictions were still in force in 1949) for army coupons for sweets and soap.

After documentation, the other new arrivals and myself were marched to the Quartermaster's Stores. Battledress, denim fatigues, berets, boots and greatcoat were hastily handed out with only scant attention to fit. Then, even more rapidly I was issued with shirts, pullover, underwear, PT kit, 'housewife' (a cloth bag containing darning wool, needles, cottons and thimble), mess tins, eating irons, mug, webbing belt, ammunition pouches, water bottle, small pack, valise and other items, all of which I hurriedly packed into my kitbag with corporals repeatedly snapping: 'Come on! Get a bloody move on!'

We were next instructed to take a shower and dress in our denims, after which we were directed to the first floor of one of several red brick barrack blocks which constituted Quebec Barracks. On entering my assigned barrack room bowed beneath the weight of the bulging kitbag across my shoulder, I saw four rather despondent-looking young men clad in ill-fitting denim fatigues who were seated on chairs by the far wall. As I laid down my kitbag feeling rather shy and awkward, one of the four – a short, fat lad – greeted me: 'Heavy, ain't it, mate?'

I quickly relaxed and soon learned that the four of them had arrived earlier in the day and were glumly awaiting developments. As I dumped my kitbag on the nearest available bed, other new recruits laden with kitbags came in to lay claim to the remaining beds and lockers.

There was a prevailing atmosphere in the barrack room of mutual sympathy between people drawn close together by a situation of shared adversity. A big fellow with boils around his lower face, who introduced himself as Johnny Grose, told me: 'My girlfriend's a peach. We was going to get married. Then this come along. She fainted on the platform when I left on the train this morning.' I made sympathetic noises, even though I didn't believe a word of it. Grose continued: 'I'll tell you this, Jock; none of these people here had better try pushing me around. Old Johnny's as tough as a bull and as strong as an ox. I'll break their backs if they try anything with me!'

When, in due course, our instructors did start 'pushing him around', needless to say there wasn't a murmur out of him!

Another National Service recruit was Harold 'Ginger' Thompson – a lean, sandy-haired ex-miner from Bishop Auckland, County Durham. 'Thoo's a long way from home, Jock,' he said to me. 'Couldn't thoo have got theeself into the Black Watch or something?'

'Well, I've got relations from Tyneside,' I explained. 'So I decided I'd try the Durham Light Infantry.'

'Is thoo DLI an'all?' Ginger exclaimed with approval, offering his hand. 'Shake!'

Little did we know as we clasped hands that neither of us would serve in the DLI, but we would nonetheless soldier together in the KOYLI in Malaya. Both Johnny Grose and Ginger Thompson had automatically labelled me 'Jock' on that very first day and this would remain my name throughout my army service. I never resented it. In fact, in a short space of time I began to think of myself as 'Jock'.

Our barrack room corporal was a cynical, rough-and-ready, desert and Burma war veteran called Peacock who, I recall, had a very poor opinion of Field Marshal Montgomery. Once everyone had arrived, Peacock instructed us to parcel up our civilian clothing for posting back to our homes. One recruit had something extra to return home. He had naively brought his dog with him and was very upset when told that he couldn't keep it. The dog was duly kennelled somewhere in the camp until the lad's father came to collect it a few days later.

Intake Group 4917 totalled about 70 men and constituted 3 and 4 Platoons of 'A' Company of the Light Infantry Training Battalion. Those in my room were in 3 Platoon. That first evening, we were visited by our platoon commander – a smartly attired and good-looking second lieutenant, with very fair hair, called Waite. Accompanied by Corporal Peacock, he moved from bed-space to bed-space, speaking to us individually in a fairly sociable if cautiously restrained manner. When they halted by my bed, Mr Waite asked me my name and then enquired: 'How d'you feel about being conscripted?'

'I don't mind at all, sir,' I answered enthusiastically. 'In fact I've been looking forward to it. I was in the army cadets for three years and I really enjoyed it.'

'Well, you won't enjoy yourself here,' Mr Waite assured me ominously. After questioning me about the reasons for my choice of regiment, he shook his head and commented: 'You should have joined the Royal Scots.'

As the pair moved on to the next bed-space I felt slightly disheartened. Although he had been quite civil, the young officer's remarks had not exactly been encouraging.

Later, Mr Waite gathered the whole of 3 Platoon together in our room and explained to us exactly what lay ahead of us during our ten weeks of basic training. First of all, he formally introduced Corporal Peacock, who was slouched against a window sill, smoking a cigarette.

'Corporal Peacock here is a bastard!' Mr Waite announced. 'That is, on parade. Off parade, you'll probably like him. I hope you do.' He paused and then continued: 'They call me "the blond bastard". You can start calling me that now if you like – not to my face, of course!'

During all the time that I was in that camp, I never once heard anyone refer to Mr Waite as 'the blond bastard'. This made me wonder if this was a name that he had perhaps thought up for himself and had fed it to us in the hope that we would establish the title for him.

Mr Waite then explained to us that as from reveille the following morning, our lives would dramatically alter and that he and his NCOs would be constantly chasing us throughout the hours of daylight. 'You might think we treat you very hard,' he said. 'But we have to get you ready for war and we only have ten weeks to do it in. We train you hard because war is hard, and we really haven't got time to be nice to you. We'll be saying some pretty harsh things to you but we don't mean all the things we say – not all of them.' Then, he said very seriously: 'You chaps are going to hate me. You'll hate me worse than you've hated anyone in your lives before. You may not believe it now, but you will – you'll see.'

He was right. We did. At least, I know I certainly did. At that moment, however, I did not really believe it. I had no conception of what was to come. When I retired to bed at the close of my first day in the army, I supposed that it would take me a week or so to adjust to my new surroundings and lifestyle and that after that I'd be very happy.

In those days, there seemed to be an unwritten law that men in the ranks slept in their shirts. To have worn pyjamas would have been regarded as 'cissy'. I can remember awakening early the next morning, aware of the rough texture of my shirt and the hard mattress and staring into the pitch darkness, wondering where the hell I was. Oh, I'm in the army! I remembered with dismay. I lay awake, feeling lost and miserable until the bugle sounded reveille. Then I joined the mad scramble to form queues at the few wash-basins in the adjoining ablutions room. It all seemed so uncivilised!

September 1949 was a glorious month of hot, sunny days in which shirtsleeve order – shirt with sleeves rolled up, denim trousers, web belt, boots and anklets – was the normal parade dress for training. On our berets we wore a non-specific Light Infantry badge of a silver bugle. So attired, we were assembled on that first morning in a lecture hall to be addressed by 'A' Company Commander, Major Armistead. He spoke to us in rather cold, unwelcoming terms: 'If you behave yourselves, we'll treat you all right. If you don't, we'll come down on you like a ton of bricks! But you can forget any stories you might have heard about bullying, Foreign Legion-type sergeant majors. We don't have people like that here. They wouldn't stay.'

We were next addressed by Company Sergeant Major Barnes – a small, wiry man with fierce, dark eyes – whose presence would always inspire instant terror. 'When I was a lot younger than any of you,' he told us in a high-pitched growl, 'I was fighting on the North-West Frontier. I learned then the essentials of being a soldier: self-respect and pride – guts!' His eyes glared malevolently as he continued: 'Now let me make one thing clear. I don't like idle men and I don't like malingerers and I especially don't like men who report sick without proper cause. If you're genuinely ill and are hospitalised, I'll have every sympathy for you. But if the Medical Officer gives you M and D – Medicine and Duty – then as far as I'm concerned, there's nothing wrong with you and by the time I'm finished with you, you won't want to report sick again in a hurry!'

I made a mental note never to attend sick parade unless I was carried there on a stretcher!

The remainder of that day was spent having our battle-dress uniforms tailored and our hair cropped extremely short, being issued with .303 Lee-Enfield No.4 rifles and being shown how to make up our beds and lay out our kit for inspection. We also learned how to polish our brasses and how to blanco our webbing equipment with 'khaki-green No.3' paste. When I asked Corporal Peacock how often we would be required to blanco our webbing, he replied: 'That will depend on what kind of a mood I'm in. If I'm in a bad mood, I might make you blanco your equipment three times a night!'

Peacock also explained to us that we should put heavy layers of boot polish on the toe and heel caps of our best boots and then set fire to the polish. The purpose of this seemingly risky procedure was to burn the crinkles out of the leather and thereby provide a smooth foundation for polishing the caps to the required 'bulled-up' shine. He then said: 'It's against regulations to set fire to boots in this way and if I catch any of you doing it, you'll be on a charge!'

That evening, we all duly went ahead with the forbidden instruction, and despite considerable anxiety on seeing our boots engulfed in flames, the process proved effective without rendering any other damage. Bulling up the caps, however, would take hours and hours of spit and polish – weaving minute circles with a duster over the surface of the caps night after night.

'Old soldiers' – who had been in the army for three or four weeks – tended to pop into our barrack room to give us advice. I remember that one put his head round the door and said: 'Listen, boys, stay away from these ATS girls in the camp up the road. Some lads over here got the pox!' His advice certainly wasn't needed by me. There was as much chance of me approaching an ATS girl as there was of me starting a barrack room brawl. During basic training, it was always believed that the cooks were instructed to put bromide in the tea in order to prevent recruits from feeling randy when they needed all their energy for training. Some of the chaps were quite adamant that they noticed the difference, but perhaps they were just worn out by all the hard exercise.

On the evening of our first full day, the short, fat lad who had first greeted me when I had entered the barrack room the previous afternoon suddenly burst into tears.

'What's the matter, mate?' someone enquired.

'I want to go 'ome,' the lad sobbed.

We tried to console him. Each of us in turn declared how much he'd like to go home also. But we couldn't go, we said, so we'd all just have to stick it out together. Although a sturdy lad, it soon transpired that he was neither physically nor mentally apt for the infantry, so that within a fortnight he was told to pack his kit and was sent off to join the Pioneer Corps. He was not the only man that I saw weeping during those ten weeks of basic training. However, tears were something to which I was never reduced. I managed to keep going on my hate and resentment, which were kindled within a few days but which took months to subside.

My hate was principally concentrated upon Second Lieutenant Waite, as indeed he had predicted. I had always believed that British Army officers would be gentlemen like Major Vickers (Errol Flynn – *The Charge of the Light Brigade*), Captain Durrance (Ralph Richardson – *The Four*

Feathers) or Captain Carruthers (Roger Livesey – *The Drum*). Mr Waite had a short service commission but his behaviour always seemed to me to be that of a frustrated drill sergeant. 'The blond bastard', as he hoped we would call him, was a far greater holy terror than any of his NCOs.

From the start Mr Waite appeared determined to knock out of me any idea that my cadet training had any value. It was always: 'Pull your stomach in, you Scotch thing! This isn't the cadets, you know!'

Commencing 3 Platoon's very first lesson in elementary drill outside the barrack block, Mr Waite selected me to act as 'right marker' upon whose position the remainder of the platoon would 'fall in'. When I promptly marched forward as I had always been taught, he exclaimed: 'No! No! In the Light Infantry the right marker doubles out. Get back and do it again!'

I retraced my steps and then doubled forward as smartly as I could.

'Oh, my God!' Mr Waite protested. 'Absolutely hopeless! Get back to the ranks out of my sight!'

Feeling very crestfallen, I hurried back to a place in the front rank.

'I can still bloody see you!' Mr Waite screamed. 'Get in the rear rank, right out of the way!'

Although CSM Barnes could strike terror in me by merely casting his eyes in my direction, this was what I would expect from a training camp sergeant major, and he always distributed biting, critical remarks among us with complete impartiality. Mr Waite, however, appeared to heap personal humiliation upon me at every opportunity. It was this that principally aroused my hate and completely erased my original supposition that after a couple of weeks of adjustment, I would be happy with my new life in the army.

On the parade ground I received what today might be called a 'culture shock'. I had not previously known what differentiated Light Infantry from other soldiers. (Light Infantry regiments had, in fact, developed out of the original

19

light companies during the Napoleonic Wars and were designed for rapid mobility and skirmishing with initiative.) Marching at 140 paces to the minute instead of the normal 120 and automatically standing at ease after every drill movement took some getting used to, as did marching with rifle at the trail and never at the slope. Holding a rifle at the trail for any length of time always caused considerable strain to my fingers and wrist. Even after two years, I never found marching at the trail comfortable although it certainly looked distinctive.

It was a few days before we were introduced to our platoon sergeant, who had been on leave at the time of our arrival. Sergeant Bolton always held himself very erect and looked every inch a soldier. Although he could be severe on the parade ground, he was never vicious or improper. One day, obviously dissatisfied with our efforts at drill, he clasped his hands together and, looking up at the sky, pleaded: 'God, send me some soldiers! Wooden ones will do!' Sergeant Bolton always appeared to me to stand slightly aloof from the rest of 'Waite's gang' and seemed to be with us less than the others. Perhaps he had other duties.

Waite's gang (as I called them) comprised Corporal Peacock and three other corporals – Wright, George and Puddy. Being nasty on parade seemed to come more easily to Peacock and Wright than it did to the other two, but all inspired terror when acting in concert with Mr Waite.

At that time I continued to be rather shy and was inclined to have occasional bouts of self-consciousness. One day, we were required to report to Mr Waite in a hut, one by one, in order to complete some further detail of documentation. When I had left the hut and descended the steps outside, Corporal Peacock suddenly appeared in the doorway behind me and yelled: 'Scurr! Get back in here!'

I immediately doubled back in and stood to attention. Mr Waite was seated behind a table, while Corporals Peacock, Wright and Puddy stood around him.

Mr Waite looked up at me with undisguised hostility.

'Why was your face red when you came in here just now?'
he asked abruptly.

Always a difficult question to answer, I decided to try to
make light of it. 'It's just a habit of mine, sir,' I replied,
trying to sound casual.

'Did you think we were all sitting in here admiring you
or something?'

'No, sir.'

He stared at me intently and then said in slow, measured
tones: 'You gorgeous creature, you!'

My face now flushed with genuine embarrassment.

'Oh, get out of here!' Waite snapped. 'You make me sick
to look at you!'

I turned to go, smarting inside with anger and humiliation. Immediately, the three corporals started screaming at
me: 'Go on, get out of it!' – 'Get to fuck out of it, you
fucking idiot!' – 'Fuck off, you fucking stupid bastard!'

Once I had rejoined the platoon ranks outside, Ginger
Thompson looked at me and said: 'Is thoo all right, Jock?
Don't let those sods bother thee!'

I attempted to smile but couldn't. 'Those sods' *had* bothered me and that was that.

Perhaps wrongly, I always believed at the time that Mr
Waite especially had it in for me. But he was certainly also
nasty to other people and always seemed intent to prove to
the rest of his gang and to us that he was the biggest
'bastard'.

I remember one occasion when we had spent hours
painstakingly laying out our kit for inspection. Our blankets,
sheets, shirts and even our socks were all neatly folded and
squared off around pieces of cardboard. All our webbing
equipment was freshly blancoed, our boots, brasses and
mess tins were brightly polished and all items of kit were
placed in precise display positions on our mattresses. In
fact, everything was as perfect as it could be. Then came
the order: 'Stand by your beds!'

The atmosphere of communal tension and fear was painfully acute as Mr Waite, followed by Sergeant Bolton and two corporals, made his inspection, criticising everyone for one supposed fault or another. He finally stopped opposite one poor fellow's bed. 'My God!' he exclaimed, surveying the lad's laid out kit. 'What a bloody shambles!'

With that, Mr Waite opened the adjacent first-floor window and, assisted by the corporals, picked up the recruit's mattress, complete with blankets and displayed kit, and heaved it all out of the window. I could hardly believe it.

Our daily training schedule was non-stop: close order drill, rifle drill, PT, weapon training with rifle, Bren light machine gun, Sten sub-machine gun and No.36 grenade, bayonet practice, fieldcraft, route marches ... And all the time it was: 'At the double! At the double!' – 'Get a bloody move on! You're like a pregnant NAAFI woman!' – 'Come on, you useless lump of shit! Move your fucking arse!'

All of these activities, which I'd always found exciting and enjoyable in the cadets, now seemed to be the components of a never-ending nightmare. Not once did we receive a pat on the back or a word of encouragement; only repeated verbal abuse, usually laced with the crudest of obscenities.

It may well be that this harsh and even cruel treatment was the proved best method of converting free-and-easy civilians into disciplined soldiers, but I certainly couldn't see it that way at the time.

Most of our 'free time' in the evenings had to be spent bulling up our kit but we nonetheless found time to have a few laughs and play childish pranks upon one another. One of the recruits was a gypsy who could neither read nor write. At his request, a couple of his mates agreed to write a letter from him to his mother, which she could get a friend to read to her. The letter that his 'mates' then composed began: 'Dear Mum, I'm really pissed off with this place. The grub here is fucking manky...' and continued in similar vein. Regrettably, I never learned of his mother's reaction to her son's first letter home.

In actual fact, the 'grub' provided during basic training at the LIBTC was excellent; large platefuls of varied and well-cooked meals. This good feeding, combined with all the outdoor exercise, caused me to put on several pounds of weight by the end of the ten-week period and without a doubt made me both bulkier and stronger.

During theoretical instruction periods, there was no need for me to pay too much attention. I knew all the infantry training lessons by heart and had been delivering them myself only a couple of months before. However, like everyone else, I found the physical side of the training very tough and gruelling and the constant harassment from Waite and his gang extremely wearing. 'Lights Out' at 10 p.m. was the time I always longed for. Once I was between the sheets, I had a luxurious feeling of being safe and secure, knowing that until reveille at 6.30 a.m., no one could hound me.

I usually awoke around 5 a.m. and would look at the luminous dial of my watch, taking great comfort in the knowledge that I still had another one-and-a-half hours of peace. After that, I would glance at my watch periodically, growing dismayed and alarmed once the hands had passed six o'clock. From 20 past onwards I would keep the minute-hand under constant surveillance, aware that I was power-less to keep it from moving on, yet hoping that somehow the dreaded bugle call would be miraculously delayed. Every morning, however, it was always the same. At 6.30 on the dot, that bloody bugle would sound out, heralding another day of torment and tribulation.

After the first week, we were given aptitude and intelli-gence tests. In the aptitude tests – assembling a bicycle pump and other such practical tasks – I achieved moderate results. However, in the intelligence tests – puzzles involving figure calculations, etc. – my results were very poor. Then, towards the end of the second week, we were interviewed individually by the Personnel Selection Officer – a florid-faced captain who looked and acted as though he were recovering from a colossal hangover. He was in a foul mood and seemed to be forcibly restraining his irritation every time he spoke.

He had a fixed idea in his mind that I had been promoted to CSM in the cadets only because I was soon to be called up into the army and would not accept my truthful declaration that this was not the case. When he then saw that I had War Certificate 'A' and the Scottish Higher Certificate, he immediately summoned an Education Corps sergeant from the adjoining room and instructed him to take me away and give me another intelligence test. I returned shortly, this time with high results. The PSO now asked me what I wanted to do in the army.

'Is it too early to think about a commission, sir?' I asked cautiously.

'No, it's not too early,' he replied, still irritated, and made a note on the report sheet in front of him. He then told me that I would be allocated to 'X' Cadre – a special squad for recruits who were potential officers and NCOs. I came away from this interview feeling pleased and a little excited. My growing anti-army feelings were momentarily forgotten as I basked in the thought that I was now listed as a potential officer.

When Mr Waite heard the result of my interview, he shook his head and said to me sullenly: 'You'll have to pull your finger out if you're going to be an officer!'

He turned and walked away. My previous elation quickly dwindled. What he had said was no doubt absolutely true, but a few words of encouragement from him would have done me the world of good.

With more than a dozen others from the intake, I packed my kit on Saturday, 17 September and moved to a ground floor barrack room in the 'X' Cadre block. My companions were mostly well educated like myself. There was Johnny Ainsworth, a Yorkshire theological student who couldn't open his mouth without swearing, Geoff Clarke, Tony Roberts, Sam Coster, Phil Cox, Jim Lancaster, Bagnall, Brown and Ledsome – who the men in 3 Platoon had nicknamed 'Jolly hockey sticks' because of his posh accent and fresh, slightly girlish features.

Among the others, whose names I don't recall, was a scruffy, lazy individual (and excellent piano player) who seemed incapable of keeping himself or his kit clean. He consequently spent most of his time on 'jankers' – CB (Confined to Barracks) – parading at the guardroom in the evenings for extra fatigue duties. He quite honestly did not give a hoot about anything and although he sometimes drove the rest of us to the limits of exasperation, we couldn't help liking him. In a strange way I rather admired him. After a couple of weeks, he was pronounced unsuitable for 'X' Cadre and returned to 'A' Company.

There was also a quiet and very likeable Cornish lad who was constantly homesick and very depressed about being in the army. He had a corner bed space, and when off duty, he would lie on his bed facing the wall and just would not respond to our many efforts to buck him up. At weekends he would lie like that for a whole afternoon. Sometimes at night he would cry.

In 'X' Cadre we had two sergeants as instructors. One of them was a big, powerfully built, very serious man called Black. On the morning of our arrival, he told us: 'You'll find you'll be treated a bit more intelligently here. We know how they chase you around in "A" Company. Well, I don't see any need for that. Mind you, make no mistake, if any of you try to mess me around, I'll make you wish you'd never been born!'

There was no fear of any of us trying to mess Sergeant Black around. He exuded power and authority without even needing to raise his voice. I always had the impression that he had been in his element during the Second World War. His eyes used to light up every time he spoke of it. Every day, he practised firing his rifle and Sten gun as though itching for another opportunity to use them for real.

The other sergeant – a small, cheery, ginger-moustached man with an unusual name that I cannot recall – treated us very civilly and with humour. On one occasion when he was speaking to us about the war, he said with a mischievous gleam in his eye: 'There's a sergeant in this camp – you could never leave him with a prisoner. If you took a prisoner and then turned your back, he'd bump him off!' Some of the lads were convinced that he was talking about Sergeant Black, but I didn't think so.

Unfortunately, we only received instruction from these two splendid sergeants in map reading, fieldcraft and weapon training. For drill, PT, firing range and route marches, we had to report to 'A' Company as before. We were readily identifiable as members of 'X' Cadre by the narrow, dark green bands that we wore on our shoulder straps. Consequently, we took a lot of 'stick' on parade – '"X" Cadre again! Potential officer? You dozy sod! You couldn't lead a NAAFI queue!' – or, as CSM Barnes said on one occasion to 'Jolly hockey sticks' Ledsome: '"X" Cadre? You got about as much brains as I got, and I ain't got none!'

To our considerable relief, we didn't see much of CSM Barnes except during drill instruction periods. When we were on the square, he was inclined to hover in the background at first, making us all nervous by his very presence. Then he would step forward and take over from the NCO instructor for a while, issuing commands with a strange, high-pitched snarl. He had two stock remarks which he uttered every time that he drilled us. One was: 'Swing your arms from front to rear!' How else you might swing them I could never imagine! The other was his favourite evocation of soldierly qualities: 'Self-respect and pride – guts!'

He would normally spout the latter when we were standing rigidly to attention, endeavouring not to sway or even blink. Although self-respect and pride were qualities that I had always previously associated with being a soldier, they just could not be inspired by CSM Barnes screaming down my ear: 'Keep still, you bloody nig-nog!' At such a time, the only thing that I felt was terror.

The most frightening thing about the army, particularly

in those early days, was the inordinate power which superiors – sometimes of low intelligence and little common sense – held over us. Almost at whim, they could charge a man with some supposed offence and have him sentenced to 'jankers' or close arrest, against which the accused had virtually no redress. I was never placed on a charge during my basic training, but I observed others who were and lived in constant dread of the possibility.

After the first two weeks had passed, we were allowed to leave the camp during off-duty hours. However, there was so much bull to do on our kit that most of us spent the greater part of every evening occupied with the various tasks involved. Shining up boots, bayonet scabbards and mess tins to the required 'see your face in it' standard was unbelievably time-consuming, in addition to blancoing webbing equipment, polishing brasses, pressing uniforms and cleaning rifles. We would normally have a short break in the NAAFI canteen for tea and cake. Popular songs of the era most played in the NAAFI were 'You're Breaking My Heart', 'Forever and Ever', 'When the Angelus was Ringing' and 'The Wedding Samba'.

On Saturday and Sunday afternoons I could afford to relax. I used to journey by bus to Aldershot, always on my own. Although I had good friends in the 'X' Cadre squad, I treasured the opportunity to be alone. In Aldershot I would always go to a cinema, still preferring adventure films, and afterwards would enjoy a meal at the luxurious NAAFI Club. The total cost, including fares, would be about ten shillings (50p). In my young and innocent mind I really thought I was living it up on these trips.

This became my pattern for most weekends. At the end of the third week of training, however, we were granted a 36-hour pass. I happily travelled up to London by train to spend the weekend with cousin John, staying overnight in his hostel. I remember saying to a couple of the hostel's residents who were approaching call-up age: 'Dodge out of it if you can. But if you have to go into the services, don't go into the army; if you have to go into the army, don't go into the infantry; and if you have to go into the infantry, don't go into the Light Infantry !'

On the Saturday evening, John and I went to see Tyrone Power in a new swashbuckler called *Captain from Castile* and afterwards returned to the hostel, where we got tipsy sharing just one large bottle of cider! Next day, we went to Hyde Park, enjoying the sunshine among the usual Sunday crowds. The peace and freedom taken for granted by civilians seemed unbelievable. People could stroll around without anyone yelling at them to smarten up and keep their stomachs in. They could even put their hands in their pockets if they wanted to. How I envied them all, and how heartbreaking it was when I had to leave that civilised tranquillity to take the train back to 'jail'!

My pay book (AB 64 Part I) recorded that I received vaccinations on 10 and 16 September, a schick (blood) test on 14 September and TAB inoculations on 17 September and 15 October. The inoculations were the worst. I actually saw one chap faint when he caught sight of the needle, as happens in comedy films. Our arms remained stiff and painful for days afterwards but we were still expected to continue with rifle drill, PT and other physical activities as normal. Jabs affected some men quite seriously, causing them to shiver or sweat with temporary fever symptoms. Fortunately, I was spared such ill effects.

From those weeks of constant fatigue, anxiety and humiliation, there is one day that particularly stands out in my memory which was nonetheless typical of so many others. On this day, we paraded immediately after breakfast with our rifles and wearing battle order, ready to go to the firing range as scheduled. Trucks were always provided to take platoons to the range – approximately 4 miles from the camp. Mr Waite, however, dismissed the trucks and announced that we were going to march there.

Once on the road, he gave us the customary choice: 'Sing or double!' We hastily gave discordant voice to the obscene version of 'She'll be coming round the mountain when she comes.' It was to no avail.

'Call that singing?' Mr Waite exclaimed. 'Light Infantry! Double march!'

We now broke into a trot, carrying our rifles at the port position across our chests. The undulating country road seemed endless. By the time we eventually reached the firing range, which was situated in bleak moorland, we were soaked in sweat, out of breath and near exhaustion. This, combined with the constant abuse hurled at us by Mr Waite and his gang, hardly provided the physical or mental conditions for achieving high standards of marksmanship. On this and other occasions, my shooting scores were erratic and noticeably below the standard that I had acquired in the army cadets.

Around 11 a.m., the NAAFI mobile canteen drove up with canisters of hot tea and the usual selection of cakes, buns and rolls. Mr Waite immediately assembled us from the firing points and butts, and we happily formed up in three ranks facing the mobile canteen.

To our consternation, Mr Waite now gave the order: 'Light Infantry! Right-turn!'

When we had duly complied, Mr Waite then ordered us to hold our rifles over our heads with our right hands. 'Keep your arms straight!' he bellowed. 'Anyone who bends his arm doesn't get a NAAFI break!'

The NCOs now began barking at us: 'Come on! Get those fucking arms straight!'

Then, to our further dismay came the order from Mr Waite: 'Light Infantry! Double march!'

We doubled for 20 yards, received the order to about turn and so continued to double back and forward. Needless to say, no one could keep his arm straight beneath the weight of his rifle for more than a few minutes while running at the same time.

After ordering us to halt and turn to the front, Mr Waite then announced: 'Right! None of you gets any tea!'

By this time Corporal Peacock and the other NCOs had bought their own tea and buns, so Mr Waite slapped the side of the van and ordered: 'OK! Take it back to camp!'

Gasping for breath and enraged to the verge of tears, I watched the mobile canteen disappear down the road. We now returned to target practice, no doubt in even worse condition to obtain good results.

At the end of the morning, as scheduled, transport arrived to take us back to camp. Mr Waite immediately instructed the drivers: 'Off you go! These people don't deserve to ride back!'

As the trucks drove off, we formed up on the road and then alternately marched and double marched the miles back to barracks.

On the fifth weekend we were allowed a 48-hour pass. This enabled me to travel up to London again and spend almost two full days with cousin John. London once more seemed like a haven in which I was acutely aware of the contrast between the lives of free civilians and my own. John's enlistment date was fast approaching. No doubt he was increasingly apprehensive after listening to all the stories that I told him of life in a training company. On the Sunday, in the late afternoon, we went to see Errol Flynn in *Edge of Darkness*. It was not one of Flynn's best films but in any case I was unable to enjoy it, being ever aware that after the show I would be catching the train back to Bordon. The prospect was very hard to bear.

During our sixth week of training, orders came for 'X' Cadre potential officers to attend for examination by War Office Selection Board that coming weekend. There were about seven of us – Tony Roberts, Jim Lancaster, Ledsome, Brown, a couple of others and myself. Johnny Ainsworth – the hard-swearing theological student – had been originally listed as a potential officer but he was now informed that he would not be suitable to attend WOSB. No reason was given. As Johnny was as well educated as any of us, we could only assume that he had been excluded due to his broad Yorkshire accent.

The candidates were divided into two groups to attend for examination at two separate locations. My group went to a place called Barton Stacey, near Warminster in Wiltshire, and on the whole I enjoyed the experience. Everything was very civilised. Accommodation (two to a room) and food were excellent and officers and NCOs addressed us throughout as 'gentlemen'. There were candidates from numerous units; all nice chaps and good company.

It seems to me now that in my initial interview I gave all the wrong answers. The interviewing officer told me that he had never heard of Boroughmuir School in Edinburgh. 'But I've heard of Watsons,' he said, referring to one of Edinburgh's top private schools – a school that my brother had, in fact, attended. 'Is it as good as Watsons?' the officer enquired.

'No, sir,' I replied. 'It's not quite as good as Watsons.'

Then, when asked if I played rugby, I answered: 'No, sir. I play hockey though.'

Being an honest lad who had learned no wiles, it had not occurred to me to respond with a positive 'yes' to both of these questions – that Boroughmuir was on a par with Watsons and that I had played rugby in my school's Ist XV as a matter of fact! I doubt if any verification would have been sought.

As far as I can recall, we did not commence the practical tests until first thing on the Sunday morning. We were divided into teams of five and wore orange-coloured pullovers which were numbered on the front and back. There were physical ability tests, such as climbing ropes and clambering over high walls, which did not present any great problem. The initiative and leadership tests, however, did not appear to reveal that I had much potential.

There was one 'situation' in which we had to transport an empty oil drum across a low wall, employing only a rope and two short planks. The examining officer was watching, of course, to see which member of the team took the initiative. While I and three others pondered, one candidate – a definite bright spark – immediately exclaimed: 'Right, chaps! What we need here is a system of elevation and locomotion.' He then proceeded to issue instructions which enabled us, after a struggle, to propel the oil drum to the other side of the wall.

We were then presented with a succession of five similar situations in which we each took a turn at being in charge. When it was my turn to take command, I had to resolve a problem which also involved the transportation of an oil drum with the same limited means; this time across a ditch. I formulated a plan quickly enough but when I issued my orders, the other members of the team shook their heads and said that it wouldn't work. Bright Spark then suggested what should be done. Like the good private soldier that I was, I immediately joined the others in the team in carrying out his instructions!

Later, we all sat in a circle in a small room, and the examining officer placed a pound note on the floor and told us to discuss it. Without hesitation, Bright Spark spoke up: 'It's remarkable the number of things you can do with a pound note . . .' After he had given us several examples and a dissertation on finance in general, other members of the team began to join in. I only managed to make one brief comment regarding a current problem in which Argentina was refusing to sell beef to Britain, and then dried up.

Following that, each of us had to talk for five minutes on any subject of our choice other than the army. Prior to call-up, my two principal interests had been the army and pirates. I therefore delivered a discourse on the battles cousin John and I had fought in the bath with our model galleons. Actually, I had the impression that my team-mates thoroughly enjoyed my talk. The next speaker went so far as to 'heartily congratulate' me for it, but what the examining officer may have thought I wouldn't like to say!

Finally, I was personally interviewed by an ageing major of the Seaforth Highlanders. He was a real gentleman, with white hair, drooping white moustaches and a very kindly manner. He seemed quite impressed when I told him that my brother had been a lieutenant in the 3rd Gurkha Rifles.

When I then went on to describe how Bill was killed while leading a platoon attack in Burma, I was most surprised by his reaction. Although the major wore two rows of medal ribbons on his chest and had no doubt seen many men shot to pieces around him, deep furrows now formed across his brow and he bowed his head, shaking it slowly from side to side. 'Oh, dear!' he said. 'Oh, dear, dear me! What a terrible thing to have happened!' Then he asked me: 'Have you any plans for a career?'

'I'm afraid not, sir,' I replied. 'I did intend to make a career out of the army, but now I'm in the army I've found that I don't like it.'

'How can you say that?' the major protested gently. 'You've only been in the army a few weeks. It's far too early to tell.' He looked at me carefully for a moment and then asked: 'Would you like to go to Sandhurst?'

So here it was. My dream of only two months before – a place in Sandhurst Military Academy – was now being offered to me. Before I could reply, the major continued: 'You see, if we can get a chap at Sandhurst for eighteen months, we can develop qualities which may be lying dormant in him at the moment.'

I did not hesitate. 'Oh no, sir,' I replied. 'I don't want to go to Sandhurst.'

'Well, this interview is the final part of your examination . . .' The major paused, seeming a little distracted, and then made his final plea: 'Are you sure you wouldn't like to go to Sandhurst?'

'Yes, I'm quite sure, sir,' I said.

And that was that.

At the end of it all we lined up in the grounds to receive our results. An officer walked along the line, placing a folded, numbered slip of paper in each man's hand. The paper could reveal that the candidate was recommended for Officer Cadet School training or that he would be reconsidered in three months' time or that he was – as it stated simply on my slip – 'not recommended'. Even though I had been fully expecting that result, I still felt a pang of disap-

33

pointment when I read those words. Considering I had so firmly turned my back on the idea of becoming a regular officer, it may seem strange that I cared about not obtaining a National Service commission. I suspect that although my illusions had been shattered and my world turned upside down in just a few short weeks, deep down the army still mattered to me. Bright Spark, of course, quite rightly passed the examination. He was a very nice fellow and genuinely commiserated with me when I congratulated him on his success.

Of our 'X' Cadre candidates who had been to both WOSB locations, Jim Lancaster, 'Jolly hockey sticks' Ledsome and Brown had passed, Tony Roberts was to be reconsidered in three months and the rest of us had failed. Like the remaining members of the 'X' Cadre squad, the failures could still be considered as potential NCOs.

Towards the end of October the weather grew bitterly cold. This provided an added discomfort to our daily training and meant that we froze in our barrack room at night and in the early morning. There was a stove in the room, but we soon learned that it was wise not to light it as it had to be cleaned out and spotless for morning inspection. Although kit and barrack room inspections in 'X' Cadre were not quite the ordeal that we had known in 'A' Company, Sergeant Black was very meticulous in seeking out genuine imperfections. In fact, Sergeant Black never actually bullied any of us but the sheer aura of power which emanated from his bulky frame and commanding personality made us all anxious not to displease him.

In the final weeks of our basic training, we underwent physical proficiency tests involving rope climbing, exercises on the parallel bars and various other fitness trials, all of which culminated in a 5-mile run that had to be completed within an hour. It was essential to make the grade in these tests in order to be pronounced a trained infantry soldier and, happily, I came through it all rather well.

On Thursday, 3 November, my cousin John arrived in

Bordon Camp to commence his National Service. Like me, he was enlisted with the Durham Light Infantry as his parent regiment. His intake was sufficiently fortunate to be allocated to 'B' Company, which did not have the severe reputation in the camp that 'A' Company had. To my considerable envy, John described his platoon officer, Mr Cannon, as 'a really nice bloke' and his platoon sergeant as 'a nice old guy. He treats us like a father'. His barrack room corporal was a bit of a comedian. On the first day, with a lance corporal by his side, the corporal addressed the platoon as follows: 'From now on, as far as you blokes are concerned, I'm God – and this is my mucker, Jesus Christ!'

Of course, basic training was always a tough and trying experience, no matter what – as John was to find out. In due course, he would be selected for 'X' Cadre as a potential officer, as I had been. Needless to say, I was delighted to see him, but the exigencies of bulling our kit meant that we saw little of each other in the evenings beyond a brief half-hour in the NAAFI.

Hard marching was a regular feature of our training – endurance marching in PT kit, marching to and from the firing range (as ordained by Mr Waite) and route marches in full battle order. After route marching 5 miles and 7 miles on different occasions, the climax came in our ninth week when we had to complete a 9-mile march. During the shorter marches, if anyone collapsed, Waite and his gang used to stand around the prostrate figure and scream: 'Get up on your feet, you fucking useless bastard!' However, it seemed to be expected that on the 9-mile route march, people would go down.

As we proceeded along the never-ending country road that day, complete with rifles, steel helmets and full battle equipment, the speed of 140 paces per minute was never allowed to slacken. All the time, the NCOs kept barking: 'Come on! Keep up the pace! You're supposed to be Light Infantry!' Occasionally, we were ordered to double for a short distance, which we actually welcomed as it relieved the pressure on our leg muscles. As the time went by, however, the strain of continually forcing our legs forward at that pace, carrying our heavy loads, began to take its toll.

After we had completed 5 or 6 miles, men began to stagger out of the column and collapse at the side of the road. Some of them, I noticed, appeared to be bigger and stronger than I was. Although weak, breathless and soaked in perspiration, I was determined that I would not fall out; I never had done yet. Then, after about 7 miles, Johnny Ainsworth – immediately in front of me – muttered: 'I'm sorry, chaps,' and staggered out of the column towards the grass verge. I was now gasping for breath and the pressure on my calves was quite unbearable. Thinking to myself, I can't go on! I stepped out of the column and stood there on the road, swaying back and forth like a drunk.

Suddenly, I felt a hand grasp hold of the harness of my pack and swing me back into the column. I automatically fell into step and forced my aching legs forward, and for two more miles I somehow managed to keep going. Then, the camp came into sight just ahead. It was wonderful! Mr Waite yelled: 'Come on, you people! We're almost there! March to attention! Straighten up! Shoulders back! Come on! Come on! Keep your heads up!'

Soon, to my joy, I saw that we were approaching 'A' Company barrack block. Mr Waite gave the order: 'Light Infantry! Halt!'

We halted and stood at ease. For several minutes we remained in that position, reeling on feet which felt like they were blistered raw and with our lungs heaving desperately. I could hardly believe what had happened. Somehow, I had marched for two more miles after I had become convinced that I could go no further. It was a lesson that I was never to forget and that would stand me in good stead months later in Malaya.

I gratefully turned towards the man behind me. It was Charlie Walker – a dark-haired Durham lad of about my height, though of a stronger build.

'Thanks for pulling me back in, Charlie,' I said between gasps.

He smiled weakly as he still struggled to regain his breath. One-and-a-half years later – as will eventually be related – Charlie would be shot dead in a terrorist ambush.

When we were dismissed, I found walking both difficult and painful and literally hobbled to my billet in 'X' Cadre block. I nonetheless was feeling very pleased with myself – thanks to Charlie Walker!

Shortly after that day, I went up to 3 Platoon's barrack room one evening to collect some mail which had been misdirected. On reaching the first-floor landing, I noticed that the door to Corporal Peacock's small room was open and that the intake's skill-at-arms books were piled up on the table. I hesitated for a moment. The light was on in the room but there didn't appear to be anyone inside. Cautiously, I tiptoed in and then hurriedly searched through the piles of slim books until I found mine.

At this stage in my service, I was classified as a second-class rifle shot but as first class with the Bren LMG. What interested me at that time, however, was the report on my potential which was annotated on the rear cover. It read: 'Lacks go and initiative. He will not make an NCO.' The contrast with the character reference on my Cadet Discharge Certificate could not have been more complete. At that moment I felt deeply wounded. It seemed that the army had nothing to offer me and that I had nothing to offer it. I had yet to learn that even a private soldier has a valuable contribution to make and indeed attains his own rewards.

During my search, I had come upon Tony Roberts' book. His report briefly stated: 'Too weak-willed to be an NCO.' Several months later, Tony would be wearing the stars of a second lieutenant! When I later told Tony about the two reports, he commented: 'Well, I'll tell you, Jock – I think you showed great initiative in sneaking into the corporal's bunk to look up the books!'

The news eventually reached us that on completing our training, the few regulars in our intake would be posted to their own regiments, while the National Servicemen would be divided into two drafts – one for the King's Own Yorkshire Light Infantry stationed in Malaya, and the other for the Duke of Cornwall's Light Infantry based at Mogadishu, Somaliland, in East Africa. We all knew that soldiers were being killed in Malaya, so Somaliland was the favoured location.

Then, late one afternoon at the beginning of November, the whole intake was assembled in a lecture hall. Seated on rows of benches, we waited in hushed anticipation as 'A' Company Commander, Major Armistead, mounted the small platform before us. Mr Waite, CSM Barnes and the NCOs were all present at the side of the platform.

After Major Armistead had confirmed the two intended destinations, he looked around the hall and announced: 'I want thirty-five volunteers for the King's Own Yorkshire Light Infantry in Malaya.'

Johnny Ainsworth and half a dozen others stood up. They were all Yorkshiremen whose parent regiment was the KOYLI.

Major Armistead grimaced. 'Come on!' he urged. 'I said I want thirty-five volunteers!'

I stood up. No one else did. I was aware that Mr Waite was looking at me. At that moment I felt immensely proud and very excited. I thought that perhaps I was indeed a soldier after all.

CSM Barnes now came round with a notepad, taking the names of the volunteers. 'What's that, son?' he asked gently when I pronounced my unfamiliar surname.

Looking round the hall again, Major Armistead asked: 'Any more volunteers?' There was no response. 'Very well,' he continued. 'Men from the northern regiments will be drafted to the KOYLI.'

This meant the Durhams and the Shropshires. So, as the DLI was my parent regiment, I would have been drafted to Malaya anyway. Of course, I had not previously known that, therefore I could remain proud that I was a genuine volunteer.

After we were dismissed, I was walking up the road from the lecture hall when I heard Mr Waite's voice call amiably from close behind me: 'So you're off to the jungle, are you, Scurr?'

I turned my head. 'Malaya, sir,' I confirmed. He gave me a friendly smile. I smiled back and continued on my way, feeling very content. Regrettably, I cannot say that at this point all was forgiven. My hatred for Mr Waite would linger inside me for many months to come. (Later, in Malaya, I would meet men who had served under Second Lieutenant Waite, other than in basic training. They assured me that he was 'a pretty good bloke'. I'm sure he was.)

To our delight, our ten weeks' basic training period had finally come to an end. On Tuesday, 8 November 1949, we jumped out of bed at reveille, rejoicing. At breakfast in the dining hall, newly arrived recruits – cowed and bewildered, with weeks of hell still ahead of them – eyed us with envy. We looked back at them, feeling very smug and superior.

An hour or so later, with best battledress uniforms neatly pressed, webbing belts and anklets freshly blancoed and cap badges, brasses, boots and bayonet scabbards bulled up to a dazzling brilliance, we formed up on the main barrack square for our passing-out parade. A rather stern brigadier general delivered a short speech, congratulating us on achieving the status of trained soldiers. Among other things, he told us: 'Those of you who are going to Malaya have got to get in as much shooting practice as possible. Too many Malayan bandits are getting away because of poor army marksmanship. This situation must be altered and I'm depending on chaps like you to do it!'

After his speech, the general began his inspection, passing along our ranks with his entourage and halting quite frequently to speak to someone. When he reached me, he stopped and looked me coldly in the eyes. 'Where are you going?' he asked.

'Malaya, sir!' I snapped out proudly.

'Are you a good shot?'

'Yes, sir!'

'Then, you've got nothing to worry about,' he stated positively and walked on down the rank.

His inspection complete, the general took his place on the saluting base. To the stirring tune of *Light Infantry* played by the Band and Bugles of the Somerset LI, we marched past in review order with rifles at the trail. I have to say that despite all hostile and bitter feelings engendered within me during the previous ten weeks, I now found myself tingling with pride; firstly, at having been declared a trained Light Infantry soldier, and secondly, at having been addressed as someone shortly to embark upon active service.

After the parade, we deposited our packed kitbags in the stores in readiness for our departure on leave. Those drafted to the DCLI in Somaliland were going home on 14 days' embarkation leave. The rest of us were being granted only seven days' leave, due to the fact that we had to return to Bordon for a further six weeks' training. Apparently, there had been some fuss in Parliament to the effect that young National Servicemen were being sent to the Malayan war with insufficient training. That was why we were required to undergo further training in FARELF (pronounced Farelf and meaning Far East Land Forces) Cadre before being considered ready to sail for Malaya.

With a group of others I was standing outside the stores, after depositing my kitbag, when CSM Barnes came along and climbed on a bicycle that had been leaning against the wall.

'Well, cheerio,' he said brightly.

'Cheerio, sir!' we all responded with great enthusiasm. CSM Barnes smiled – the first time I'd ever seen him smile – and then pedalled off up the road whistling 'My Happiness' – a hit song of the period. We gazed after him in total silence. Had we really been terrified of this cheerful, smiling, whistling little man?

In happy mood, Intake Group 4917 now departed for a

well-earned and desperately needed rest. Wearing my new KOYLI badge – a golden bugle with a silver rose centre-piece – on my dark green beret and carrying a few essentials in my pack, I set out from Bordon on the first stage of my long journey home. From King's Cross I travelled up to Edinburgh overnight, sharing a compartment with a friendly merchant seaman. Around 10 p.m., we removed the electric light bulb from its socket and, having pushed up the arm-rests, each stretched out on a row of seats.

Before dropping off to sleep, I reflected briefly on the extent to which my world had altered since I had made the train journey south just ten weeks earlier. At that time, I had been eager and filled with hope as I embarked upon the first stage of my intended career. I had fully expected that I would be very shortly signing on as a regular soldier with my path firmly set towards obtaining a commission. Now, I was returning home bitterly disillusioned with the army and with its apparent opinion of me, yet strangely proud that I was now a trained soldier and a volunteer for active service in Malaya.

However, I did not ponder over my complex plight for long. I was very tired and soon sank into slumber with the joyful realisation that I had now left Bordon Camp far behind me and that nobody would be able to hound me for seven whole days.

3

FARELF Cadre and Holding Company – Bordon November 1949 – January 1950

At no time in my life had I ever appreciated the comforts of home as I did during that week's leave in Edinburgh.

It was sheer luxury to sleep in pyjamas, instead of in my coarse khaki shirt, and to be able to lie in bed late in the morning without being roused at 6.30 a.m. by that dreaded bugle-call. After rising at my leisure, I could then wash and shave without being required to queue up first at a wash-basin. At mealtimes I so much enjoyed my mother's home cooking and the tranquillity of not being surrounded by about 200 other diners. Life as a temporary civilian was so civilised and comfortable. I treasured every moment of it.

Of my visits to my old haunts during those few days, only one stands out in my memory. That was the morning I spent at Boroughmuir Secondary School. Here, I saw again the large mural painting that I had completed earlier that year, depicting scenes of the Scottish timber industry. I chatted happily with my former art teachers, Mr Fisher, Mrs Smutts and Miss Anderson, and with the school's splendid head-master, Mr Carswell. When I eventually left the school to walk home, I was feeling very nostalgic for happier days which I knew would never come again.

My leave ended all too soon. On Tuesday, 15 November, I journeyed back very reluctantly to resume my life as a soldier.

When I alighted from the train at Bordon station, I was aware that another passenger – a sturdy, dark-haired man in civilian clothes – was eyeing my KOYLI cap badge. He introduced himself as Jim – a former soldier of the KOYLI who had just signed on again. As we turned down the road towards the barracks, I expressed to him my utter amazement that anyone who had escaped from the army could possibly wish to return to it.

'It's like hell on earth in this camp!' I told him.

Jim shook his head disdainfully. 'It'll be all right once we get to Malaya,' he said. 'The KOYLIs are having the time of their lives out there.'

I felt perplexed. 'What about the bandits?' I asked.

'Aahh!' he grunted. 'They're fuck-all! You never see them.'

'Well, somebody must see them,' I retorted, thinking of the news reports of soldiers being ambushed and killed.

'Yeh, but you won't,' Jim replied positively.

On reaching Bordon Camp, we went our separate ways, though I would meet up with Jim again some weeks later. (Traditionally, soldiers in the KOYLI were supposed to be offended if anyone referred to them as 'KOYLIs' – pronounced Koylis. Nonetheless, most of us called ourselves 'KOYLIs' in daily conversation.)

Reporting to the FARELF Cadre block in St Lucia Barracks, I was allocated to a ground floor barrack room in which I was happy to discover that there was a concentration of former 'X' Cadre members – Johnny Ainsworth, Geoff Clarke, Tony Roberts, Sam Coster, Phil Cox and others.

When I went down to the stores with Geoff Clarke to draw out our kitbags, the storeman nodded towards a packed grey bag lying on its own.

'He won't be needing his kitbag,' the storeman said. 'He's dead!'

Startled, I read the name that was stencilled on the grey cloth and instantly pictured the small, wiry lad with tightly curled black hair who had been drafted to the DCLI. Immediately prior to their departure on leave, all of the men going to Somaliland had been given jabs against yellow fever. That night, apparently, this lad had gone out drinking with friends in his home town and had dropped dead.

Late that afternoon, our FARELF Cadre Platoon paraded outside our barrack block to be introduced to our Platoon Commander and Sergeant – Lieutenant Ryall and Sergeant O'Hare. The latter had been 4 Platoon's sergeant during our basic training and was well reputed to be a 'bastard'. Mr Ryall, on the other hand, proved to be a mild-mannered, thorough gentleman who had served in Burma during the Second World War and therefore felt well qualified to train us for Malaya. Slim and sandy-haired, Mr Ryall impressed me favourably from the start.

He told us: 'You'll find life a bit cushier here than it was in basic training. After all, you're trained soldiers now. When I come round, I won't expect to find your cap badge shining too brightly. If I pick up your rifle, I'll expect there to be a little dust on it. In fact, I won't be making you do any bull. I hope to teach you something else.'

My heart leapt with joy. This sounded much better, I thought. After telling us finally that our training would commence the following morning, Mr Ryall left us.

Stout and brawny Sergeant O'Hare now addressed us with unpleasant severity. 'Right!' he said. 'You can forget what you just heard about having a cushy time. Trained soldiers? You lot? As far as I'm concerned, you're recruits and I intend to treat you like recruits! And I can tell you this – if I catch any of you without your cap badge shining or with dust on your rifle, you'll be straight on a charge!'

My short-lived joyous feeling was now replaced with disappointment and despair. It just wasn't fair!

Sergeant O'Hare was true to his word. Over the following six weeks, he kept us doing bull as much as he could and always behaved like an absolute pig. However, despite his efforts, life in FARELF Cadre proved to be considerably better than it had been in 'A' Company. By now, I was coming to accept being verbally abused as a normal part of army life. I still didn't like it, of course, but I no longer allowed it to hurt me to the extent that it had previously.

Anyway, Sergeant O'Hare was the only one who now tried to make our life a misery. Mr Ryall was an absolute gem and when he was around, O'Hare had to toe the line.

Our barrack room corporal was a tall, well-built, handsome young man. I am not sure but I think his name may have been Sampson. One day while giving us a lesson on the Bren gun, he told us that he had formerly been a National Serviceman and that after a few months in Civvy Street, he had signed on as a regular. He said that he was sure that some of us would do the same. When we poured scorn on this suggestion, he retorted: 'When I finished my National Service I was just as determined as you are never to have anything to do with the army again. But it's only when you go back to Civvy Street that you begin to appreciate the good things about the army.' I doubt if many of those present that day ever did sign on again, but his basic premise about appreciating the army later was correct, as I was to discover.

On parade, Corporal Sampson was aloof, sometimes cutting. Off parade, he could be reasonably friendly with some members of the platoon, though never with me. I don't think he liked me much but apart from a few sarcastic 'You're not in the cadets now'-type remarks, he didn't take it out on me.

Someone who did like me and who chatted to me frequently was our junior NCO, Lance Corporal Scott. He had a good sense of humour and only rarely got cross. One time, he was drilling us and when due to give the order 'Light Infantry! Halt!', he could not resist ordering: 'Shite Infantry! Halt!' Well, I thought it was funny anyway.

On the first Saturday afternoon following my leave, I called at 'B' Company barrack block, intending that cousin John and I would journey into Aldershot to see a new Errol Flynn swashbuckler, *Adventures of Don Juan*. I found John lying on his bed, sweating and quivering and hardly able to speak to me as a result of the inoculation that he had received that morning. Consequently, I had to go to Aldershot alone but I thoroughly enjoyed the film. At that time

Errol Flynn had already begun his sad, debauched decline, although it was not yet apparent on the screen.

Our training in FARELF Cadre consisted principally of weapon training and fieldcraft, with plenty of shooting practice on the firing range. For the first time we learned to fire the 2-inch mortar and the PIAT anti-tank weapon. We were also shown a film about jungle fighting in Burma that had been used for training troops during the war. I remember that the film commentator advised the British soldier that he should not be afraid of his Japanese counterpart: 'Remember you're twice the man he is, physically and mentally!' If they believed the film, the troops would have been in for a shock when they got to Burma.

One night, we went on an all-night exercise. Former members of 'X' Cadre were each put in charge of two men. These teams were then sent out independently with the mission of locating an 'enemy' base, manned by Lance Corporal Scott and his squad. Early on, I fell into a waist-deep stream. It was a cold night, so I was extremely uncomfortable in wet trousers during the rest of the exercise. Despite this mishap, I managed to locate the enemy base and led my team in an attack, firing blank cartridges, after which we successfully escaped the pursuit of Lance Corporal Scott and his men. My team was the first to locate the base. I consequently felt that I had done rather well for someone who 'lacks initiative and will not make an NCO' – as reported in my skill-at-arms book!

Soon after that, John went for his WOSB examination but – like me – was 'not recommended' for Officer Training School. At weekends we normally went to Aldershot together for movies and meals at the NAAFI Club. During the week, we usually went to the camp NAAFI for a while in the evenings to enjoy a snack and a chat. I remember one particularly cold night when we managed to secure two armchairs by the NAAFI fireplace. Cosy and warm, we swapped reminiscences of our 'sea battles' in the bath and various other holiday incidents and laughed until the tears were streaming down our cheeks.

Whilst in FARELF Cadre, I became especially friendly with one of the former members of 'X' Cadre, 'Sam' Coster. Sam was not his real name but we called him that after Sam Costa, the famous radio comedian of that era. A lanky chap with rather a high-pitched voice, Sam was a very amusing companion. He was also a conscientious objector who had not, however, given voice to his convictions at the time of his call-up.

Once a week, our platoon used to assemble in a lecture hall to be addressed for an hour by the regimental chaplain on such subjects as writing home to our mothers, staying clear of ladies of easy virtue and keeping in tune with God. The chaplain was a burly, red-faced officer with a couple of rows of medal ribbons on his chest. One day, he was speaking to us about our approaching active service in Malaya. Sam suddenly stood up and asked: 'Sir, do you think God would approve of me killing my fellow men?'

The chaplain's normally red face turned absolutely crimson. 'It's your duty to kill your fellow men!' he roared. There was a moment of complete silence. Then, the chaplain said more calmly, though still obviously angry: 'It's just something that has to be done.' Unable to provide a satisfactory answer to an admittedly difficult question, the chaplain quickly moved on to another topic. Sam wisely remained silent.

On another occasion, the chaplain delivered a lecture as follows: 'Now today, boys, I want to talk to you about bad language. Now there's one word – and you all know which word I mean – that you boys use repeatedly. The other day, I was walking along the road to Bordon station behind two young fellows who employed this word no fewer than thirty times in a hundred yards. Now you all know the word I'm talking about. I'm talking about the word "fucking". Now what's the first thing you boys say when you get up in the morning? You say "Where's my fucking socks? Where's my fucking boots?" Now I ask you, boys, have you ever seen a pair of boots having sexual intercourse?'

One morning, we had to lay out our full kit for inspection.

Sergeant O'Hare walked round the room, criticising everything and everyone. He then told us that we'd obviously made no effort to display our kit properly and that the floor didn't look as though it had even been swept, never mind polished. Therefore, he told us, we would be submitted to another inspection at 6 p.m., and God help us if there wasn't a big improvement!

We then proceeded with our scheduled training for that day. In the afternoon we were on an exercise and did not get back until just before six o'clock. The barrack room and our kit were exactly as they had been at morning inspection. There wasn't time to do a single thing before Sergeant O'Hare strode in and ordered us to stand by our beds. We stood to attention, inwardly quivering as the perpetually scowling O'Hare moved from bed space to bed space, surveying our laid out kits. He remained silent throughout and having completed his inspection, halted at the door and faced towards us. 'Now that's much better,' he declared. 'If you'd only done it like that this morning, you'd have saved yourselves a lot of trouble!'

Actually, bull was not too much of a problem for me in FARELF Cadre. One chap in my room, Johnny Grose, acted as an errand-boy and general dogsbody for Corporal Sampson and was also my paid manservant. He bulled my boots and mess tins, blancoed my webbing and pressed my uniforms at sixpence (2.5p) per task, and always did a fine job, I must say.

Well into December, the platoon set out on a two-day 'jungle exercise' in some nearby woodlands – minus Sergeant O'Hare, we were relieved to find. On the way to the woods, we called in for a morning break at a country pub called The Bluebell. I had a definite impression that Lieutenant Ryall fancied Pauline, the barmaid, but he was too shy to make any direct approach. Corporal Sampson pushed his beret to the back of his head and played darts with some of the lads, temporarily calling them by their first names. Apart from this pleasant interlude the only thing I can remember about the jungle exercise is that we dug slit-trenches in the woods and slept in them. When we woke up next morning, we were covered in snow. Anything less like jungle training I couldn't imagine!

My pal Sam Coster remained very concerned about the possibility of finding himself in a kill-or-be-killed situation in Malaya. Eventually, he resolved his dilemma by applying for a storeman's job that would shortly become vacant on the LIBTC staff in Bordon. When he delightedly gave me the news that the job would be his in two weeks' time, I said to him: 'Good for you, Sam! I'll miss you, though. I mean, I was looking forward to having a good mate with me when we sail.'

Sam looked at me for a moment and then declared very resolutely: 'To hell with it! I'll see it through! I'll go to Malaya!'

'But then, you might get killed,' I pointed out.

'Oh yes,' Sam said hesitantly. 'Oh well, I'd better not go then.'

I burst out laughing, despite my considerable sorrow that Sam would not be accompanying me to Malaya after all.

As Christmas approached, Mr Ryall organised a platoon party to be held one night in The Bluebell pub. Before we set out on the appointed evening, Mr Ryall assembled the platoon and made a surprise announcement: 'I've bet Pauline a pair of nylons that she'll be kissed over Christmas. So if any of you gets the opportunity, don't hesitate to do it.'

It seemed to me rather odd that Mr Ryall should be urging the rude soldiery to take liberties with his fancied young lady. Not that Pauline appeared the type that anyone could take liberties with. She was a very pretty brunette with a full and shapely figure; yet her demeanour, though friendly, was quite prim and proper. Perhaps Mr Ryall believed that it was perfectly safe to say what he did.

The party was a success, with Sergeant O'Hare noticeably and happily absent. Most of the lads got pretty drunk and sang all of their repertoire of the more respectable army songs, to the apparent enjoyment of the pub's other customers. I only drank a couple of shandies but spent a fair amount on buying drinks for others. A Durham lad called Bill Aisbit was even more of a comedian than normal after I'd bought him a few rums!

Towards the end of the night, Corporal Sampson was chatting with Pauline across the bar. He was a handsome hunk who could turn on the charm when he wanted to. Suddenly, his arm slipped around Pauline's shoulders and he drew her towards him. She did not appear to offer any resistance. As the corporal kissed her fully on the lips, a loud cheer arose from the boys of the platoon. So presumably poor Pauline did not get her nylon stockings. Just what Mr Ryall hoped to gain from the enterprise though, I cannot imagine.

When we got back to the barracks, Mr Ryall assigned the handful of us who had remained sober to the task of putting all the drunks to bed and helping them to the toilets to be sick. At that time I was unable to understand why anyone would allow himself to get in such a state. Little did I realise, then, that the time was not too far distant when goody-goody, innocent little me would be behaving in a like manner – and smoking and swearing as well!

Our six weeks of FARELF training now came to an end. Mr Ryall gave us a farewell speech in which he said that if any of us were ever in any trouble, wherever we were we could write to him and he would always help us if he could. An officer and a gentleman, to be sure!

On 23 December, most of the platoon departed on four days' Christmas leave plus eight days' embarkation leave. Being Scottish, I was asked if I would like to stay behind over Christmas and then go home for New Year. Although New Year meant nothing special to me, I agreed to do this and several others, mainly Geordies, also remained. The camp was practically empty over Christmas and we had a cushy and very enjoyable time. Even guard duty at night was pleasant and relaxed.

As was traditional in the army, Christmas dinner was served to us by the officers. The cookhouse that we attended in FARELF Cadre had consistently produced meals of a far poorer standard than those we had enjoyed during basic training. However, on this occasion, the cooks managed a reasonably good turkey dinner. I have to say, though, that the officer who served our table had resentment written all over his face!

On Saturday morning, 31 December, those of us who had remained now set off on our four days' 'Christmas' plus eight days' embarkation leave. I was granted an additional two days' travelling time which, I hate to admit, had been obtained for me by the despised Sergeant O'Hare! This made my leave up to a fortnight.

I do not remember much about this second leave in Edinburgh other than that I went to see three films – *Captain from Castile*, *Adventures of Don Juan* (twice) and an Errol Flynn western, *San Antonio*. I left my home in Edinburgh on Wednesday, 11 January 1950, and broke my journey south at Wallsend-on-Tyne to stay with cousin John and his family for a couple of days. I had always been fond of my aunt Agnes (John's mother) and of my beautiful cousin Gladys, who bore a considerable likeness to the film actress Lynn Bari. Gladys's husband Wilfie had been in the Merchant Navy during the war, and I had always been an avid listener to his many salty tales.

John arrived home on leave that same day, upon completion of his basic training. He too had been drafted for the KOYLI in Malaya and had six weeks' extra training ahead of him in FARELF Cadre. On the Thursday afternoon, we both went to visit John's friend John Patton, who lived in nearby South Shields. While we were in this friend's house, there was a news report on the radio from Malaya in which the BBC correspondent spoke of '. . . this savage war in jungle and swamp'.

John Patton's mother looked at me, very startled, and exclaimed: 'Oh, my goodness! That isn't what you're going to, is it?'

I proudly and happily declared that it was. At that time,

of course, I knew little about jungle and swamp, other than the fact that they did not appear to present too great a problem to Johnny Weissmuller, Sabu or Dorothy Lamour.

On arrival back at St Lucia Barracks, Bordon Camp, late on Friday, 13 January, I reported to the Holding Company barrack block. Holding Company – which 'held' drafts that were waiting to go overseas – was rigidly controlled by a well-known character in the camp, Corporal 'Jackie' Diamond. I had been told that this NCO had completed almost 30 years' service and that he had a reputation for being a bit of a swine.

When I entered his room, Corporal Diamond was standing in front of a roaring fire, wearing only a towel wrapped around his enormous, fat belly. On this occasion, he was very friendly and chatted to me quite affably for about ten minutes. As I was the last to arrive back from leave, having had two extra days' travelling time, he told me that he would be unable to place me in a barrack room with other members of my intake group. Instead, he would have to put me in a room with some 'old soldiers' who had been mustered in to join our draft for Malaya. 'At least, they think they're old soldiers,' Jackie Diamond explained. 'Most of them have only been in the army a couple of years. You have to be in for thirty years before you can call yourself an old soldier!' He eyed me for a moment and then said: 'Don't you let any of these old soldiers mess you around, now. If any of them try to give you any old malarkey, you come straight to me, understand?'

After receiving this warning, I made my way to the indicated first-floor barrack room with considerable feelings of trepidation. However, I need not have worried. The old soldiers turned out to be a great bunch of characters who made me feel welcome from the start. There was 'Mac' McAllister – a veteran of World War Two and former NCO in Malaya; Jim Walters, also a war veteran, who looked very old to me and certainly must have been in his forties; Bert Marsh – a blond, muscular chap who would later become a regimental policeman; Stan Swalwell – who had rejoined after completing National Service due to domestic problems; Jim Brown – a good-looking chap with an Errol Flynn moustache who often spoke fondly of his wife and child; 'Signor' Pinchbeck – a big, lanky fellow with mischievous, dark eyes and a black moustache which twirled up at the ends; and I also recognised 'Jim', who I had met at Bordon station when returning from my first leave and who had told me that the men of the KOYLI were having 'the time of their lives' in Malaya. Like McAllister, the last four had all served previously in Malaya. Far from messing me around, most of these old soldiers adopted protective, big-brother attitudes towards me – 'Don't worry, Jock. We'll look after you.'

Every morning, the whole draft formed up outside the block and Corporal Jackie Diamond allocated us very abruptly to various fatigue duties; normally peeling potatoes, washing greasy pots and pans, scrubbing floors, cleaning out fireplaces or stoves – in fact, every dirty or disagreeable job that was going. These fatigues and the harsh, cutting tongue of Jackie Diamond made us long for notification of our sailing date. The food in Holding Company was quite abysmal, so I began eating regular suppers at the NAAFI with cousin John, following his return from leave.

The one redeeming feature of my time with Holding Company was the entertaining banter in the barrack room. I listened with fascination to my companions' many tales about their previous service in Malaya. They spoke mostly about the KOYLI headquarters on Penang Island, of a dance hall called the City Lights and of prostitutes with names such as Suzie Li and Nancy Yap. Signor Pinchbeck spoke enthusiastically about someone known as 'Big Mary'. Jim – whose last name I won't mention – knew her too. Well, Jim appeared to know them all. He told so many wild tales about women and his army service in general that the others nicknamed him 'Jungle Jim'.

Jungle Jim had first served with the Somerset LI in India before transferring to the KOYLI in Malaya. His numerous stories included: finding a naked woman in the toilet when he was on a train bound for Bombay; being filmed by a British Movietone News cameraman while he was supposedly leading a patrol into action in the Malayan jungle, when he was actually leading a retreat from a snake in the bushes; and being taken by Chinese youths to a place in Penang where naked women were lying in a circle on gigantic cushions and Jim did the rounds, rolling off one woman onto the next one!

When such stories were being told, old Jim Walters would look over at me and say with concern: 'Poor Jock must be shocked. He comes from a good home.' Actually, I was quite enthralled by these yarns, even if I didn't always believe them. At that time, the idea was firmly implanted in my innocent and fairly religious young mind that sex outside of marriage was sinful. Even so, like all other youths, I was very curious about the subject and inclined to fantasise about it.

Whenever I asked any of these old soldiers about the Malayan bandits, they always answered evasively. Finally, all of them admitted that they had never actually fought any bandits themselves – even Jungle Jim. At the same time, they did speak of actions that others had been involved in and told me about a young conscript called Ward who had been killed on patrol fairly recently. Consequently, no matter what anyone said, I remained convinced that within weeks of my landing in Malaya I would be shooting it out with the bandits – like Errol Flynn, Gary Cooper or John Wayne.

In those days I knew little about the situation in Malaya. I had a fairly simple view of world affairs in general but, of course, simple views are not necessarily inaccurate. The Second World War had ended five years earlier with the Soviet Army occupying Eastern Europe and installing Communist dictatorships in several countries, including Poland, that Britain had gone to war to keep free in the first place. Soviet Russia and these Eastern countries were then under the iron grip of the malevolent dictator Joseph Stalin, whose policies had been responsible for the deaths of many millions of people, even in peacetime. In 1948, the Berlin blockade had intensified the Cold War between East and West, and in 1949, the Communist forces of Mao Tse-tung had finally achieved victory in China.

Over the years, there has been much talk of the 'anti-Communist hysteria' in the United States and Britain during that period. However, there was, in fact, plenty to be 'hysterical' about. Communist subversion was active in many parts of the world and a third world war between the Eastern bloc and the Western democracies not only seemed possible but extremely probable. Only the existence of nuclear weapons might prevent it, people told one another anxiously.

Consequently, I saw the terrorist actions of Communist guerrilla forces in Malaya, and Britain's response to them, as another facet of the struggle to establish either a free or a Communist world. I also understood that it was vital that Malaya's rubber and tin industries should not fall into Communist hands. So, on both these counts, I believed it to be right and just that I and my fellow draftees should soon be proceeding to Malaya in order to fight the Communist 'bandits'.

Our departure date finally appeared on Company Orders. We would be sailing from Liverpool on His Majesty's Transport *Devonshire* on 24 January. Our draft appellation would be DAFJZ which we now began stencilling on our kitbags beneath our numbers and names. We each had two kitbags: one to be packed with items needed on the voyage and the other to contain remaining kit to be stowed in the hold of the ship. It was an exciting time, if tempered by some anxiety.

My last full day in Bordon Camp was a Sunday, which I spent quietly in barracks, saying my goodbyes to cousin John, Sam Coster and Tony Roberts. Sam was now safely established in his storeman's job and Tony was also being retained in Bordon with a view to attending a second WOSB examination – which he was to come through successfully this time. John would be joining me in Malaya in a couple of months.

(In the KOYLI, 'Serjeant' was always spelled with a 'j'. From this point in my narrative, that traditional spelling will therefore be employed when referring to KOYLI-NCOs of that rank.)

On the morning of Monday, 23 January 1950, four days after my nineteenth birthday, Draft DAFJZ departed from the LIBTC, Bordon, never to return. Forty-eight of us boarded that train for London. In command of the draft was a 21-year-old Royal Army Ordnance Corps officer – on temporary attachment to the KOYLI – Lieutenant George Styles. There were no fewer than four serjeants – by name Dee, Hall, Hogan and Lynn – and there were 43 private soldiers, the majority of whom were National Servicemen.

From Waterloo we travelled by underground train to Goodge Street station, which at that time was still being used as a transit camp for troops, as it had been during the war. We were allocated bunks for the night in the underground tunnels and provided with a meal. Then McAllister and Jungle Jim asked Lieutenant Styles if they could go out that night. 'We're not going to run away,' McAllister insisted. 'We're volunteers.'

'So am I,' Mr Styles answered. 'But I don't know if I'm going to be allowed out tonight.'

Soon after, Mr Styles informed us that we could all go out on the proviso that we had to be back by midnight. Unbeknown to us, Mr Styles then went to meet his wife Mary, who was a student nurse at the nearby University College Hospital. I had mixed feelings about Mr Styles at that time. While I resented the idea of Light Infantrymen being put under the command of an RAOC officer, I had to admit that he seemed a pleasant, down-to-earth sort of chap; firm enough but sensible.

Johnny Ainsworth, Geoff Clarke and I went to the Dominion cinema in Tottenham Court Road to see Gary Cooper in a wartime naval drama, *Task Force*. It was not a particularly good film but, in any case, I found myself unable

56

to relax sufficiently to enjoy it. The reality of my present situation had suddenly leapt to the forefront of my mind, ringing alarm bells. I would actually be leaving the country the following day to go to the other side of the world and take part in a war. For all I knew, I might never return. This wasn't a game or a Hollywood fantasy. I was really going! Tomorrow! After the show, I told Johnny and Geoff that I had been unable to enjoy the film because I had been preoccupied with thoughts of what lay ahead of us, and they both immediately confessed that their minds had been in similar turmoil.

Very early the following morning, our draft set out from Goodge Street and marched in column-of-threes to Euston station, carrying our heavy kitbags on our shoulders. At Euston we boarded the train to Liverpool. As we sped on our way, I was very aware of a feeling that time was running out and that nothing was going to stop this thing from happening. We were going to Malaya.

About halfway to our destination, while halted in a station (I can't recall where), old Jim Walters grew very tense and agitated as the minutes ticked by and the train did not move. 'I wish we'd get out of this place, Jock,' he muttered to me. 'I live just round the corner from here.'

'You mean it makes you feel like jumping off and making a run for it, Jim?' I asked.

'It does!' he exclaimed, gripping the armrests of his seat. Fortunately, the train lurched into motion at that moment. Jim shook his head and sighed: 'By, that were a close one!'

After alighting at a station in Liverpool, we commenced what I remember as a fairly long and depressing march through grim, dismal streets to the docks.

There, at the quay, stood the troopship *Devonshire*.

4

HMT Devonshire
January–February 1950

It was late in the afternoon of Tuesday, 24 January, when we filed up the gangway of HMT *Devonshire* and were immediately ushered below to the mess deck where we were to live, eat and sleep for the next four weeks. On that first evening, I noted that there were drafts on board for the Scots Guards, Seaforths, Devons, Suffolks, West Kents, South Staffords, King's Own Scottish Borderers, Middlesex Regiment, Royal Engineers, Royal Marines and RAF. In fact, there were drafts on board for these and many other units – approximately 1,500 men altogether – all bound for Malaya or Hong Kong.

Just before 10 p.m. as the time for sailing approached, I stood at the ship's rail and looked down through the darkness towards the quay, where sparse groups of relatives and well-wishers were continuously waving. Hundreds of servicemen, lining the rails all the way along the side of the ship, were alternately singing:

Far away places with strange sounding names,
Far away over the sea . . .

and

Now is the hour when we must say goodbye.
Soon, I'll be sailing far across the sea . . .

Then, suddenly, the ship was under way and the lights of Liverpool gradually receded. I remember thinking how final everything was. There was no going back now. I was on my way to the Malayan war. It seemed to me inevitable that on board that ship, there must be some young men who would never see their homeland again. I wondered if I would be one of them.

My mind was strangely calm while making these deliberations. The anxiety of the previous night was gone. Now that we were actually on our way, it didn't seem so bad. Packed in my kitbag was a large, hard-cover notebook which I had bought for the purpose of recording my great adventure in the form of a journal. Over the following 18 months, I would completely fill this book and another one like it. I lost no time in starting to jot down my impressions of life aboard a troopship.

Our mess deck, down below, was furnished with row upon row of long wooden tables with wooden benches on either side of them. Every draft billeted on the mess-deck was allocated its own space with its own tables and overhead racks in which kitbags were stored. At night, we slung our issued hammocks on hooks in the ceiling above our space. After reveille at 6 a.m., hammocks were rolled up and stowed away in a gigantic pile at the end of the mess deck. Although we wrote our names on our hammocks, considerable time was often spent at night trying to locate them in the pile.

The tables, benches and floor had to be scrubbed every day. This task was performed by mess deck orderlies on a rota system. Two mess orderlies were also appointed each day to go to the galley at mealtimes, bring back large dixie cans of food and tea for their particular table and then serve out the meal. This duty could be absolutely nauseating when there was a rough sea. Sometimes, an orderly would have to hastily abandon his task and rush up on deck to heave up over the side. This happened to me at least once.

Seasickness was undoubtedly the worst thing about the voyage. I had never known a feeling like it. On a couple of occasions, Ginger Thompson – one of the few hearty souls who were never sick – had to sling my hammock for me at night and help me into it. I hated when I then awoke the next morning in a swaying hammock, immediately aware that I still felt as ill as I had when I'd fallen asleep the night before. After attempting to eat breakfast, I would hang over the ship's rail and vomit, and afterwards my empty stomach would suffer agonies of continuous retching. Fortunately, we only had a few spells of really rough seas, but during those times life was unbearable for me and for many others like me. I recall that a Durham lad, Arnie Bowron, was a noted fellow sufferer.

The other main drawback was the cramped conditions on the crowded mess deck. This, combined with boredom, tended to make men get on each other's nerves and tempers frequently flared. On two occasions, disputes exploded into fisticuffs. Fifteen minutes' PT every morning and an hour's training in the afternoon still left us with a lot of time to laze around when not on one of the duty rotas.

Since boarding the troopship, the 'old soldiers' who had been my companions in Holding Company no longer recognised me as part of their group, although they were always friendly towards me as individuals. However, old friends from 'X' Cadre, Johnny Ainsworth and Geoff Clarke, provided company when required.

Sailing through the Bay of Biscay on Thursday, 26 January, the sea grew pretty rough. The constant rising and falling of my stomach in unison with the motions of the ship, aggravated by the horrible, greasy smell of food which seemed to linger everywhere, even between mealtimes, brought me close to being sick by nightfall.

At 2 a.m. on Friday the 27th, we passed Cape Finisterre, but on leaving the Bay of Biscay the sea did not become any calmer. That night was very stormy and nearly everyone was feeling ill. On the Saturday morning, I awoke with that same ill feeling and, after desperately assuring myself that it would soon pass off, I rushed up on deck to be sick over the side for the first time. Even this did not reduce the wretched effects of the malady. At 9 a.m., we saw Cape St Vincent and had quite a clear sighting of the Spanish coast, though I was in no condition to appreciate it. Around midnight, our ship passed through the Straits of Gibraltar and into the Mediterranean Sea.

Early in the morning of Sunday the 29th, two chaps from our draft had a fist fight. One of them was knocked out cold and had to be carried off to the ship's hospital for treatment. That morning, we had a good view of the southern coast of Spain and could see snow-covered mountains in the distance. In the afternoon, I was delighted by the sight of shoals of porpoises jumping up out of the water and later had a faint, distant glimpse of North Africa.

That day was a good deal warmer, the sun was shining quite brightly, the sea was lovely and calm and blue, and I felt fine all day, as did everyone else that I spoke to. Our appetites had improved, the food tasted better and, on the whole, life on board had grown decidedly more pleasant. The principal amusement aboard ship seemed to be gambling. Large amounts of money were squandered on cards by both NCOs and men – but not by me!

We passed Algiers at 4 a.m. on Monday the 30th and at times during the day sailed quite close to the North African coast. It looked very desolate country; just mountains and woods with an occasional village. The following day, we saw more of the African coast and passed Malta at 9 p.m.

When our ship reached the Middle East, the voyage suddenly became more interesting and exciting. For the time being, we forgot all our discomforts and petty annoyances and enjoyed the sights and sounds of exotic locations.

On Friday, 3 February, we were disappointed to hear that our expected shore leave at Port Said had been cancelled. Apparently, elections just held in Egypt had produced hostility towards the British government, so there might have been trouble if we went ashore. However, we were now promised shore leave when we reached Aden.

We sighted Port Said at 4 p.m. as we sailed through a brown, sand-coloured sea, and our ship moored in the harbour an hour later. Port Said looked a really nice place, with palm trees growing along both sides of the streets.

There were ships of several nationalities in the harbour, including two British liners.

As soon as we arrived, Egyptians in bumboats came alongside, hoping to sell us souvenirs and foodstuffs. Before making a purchase, you first had to bargain until the price was suitably reduced. Then the vendor threw up a line and you pulled up a basket into which you put your money. After lowering the basket, you then hauled it up again, now containing your purchase. These salesmen spoke very good English and could imitate Geordie, Scouse or Scots accents. One of them kept saying: 'Och away, man!' They knew plenty of English swear words too!

Some of the bargaining was quite amusing. A vendor proclaimed: 'Lovely lady's purse – one pound!'

'Two bob [10p]!' a soldier called down.

'Three bob [15p]!' the vendor insisted, and made his sale.

The bumboats remained alongside until late that night. Just after dark, an incident occurred which seemed amusing at the time but in retrospect was not. Some chaps from another unit brought a large, tin bathtub full of steaming hot water up on deck and poured the contents down on top of two Egyptians who were standing in a large-sized bumboat below. The two Egyptians uttered loud yells. Then one of them looked up towards us and said contemptuously: 'So this is the English!' Picking up an iron bar, he continued: 'Give me two Englishmen down here! Two Englishmen!'

Neither the culprits nor anyone else went down. The Egyptian then removed his wet jacket and for a moment seemed to be about to climb up onto the ship. However, he thought better of it and he and his fellow countryman soon resumed their business.

We left Port Said at midnight and began our journey through the Suez Canal. When I came up on deck the next morning, the canal banks were close on both sides of the ship and the first thing I saw was a dromedary on the sand of the left bank. For the first time seeing real desert, with occasional clumps of green palm trees, made me think of *The Four Feathers*, *Beau Geste* and other such adventure films. I felt immensely excited and could hardly believe that I was seeing such things. (It should be remembered that in those days, holidays abroad were almost exclusively the domain of the well-to-do and opportunities for foreign travel were very restricted.) Periodically, we saw Egyptians in long, coloured robes strolling along the banks, often leading donkeys. We also passed small army camps and aerodromes. From British troops on the banks came the customary call: 'Get your knees brown!' One Egyptian civilian took out his penis and waved it at us!

At 10 a.m., the canal widened out and there wasn't so much to see. It seemed strange to me that we were in the Suez Canal and yet it was hardly as warm as an English spring day. Around noon, the canal narrowed once more and I continued to be fascinated by our close view of Egyptian men and women, dromedaries and palm trees. When we reached Port Suez at 2 p.m., a boat came alongside to take off the pilot who had guided the ship from Port Said. The past two days had been most enjoyable.

As we sailed on into the Red Sea, the weather grew much warmer. On Monday, 6 February, we changed into our jungle-green tropical kit – bush shirt and shorts. With the change in climate, the cramped conditions down below on our hot, stuffy mess deck could be quite unbearable; especially when trying to sleep at night in our rows of hammocks all jammed together. During the daytime we had frequent glimpses of the Arabian coast and on the morning of Wednesday the 8th enjoyed watching porpoises leaping up out of the sea, quite close to the ship. Just before noon that day, we sighted Aden. I noted in my journal that Aden looked like 'a set of ivory dominoes standing among a lot of rocks and sand'.

The following afternoon, while we were waiting for permission to go ashore, I saw some sharks swimming along by the side of the ship. The promised Indian currency (which apparently they used in Aden) had not arrived but we were told that our English money would be accepted without problem.

At last, at about 8.45 p.m., launches came alongside to take us ashore. We were instructed that we had to be back by 10.30, which didn't give us much time. When we landed at the port, we were greeted by a host of taxi drivers imploring us to ride in their vehicles. Geoff Clarke, Johnny Ainsworth and I took a short walk first, pestered all the way by vendors of postcards, slippers, chewing gum, etc. We decided to go to the NAAFI for something to eat and at that moment a taxi drove up and its Indian driver called out: 'You want to go to the Lido?'

'The Lido? Is that the NAAFI?' Geoff asked.

'Yes. The NAAFI.'

'How much?'

'Two rupees.'

'Will you take English money?'

'English money – two shillings [10p].'

We climbed in and the taxi drove off. Our driver was wearing European-style shirt and slacks and spoke quite good English. He shortly said to us: 'I can show you Aden town for eight shillings [40p], sahibs. The whole town for eight shillings.'

We considered this proposition and decided to accept it. The taxi drove up a steep, winding road round the hill slopes and then down through a tunnel into Aden town, known as 'Crater'. Our driver pointed out several places to us, such as a police station, a prison and a Jewish cemetery, all of which we glimpsed briefly as we drove past in the darkness.

Soon, we drove through some gardens with beautiful trees and bushes. Everything was very silent and still, apart from one or two Arabs moving quietly in the shadows. After a while, the taxi stopped and our driver told us that we could visit some other gardens if we cared to. We all got out and approached an iron gate where some Arab men and boys

64

were standing silently. After the driver had spoken to them in Arabic, we continued through the gate with one of the Arabs as a guide. We were led up a path between large rocks until we reached some deep arenas. A plaque explained that these 'tanks' had been discovered by a British officer in the 1930s and were remnants of an ancient irrigation system.

After we had walked round these arenas, we returned to the gates. Here, we entered a small museum in which we were shown some ancient coins, skulls, swords, knives, etc. Then, we tipped the guide, giving him a shilling (5p), and with the rest of the Arabs now holding out their hands and asking for 'baksheesh', we returned to the taxi. Arab children kept calling to us: 'You give us English money? English very good, yes?'

When we had left the gardens, we asked the driver to take us to the Lido. He drove us slowly through the Indian and Arab markets, where a mass of robed and turbanned figures sat with their animals and baskets of goods or stood by their stalls, bargaining with potential customers. The markets were thronged but we drove carefully through them and then on down some less busy streets. In an effort to amuse us, our driver began shouting at any British soldiers that we passed: 'Hey, you bastards!' and other such comments. Then, he said to us: 'Plenty to drink at the Lido. As much as you want. Lido good place, sahibs. Lots of Arab bints!'

As we drove up to the brightly-lit Lido, we saw a young woman pick up a British serviceman on the pavement outside. 'Are you going to come with me, darling?' I heard her say as we climbed out of the taxi.

'An Arab bint!' our driver commented.

When I waited behind to pay the driver, the serviceman and the Arab girl passed close by me. Her skin wasn't very dark – in fact, it was almost white – and she had flashing eyes and a mass of dark hair in small curls all round her head. She was wearing a tightly fitting black dress and had a terrific pair of breasts. She was really lovely. I was immensely impressed by her vital beauty, which I later described in my journal and also in a letter to cousin John.

We entered the Lido and found it to be a large, open place, crammed with service personnel. There didn't seem to be much food for sale, just lots of beer. We settled for lemonade and cakes. If it really was a NAAFI, it was pretty poor compared to those at home.

When we left the Lido, it was a quarter past ten, so we took a taxi back to the port, accompanied by some Scots soldiers who got off without paying! We were then conveyed in a launch back to the ship. It had been quite an exciting night.

After sailing across the Gulf of Aden, our ship continued into the Arabian Sea on Friday the 10th. Owing to the strong wind, the sea grew pretty rough once more. I was sick five times in about two hours and felt ill for the rest of the day. During the days that followed, though, I felt fine again. We saw large numbers of flying fish in the Arabian Sea. At a distance they looked like little sparrows flitting from one wave to another.

One night, there was an amusing incident involving Ginger Thompson. Back in Bordon, Ginger had told me that he had originally been exempt from call-up, due to his employment as a coal miner. However, he had quit the pits after a row with a deputy and had subsequently been conscripted. Sometimes during the voyage, he somewhat annoyed me by insisting in his Durham accent: 'Thoo reminds me of wor lass.' I always responded by asking him if this meant that his girlfriend had a moustache!

Ginger had a regular fatigue duty in the ship's galley, peeling potatoes, etc. He sometimes returned from the galley at night with a few beers under his belt. On the night in question, I was lying in my hammock when Ginger appeared on the scene and tried to clamber up in beside me, exclaiming: 'Let's have a fuck at thee, Jock!' In the ensuing struggle, he managed to heave himself into the now violently swaying hammock. Then, he took a kitchen knife from his belt and began to saw through the strands of rope at one end of the hammock, singing merrily as he did so. Soon, the rope snapped and the hammock crashed down, spilling the pair of us out onto the floor, much to the amusement of the rest of the lads.

It was all just in jest, of course. Ginger was definitely a man for the girls. And so was I – in my dreams!

After passing some small groups of islands, we sighted Ceylon (now Sri Lanka) at about 2.30 p.m. on Wednesday the 15th. My first view of the island was of a long stretch of low-lying land covered in thick green jungle. At 4 p.m., we sailed through the very picturesque entrance of the palm-surrounded port of Colombo, passing a few ships, including one that was awash and half-sunk, before we anchored.

Shore-leave was scheduled for 6.30 p.m., with orders to be back by ten. Between us, Geoff, Johnny and I drew 30 shillings (£1.50) worth of rupees, i.e. 20. Before we went ashore, our mess deck serjeant came below and announced: 'If any of you are that way inclined, you can draw a French letter from the ship's hospital free of charge.'

A Scots Guardsman beside me commented: 'I niver use thon things. It's like takin' a bath wi' yer clathes on!' No doubt this was a well-worn description but it was the first time I'd heard it and I was greatly amused.

We were promptly taken ashore in launches. My two pals and I made our way to a nearby shopping area, where two jewellers enticed us into their shop. I bought a small moonstone necklace and two tiny ivory elephants for 3 rupees and 50 cents, and Geoff and Johnny purchased similar articles. From here we proceeded to the GPO. On the way, we passed a beggar with no feet, one of his legs being cut off at the calf and the other at the ankle.

After posting our mail at the GPO and shaking off a small Ceylonese who kept pestering us to let him show us the way to 'beer', we walked on through the town, looking at the shops. While strolling down one dark street, we encountered a tall, muscular, wild-looking man with long, rugged hair and beard who was stripped to the waist. I considered that perhaps he was a lunatic but Johnny suggested that he might be a Sikh. He offered us no hostility and, in fact, seemed quite oblivious of our presence.

We eventually dined in a small Chinese restaurant. Egg and chips and orange squash made a very nice change from the ship's meals. Then we continued our tour through an area of narrow streets with few shops. Here we were approached by hosts of rickshaw men making us offers such as: 'Jiggy-jig, sahibs? Me take you to jiggy-jig shop. Only three rupees!' or: 'Me take you to white lady. Very nice!'

Ignoring these proposals, we soon came to a NAAFI which was a very pleasant little place – very different from the Lido in Aden. We bought lemonade and cakes and sat back on a comfortable couch to consume them. When we left the NAAFI, we began our return journey. On the way, we again saw the beggar with no feet, creeping along the road and onto a tramcar on his hands and the uneven stumps of his legs. Despite his handicap, he seemed as agile as a monkey.

Soon after this, we arrived back at the jetty and took our places on one of the many waiting launches. There was some delay while the launches filled up with returning servicemen. Someone started to sing 'The Rose of Tralee'. Soon, men joined in from all of the waiting launches until hundreds of voices were raised in song. It sounded very beautiful as I stood there, looking across the moonlit water to the lights of our ship. All these young men, thousands of miles from home, singing that lovely air; I was very moved.

We sailed at 7.30 the following morning, and that day we saw quite a lot of the Ceylonese coast. It consisted of mile upon mile of jungle-covered hills in various shades of green with a few white buildings dotted here and there. Happily, the Indian Ocean remained as smooth as glass.

On Friday, 17 February, it was announced that the 14 men in our draft whose parent regiment was the King's Shropshire Light Infantry would now be going on to join their own regiment in Hong Kong. This included my friend Geoff Clarke. The KSLI had a notorious RSM, formerly of the Somerset LI, called Rocky Knight, whose reputation was known throughout the Light Infantry Brigade. Cursing Rocky Knight's memory, Jungle Jim said to me: 'I had enough of that bastard in India! If I'd thought there were any chance of me going to the KSLI, I'd have jumped ship at Port Said!'

However, the news was generally welcomed by the men affected as there was no terrorist 'emergency' in Hong Kong. None of us could possibly have known that in a matter of several months, some of the 14 would be fighting in the major war that was to erupt in Korea in June of that year.

We entered the Malacca Straits at about 9 a.m. on Sunday the 19th and sailed for a long while with Sumatra in sight on one side and some large islands on the other. All of this land was pretty close, providing us with a good view of rugged hills and mountains completely carpeted in thick jungle of several rich shades of green.

Early the following day, I saw some dolphins leaping through the water. They looked similar to porpoises, I considered, though not as big. At 10 a.m., we paraded to draw our stowed-away kitbags from the hold. Then in the afternoon we were ordered to scrub all of our webbing equipment in preparation for disembarkation at Singapore next day.

Secure in the belief that they were bound for peaceful garrison duties, the 14 KSLI wished the rest of us the best of luck when, on Tuesday, 21 February 1950, we came to the end of our voyage. HMT *Devonshire* was about to dock at Singapore, from where 34 members of Draft DAFJZ would proceed up-country to join the 1st Battalion, KOYLI.

5

The King's Own Yorkshire Light Infantry – Malaya September 1947 – February 1950

The regiment which was later to become the King's Own Yorkshire Light Infantry was raised in Leeds in 1755 as the 53rd Regiment of Foot and renumbered 51st in January 1757.

The 51st won its first battle honour and undying fame at the battle of Minden on 1 August 1759 during the Seven Years War (1756–63). While fighting in the Peninsular War (1808–14), the 51st gained eight battle honours and was converted into a Light Infantry regiment on 2 May 1809 as a reward for its gallant conduct at Corunna. Being on the extreme right of the line at the Battle of Waterloo on 18 June 1815, the regiment had no opportunity to distinguish itself that day. However, it won further battle honours during the Second and Third Burmese Wars (1852–54 and 1885–87) and in the Second Afghan War (1878–80).

On 1 July 1881, the 51st Regiment of Foot and the 105th Madras Light Infantry became the 1st and 2nd Battalions of the King's Own Light Infantry (South Yorkshire Regiment). This title changed six years later when on 2 July 1887, the regiment was redesignated the King's Own Yorkshire Light Infantry. The 2nd Battalion distinguished itself at the Shin Kamar Pass during the Tirah expedition of 1897–98.

The KOYLI's reputation for fast marching and endurance was enhanced during the Boer War (1899–1902), when it was nicknamed 'French's Foot Cavalry'. In the First World

70

War (1914–18), the KOYLI fielded 26 battalions, won 59 battle honours and 8 awards of the Victoria Cross. During the Second World War (1939–45), four battalions of the regiment fought in Norway, North Africa, Sicily, Italy, France, Holland, Germany and Burma. In this last location, the 2nd Battalion, KOYLI, gained two battle honours: 'Sittang 1942' and 'Burma 1942'.

The 2nd Battalion was posted from India to Malaya in 1947 and was one of the first units to undertake security operations there. At that time, Malaya had a mixed population of 2,428,000 Malays, 1,885,000 Chinese, 531,000 Indians and 12,000 Europeans. During the Japanese occupation of Malaya in the Second World War, the Malayan Communist Party, which was predominantly Chinese, had formed a 'Malayan People's Anti-Japanese Army'. From base camps in the dense jungle which covered four-fifths of the country, the MPAJA inflicted more than 2,000 casualties upon the Japanese in guerrilla actions, while its 'Traitor Killing Squads' assassinated an even greater number of Malayans who were either alleged collaborators or persons known to be opposed to Communist domination. British officers of Force 136 made contact with the MPAJA towards the end of 1943, supplied instructors and arranged for thousands of small arms and large quantities of ammunition and other equipment to be parachuted to the Communist guerrillas by mid-1945. The intention was that the MPAJA would be able to cause havoc behind the Japanese lines when the British launched their invasion, planned for September of that year.

However, the dropping of atomic bombs on two Japanese cities brought about Japan's surrender in August 1945, enabling the British to return to their former colony without a fight. In early September, sufficient British and Indian troops landed to convince the MCP to forget for the time being its aspiration to establish a Communist People's Republic in Malaya. By 1 December, the MPAJA had reluctantly agreed to hand in its arms and disband. Despite this agreement, several thousands of Japanese and British weapons, as well as ammunition and explosives, were stored away in secret caches in the jungle and many disbanded guerrillas remained on underground lists and kept in contact with each other.

During the next two years, the MCP concentrated on achieving power in the trade unions and fomenting industrial unrest both in Malaya and in Singapore. MCP representatives attended the Asian Youth Congress in Calcutta in February 1948 and upon their return, the 26-year-old Secretary General, Chin Peng, and his Central Executive Committee laid their plans for armed insurrection in Malaya. The former Chairman of the Central Military Committee of the MPAJA, Lau Yew, began calling up his 'reservists' to form a Malayan People's Anti-British Army. By June, the MPABA had reached a strength of 3,000. In that month, the Communist strategy of murder and intimidation of Chinese, Malay and Indian workers in European-owned enterprises had reached its peak. Thousands of trees on the vast rubber estates had been slashed and machinery in the tin mines sabotaged.

On 16 June 1948, three European managers were assassinated on rubber estates near Sungei Siput in Perak. The High Commissioner of the new Federation of Malaya, Sir Edward Gent, immediately declared a State of Emergency in parts of Perak and Johore, and the following day he extended this measure to the whole country. The MPABA now began to launch its planned armed attacks upon village police stations, rubber estates, tin mines, road convoys and trains. After each terrorist action, the 'bandits' – as they were universally labelled at that time – withdrew to their camps concealed within the fringes of the jungle, often close to Chinese villages or squatter areas from where they could obtain either willing or coerced assistance.

So began the war that would last for 12 long and bloody years; a war which would officially only be called an 'Emergency'. On 1 February 1949, the MPABA altered its title to Malayan Races Liberation Army, but this did not attract many recruits from either the Malay or the Indian communities. By 1950, the MRLA had a strength of 5,000 full-time guerrillas, increasing to 8,000 by 1951. It was organised in 11 state regiments, plus several independent companies and platoons. Ninety per cent of the membership was Chinese. In the jungle, bandits normally wore khaki drill uniforms with red stars on their five-peaked caps. Supporting the jungle units were 60,000 members of the underground Min Yuen (People's Movement), which provided funds and food, extorted from villagers and squatters, and which also had its own part-time armed units.

On arrival in Malaya from India on 29 September 1947, the 2nd Battalion, KOYLI, was stationed at Taiping in the State of Perak. The battalion was commanded by Lieutenant Colonel W.S.F. Hickie, OBE, and formed part of the 99th Brigade in the 17th (Gurkha) Infantry Division. During the closing months of 1947, the battalion mounted security patrols on the roads in response to the increasing unrest and lawlessness in the country. Tragedy struck at this time when one of 'D' Company's 3-ton trucks, returning from a swimming trip, crashed over the side of a small bridge onto the rocks below. Privates Mayoh and Morton were killed and a dozen others were injured.

In November, 'C' Company undertook the battalion's first jungle patrols in the Sitiawan Police District, hunting – without success – for bandits, pirates and smugglers. On 8 December, 7 Platoon, 'C' Company, was sent on operational detachment to Grik, near the Siamese border. Within eight days, due to incessant heavy rainfall, the platoon was called upon to rescue Chinese squatters from low-lying villages beyond the flooded Perak river. After managing to locate a boat, the men of 7 Platoon brought 250 Chinese safely across the enormously swollen river over a period of three days and two nights. After Christmas relaxation, 'A' and 'C' Companies went on detachment to Ipoh, the capital of Perak State, on 6 January 1948.

In March of that year, Lieutenant Colonel A.B. Brown

took over command of the battalion. He had lost an arm in Normandy in 1944 and was consequently nicknamed 'Winger' by the other ranks.

On 9 April, due to the deteriorating national situation, 'B' Company began an anti-bandit operation in the jungle bordering the Perak river, near Lenggong. Two weeks later, during a heavy rainstorm on the 24th, a rolling tree stump killed CQMS Price and Private Foley, seriously injured the company commander, Major Bell, and slightly injured three others. 'B' was later joined by 'C' and 'D' Companies who continued the operation – without contact – until June. Private Marritt of 'D' Company died of malaria in the British Military Hospital, Ipoh, on 31 May.

Meanwhile, 'A' Company had been sent as an advance party to Penang Island, off the coast of Province Wellesley, where during May, the battalion established its new headquarters in Glugor Barracks. In Penang, the battalion mounted a guard of honour for the High Commissioner of the Malayan Federation, Sir Edward Gent, on 19 June – three days after the first official declaration of a State of Emergency.

A tragic accident occurred on 30 July when a pressure cooker exploded in 'B' Company's cookhouse at the Caledonia Estate, Province Wellesley. Severe burns were suffered by Privates Guy, Boddy and Taylor. Private Guy consequently died the following day.

Another tragedy took place on 5 August at 'D' Company's location in the Cameron Highlands, north-west Pahang. Private Elliott was accidentally shot by a fellow soldier and died a day later.

The battalion's normal operational area comprised of the southern half of Kedah, Province Wellesley and Perak. Its first success came in August in the Kroh area, near the border with Thailand – in those days still frequently referred to as 'Siam', as it will be sometimes in this book. A patrol of 9 Platoon, 'C' Company, commanded by Lieutenant Haddon, discovered a bandit lurking in a clump of bamboo

74

close to their camp, and promptly eliminated him with a hail of rifle and automatic fire, plus a hand-grenade.

At the beginning of September, 'D' Company killed two bandits in South Kedah – reported in the regimental journal without further details.

Also early in September, two platoons of 'B' Company were cordoning a Chinese hut on the edge of the jungle at Papan, near Ipoh. An armed bandit emerged from the doorway and was killed by Private Lyons with a burst from his Bren gun.

'A' Company also struck lucky that month. Second Lieutenant Storey, commanding 3 Platoon, had received information that the enemy had set up an observation post on a hill overlooking the platoon's base in a kampong (village) called Bondor, on the Weng–Baling road in Kedah. Early one morning, 3 Platoon climbed the hill, then began to descend the other side with the intention of attacking the small camp from which the OP was being manned. Suddenly, the leading scout, Private Latcham, came face to face with the ascending enemy observation party. Latcham fired a burst from his Sten gun, seriously wounding one of the bandits. Though the man fell to the ground, he somehow managed to get up again and stumbled off down the hill, disappearing into the jungle with his fleeing comrades.

The platoon then hastily made its way to the presumed location of the camp but passed the correct spot. Luckily, Private Latcham, the second scout and Second Lieutenant Storey found themselves on the exit track just as the occupants of the camp were making their escape. The trio opened fire, bringing the leading bandit down with a broken leg, while the others fled. The platoon burned the camp and marched off, bearing the wounded prisoner. A few days later, 9 Platoon, 'C' Company, patrolling the same area, found the body of an armed and uniformed bandit who 'A' Company claimed must have been the first man shot by Private Latcham. This claim is dubious, however, as the 'C' Company patrol reported that the state of decomposition of the body suggested that the bandit had been dead for a few weeks. This estimation may have been mistaken, of course.

It was on 14 September that 'C' Company suffered its first casualty. Serjeant Dolby was shot in the left shoulder by a hidden assailant while on a patrol from Kroh. Fortunately, the serjeant made a speedy recovery.

The first serious casualties inflicted upon the battalion occurred near Bidor in Perak on 2 October when a party from 4 Platoon, 'B' Company, was ambushed while bathing in a jungle pool. Captain Lock, Lance Corporal Hutchinson and Privates Woodhouse and Dobson were all killed, and Privates Ridden, Hawksworth and Buckland were seriously wounded. Two bandits were also killed in the engagement, one being shot by Private Pidgley, who had come under fire while guarding the party's transport. Pidgley had only recently joined the company from the latest draft from Blighty.

Two weeks later, on 16 October, 6 Platoon, 'B' Company, led by Lieutenant Handley, surprised some bandits who were working in an armourer's shop in the jungle, east of Bidor. The platoon killed one bandit and wounded two and brought back considerable quantities of arms, ammunition and other equipment.

Early that month, while operating with 1/6th Gurkha Rifles in the Kroh area, two sections of 'C' Company, under the command of Second Lieutenant Burrows and Serjeant 'Taggy' Bell, came under enemy fire from a village. After a stiff fight, the KOYLI and Gurkha troops launched an attack during which two Gurkha soldiers were killed. The bandits nonetheless withdrew from the village, taking their casualties with them.

Late in October, 12 Platoon, 'D' Company, captured a bandit who was so preoccupied with cleaning his rifle that he failed to notice the approach of hostile troops. This happened near Baling; while further south, 10 and 11 Platoons attacked a bandit camp in the Bongsu Forest Reserve, achieving no kills but recovering documents and ammunition. Shortly after, at Badenoch Estate in South Kedah,

12 Platoon had several running fights with a troublesome bandit gang who even had the temerity to attack the estate buildings where the troops were based. The platoon sustained no casualties, however.

During the following month, the battalion underwent a fundamental structural alteration. The 1st Battalion of the KOYLI had been phased out in April of that year. Then, on 7 October, an Amalgamating Cadre from the 1st Battalion had arrived in Penang from the UK. Three officers, one colour-serjeant, one serjeant and ten other ranks had brought over the 1st Battalion's colours and a portion of the officers' and serjeants' mess silver and other property. Now, on 18 November 1948, an amalgamation took place in which the 2nd Battalion became the 1st Battalion of the King's Own Yorkshire Light Infantry (51st and 105th).

In mid-December, in the Kinta Valley, near Ipoh, 4 and 6 Platoons, 'B' company, located a bandit camp which was well-concealed in thick, swamp jungle. The occupants had fled but the platoons decided to maintain a seven-day vigil. On the very first day, an unsuspecting bandit turned up and was promptly shot by Private Brown of 4 Platoon. The bandit was only wounded, however, and escaped into the swamp, where he must have spent an extremely uncomfortable night. Endeavouring to crawl away the following morning, the bandit was spotted by Private Denvers and Lance Corporal Round, who duly finished him off.

Based at Papan in the Ipoh area, 'C' Company also experienced some excitement towards the close of the year. During a screening operation, Privates Chase and Edwards of 9 Platoon captured a wanted bandit and his girlfriend who were hiding in the undergrowth. Some time later, as Christmas approached and the company had discovered a succession of abandoned camps and dead and buried bandits, Private Rowe of 7 Platoon came face to face with a lone, live bandit. The bandit instantly turned and ran. Rowe fired at the man, causing him to stumble, but he managed to escape through the dense jungle. In the early hours of 28 December, Second Lieutenant Thorne, acting on good information, led 8 Platoon to investigate a particular hut. On arrival, they opened fire upon some figures fleeing into a nearby swamp. Then, upon searching the hut, they found a wanted bandit hiding under a bed. The swamp was cordoned and searched after first light, resulting in another two men and a woman being detained.

As the year ended, 12 Platoon, 'D' Company, attacked an important camp near Badenoch Estate in South Kedah, shooting one bandit dead and capturing four others. Large quantities of documents, ammunition and other stores were recovered. Yet another bandit was shot dead and a good haul of ammunition captured when a 'D' Company patrol attacked another camp early in the new year.

The battalion's greatest success was gained on 11 January 1949. A small patrol of 11 Platoon, 'D' Company, consisting of Serjeant Chadwick and six other ranks, spotted five bandits walking along by a river in a rubber estate near Karangan, South Kedah. Diving for cover behind the river bank, the bandits opened fire at the patrol's leading scout at a distance of about 40 yards. Swiftly taking cover themselves, the men of the patrol returned fire down the hill, killing one of the bandits, whose body floated downstream. Although the enemy were behind superior cover, they kept raising their heads in order to fire, which eventually enabled the patrol to kill another one. All the while, the KOYLI soldiers were gradually closing in, drawing a hail of enemy fire at every movement. After a quarter of an hour had passed, one of the bandits tried to halt the advance by throwing a grenade. However, the missile fell short and rolled back down into the river.

Eventually, a bandit tried to run for it. Attempting to jump a fence, he was shot dead by the patrol. There were now only two of the enemy left – a man and a woman. Though wounded, the woman was full of fight and kept firing with her pistol to enable her comrade to reload his rifle. Seizing his opportunity, Corporal Battersby took two men around the flank. As the two surviving bandits continued to return fire at the four men on the hill, Corporal

Battersby and the other two crept to within a few yards of the man and woman and riddled them with close-quarter fire, killing them both.

The patrol recovered the bandits' weapons and a red and white silk Communist flag. For his brave leadership in this well-executed action, Serjeant Chadwick was subsequently awarded the Military Medal.

Shortly after this engagement, on 27 January, a patrol of 12 Platoon, 'D' Company, was reconnoitring in a hilly rubber estate in the same area. The patrol divided into two groups. Second Lieutenant Wigg and his batman, Private O'Reilly, accompanied by a Bren gunner, decided to investigate some houses near the top of a hill. Suddenly, they spotted a bandit who dashed out of a house 200 yards away. The bandit then ran up a steep hill and hid behind a large boulder. He paid no heed to calls to him to surrender, so the group opened fire.

Private O'Reilly, meanwhile, crept round the side of the hill until at only a few yards' distance he saw that the bandit was clutching a grenade. Quickly, O'Reilly aimed his Sten gun and pressed the trigger but the weapon jammed. Seeing that the bandit was about to hurl the grenade at his officer and the Bren gunner, O'Reilly made a flying leap and brought the man down with a rugby tackle. The pair of them rolled together down the hillside, with the grenade rolling after them. As they became jammed between two rocks, the grenade exploded, wounding O'Reilly in the face and left side. Despite this, O'Reilly held on to his man until Mr Wigg and the Bren gunner ran up and shot the bandit dead.

In the meantime, the other group from the patrol had seen another bandit jumping from the loft of one of the houses. The group instantly opened fire, wounding the bandit and subsequently taking him prisoner. For his brave deed, Private O'Reilly would be awarded the Distinguished Conduct Medal.

On 18 March, the final day of a screening operation in the Kulim area of Kedah, 7 Platoon, 'C' Company, flushed three bandits from a hut. Two surrendered but the third started to make a run for it. Suddenly, he turned, threw a home-made hand-grenade at Corporal Goodall and fired at Serjeant Hutchinson with an automatic pistol. Serjeant Hutchinson immediately returned fire with his Sten gun, putting 14 rounds into the bandit and killing him.

While participating in a battalion operation in the same region during the following month, 3 Platoon, 'A' Company, achieved the rather unspectacular success of capturing two bandits who were discovered asleep in bed!

Based at Lubok Segintah Estate in Central Kedah, 'B' Company received information early in June that six bandits were living in a hut, situated in a squatter area. Consequently, at dawn on the 6th, Serjeant Sanders led 5 Platoon to the indicated location. As the serjeant crept stealthily to within 10 yards of the hut, a dog suddenly began to bark and raised the alarm. This caused four bandits within the hut to hastily abandon their breakfasts and bolt out of the door. All four were promptly shot down and killed by the men of 5 Platoon positioned around the hut. A fifth bandit, who had been hiding in a nearby swamp, now decided to surrender. In his possession were many Communist documents, mostly receipts for money extorted from the local population. The sixth bandit, who had not been in the area, was caught by the police a few days later. The success of this operation encouraged a number of local Chinese to come forward with useful information about enemy activities, which enabled the police to secure the entire area.

On 10 July, 8 Platoon, 'C' Company, under the command of Second Lieutenant Thorne, effected an ambush on a track crossing the border between the State of Perlis and Thailand. A bandit 'sergeant' was shot dead and his Thompson sub-machine gun and ammunition were recovered. Following up with 9 Platoon, Second Lieutenant Walby found 16 sacks of opium, valued at 500,000 dollars, which were doubtless being brought across the border to finance the Communist terror campaign.

'C' Company suffered two unfortunate losses within a

short period of time. Serjeant Gilpin of 8 Platoon contracted scrub typhus in the jungle, rapidly deteriorated and died on 25 July. Only ten days later, on 4 August, during a transport escort duty on the Baling road, one of 'C' Company's 3-ton trucks overturned and Private Gee – a soldier in 9 Platoon who was shortly due to go home – was killed.

On 3 November, 'B' and 'D' Companies co-operated in an operation in the Kulim region. After midday, 'B' Company Commander Captain Sutcliffe left his men to 'brew up' and set out, accompanied by Private O'Brien, to locate a spot that the captain had decided from his map would make a good place to set up his company base. After struggling for an hour through thick *belukar* (secondary jungle), the pair arrived in a small valley of *lallang* (elephant grass). It was raining steadily and mist shrouded the sides of the valley, but at the far end, they discovered a man-made waterhole. Placed across the hole was a plank and on the plank stood a tin which contained a freshly-used cake of soap. The two men also observed that a track led from the waterhole up into a re-entrant in dense woodland.

Captain Sutcliffe immediately hurried back to summon his company. On returning to the waterhole, he deployed his men to surround the area and then close in. Corporal Pudwell, Private Brown and a Bren gunner, Private Lyness, were left behind in concealed positions to cover the approach to the waterhole. Very shortly, Lyness saw two bandits, carrying rifles, walking down the track towards him. Aware of the necessity not to raise the alarm before the remainder of the company were in position, Lyness had the sense and restraint not to open fire. To his relief, the bandits stopped to wash in the waterhole and then returned up the track.

The enemy's camp, which contained three *bashas* (huts), was soon surrounded. Corporal Walker's section approached one of the *bashas*. Upon entering, Lance Corporal Mills and Private Carter were confronted by two men and two women who were seated at a table studying some papers. One of the men reached for his gun and was shot dead. The other man ran out of the *basha* and down a track, where he was shot down by Corporal Flint's section or possibly by Private Lyness' Bren gun. The two female bandits were taken prisoner. Also captured were a rifle, a shotgun, three pistols, a Gestetner duplicating machine and a large number of documents.

Captain Sutcliffe decided that the company should stay in the camp overnight. At about 9 p.m. while on sentry duty, Private Smith spotted an electric torch shining in the darkness. He fired a shot and the light went out. Next morning, Lance Corporal Collins located the wounded bandit and finished him off as he tried to escape.

In a follow-up patrol, Second Lieutenant Huxley captured two food suppliers, one of whom had been on his way to the camp carrying a sack of rice. This successful two-day encounter put out of action the MRLA's South Kedah and Penang Propaganda Section. The two female prisoners were each sentenced to seven years' imprisonment. Private O'Brien, who had accompanied Captain Sutcliffe on the original recce, was awarded the Military Medal.

On 9 November, a patrol of 10 Platoon, 'D' Company, was ambushed by 60 to 70 bandits whilst patrolling in a rubber estate in the Anak Kulim area of Kedah. Marching in file up a hill of *lallang*, the patrol came under heavy fire from a flat earth mound on the summit. The ensuing action continued from 4.45 to 7.30 p.m. with gunfire constantly echoing round the hills. Private Ward received a fatal chest wound early on in the battle. Close at hand was Private Slade, who endeavoured to apply a field dressing to the hole in Ward's chest, but had to abandon the attempt when he came under direct enemy fire. Shortly after that, Serjeant Holmes crawled to within 15 yards of the bandits and threw six grenades among them, preventing them from enveloping the patrol's flank. Although outnumbered five to one and in a disadvantageous position, the patrol continued to fight off the enemy until darkness fell. To the patrol's surprise, there was then a sudden cessation of fire from the other side. This prompted a sturdy private to yell out: 'What's the matter,

Johnny? Have you gone for a NAAFI-break?' There was no reply of any kind. The bandits had withdrawn, leaving two dead on the field and, it was believed, carrying off six other dead with them as well as the wounded. The Platoon Commander, Second Lieutenant Richards, was awarded the Military Cross and Serjeant Holmes the Military Medal for their gallant leadership in this well fought action.

A month later, on 3 December, 'B' Company Commander Major Sutcliffe and a party of five other ranks were driving along the Kroh–Klian Intan road, near the Siamese border, in a jeep and a 15-hundredweight truck. Twenty bandits were lying in wait along a V-shaped bend in the road. When the first shots were fired at the jeep, Major Sutcliffe ordered Private Kelly to drive on while he jumped out onto the road, intending to stop the truck and organise its occupants into action against the ambushers. By this time, however, the truck was also under heavy fire and drove past the major, who, now isolated with only a pistol and five rounds of ammunition, had to make a run for cover in the *belukar* at the side of the road.

Enemy fire had now hit all five of the private soldiers and halted both vehicles. Privates Kelly, Mills, Carter and Godfrey were all killed at close range when the bandits descended from their ambush position to finish off the wounded and collect their arms and ammunition. Private 'Ginger' Fry was lying on the road, severely wounded. Fortunately, he did not flinch when a bullet that was fired at him struck the road close to his head, nor when a bandit removed the bandolier of ammunition from around his waist. The bandits presumed that he was dead and began to hunt around for Major Sutcliffe, who had concealed himself in the jungle. The Communists were especially keen to eliminate the major as he had served in Sumatra as a member of Force 136 during the war against the Japanese and was therefore an experienced jungle adversary. Yelling 'We'll get you, Sutcliffe!' the terrorists probed around for some time, but finally gave up and departed just before relief parties drove up to the scene from Kroh and Klian

Intan, commanded by CSM Shelton and Second Lieutenant Huxley respectively.

From 9 to 23 December, 'C' Company undertook an unusual operation, starting out from Grik and disappearing into the remotest regions of Upper Perak, accompanied by Sakai aboriginals and elephants complete with mahouts to drive them. The elephants carried supplies that were normally packed by the troops on their backs. Men who took part later told me that on the march they kept falling down holes in the mud made by the elephants' heavy feet and that, in fact, the elephants became very tired and couldn't stand the pace! Certainly the experiment was never repeated.

One person for whom this last operation proved disastrous was Private McAdam. He developed severe stomach pains in the jungle but was not brought out until the operation ended. After being operated upon for appendicitis in a Singapore hospital, Private McAdam died.

'A', 'B' and 'D' Companies participated in operations in South Kedah from 10 to 20 and 24 to 29 January 1950. On 20 January in a region to the east of Junjong, two patrols of 'A' Company, led by Second Lieutenants Carter and Sibbald, chased a man into a camp that was found to be occupied by 20 bandits. In the ensuing firefight, a wounded bandit continued to shoot back, inflicting wounds upon Privates Carey and Jones before being finished off by Mr Sibbald, and a second bandit was also killed. Private Jones had previously lost a finger from his right hand in a civilian industrial accident. Now, on his first patrol in Malaya, he had two fingers shot off his left hand. After that, he was rather unkindly nicknamed 'Fingers' Jones!

Commencing the second operation on the 24th, 1 and 3 Platoons of 'A' Company, under the command of Captain Rome, came under fire whilst on an uphill track in Dublin Estate. As he took cover behind the large root of an ipoh tree, leading scout Lance Corporal Caldecott was relieved that a terrorist grenade which exploded only 3 yards from him only blew his hat off! The men behind him were moving up from tree to tree under a heavy fire. As Serjeant Wilson came up with his platoon on the left flank, Serjeant Battersby shouted to him: 'Tally ho!' Then, while Private Whitehead sprayed the area in front with bursts from his Bren gun, Battersby took the EY (grenade-throwing) rifle and fired a grenade up the hill, dispersing the enemy. The two platoons were now able to advance to the top, where Serjeant Battersby surprised a bandit taking aim from behind a tree and shot him in the head with his Sten gun.

As the remainder of the enemy fled, Signals Lance Corporal Brown speedily erected his wire aerial and made wireless contact with 'B' and 'D' Companies, who, between them, killed another two of the escaping bandits.

In February, 'A' Company was stationed at Grik in Upper Perak and 'C' Company at Tapah in Lower Perak. On the 16th of the month, Tactical HQ, together with 'B' and 'D' Companies, moved south to Ipoh, Perak State capital. Between 8 and 18 February, 'C' Company cooperated with the Green Howards, the Coldstream Guards and the Malayan Police in two large-scale operations. On the first of these, Second Lieutenant Suckling, with a small ambush party, captured one bandit and wounded another, while on the second, Second Lieutenant Storey sprang another ambush, in which he killed a strolling bandit with one shot and his batman, Private Plummer, wounded a second man, who nonetheless managed to get away.

This brief resumé of the KOYLI's armed encounters with the enemy up to February 1950 may read like a story of regular action. However, it should be remembered that for every patrol that made contact with bandits, there were dozens that did not. After the Malayan Emergency ended in 1960, it was calculated that the security forces had achieved one kill for every 1,800 man-hours of toil and sweat in the jungle. Even in the peak years of terrorist activity during which my story unfolds, the ratio of man-hours to one kill was estimated to average at 700. I presume that these ratios were calculated only on the operational hours of those personnel who had the opportunity and the skill to shoot straight and true. Most infantry soldiers endured thousands of hours on patrol without ever scoring a fatal hit.

At the time of my disembarkation, though, this was a lesson that I had yet to learn. As HMT *Devonshire* approached Singapore docks, I was convinced that mortal combat lay just around the corner.

6

Glugor Barracks – Penang
February–March 1950

We sighted Singapore at 7.30 a.m. on Tuesday, 21 February 1950, and moored at the harbourside an hour later. On the quay to welcome us was the brass band of one of the Highland regiments and several 'brass hats'. During the morning, a detachment of the 10th Gurkha Rifles embarked, bound for Hong Kong, and Chinese women, clad in brightly coloured pants and blouses but barefooted, were employed carrying hammocks aboard the ship. As we waited all morning for orders to go ashore, I felt no qualms about what might lie ahead. I was only too eager to be freed from our cramped, restrictive life aboard the troopship.

At long last we disembarked at 3 p.m., loaded up with our kitbags, and were taken by truck to the railway station. On arrival, we were provided with a meal by the Army Catering Corps, and then allowed out until six o'clock. Johnny Ainsworth, a lad called Blunsdon and I went for a walk through the adjacent quarter of Singapore. Everywhere we went, seeing Chinese faces and hearing Chinese voices and Chinese music, it was difficult to believe that we were not, in fact, in China. In my youthful ignorance I had presupposed that Malaya and Singapore would be similar to my movie-inspired images of India, even though Chinese inhabitants had figured prominently in the tales of Jungle Jim.

When we returned to the station, another meal was served. Each member of the draft was then issued with a

Lee Enfield No.5 rifle – shorter and two pounds lighter than the No.4 rifle that we had used in training – a short sword-bayonet and a bandolier containing 50 rounds of ammunition. Rightly or wrongly, taking possession of the lethal power of my rifle and 50 rounds gave me a happy feeling of strength and security. I remember commenting to Johnny Ainsworth that for the first time since I had joined the army, I felt like a soldier.

On boarding the train, we were allotted sleeping berths. The train departed for the north-west at 8 p.m. There was an escort of Malay Police on board, armed with old Mark III rifles. The police also manned two Bren LMGs and a searchlight, at the front and rear of the train. Orders conveyed to us by our serjeants stipulated that if the train was ambushed, all lights were to be put out and troops were to stand by ready to return fire.

I was one of eight from our draft who were picked for guard duty. We mounted guard in pairs; one to stand on each platform at the front and rear of the coach whenever the train stopped. Serjeant Hogan instructed us not to allow anyone to board the train, no matter who it was. He warned us not to shoot unless we had to, but if the necessity did arise we should shoot low, as there would be an enquiry into any shooting that occurred. Finally, he informed us that there would be no need for us to go out on the platform except when the train came to a stop.

My two periods of duty were from eight till ten and from four till six. During my early spell, I went out onto the platform when the train reached its first stop. An Indian beer-merchant tried to board the coach and I had to force him back with my rifle when he attempted to push past me. Standing down on the step, I then saw him board the train further down. I suppose he was just going about his normal, lawful business but I had followed my orders.

When the train set off again, it occurred to me that it was far more pleasant out on the platform in the night air than it was inside the hot, stuffy coach. So I decided to stay out there and settled down to reading a film magazine that I had bought in Singapore. Suddenly, I became aware of the presence of Lieutenant Styles, the RAOC officer in command of our draft.

'What are you doing?' he snapped angrily.

'I'm on guard, sir,' I replied.

He eyed my magazine. 'Put that away!'

'I was told, sir, that I didn't need to come out here except when the train stopped,' I tried to explain.

'And I'm telling you to stay on guard!'

'Yes, sir.'

Such is the army! I thought to myself.

After completing my first spell of guard, I drank my first bottle of the famous Tiger beer, which Johnny had waiting for me. It tasted rather strong but really lovely, I considered. Throughout the night, the searchlights swept the surrounding bush country but there was no trouble.

Next morning at 8.30, we arrived in Kuala Lumpur, capital city of the Federation of Malaya. Here, the Scots Guards draft left us, and after breakfasting on the platform, we boarded another train for the next stage of our journey. As we proceeded further northwards, we passed through some rubber plantations and paddy fields, but the scenery was mostly just desolate jungle. The journey seemed endless. Nonetheless, at 5.30 p.m. we finally arrived at Prai on the coast of Province Wellesley. Stiff and weary, we gladly alighted onto the platform, where we were awaited by the rather stout CSM Potts of HQ Company, KOYLI.

Shouldering our kitbags, we boarded the ferry that was to convey us over to the Island of Penang. At that time, McAllister – the Second World War veteran who had been with me in Holding Company – was inclined to get on Jungle Jim's nerves by announcing at every opportunity: 'I've been out here before!' To some extent it also irritated the rest of us, though Mac was normally a very likeable fellow. Once the ferry was under way, McAllister – no doubt keen to create an impression and hopefully regain his corporal's stripes – approached CSM Potts and requested: 'Can the men take their packs off, sir?'

Potts scowled at McAllister. 'No, they can't!' he snarled. 'It's only a five-minute journey.'

'It's not, sir,' McAllister asserted. 'It takes fifteen minutes. I've been out here before!'

'Look!' Potts exploded. 'Don't try to come the old soldier with me! I've seen more service than you've ever seen! As far as I'm concerned, you're a recruit! So fall out!'

McAllister withdrew, absolutely fuming with anger and humiliation. Although I felt sorry for him, I must confess that I also found the incident quite amusing.

Upon reaching the island, we landed on the quay and boarded a couple of waiting 3-ton trucks. These conveyed us through the bustling periphery of Georgetown and along the palm-lined coast until we reached Glugor Barracks – the headquarters of the 1st Battalion, KOYLI.

I was instantly impressed by Glugor Barracks, which presented a delightful contrast to Bordon Camp. Mostly constructed between 1939 and 1941, Glugor had been justifiably described as the best barracks in the Far East. Built on high ground and surrounded on three sides by lush hills, embellished with masses of coconut palms, the two-storey, yellow-walled barracks blocks were very picturesque and well designed for a tropical climate.

Our draft was assigned to an upstairs barrack room above the dining hall. The ceiling supported large, electric propeller fans and the side walls were, in fact, rows of double doors, left permanently open, which gave access to the wide verandah. Within the room, which was 'halved' by six stone pillars down the centre, were four rows of familiar iron bedsteads and wooden lockers. At the far end was an ablutions room, fitted with washbasins, showers and toilets.

Off-duty facilities in the camp included a very nice NAAFI, an AKC (Army Kinema Corporation) cinema providing two shows nightly, a large sports field and an open-air swimming pool. Although, as I have said, I was instantly impressed, it would take some time for all of the benefits of Glugor Barracks to be learned and appreciated. On the night of arrival, confusion, uncertainty, weariness, constant perspiration and the realisation that I was a long way from home – and would be for a long time – left little room for other considerations.

After a kit check the following morning, CSM Potts – no doubt merely for his own amusement – asked each of us which job he would prefer upon completion of initial jungle training. Storeman and driver emerged as the most sought-after employments. In my turn, I replied: 'I want to be a rifleman, sir.'

'You want to be a rifleman?' Potts looked at me, surprised, and then commented: 'I don't think you'll have much difficulty in getting that job. We need plenty of them around here!'

McAllister had lost no time in making an official complaint to HQ Company Commander that, wearing a worthy row of medal ribbons, he had been called a recruit by CSM Potts. To his credit, Potts agreed to apologise to McAllister.

The warrant officer who was in overall charge of our training was Company Serjeant Major Taylor. A tall, lean, bespectacled man, Taylor could indulge in biting sarcasm and occasionally explode into anger, but most of the time he treated us pretty fairly, for a CSM. He had apparently taken note of my 'Trade on Enlistment' and frequently addressed me rather contemptuously as 'student.'

The factor which had most effect upon us since our arrival in Malaya was the clammy, damp heat which drained all our energy and kept our clothing constantly soaked in perspiration. It was normal for troops in barracks to walk around in shorts with no garment on the upper body. As part of our 'acclimatisation', we had been instructed to follow this practice for a graduated period every day. Even with this precaution, the hot sun tended to burn our skins, sometimes to an alarming degree. My shoulders became so red and painfully blistered that CSM Taylor rather reluctantly granted me permission to keep my shirt on for a couple of days.

In that heat, during NAAFI breaks, a variety of Fanta minerals in ice-cold bottles – orange, cream soda, lemon, cherry and pineapple – were greatly appreciated. There was also a delicious coconut cake, the like of which I never tasted anywhere else.

On Friday morning, 24 February, CSM Taylor told us: 'I want you all to bear in mind that you must at all times treat the local people properly. There was a time in India before the war, and even during the war, when if a native gave a soldier any lip, the soldier would boot the beggar up the arse without hesitation. Nowadays, we're not allowed to do things like that. We have to treat them with respect – as equals.'

It wasn't really clear to me whether Taylor was saying that it was a good thing or a bad thing that we could no longer boot natives up the what's-it!

That afternoon, we were assembled in the dining hall to receive another lecture; this time, on the dangers of venereal disease.

Major 'Porky' Gowans, HQ Company Commander, addressed us first: 'I know when you're so far from home, away from your wives and girlfriends, the temptations are very great. I also know that you'll meet chaps who will say to you: "VD? It's nothing. I've had it twice!" Well, of course, nowadays, since the advent of penicillin, if it's caught in time VD can be cured, as far as we can tell. But no one can say what the long-term effects might be. There are men dying today as a result of VD they contracted during the First World War.

'Now I know that no matter what I say to you, there are people here who will go downtown and get VD. I could tell you who those people are now.' Major Gowans looked towards Jungle Jim and a few others and then continued: 'I also know that there are others among you who wouldn't dream of going with a woman downtown. I could tell you who they are now.' He looked at me and some others. 'But the chaps I'm trying to reach are the rest of you who, if you come across a woman, you will and if you don't, you won't bother. Believe me, the women you see down there may look very attractive when they're all painted up and wearing their finery, but underneath they're filthy – absolutely filthy! My advice to you is – keep it inside your trousers!

'Now, for those of you who aren't prepared to take my advice, here's the Medical Officer to tell you what precautions to take.'

The MO, Captain Daly, then stood up, his face beaming from ear to ear. 'Now, chaps,' he said brightly. 'When you go downtown for a jolly, always be sure to wear a rubber sheath. You can get one free of charge at the PAC [Prophylactic Aid Centre] and a tube of cream to go with it. You also get a chitty to prove that you've been to the PAC, so that if you get a dose, you won't be put on a charge.'

Captain Daly continued with the clinical details of preventative action. Afterwards, Jungle Jim said it was all 'a load of bollocks' and that we should all just enjoy ourselves!

Johnny Ainsworth and I made our first visit to Georgetown on the night of Sunday the 26th. We travelled in by bus and found that, like Singapore, Georgetown was predominantly Chinese. Both of us being 'good boys', we had no problems with temptations, but merely enjoyed simple pleasures such as a ride in a trishaw, a visit to the Odeon Cinema in Penang Road and a meal in the Chinese Town Hall NAAFI. Finally, we took a taxi back to barracks.

The following night, I found myself on guard. My spells of duty were: guarding the Motor Transport Park from 6.30 to 8.30 p.m. and guarding the magazine from half-past midnight to 2.30 a.m.

The magazine was situated in a large fenced-off compound on the far edge of the camp. I had been told that it was a very creepy sort of place; lonely, full of snakes and with its own ghost. The compound was supposed to be haunted by the spectre of a Chinese girl whose body had been thrown down into one of the deep caverns after she had been shot by the Japanese during the war. I was told that on one occasion, a sentry had run the half-mile back to the guardroom and arrived there as white as a sheet, with his hair standing on end, babbling about having seen the girl's spirit. One informant maintained that the ghost had actually spoken to the sentry, ordering him to open the compound gate. When he complied, the Chinese girl had walked in, followed by her Japanese execution squad! Even long-service regulars, I was told, did not like guarding the magazine.

The man with whom I was paired for guard made it clear that he was not at all keen to do the after midnight shift at the magazine, so I said I would do it while he guarded the MT Park at that time. A 15-hundredweight truck dropped me off at the compound and picked up the relieved sentry. The truck drove off, leaving me alone in the darkness. I was not exactly cheered by the wooden noticeboard on the gate which proclaimed 'DANGER OF DEATH'. I closed the gate behind me and stood for a moment by the small white building (intended to be a guardroom) on the left-hand side. Cautiously, I surveyed the circular road which wound around a large central 'island' that was overgrown with trees and shrubbery. The magazines – containing ammunition and explosives – were in caverns in the rocky slopes that bordered the compound.

I patrolled round the road with my rifle in the crook of my arm. I found the place lonely enough but not too frightening, despite the strange noises which I presumed to be birds or animals and the tree stumps which could so easily be mistaken for figures in the bushes. Once, I stopped to point my rifle at someone moving through the grass on my left – which proved to be my own shadow! My only live visitor during the two hours was a strange-looking cat. Altogether I found it quite an interesting and satisfying experience insofar as I had expected to be scared but was not. (Later in my service, a lad from my draft assured me that one night in the magazine, he had seen what he described as a white mist, in the shape of a Chinese girl, hovering over the roof of the unused guardroom. I suspect that sentries generally spent most of their time in the magazine watching out for ghosts and paid scant attention to the possibility of a terrorist raid to acquire ammunition and explosives!)

On Tuesday, 28 February, I noted in my journal: 'A year today is my Date Due for Discharge. What a lovely thought!' Little did I know, then, that my discharge date was destined to be postponed for a further six months. Being demobbed was the dream of every National Service-man and, I don't doubt, of many regulars also. During those early days in Malaya, going home was all I ever thought about – just to be safely back in Britain and out of army uniform. Beyond that, I had no plans. Back in my school-days, no civilian employment had ever appealed to me; nor could I foresee any suitable civilian career for me now. Sometimes, I did entertain illusions of becoming a novelist or an artist, but I was not so naive that I didn't appreciate that only a lucky and particularly talented few ever earned a decent living in either field. My disillusionment with my long-cherished dream of an army career had left a decided void in my life. I felt bitter and resentful and was inclined to brood. Yet, despite everything, I suspected that there was still a part of me that yearned to be a soldier.

Our training in Glugor Barracks consisted mostly of fieldcraft and firing on the ranges. The NCOs who instructed us were the best I had met since I joined the army and generally treated us like human beings. One afternoon, we were given a lecture on jungle warfare by Serjeant Thomas of 'A' Company. He was a rather flamboy-ant character who was very popular in the battalion. Towards the end of the lesson, someone asked him what was the largest number of bandits that had been killed in one action. Serjeant Thomas answered: 'The Gurkhas killed twenty-two in a battle in Johore last month.'

'Ah, well,' one of the lads commented. 'The Gurkhas are the boys!'

Thomas seemed to bristle. 'The Gurkhas are the boys!' he repeated disdainfully. 'Don't say that! We're the boys! The KOYLIs are the boys! Any time we've come up against bandits, we've always given a good account of ourselves.' Then, he said very seriously: 'If you ever come across any of these people in the jungle, don't show them any mercy.

95

If you wound one, don't feel sorry for him. Finish him off! If you can, stick a bayonet in him and save your ammunition. Because, I can assure you, if you were to feel sorry for one and leave him alive, he'd shoot you in the back as you walked away. That's the kind of sods they are! One time when a Fourth Hussars vehicle was ambushed, the bandits came down to the road to collect the weapons of the dead. There was one wounded Hussar who held onto his Sten gun and wouldn't let go. So the bandits took a can of petrol from the truck, doused the lad with it and set him alight. And you must have heard what they did to our blokes on the Kroh–Klian Intan road. So never hesitate. Kill any of them that you can find!'

At that time, I could see no incongruity in Serjeant Thomas first complaining that the enemy were 'sods' and then recommending that we behave like 'sods' ourselves. In fact, I can remember being quite impressed by his speech. To give the bandits a taste of their own medicine seemed to me a worthy objective.

In our barrack block, we were visited several times a day by the char wallah who had come with the 2nd Battalion from India. He was a very jovial chap who always called me 'Tashy' because of my moustache. As well as tea, he sold 'banjos' (sandwiches), biscuits and chocolate. He was usually assisted by his small son, nicknamed 'Chico'. Another regular visitor was the dhobi wallah, whose normal laundering was paid for by the army but who also operated a 'flying dhobi' whereby we could pay for clothing to be washed quicker and to be more neatly starched and pressed. Finally, there was the book wallah who sold dirty books such as *Frenchy Frolics*, printed in Calcutta, American magazines and British comics – *Dandy*, *Beano*, etc.

The night of Saturday, 7 March, saw me on guard again. This time, I was on prowler guard, which consisted of patrolling in pairs round the entire camp for two two-hour spells. It was the most tiring guard I had ever done; the boredom only being relieved by the numerous fireflies, which looked like glowing cigarette ends, floating through the darkness around us.

On the following Monday morning, CSM Taylor organised a jungle ambush exercise. After carefully concealing half of the draft in ambush positions amongst palm trees, shrubs and long grass, he then decreed that the other half should take the part of a patrol on reconnaissance. Thinking that I might be sufficiently inalert to walk right into his planned ambush, he intentionally – I am sure – chose me to be leading scout of the patrol. Taking the lead as instructed, I duly set out along the path, with the rest of the lads strung out in single file behind me. After covering about a hundred yards, I spotted a head bobbing in the grass to my left front. Immediately, I turned and waved the other chaps into cover, from where we crept round through the shrubs and long grass and 'opened fire' upon the would-be ambushers.

Far from receiving any praise for spotting the ambush and saving the patrol, I merely incurred the serjeant major's wrath for ruining his carefully prepared trap. Absolutely livid, Taylor strode up to me and exclaimed: 'Listen, student! If that had been real, you would have been as dead as a doornail, standing in the middle of the path and waving your arm like that!'

'But I had to warn the others, sir,' I protested.

'Yes, you dolt, but you should have dived for cover as you waved,' he insisted. 'Two or three of my men said they could have shot you.'

Maybe so – I thought to myself – but I still saved the rest of the patrol!

We spent our final day in Glugor Barracks preparing for our imminent move to Grik, near the Siamese border, where we were to undergo our jungle training. Five days earlier, we had been issued with jungle hats, jungle boots, poncho capes, bedding lines (coils of rope) and matchets (army-issue machetes) from the stores. We now followed instructions and sprayed the seams of all our jungle clothing with a solution which deterred the mites that carried scrub typhus. This was no doubt a wise precaution but it was something I never did again during my 18 months in Malaya, nor did I ever see anyone else do it.

On that final afternoon, we practised MT ambush drill in case of trouble the following day. In the event of an ambush, men on one side of each truck would give covering fire while those on the other side dismounted and took cover. These men would then provide fire cover to enable those still on the truck to dismount. If, as was most likely, only the leading trucks came under immediate fire, all. men in the rear trucks would dismount and attack the ambushers from the flank.

It all sounded simple in theory. CSM Taylor knew better, however, and made a final plea to us: 'If we do get ambushed on the road tomorrow, debus and take cover as quickly as you can. And for God's sake, fire back! Don't just lie there paralysed, the way green troops tend to do when they first come under fire. I'm not a windy type but I'm not a brave type either. So for God's sake, don't put me in a position where I have to go round kicking your arses to make you fire back!'

Lieutenant Styles then briefly addressed us: 'If anything does happen tomorrow, try to keep calm. Don't regard being ambushed as something to dread. In fact, welcome it as an opportunity to hit back at them.'

CSM Taylor grimaced at this, but I was 100 per cent with Mr Styles. Earlier on, I had said to Johnny Ainsworth that I hoped we would be ambushed so that we could see some action and I would have something really exciting to write about in my journal.

Of course, Mr Styles and I were both completely green and had no conception of what being caught in a murderous road ambush really entailed.

7

Jungle Training – Grik and Kroh March 1950

Reveille was at 4.30 a.m. on Wednesday, 8 March, and by 6.30, we were on our way. Once on the mainland, our convoy set off towards the north-east. There were four 3-ton trucks, each with a Bren gun mounted on the cab, maintaining a distance of 200 yards between each two vehicles. I was in the fourth truck, commanded by Lieutenant Styles.

Some time after 11, we reached Baling, where we were met by two armoured scout cars from 'A' Company. We stopped for a break here and ate our haversack rations. Then we continued on our way up the winding road to Kroh, with one scout car leading the convoy and the other at the rear. From Kroh we turned eastward onto the road to Klian Intan, which wound its way through hilly terrain and was considered very dangerous. Nonetheless, at about 2.30 p.m., we arrived safely at 'A' Company's base, near the small town of Grik in Upper Perak. In a nearby grassed area, we made our own camp, constructing bivouacs with our poncho capes and lengths of bamboo chopped from an adjacent thicket.

We camped at Grik for eight days, living on tinned 'C' (composite) rations. During this time, we attended to all personal needs in pairs. While one man washed in the stream, the other covered him with a loaded rifle; likewise when answering a call of nature. Such rigid security precautions were probably quite sensible but were not maintained when we later went to our companies. We also performed guard duty in pairs, patrolling round the perimeter of our bivouac area, listening to the strange night noises and the occasional rustling sounds of some unknown animal in the bushes.

On Friday the 10th, Serjeant Howgego (known in the battalion as 'Bamboo John') taught us various uses of bamboo: how to make *bashas* (huts), ovens, pipelines, water carriers, plates, knives and *panjis*. The latter were stakes which could be concealed in pits in the ground with the purpose of impaling animals or men upon them. The Sakai aborigines used the sap from the ipoh tree to poison *panjis*, as well as using it on the darts of their blowpipes. On operations later, I never knew bamboo to be used for any purpose other than building *bashas*.

We spent most of the following two days building very elaborate two- or three-man *bashas* out of bamboo, attap leaves and grass. It was very hard work which really made us sweat. Johnny and I were very proud of ours and took up residence in it. Some of the other chaps were not so happy with their finished products and preferred to continue sleeping in their bivouacs. (Irrespective of the precise meaning of the term 'bivouac', we always applied this description to shelters made with our poncho capes; at other times calling them 'bivvies' or '*bashas*'.)

Our training schedule was very gruelling and continued throughout the daylight hours – all work and no play. As we were not yet fully acclimatised, we suffered considerably from the debilitating effects of the damp heat. Sometimes I felt so tired that I seemed to be wandering around in a daze.

Most days, we spent hours on 'A' Company's firing range. Good shooting was the number one requisite for the usually sudden and brief encounters with the enemy in the jungle. More often than not, we practised firing at figure targets rather than the conventional round, ringed variety. Also, we fired at comparatively close range, shooting usually in standing or crouching positions and often from the hip with rifle, Sten and Bren gun.

Firing accurately from the hip was extremely difficult. It made me realise how ludicrous was all the fancy pistol-shooting from the hip in cowboy movies. However, we practised this for the simple reason that in a sudden face-to-face encounter in the jungle, there would often be no time to raise your weapon to your shoulder and take aim. At the same time, we were advised by our instructors that if we were unable to shoot reasonably well from the hip, our chances of survival might be greater if we risked the extra time involved and shot from the shoulder.

CSM Taylor kept drumming into us: 'The tendency is always to shoot high – so aim for his goolies!'

After my unhappy experiences on the firing ranges at Bordon, I was pleased to find that my rifle-shooting, from the shoulder, had improved a little, although it had not returned to the fairly consistently high standards of my army cadet days. In addition to the small arms mentioned, we also practised firing the EY rifle. This was an old Lee-Enfield Mark III, with a discharger cup fitted to the muzzle, which could lob hand grenades to distances just over 200 yards. Any interest that I managed to derive from this training was very much deflated by the fact that I was always so hot and weary.

One person who definitely brightened up the scene was Serjeant 'Geordie' Dee, one of the four serjeants who had come with us from Bordon. Dee was a big, brawny, loud man, full of boisterous energy and humour.

Late one afternoon, Johnny Ainsworth ran up to me, very excited, and said: 'Jock! I've been looking for you everywhere. Geordie Dee's taking names of people who want to go on a painters and decorators course. You get posted to a special unit that goes round the country, decorating officers' messes. It sounds like a really great skive – better than all this crap. I've put my name down. You'd better hurry if you want to do the same.'

I immediately rushed off and located Geordie Dee. 'Serjeant,' I gasped. 'Can I put my name down for the painters and decorators course?'

Dee smiled faintly. 'Well, I've got all the bods required now,' he said.

'I'd really like to go on it,' I persisted.

'I wouldn't worry,' he said. 'Just forget it.'

'But I think I would be good at it,' I pleaded desperately. 'I studied art at school.'

Geordie grinned. 'OK. I'll take your name in case there's a further vacancy.'

That gave me a little hope but I walked away cursing the fact that I had not been there when he first compiled the list. About half-an-hour later, Geordie Dee assembled the men on his list and marched them all off to the firing range to do their 'painters and decorators course' – pasting up the perforated targets!

On Monday, 13 March, Second Lieutenant Sibbald of 'A' Company took us into the jungle on an all-day training patrol. My first impression of the jungle was not favourable. It did not seem at all exotic like the jungles which made Dorothy Lamour burst into song in her films. It was dark and gloomy and hostile. The surrounding trees, vines and dense undergrowth seemed to close in on me and bruised my arms as I pushed my way through, trying not to lose sight of the man in front of me. Underfoot, there was either rotting leaves or squelching mud. In no time at all, my shirt, slacks and jungle boots were drenched in sweat and slime. We climbed and slithered up and down hill slopes, gasping the stale jungle air into our lungs, and at one time waded waist-deep across a fast-flowing river.

When we halted for tiffen (lunch), I wearily flopped to the ground and soon noticed a large snake coiled around a tree stump, close to where I was sitting. I was too tired to move away, so just kept cautiously watching it as I ate my haversack rations. Fortunately, the snake remained motionless and displayed no unfriendly intentions.

After our break, we moved on again and eventually stopped on a track leading to a small Sakai village. Mr Sibbald and a Malay guide went on by themselves to speak to the headman. Soon, they returned and summoned us into a small clearing containing a cluster of bamboo huts with attap roofs. The Sakai aborigines were very small and the women seemed to be lighter in colour than the men. Some of the young women were quite nice-looking. They wore dingy, flower-patterned cloth garments and their breasts were so poorly covered that they were almost fully displayed. The women gave us a demonstration of how to weave attap leaves together to form a roof, while the men showed us how they fired their 8-foot bamboo blowpipes. These proved to be very accurate at close range. When Mr Styles had a shot, however, the dart flew dangerously wild!

Never again, during all my time in Malaya, did I ever visit a Sakai village. The nomadic Sakai tribes normally lived in the depths of the jungle and painstakingly avoided contact with strangers. It was therefore a great privilege to have that opportunity on our first patrol in the jungle, although I did not fully appreciate my good fortune at that time. (I believe that these particular 'Sakai' were, in fact, Negritos.)

The march back through rough and muddy terrain was quite exhausting, so that by the time we reached our camp at Grik, we were all on our last legs. We gladly retired to our *bashas* or bivouacs to rest up and nurse our tender feet. On passing a bivvie, I heard the chaps inside moaning to one another about the hard jungle march. One of them commented: 'I wonder if Jock Scurr still wants to be a rifleman? He's a stupid cunt!'

Yes. Well, leaving aside whether or not I was a stupid what-he-said, the speaker was absolutely correct to wonder if I still wanted to be a rifleman. I was seriously beginning to wonder myself. Did I really want to live a life of continual exhausting treks such as we had just experienced? Little did I realise that that day's 11-mile hike had been an easy stroll compared to many jungle marches that lay ahead of me.

At that time, several of the draft were on the sick list with diarrhoea. Sweat rashes and prickly heat were also very common ailments. As a preventative against malaria, we each had to take a Paludrine tablet every day, and this continued throughout our time in Malaya. Paludrine proved to be fairly effective, as surprisingly few men succumbed to the disease. Some of us, however, were to find that the malaria in our bloodstreams would later get the upper hand, once we had returned home and ceased taking the tablets.

On the morning of Tuesday the 14th, our kitbags were taken by truck to Kroh, a location close to the Siamese border to which we would be proceeding in two days' time.

That afternoon, we practised throwing hand-grenades. CSM Taylor summoned us one by one to join him in a ditch on top of a ridge of high ground. I waited with the others at the foot of the hill, listening to the periodic explosions just beyond the ridge. When I was called, I hastened up the slope and dropped into the ditch beside the serjeant major.

Taylor handed me a Mills No.36 grenade. 'Have you thrown one of these before?' he asked.

'Yes, sir,' I affirmed.

'Right,' he continued. 'Now, back in Blighty, you used to throw grenades at a range of twenty-five yards or so. But out here in the jungle, when you spot the enemy, he's liable to be a good deal closer. Now, you see that tree stump?' He indicated a stump about 3 feet high, only 10 yards away.

'Yes, sir.'

'Right, student. I want you to aim for that stump. But when you've thrown, I don't want you to duck into cover right away. I want you first to observe where the grenade lands. Now, I'm telling you this, just as I've told it to all the others, but every one of them, so far, has ducked immediately.' He paused, looking at me with undisguised contempt, and then emphasised: 'And I know that you will!'

That's it! I thought to myself. I don't care what happens, I'm not going to duck.

'All right,' said Taylor. 'Pull pin. Prepare to throw.'

With my left middle finger through the ring, I drew the grenade away from the pin in the prescribed manner with my right hand and swung my arm back.

'Throw!' Taylor yelled.

I threw the grenade, determinedly keeping my head and shoulders above the parapet of the ditch, and watched the lethal missile arc through the air, bounce on the ground and roll to less than a foot from the stump. I could hear Taylor's voice muttering quietly: 'Good – good.' I continued to observe.

'Get down!' Taylor screamed, frantically grabbing my shoulders with both hands and shoving me down upon the earth-floor of the ditch. Instantly, I heard the explosion and the whirring of the shrapnel flying overhead. When I straightened up, I looked CSM Taylor in the eyes with a feeling of immense satisfaction. He stared back at me with an expression of complete exasperation. 'All right,' he said disdainfully. 'Send up the next one.'

Whatever he thought of me at that moment, I was very pleased with myself.

The following morning, our draft paraded with 'A' Company to be inspected by General Sir John Harding, KCB, CBE, DSO, MC, Commander-in-Chief of Far East Land Forces, who was accompanied by Brigadier K.N.M. Jones, CBE, i/c Administration Malaya District. Knowing that the two generals were going to observe our shooting practice in the afternoon, CSM Taylor ordered the party in the butts of the firing range, whose job it was to mark up our scores on the targets, to keep signalling bull's-eyes and inners, irrespective of where our bullets actually struck. The result was that we produced a phenomenal display of marksmanship, but whether Sir John was fooled by it all, I wouldn't like to say!

At 6.30 a.m. on Thursday, 16 March, we left Grik in trucks, once more escorted by 'A' Company's two armoured scout cars. We were dressed in full jungle kit and our packs were heavy with tins of 'C' rations in addition to our personal gear. About 9 a.m., we debussed at Kampong Lallang, where we were met by three Malay guides. After eating breakfast, we marched off in three sections along a winding path until we eventually reached a bridge over a river. On the other side, we were confronted by a steep, jungle-covered hill.

Johnny Ainsworth and I were with the first section.

Lieutenant Styles selected us to act as leading scouts. It seemed that Mr Styles had more confidence in my worth than CSM Taylor. For a long time we proceeded slowly up the hill, cutting a path through the undergrowth. Johnny and I had one matchet between us and took turns in the lead, hacking at the shrubs, branches and creepers which constantly barred our way. I soon found that I was close to total exhaustion and was swinging the matchet with little effect.

Suddenly, CSM Taylor pushed his way to the front and seized the matchet from my hand. 'What's the hold up?' he demanded impatiently. He began to hack at the obstructing branch that I'd been tackling but found that he was unable to sever it either. 'This matchet is about as sharp as you are, student!' he concluded, and threw the implement on the ground. He then brought forward Ginger Thompson and Blunsdon and told them to take the lead. They managed to make a little more headway but we soon reached a ridge with a sheer drop on the other side.

Mr Styles, who was in the role of patrol commander under Taylor's supervision, now came forward and announced to us: 'All right. We've tried this way but we can't get through. So now we're going to retrace our steps and start again.'

CSM Taylor shook his head as the young lieutenant turned to go. 'You knew!' he scolded Mr Styles. 'You fucking knew!'

By this time, we were all soaked in perspiration, out of breath and tottering on our feet. The idea that we had made this long climb, struggling against the jungle all the way, for nothing seemed utterly unbearable. However, we had no choice other than to bear it, so we started back down the hill. By the time our section – now in the rear – arrived back at Kampong Lallang, contact had been lost with the other two. We stopped for a short, much needed rest and then made our way along a track beside the river, which presumably was the original, intended route. Soon, we

106

caught up with the rest of the patrol who had stopped for tiffen.

Eagerly, we filled our brew cans with water from the river to make tea, but CSM Taylor reprimanded us for not asking his permission, saying that the water was not safe for drinking. As a punishment, he refused to allow us to make tea with the water in our water bottles as the other two sections had done. 'If I catch any man taking water from a river again without my permission,' he warned us. 'I'll send him out in front with no water and no weapon!'

We continued our march throughout the afternoon. Though we were now following an established track through the jungle, it was still very hard going and drained all the strength out of us. When we finally halted just before nightfall, Serjeant Hogan flopped down with his back leaning against a tree, gasping for breath. He looked at Johnny and me, who were equally shattered, and said between gasps: 'It's no use me trying to pretend to you youngsters that I can take all this because I'm an old soldier. I'm just as fucked as you are!'

We utilised our poncho capes to construct *bashas* as we had been taught and gladly ate a hot meal. During the night, we stood guard in pairs. Johnny and I did our spell between 4 and 6 a.m. We sat back to back, listening to the continuous chatter of strange jungle noises. We could see nothing in the pitch-darkness. It was just a case of sitting still and listening.

After an hour had passed, Johnny suddenly whispered: 'Jock! There's a snake wrapped round my leg!'

I hesitated, wondering if it was just his imagination. 'Just keep still, Johnny,' I said, concluding that this was the best advice for dealing with either real or imaginary snakes. 'If you don't move, it'll just go away.'

I was right. It went away.

Next morning, we set off again. Following a track up a hill slope around 10 a.m., we found a large lizard that appeared to have been shot through the back, the remains of a fire and some food pouches. The Malay guides considered that bandits must have passed along the track only four hours previously. CSM Taylor gave us this information and told us to keep our eyes open.

After a short rest, we continued our march, which grew increasingly arduous. Several times, the rear section lost contact with the rest of us and we had to halt until they caught up. Two chaps collapsed from exhaustion, causing welcome delays by doing so. Eventually, just after 3 p.m., we arrived at Kampong Jalong and stopped for tiffen.

CSM Taylor now called for volunteers to go on ahead to make contact with a 'D' Company patrol at a place called Ayer Panas (Hot Springs), which, he told us, bandits were known to frequent. Although by that time I was so tired that I didn't feel I could walk another step, I volunteered along with eight others. Taylor seemed perplexed, even exasperated, when I stepped forward. He placed Ginger Thompson in charge and told us to be careful. We duly set out and reached Ayer Panas without incident. Two 'D' Company officers met us there and said that bandits normally only came there at night. A signaller with the patrol made wireless contact with 'D' Company's base at Kroh to summon transport.

While awaiting the remainder of our own patrol, we took a delightfully refreshing bath in the hot springs which formed a sizeable pool among some rocks, discovering several leech-bites on our bodies in the process. Soon, the others arrived, as did trucks which eventually carried us all into the camp at Kroh that 'D' Company had taken over from a Gurkha company that very day. We were allotted to large squad tents and that night slept in beds for the first time in nine days. Under the protection of mosquito nets and very weary after our arduous patrol, we slept like logs.

On the Saturday afternoon, the 18th, the CSM interviewed each of us individually before preparing our reports. Seated at the table with him in his tent was Lieutenant Styles, but Taylor did all the talking.

'I know you don't like the army, student,' he said to me. 'But what I want to know is – have you got something on your mind?'

'No, sir,' I lied.

'Well, I think you have,' he said. 'You're worrying about something.' He paused, but when I didn't respond, he continued: 'You're worrying about your studies, aren't you?'

'No, sir,' I replied truthfully. I wondered what he'd say if I told him I had no interest in further study and that my only problem was the disintegration of my dream of becoming a regular soldier and the continuous gnawing pain of my disillusionment.

'You know, this could be a great experience for someone like you,' Taylor said now. 'You're educated – you're intelligent. But I'd be very reluctant to post you to a company because while you're walking around wrestling with whatever it is that's worrying you, you'd be a constant danger – not only to yourself but to the men around you.'

I didn't know what to say, so I remained silent.

'All right,' he said with a sigh. 'I'll have to decide what I'm going to do with you. I'll speak to you again.'

Later, he called me back and told me briefly that he was going to recommend me for training as a clerk. He urged me to organise myself and, as a clerk, be a useful man to my company. I came away from this second summons in a mood of considerable disquiet. The past three weeks since landing in Malaya had been very tiring; I was still not accustomed to the hot, damp climate. The two forays into the jungle had been totally exhausting and unpleasant experiences and I suppose I had strong underlying feelings of homesickness. All of these factors, added to the antipathy for army life that I had developed during basic training, had caused me to sink into a definite depression. But did I really want to be a clerk? That night, I noted in my journal: 'Although I didn't like our little patrol much, I'm still not sure whether or not I'd rather be a rifleman, as I wouldn't mind having a crack at the bandits. Still, the CSM said he couldn't guarantee I would get a clerk's job, so I might as well just wait and see what turns up.'

This resolve to 'wait and see' did not last. When I retired to bed, my mind just would not let the matter rest, and throughout Sunday, 19 March, I was continuously preoccupied with my problem. By nightfall, however, I had reached a definite decision.

I caught CSM Taylor just as he was leaving his tent. 'Have you sent off my report yet, sir?' I asked him.

'No, not yet,' he answered cautiously. 'Why?'

'Well, I've been thinking things over, sir,' I said. 'And I've decided that while I'm out here, I'd rather do some proper soldiering.'

Taylor's face reddened slightly and then grinned broadly. 'Well, what made you change your mind?' he asked, clearly delighted.

'I've just been thinking about it last night, sir, and again today, and I've realised that this is an opportunity that I mustn't miss,' I explained. Then I added, a little dejectedly: 'I'll try to do better, sir, if I haven't been good enough up to now.'

'No, it's not that,' Taylor said gently, placing a hand momentarily on my shoulder. 'It's just that I want you to buck up a bit and be more aware of what's happening around you.'

'I'll do my best, sir,' I assured him.

'Right. I'll have to write out another report but that won't be any problem.' With that, he walked away. I'm sure he was pleased. So was I.

That Sunday night was the turning point in my personal crisis. From that night on, I gradually began to relate more positively to the army – the real, flesh-and-blood army with all its faults – and to feel that there would be a place for me in the KOYLI.

Our training at Kroh was nearly all on the firing range. The purpose behind our training was brought home to us on Tuesday the 21st when we heard that a car had been

110

ambushed by bandits near Ayer Panas (the hot springs where we had bathed five days before). Two Europeans in the car had been killed and two Malays seriously wounded.

On the Thursday afternoon, our firing practice took place in a location called 'the jungle lane'. Each of us had to advance, one at a time, up a jungle track, armed with a Sten gun. Figure targets were concealed among the trees and bushes on either side. I managed to spot nearly all of them and shot them down satisfactorily with well-aimed bursts of fire. CSM Taylor seemed quite pleased with my performance.

So ended our jungle training. Our postings were announced on 'D' Company detail that night. Along with Johnny Ainsworth, Jim Walters, 'London' Line and Ron Stringer, I was destined for the Signal Platoon. The following day, we were issued with green 1944-pattern webbing equipment to replace the normal 1937-pattern that we'd used since enlistment. The new equipment was far more suitable for jungle operations and best of all, did not have to be blancoed!

On Saturday, 25 March, all of our draft, excepting those posted to 'A' and 'D' Companies, departed for Penang at 8 a.m. We travelled in two 3-ton trucks, escorted down the Baling road by two armoured scout cars. By 12.45 p.m., we had arrived safely at Glugor Barracks, Penang Island.

8

The Signal Platoon – Penang and Ipoh March–June 1950

Being an infantry signaller was something that I had never considered. It certainly wasn't a rifleman, but as I was posted to the Signal Platoon with good friends, I initially accepted the situation without complaint. My companions comprised of my pal Johnny Ainsworth, old Jim Walters, 'London' Line – nicknamed thus since his first day at Bordon – and Ron Stringer. With a few others, the latter had volunteered to transfer to the KOYLI from the King's Royal Rifle Corps and had joined our draft in Penang before we left for Grik.

On arrival at Glugor Barracks on Saturday, 25 March, the five of us were allocated beds in the Signals *basha* – a ground-floor barrack room in one of the two-storeyed blocks described in Chapter 6. From that day on, London Line spent much of his spare time with his head underwater in the swimming pool, trying to obtain 'Singapore ear' and become sufficiently deaf to be sent home. Alas, despite all his efforts, his hearing remained unimpaired!

At that time, HQ Company was commanded by the very wealthy Major 'Porky' Gowans, who had his own private bungalow and chauffeur-driven American car. He treated the other ranks pretty fairly, while CSM Potts was not too severe as serjeant majors go. There were, of course, characters around the barracks such as Regimental Serjeant Major Tanner and Bugle Major Harbisher, who were liable to pounce upon unsuspecting privates who did not have their berets on straight or who did not swing their arms while walking from place to place. But, as I now finally accepted, this was only to be expected in the army.

There was also a rather strange, though likeable, little man, Corporal Borrie, who acted as permanent 'Company Orderly Serjeant'. He organised fatigues and guard rosters and, so far as I could see, practically ran the company. He seemed to like me and certainly gave me no problems. (Two months later, Borrie was 'ambushed' in the early hours of the morning by RSM Tanner and a couple of regimental policemen as he crept out of the married quarters after visiting an absent soldier's wife. On appearing before the Company Commander, Borrie is reputed to have stated in his defence: 'Well, if she put it on a plate for you, sir, what would you have done?' Perhaps this retort was well received, as Borrie's only punishment was to be posted to Tactical HQ for a spell. When the news reached the lady's Irish husband, he threatened to 'borry' Borrie at the first opportunity. However, when the confrontation finally occurred, husband, wife and Borrie all went downtown to the races together!)

On the evening of our arrival, we were interviewed individually by Captain Saltonstall, who had been Signals Officer for the previous two years. He immediately impressed me as being both intelligent and cordial and seemed genuinely pleased to have me in his platoon. When I told him that my principal subject of study at school had been art, he commented that there was nothing artistic about signalling but he had no doubts that I would master it easily enough. He also explained that if I sought advancement I would need to 'sign on', as only regulars were promoted in the Signal Platoon.

Quite happy after this initial meeting with Captain Saltonstall, I was also gratified to find that the Signal Platoon senior NCOs liked me from the start and I liked them. Serjeant Stan Haley was a genial, highly strung bundle of energy who, when he 'flapped', practically took off into the air. He had married a very nice Siamese girl from Penang only a few months previously and seemed completely dedicated to signalling. Stan made me feel instantly welcome, as did Corporal 'Jock' McClung. The latter was described to me as 'the Scotsman from Doncaster' but, in fact, he told me that he had been born in a Royal Scots Fusiliers barracks in Bombay and that the army was the only world he knew. Another Scotsman was Serjeant Cook, an old friend of Stan Haley's, who arrived in the Signal Platoon only days after I did. Both of these fellow countrymen were consistently kind to me and concerned for my welfare.

Temporarily billeted in the Signals *basha* at the time of my arrival were three regular soldiers who had completed their three years' overseas tour and had been withdrawn to headquarters to prepare for shipping home. During that first weekend, I was very eager to talk to them about their 'jungle-bashing' experiences. Seated on an adjacent bed on the Sunday afternoon, I expressed my interest to a ginger-haired, well-built chap who had been a Bren gunner in one of the rifle companies.

'Well, I'll tell you this much,' he answered. 'I'm bloody glad to be getting out of here. I went right through the war without – well, practically without a scratch. So, I'd hate to get killed out here. You're fighting for fuck-all!'

I politely agreed with him, although even then I knew that there were important issues at stake in Malaya. 'Still,' I said to him. 'After being in the war, you can't have found it too bad out here.'

He thought for a moment and then replied: 'Well, it might have been a lot more dangerous in the war, but this is a tough campaign – make no mistake about that. The jungle is a bastard!' He smiled gently as he concluded: 'You stay out of it if you can. Find yourself a cushy number somewhere.'

Perhaps it was good advice, but I'd already turned down that option at Kroh and I had no intention of changing course now.

Also waiting to go home that month was a Signals NCO, Corporal Cockerham, who had just arrived in HQ from 'D' Company. On the first Monday morning, Corporal Cockerham took Johnny Ainsworth and me to assist him in laying a new telephone cable to the officers' mess. Every time he gave us an instruction, Johnny and I automatically leaped to attention and snapped out: 'Yes, Corporal!'

To our surprise he reacted vehemently. 'Will you stop that!' he exclaimed. 'You're embarrassing me. Just relax. And stop calling me "Corporal". My name's Geoff.' This was indicative of the 'family' relationship which generally prevailed between the ranks in the Signal Platoon.

Later that day, Geoff Cockerham confided to me: 'D'you know, Jock, I came safely through all those operations in the jungle, yet I'm worrying now in case I get killed on the train down to Singapore.' Fortunately, Geoff's fears proved groundless and he got safely home.

My journal records that on the night of Thursday, 30 March, while I was on guard in the MT Park, I became aware of a long, black form slithering through the grass towards me. Stopping dead in my tracks, I recognised the hooded head of a cobra. Following the advice that I had previously given to Johnny Ainsworth, I remained perfectly still. The cobra wormed its way past me only a couple of inches from my boots, apparently heedless of my presence.

Other brief entries in my journal during this period describe trips into town, principally to go to the cinema. For someone like me who was an action-adventure film addict, Georgetown was a veritable paradise, as the cinemas there seemed to show little else. Subtitles in the local languages were not printed on the film itself but displayed on slides either below or at the side of the cinema screen. I was always interested to note that when films about the British Empire were screened – such as *The Four Feathers* or *The Drum* – the audiences invariably clapped and cheered ecstatically whenever the British won a battle against rebellious tribes.

On the night of Friday the 31st, I dined for the first time in the very popular Broadway Café in Penang Road. This café will be fully described in a later, more appropriate chapter. On this occasion, I was accompanied by two of the men from the King's Royal Rifle Corps – fellow signaller Ron Stringer, and Lance Corporal Berry, who had been posted to the MT Platoon.

Berry was a handsome, dashing sort of character who had previously been on active service in Greece and Palestine. In several discussions that I had with him about the army, he advised me that I ought to sign on as a regular as I had originally planned and warned me that I would never be really happy unless I did. Shortly after that, the men from the KRRC were instructed that they must start wearing the badge of the KOYLI on their berets. All of them complied except for Berry, who refused to take down his KRRC badge. He was consequently placed under close arrest.

One time when reporting to the guardroom, I spotted Berry tending the lawn outside and rather pointlessly asked him why he was in the 'clink'. Berry answered: 'Because I told them to stick their KOYLI bugle up their arse and fart down it!' This remark brought a harsh admonishment from a watching regimental policeman and I immediately regretted having asked the rather foolish question.

Eventually, Berry disappeared from the scene, presumably back to his own regiment. At the time, I considered that he was being unfairly victimised, but I am no longer of that opinion. He should have worn our badge while serving with us. Despite this misdemeanour born of regimental pride, in the short time that I knew him, Berry impressed me as being a good soldier who thought very highly of the military life.

Quite frequently, I went into Georgetown alone. This may have been a foolhardy thing to do in those times of the terrorist emergency, especially as I sometimes attended the small cinemas within the confines of the Chinese amusement parks New World and Happy World. There were times during those early weeks when I felt a little anxious on my own, but no one ever offered me any hostility. In fact, the only problem I experienced in the amusement parks' cinemas – the Globe and the Lido – was trying to follow the plot of the film without being distracted by the

116

constant banging and clashing of gongs and cymbals. These sounds vibrated continuously from the nearby Chinese open-air theatres, where gaudily costumed actors performed interminable and very noisy plays apparently depicting ancient Chinese legends.

Evidence of potential dangers was, however, presented when I journeyed by bus into Georgetown on Sunday, 2 April. The bus was stopped on the way by what we used to call 'anti-bandit wallahs' (Malay Home Guards), armed with shotguns, who checked all the passengers' identity cards. Arriving in town soon after, I went to see John Wayne in *Red River* at the Cathay in Penang Road; quite a nice cinema with basket-chair seats. Later, I learned that Communist agents had shot two 'enemies of the people' in town the previous day.

I also heard that the previous day, 1 April, Lance Corporal McGee of 'C' Company had died in the British Military Hospital, Kuala Lumpur, from acute gastroenteritis. I thought how sad and unjust it was that a young soldier on active service, thousands of miles from home, should die – not from an enemy bullet but from a stomach complaint.

Whilst awaiting a Signals training cadre that we were told would be organised shortly, we new signallers were given some elementary instruction by Corporal Jock McClung and assigned to work on the battalion telephone exchange. This was not a task that I enjoyed. I made mistakes quite regularly and was bawled out more than once for making wrong connections. There was one memorable occasion when the Adjutant asked to speak to the CO and was answered by a Chinese! I was also adept at disconnecting people in mid-conversation.

This duty required us to work a night shift every third night. It was a two-man shift, and we were armed with our rifles in case of intruders. However, the only unwelcome visitors I ever saw were strange large black flying beetles which, attracted by our light, used to come zooming through the open shutters and smash themselves against the walls.

All the while, the army continued to be the army, exem-

117

plified by CSM Potts ordering a locker and room inspection at 7 p.m. on Tuesday the 4th because he wasn't satisfied with the morning's inspection. There was, however, a decided difference between this situation and similar ones in basic training. On this occasion, the platoon NCOs were on 'our side'. Only the serjeant major was 'the enemy'. The dread and terror of training company days were gone. Irritation and resentment were all that remained.

I sometimes wondered how other members of my draft were getting on. I knew that McAllister, Stan Swalwell, Phil Cox and Ginger Thompson had all been posted to 'C' Company and Jungle Jim to 'A' Company. Lieutenant Styles had gone to 'B' Company, where he did not have to wait long to experience action.

On 9 April, Easter Sunday, Mr Styles was leading a patrol through the jungle in the Pelam area of Kedah. The leading scout was hacking his way through a clump of *belukar* when a bandit leapt out with a grenade in his right hand. Private Corrie instantly opened fire with his Bren gun, killing the terrorist before he could use his grenade. The patrol then discovered a small camp nearby, from which the rest of the bandits had flown, leaving a few packs behind. In the camp was a classroom with a large tree stump serving as a blackboard. The man killed proved to be the leader – an Indian Communist called Nathan. His gang had killed a European police sergeant in an ambush only two weeks before.

This success made a fine start to Mr Styles' service in 'B' Company. He would shortly be promoted to acting captain, and would retain that rank for the remainder of his attachment to the KOYLI.

A new draft arrived in Glugor Barracks on the night of Thursday the 13th, which I was pleased to find included my cousin, John Kitchen. John was able to join me on three trips to the cinemas in town before departing for his jungle training in Kroh 13 days later.

In mid-April, there were two accidental shootings within the battalion. Private James of 'B' Company died from a gunshot wound on 18 April while on a patrol near Sungei Patani, Kedah. Three days later, Private Bennett of HQ Company was wounded during training in the Kroh–Klian Intan area of Upper Perak and responded slowly, but satisfactorily, to treatment in Penang General Hospital.

At this point, my journal again began to register discontent. Battalion operations had just begun in the Kulim area of Kedah and I had been told that our Signals training cadre could not start until they were ended. I tried, without success, to obtain permission to go to Tactical HQ for the period of the operations and also considered applying for a posting to a rifle company.

Aware of my increasing restlessness, Corporal McClung arranged for me to go on an escort duty to Tac HQ on Wednesday the 26th. At 7 a.m., we left the barracks in two vehicles; a jeep and a 15-hundredweight Dodge, carrying Captain Saltonstall, Jock McClung and half a dozen privates. After crossing to Prai in the ferry, we started up the Kulim road and arrived at Tac HQ, a few miles past Kulim, about nine. The previous morning, one of the rifle companies had chased off 20 bandits from there as the Tac HQ personnel arrived, and the CO had ordered all Chinese males in the vicinity to be put under arrest for questioning.

We made the return journey in the early afternoon, bringing back another Signals NCO, Corporal Heathcote. I had enjoyed the trip and been excited at the thought of being in a zone of active operations. I consequently asked Serjeant Haley if I could be posted to Tac HQ for a while. From the dubious way he replied that it might be arranged, I correctly assumed that it wouldn't be.

At this time, I began drinking an occasional Tiger beer. One bottle (containing a pint and a third) could render me 'happy', and I observed that the brew had a startling effect on chaps who drank several bottles. Every soldier in Malaya received a weekly free issue of 50 cigarettes (Woodbines, Players or Capstan). Consequently, for the first time in my life I began smoking. I also have to admit that my mode of speech was gradually growing saltier. Four-letter words

119

were an integral part of a soldier's vocabulary. It was sometimes essential to use them in order to make yourself properly understood!

There was one vice, however, which I continued to resist. Often when riding in a trishaw in town, the Chinese driver pedalling behind me would ask: 'You want a good woman, John?' But I always declined without hesitation. Corporal Charlie Heathcote, who had returned with me from Tac HQ, was a very amusing fellow. We got on very well together during the short time that I knew him. One day, I said to him: 'You don't go with these women downtown, do you, Charlie?'

'Not me, Jock!' he assured me emphatically.

A couple of nights later, Charlie was lying on his bed when I returned from the NAAFI. It was apparent that he had consumed a few Tigers as he began to happily reminisce: 'Oh-ho! Last night downtown with Suzie Li! Wo-ho!'

'Charlie!' I exclaimed. 'You told me you didn't go with these women.'

Charlie began to rock back and forward on his bed, his eyes rolling wickedly. 'Oh, Scu-urr!' he gently mocked. 'Oh-ho-ho, Scu-urr!'

(In July, Charlie Heathcote left us to go home, having completed his overseas tour. Weeks later, we heard that when he was returning to the KOYLI depot at Strensall, Yorkshire, at the end of his disembarkation leave, poor Charlie crashed his motorbike and was killed.)

During this period in Penang, the number of my favourite films that I was able to see within a few weeks was phenomenal: *Captain from Castile, The Sea Hawk, The Four Feathers, The Spanish Main, The Three Musketeers, The Mark of Zorro, Adventures of Don Juan, The Drum* ... I could not believe my luck! However, this succession of celluloid fantasies was not enough to keep me content.

Our Signals training cadre finally began on Friday, 5 May. I found that first day's lessons in operating a wireless transmitter difficult to comprehend. It all seemed very complicated, technical and, I considered, not for me. Corporal McClung grew quite exasperated when I stated that I had been unable to understand his instructions on how to tune and net a wireless. 'I can't make it any plainer, Jock!' he exclaimed. Next morning, I put forward a request to see the Signals Officer about obtaining a transfer to a rifle company.

Late in the afternoon of Tuesday the 9th, I was accompanied by Serjeant Cook and Corporal McClung to the Signals Office, where I was interviewed by Captain Saltonstall. Standing before the captain's desk, I explained to him that signalling didn't appeal to me and that I wanted to go to a rifle company.

'Now look, Scurr,' Captain Saltonstall said firmly. 'You don't know anything about signalling yet, and for that matter, you don't know anything about rifle companies. It isn't all charging with bayonets against lines of screaming bandits. There's an awful lot of walking to do and the jungle's no picnic! Anyway, if you really want all that, we can send you to a company as an operational signaller as soon as you've completed your training.'

'I'd rather be a rifleman, sir,' I insisted.

'All right,' Captain Saltonstall said with resignation. 'I'll tell you what we'll do. I'm going to ask you to at least wait until you're halfway through your training cadre and then see how you feel about signalling. If you still feel then that you want to go to a rifle company, I'll recommend your transfer. All right?'

'Yes, sir,' I agreed. 'Thank you.'

After we'd left the office, both Serjeant Cook and Corporal McClung spent a considerable time trying to persuade me that I'd be far better off and much happier if I remained in Signals. I was greatly impressed that afternoon that at long last, someone in the army wanted me. On returning to the barrack room, I noted in my journal: 'It's obvious that they're dead against me leaving. I think I'd better remain in the Signal Platoon. I've been assured that I'll be sent out to a company, as a signaller, as soon as the cadre's finished. But if these rumours that are floating round about us moving out of the operational zone are true, I'll just about go mad!' This last statement referred to a typical wild rumour that the battalion was destined shortly to undertake garrison duties in Singapore. Thankfully, this proved to be completely unfounded.

The start of the Signals cadre meant the end of my duties on the battalion telephone exchange. This pleased me immensely, even though it meant that I was once more available for the guard duty roster, doing a guard every six days. Cousin John arrived back in Penang on Friday, 12 May, having been posted to HQ Company as a clerk on the Quartermaster's staff. He seemed quite happy with this posting. We could now again enjoy our trips to the cinema together.

The cadre was due to last six weeks. As I recall, Corporal McClung and Serjeant Cook provided most of the instruction in wireless procedures, Morse, telephones, line-laying, etc. Contrary to my initial impression, I soon found that tuning and netting the No.62 and 68 wireless sets was neither complicated nor difficult – at least, not in theory. I loved the lessons in Morse and was very disappointed to learn that we would not be using this means of communication in the field. My biggest surprise came when I found that I was very adept at ascending telegraph poles, using spiked climbing irons strapped onto my boots, and that I tackled this task more readily than most of my classmates.

The other members of the cadre constituted a great bunch of lads. In addition to Johnny Ainsworth, Jim Walters, London Line and Ron Stringer – all from my draft – there were four others: Joy, Bentham, Jones and Schaverien. Tom Joy – a regular soldier from Liverpool – was a small, chubby bundle of energy and fun and a keen film fan. We got on well together throughout my service. Chas (Charles) Schaverien, also small, was a Jewish National Serviceman from Uxbridge who would soon become a close friend. We all worked well together, tackled our instruction with enthusiasm and had a lot of fun doing it. Long before halfway, my decision to remain in the Signal Platoon was positively confirmed.

The June 1950 edition of the KOYLI journal *The Bugle*, stated the following:

> Another cadre was started during May which turned out to be one of the best ever. Our congratulations are extended to the gallant nine for their good work and spirit. During this period, however, we had one unhappy trainee, this being Private Scurr who was straining at the leash to get into the 'ulu' [jungle] to get material for his latest book. He settled down, however, to the cadre on being promised that he would, as soon as the cadre was completed, be sent to a company.

By then, the word had got round that I was an aspirant writer. In my spare time, I was working on a short novel about gallant English pirates and beauteous Spanish ladies which was later avidly read by some members of the platoon.

Every Wednesday, the cadre was given the afternoon off so that we could all join the HQ Company swimming party. Trucks conveyed us through lush green hills of coconut palms to the golden beach below Major Gowans' bungalow at Sandycroft. Swimming in the calm sea, beneath the hot sun in the clear blue sky, I thought to myself more than once that Penang Island truly was a tropical paradise.

While I was on magazine guard on the night of Wednesday the 24th, I was startled by a loud, crashing noise which came from a dark clump of trees behind the small, unused guardroom building. Needless to say, I had 'one up the breech' in no time. With my rifle at the ready, I searched cautiously around the trees and then round the entire magazine enclosure but found no signs of anything living. Although I didn't really believe the tales of ghosts in the magazine, I still felt uneasy. I'd met several people who were convinced that the dead Chinese woman did haunt the place. When Ron Stringer arrived to relieve me, we searched through the bushes around the clump of trees very carefully but found nothing that could possibly have made any noise. Later in the night, one of the guard heard a similar crashing sound in the same place and another complained of strange noises round the magazine caverns.

That same night, in Georgetown, a terrorist threw a hand grenade through a window into the Chinese Town Hall NAAFI, where a number of soldiers were eating. The grenade landed on the billiard table. While other lads dived to the floor, Lance Corporal Hall of 'D' Company picked the grenade up and threw it back out of the window. For his brave act, Lance Corporal Hall was later awarded the British Empire Medal.

At that time, large numbers of marines from 45 Commando, 3rd Royal Marine Commando Brigade, were arriving in Glugor Barracks from Hong Kong. Eventually, there were more than 1,100 of them, accommodated in vast rows of tents which we were forced to erect during all of our available time. Although some of the marines were inclined to be cocky and to give the impression of being big-heads, there was in fact surprisingly little friction between the two units. Indeed, we were truly grateful to them when we heard that the marines were taking over guard duty at the magazine. Much to our annoyance, we then discovered that this did not mean that we would be doing fewer guards. The same numbers of KOYLI were put on guard as before, but instead of having one man guarding the MT Park, there were now two; one patrolling round the inside of the fence and the other outside.

Also grateful to the KOYLI for hospitality were men of the 2nd Battalion, Scots Guards, who frequently came to Penang for leave periods. This resulted in an impressive ceremony, held on Friday, 26 May. At 6 p.m., all of HQ Company was drawn up on parade on the sports field, as was a representative party from the Scots Guards. An inscribed silver bugle, paid for by voluntary subscription by all ranks of the 2nd Scots Guards, was then presented to the 1st KOYLI. Following our Commanding Officer's speech, thanking the Scots Guards for this most generous gesture of appreciation and friendship, the band and bugles splendidly sounded retreat.

In mid-May, 8 Platoon, 'C' Company, had been sent on detachment to Grik. One day towards the end of that month, Captain Haddon and his batman were returning to Grik in the Captain's Vauxhall car, conveying the platoon's pay. An escort truck preceded the car about a hundred yards ahead. In the cab were Private Harrison, driving, and Lance Corporal McAllister, while Privates Lloyd, Eathorne, Carter, Swalwell and Keenan rode in the back. ('Mac' McAllister and Stan Swalwell were both from my draft and had previously been two of my 'old soldier' companions in Holding Company.) When it started to rain, the men in the exposed back of the truck huddled up against the cab, endeavouring to obtain some shelter.

Halfway between Lenggong and Grik, bandits suddenly opened fire from ambush positions on a jungle hill overlooking a bend in the road. Several shots struck the front of the escort vehicle, narrowly missing the driver and Lance Corporal McAllister and peppering the engine. It is likely that the bandits had not seen the others still huddled behind the cab. However, Private Frank Keenan – a young regular soldier from Bradford – immediately grabbed his Bren gun and fired several bursts into the shrubbery of the bank above, taking the ambushers completely by surprise. As the truck came to a halt, other members of the escort also began to return fire.

The escort party swiftly dismounted from their vehicle and climbed the bank, intending to launch a flanking attack upon the rear of the bandits' positions. As the soldiers advanced, still shaken by the shock of the ambush, they warily fired into any suspicious-looking bush in their path. Realising that they were being flanked, the bandits hurriedly left their positions, crossed the road and made their escape.

Descending again to the road, Mac and his men hastened back around the bend, only to find the Vauxhall car abandoned with no sign of Captain Haddon or his batman. So they returned to their truck and, despite the damage to the engine, were able to drive off. A few miles further up the road, however, the engine burst into flames. After promptly halting once more, the party commandeered a car that came along, driven by a Chinese civilian. They then drove speedily on to their platoon base at Grik.

Early next morning, Captain Haddon and his batman turned up safe and sound with a large police escort from Lenggong. They said that they'd presumed that the men in the truck were dead, so they'd gone off to seek help.

On Friday, 2 June, John Strachey, Minister of War in Britain's Labour Government, visited Glugor Barracks. Everything had been carefully prepared beforehand with extra scrubbing and polishing. Flowers even appeared on the dining hall tables! In the event, Mr Strachey was rushed round very quickly in a car and saw little of the results of our hard work. However, he did call in at our Signals cadre lecture room during our morning instruction.

'These men are learning signalling,' our CO, Lieutenant Colonel Brown, explained to him.

Mr Strachey glanced round the nine of us and then said, a little hesitantly: 'Signalling? Oh, yes. That's a good thing to know, isn't it?'

With no more ado, the CO ushered the War Minister out to the waiting car to continue his rapid tour.

During my Signals training period, the food in Glugor Barracks deteriorated to an alarming degree. The bread was always damp and smelled horribly and the meals were often flavoured with insects, dead or alive. One day at tiffen, I was seated in the dining hall beside Corporal Charlie Heathcote. Suddenly, Charlie called over the Company Orderly Serjeant, threw his plate down in front of him and exclaimed: 'Have you seen this fucking conner? It's covered in spunking ants!'

To this, the Company Orderly Serjeant merely replied: 'Well, I can't do anything about it!'

Every morning at breakfast, cousin John used to sift

126

carefully through his porridge, always depositing a score of dead ants around the edge of his plate before eating. I preferred just to shovel the lot down while avoiding looking at the contents of my spoon!

Early in June, the battalion was in the process of concentrating around Ipoh in Lower Perak: 'A' Company at Sungei Siput, 'B' Company at Batu Gajah and 'C' Company at Tanjong Rambutan. 'D' Company was already established at Ashby Road Camp in Ipoh itself.

On Saturday, 10 June, 10 Platoon, 'D' Company, led by Serjeant Phil Hogan (the same Serjeant Hogan who had been with my draft from Bordon), was scouting ahead of the remainder of the company in an area known as 'Dead Man's Gully' near Ampang, about 3 miles from Ipoh. On coming to a fork in the track, Serjeant Hogan decided to split the platoon into two sections. He sent the newly promoted Serjeant Benny Cookson with one section to reconnoitre the left-hand fork which continued upwards through the *lallang*. Hogan led the second section along the other fork, proceeding up a slope and then down into a saucer-shaped hollow surrounded by jungle. The ten-man section was ambushed here by a large force of bandits concealed in the undergrowth by the track and on high ground overlooking it. The leading scouts – who I believe were Privates Harrison and Gough – were shot at point-blank range and practically fell upon the enemy Bren gun that slew them. Murderous fire annihilated the rest of the section in a matter of moments. Most of the lads fell without being able to fire a shot in return.

Privates Harrison, Gough, Jones, Boden, Hall and Hudson were killed outright, while Serjeant Hogan, Lance Corporal Brown and Privates Daniels and Storey all lay badly wounded. Following their usual practice, some of the terrorists now began to emerge from their positions in order to collect the soldiers' weapons and ammunition and finish off the wounded. Raising his head from the ground, Lance Corporal Vernon Brown saw a bandit jump down from his place on the adjacent bank. With a wide grin on his face, the Chinese approached him. Despite his wounds, Brown managed to rear up, swing his rifle into position and fire. Shot through the heart, the bandit went down with his grinning expression changed to one of utter surprise. The remainder of the ambushers now swiftly dispersed, carrying away only a couple of seized weapons.

12 Platoon, patrolling to the rear of 10, had heard the firing and seen Chinese civilians fleeing from the area. They now hastened towards the ambush site.

Serjeant Cookson's section, meanwhile, had seen the ambush from higher ground but had been unable to open fire because of the risk of hitting their own men. Retracing their steps, they found Serjeant Hogan, shot through the back, crawling back along the track towards them 'in a hell of a state', as a 'D' Company signaller later described to me. I subsequently recalled that at the end of our jungle training period when we had boarded the trucks to leave Kroh, Serjeant Hogan's final words of advice to us young soldiers had been: 'Keep your eyes open!'

One of Serjeant Cookson's men now ran back to Company HQ's position to report the ambush to the Company Commander, Captain Davis, MC. The men of HQ had detained some local suspects for questioning and later heard the sounds of heavy firing. When 10 Platoon's messenger arrived, he was raving excitedly about lads being killed and wounded and began to threaten the suspects with his Sten gun. The HQ personnel eventually managed to calm the man down. He then led Captain Davis with part of HQ to the ambush scene, while Signals Lance Corporal Sid Grant tried to make contact on his wireless with rear HQ, Penang. It was not a normal transmission time but Sid's call was picked up by the 4th Hussars, who then informed our battalion to make contact and also sent a patrol of scout cars to the scene.

The following day, Sunday the 11th, 'D' Company's six dead were buried with full military honours in the civil cemetery at Batu Gajah. Six days later, on Saturday the 17th, the brave Lance Corporal Vernon Brown was also buried there, having died in hospital the previous day. Vernon had been able to give a clear description of the ambush incident, but as he began to react to the horror of it all, he had been unable to close his eyes to sleep without reliving his terrible experience in nightmares. The other wounded men fortunately survived. Private Storey's knee-cap had been blown off, while Private Daniels had to have his right hand and wrist amputated.

When news of the ambush had reached HQ Company in Penang on Saturday the 10th, I remember an NCO from the MT Platoon commenting rather casually: 'Well, this is war. We've got to expect casualties.' However, my feelings – and I'm sure, those of most of the men in the battalion – were far from casual. I felt angry and longed to strike back at the enemy and avenge our dead. I am convinced that soldiers rarely fight for 'freedom', 'democracy' or other fine-sounding concepts. Soldiers fight for their regiment and to avenge their slain comrades.

As our Signals cadre instructors were required for duties with Tactical HQ, which was departing for Ipoh the following day, it had been decided that the cadre would go with them to complete its training. I was considerably pleased that I was about to get a bit closer to the action.

Dressed in full jungle kit and battle order, we left Glugor Barracks at 9.30 a.m. on Sunday the 11th. The convoy carrying the personnel and equipment of Tac HQ consisted of an armoured scout car, two jeeps with trailers, six 3-ton trucks, a water-carrier, a civvy car and two motorcycles. It rained for the first part of the journey south from Prai, so we got rather wet in the exposed backs of the trucks. After halting just past Taiping for a tiffen of cheese 'banjos' (sandwiches), we finally arrived at Ashby Road Camp, Ipoh, at about 3.30 p.m.

This was, in fact, the camp of the 2/2nd Gurkha Rifles, who were kindly providing accommodation there for both 'D' Company and Tac HQ. After we had unloaded numer-ous crates of 3-inch mortar bombs, we were allotted fairly primitive wooden *bashas* which contained equally primitive

129

wood and rope cots for sleeping. Ipoh was also 'home' to the 4th Hussars, who had a camp quite nearby.

Our Signals training cadre recommenced on Tuesday the 13th. Training now mostly consisted of practical work with the wireless sets, which I rather enjoyed. My early fears that I would not be able to master signalling were now completely banished. However, it would be true to say that my sole motivation for becoming a competent wireless operator was the prospect of thus obtaining a posting to a rifle company.

Our training schedule was finally completed on the morning of Friday the 16th. Nonetheless, as a precaution against Bugle Major Harbisher rounding us up for fatigue duties, Serjeant Cook kept the cadre members in a storeroom during that afternoon. Harbisher eventually came in and surveyed us all apparently just sitting around.

'What are all these bodies doing in here, Serjeant Cook?' he demanded.

'Signals cadre, Bugle Major,' Serjeant Cook responded without hesitation. 'There was nowhere else available for the lecture.'

Harbisher grunted and looked us over again. He was obviously suspicious but, unable to disprove the serjeant's statement, he turned and left.

'I'm not having signallers doing fatigues,' Serjeant Cook said now, with our full approval!

That night, I went into town with two of the cadre, Schaverien and Jones. Ipoh seemed a very clean, neat, little town – 'quite a contrast from dirty, sprawling, smelly Georgetown,' I observed, perhaps unfairly, in my journal. The exterior of the Rex cinema was superbly decorated and lighted, I considered. However, we were too late for the show, so we had a walk round and finished up in the Café Metropole. This establishment also impressed me, as did the well-served meal we had of ham, eggs and chips, toast, ice cream, coffee and ice-cold orange crush. There were two young Englishwomen dining at a nearby table. They were not particularly attractive but were nonetheless an unusual and very welcome sight. I found myself constantly glancing at them.

Our enjoyable trip into town was tinged with some sadness due to the fact that the following day, I was to be separated from my new pal, Chas Schaverien, and from other friends in the cadre. We were all now declared to be trained signallers and most of us were being posted to rifle companies as wireless operators. I was, of course, very glad to be at last going to a company, yet I was sorry to be leaving my friends.

Transport left Tac HQ at 1.30 p.m. on Saturday, 17 June, to deliver the new wireless operators to their various destinations: three to 'B' Company at Batu Gajah, two to 'A' Company at Sungei Siput and finally myself to 'C' Company, based in the State Mental Home at Tanjong Rambutan.

When our trucks entered the gates, we were greeted by the sight of numerous lunatics clinging to the wire mesh of their cells on both sides of the roadway. We found 'C' Company also housed in cell blocks. The communal cells were spartan but not drab. White walls were topped at chest height by wire mesh, all beneath red-tiled roofs. The company's blocks were incorporated within a separate enclosure and surrounded a central grassed area. I was pleased to find that the signallers were accommodated in a squad tent near the entrance to the enclosure.

The NCO who supervised the cadre's distribution was Corporal Ivor Lewis – not previously mentioned – who had assisted with our training. He was one of the nicest people I had ever met; a big chap, yet immensely kind and gentle with a lovely sense of humour. Ivor took me into the Signals tent and introduced me to the three men inside, none of whom I had met before.

At that moment, I felt suddenly lonely and isolated. Johnny Ainsworth had gone to 'A' Company and Chas Schaverien to 'B' – both with other members of the cadre; whereas I was being deposited here alone amongst complete strangers. Ivor Lewis now seemed to be my last link with my recently acquired Signals 'family' with whom I had been surprisingly happy.

'Well, cheerio, Jock,' Ivor said as he was about to leave, then added jokingly: 'If they don't look after you properly, you let me know!'

For an awful moment, I thought tears were going to come to my eyes but I managed to produce a laugh instead. Then Ivor was gone. I turned to face my three new companions, who, to my relief and delight, did not waste a moment before making me feel at home with their friendly chat. In a short space of time, my initial strangeness was completely dispelled as I realised that I was still with 'family'.

The senior NCO of the Signals detachment was Lance Corporal Arthur Greenacre from Manchester. Arthur was soft-spoken, quite unflappable and – I was pleased to find – an Errol Flynn fan like myself. Lance Corporal Bill Downs – a Yorkshireman – was a very lively person who regularly had me in fits of laughter with his almost constant jocular repartee. One of Bill's earliest comments to me was: 'There used to be two thousand, nine hundred loonies in Tanjong Rambutan but since 'C' Company arrived, the number has risen to three thousand!' Also from Yorkshire was National Serviceman Private Dennis Westwood, soon due to go home. He was quite a character and had a reputation as someone who could 'acquire' items of equipment or of personal comfort which were not available through normal channels.

When I eagerly enquired of these new friends if they had seen any bandits, Arthur Greenacre replied that he had seen a couple of dead ones and Bill Downs admitted that he had only seen bandit suspects. In his turn, Dennis Westwood gleefully related to me the story of when he had once arrived at the scene of a road ambush with a follow-up patrol. A dead bandit had been lying on the road and Westwood had tapped the man's head with his boot. When the bandit's cap had consequently rolled off, Westwood had quickly picked it up. He now reached into his kitbag and proudly showed me his prized souvenir – a five-peaked khaki drill cap with a Communist red star embroidered on the front.

Westwood also had a fine singing voice. On that very first night when we were all in bed after lights out, at Bill Downs' request Westwood regaled us with a beautiful rendering of 'Beneath the Lights of Home'. I listened quite moved and feeling very happy that I'd had the good fortune to be posted to 'C' Company.

9

'C' Company – Tanjong Rambutan
June–July 1950

'C' Company Commander was Major Francis Anthony Stoddart Murray, MC – a fellow-Scot who was then approaching 32 years of age. Major Murray was born in Glasgow and educated at Uppingham and Sandhurst. He was commissioned into the 2nd Battalion, Durham Light Infantry, in January 1939. Following the outbreak of the Second World War in September of that year, he served in France with the British Expeditionary Force, being evacuated from the beaches of Dunkirk in May 1940. As a War Substantive Captain – temporary Major, he landed in Normandy with the Allied forces in June 1944. Five months later, while attached to the Glider Pilot Regiment of the Army Air Corps, he was awarded the Military Cross for gallantry at Arnhem. From 1945 to 1948, he served in Palestine with the AAC, in command of the Glider Pilot Regiment, becoming a War Substantive Major – temporary Lieutenant Colonel. He had commanded 'C' Company, 1st KOYLI, since May 1949.

On the morning after my arrival at the company, I had my first, brief meeting with 'the Mad Major' – as he was aptly nicknamed. Fairly tall, with a rather prominent red nose and wearing dark glasses, he strode into the Signals tent and demanded abruptly: 'Where's this new chap?'

I immediately leapt to my feet, feeling the customary awe of a private soldier when presented to an unknown senior officer. My eyes immediately alighted on the pilot's wings above his breast pocket.

'This is Private Scurr, sir,' Arthur Greenacre introduced me calmly.

'Good morning, sir,' I blurted out, not so calmly.

Major Murray glared at me for a moment and then said: 'You'll have a lot to learn. Pay attention to what Corporal Greenacre tells you.' With that, he turned and strode out of the tent.

Arthur grinned at me and said: 'You'll find he's a bit of an oddball, Jock, but he's really quite a good sort at heart.'

When I remember Major Murray now, I do so with considerable regard and even affection, but it would be dishonest of me to pretend that these were my feelings towards him at the time. Because of his completely unpredictable moods and reactions and his often impossible demands, I soon came to dread contact with him. This dread would eventually diminish to some extent as my confidence as a company signaller grew and I learned to take the major's manner less seriously.

Despite my reservations about him, it later became quite evident that in between driving me mad, the major was nearly always well disposed towards me. Indeed, he displayed considerable interest and concern for the comfort and well-being of all the men in his charge. I noticed that he always wore dark glasses in the mornings, presumably to reduce the visibility of the effects of his daily hangovers. He was inclined to be extremely tolerant towards soldiers who committed misdeeds while under the influence of drink. The reason for this tolerance, of course, is not hard to guess.

Second in command of the company, and 8 Platoon Commander, was Captain John Haddon. He was a big mountain of a man in every way, full of energy and vitality. As a lieutenant, John Haddon had 'bagged' the battalion's first bandit in August 1948. (See Chapter Five.)

Commanding 9 Platoon was Second Lieutenant David Wride, who had been transferred from 'D' Company shortly before. Mr Wride was a tall, good-looking, intelligent and quite splendid person, who I would get to know quite well in later months, despite the barrier of our ranks.

Company Serjeant Major Allen was ex-DLI and a Second World War veteran. He was very stout and was a calm, good-natured, even fatherly figure who rarely raised his voice; yet he commanded complete respect and immediate obedience from the men.

Among the 'other ranks' in 'C' Company were four men from my draft: Lance Corporal 'Mac' McAllister, Stan Swalwell, Ginger Thompson and Phil Cox. The last named had also been with me in 'X' Cadre in Bordon and was now Company Pay Clerk. He gave me a big welcome on the first day that I arrived. As for the other men in the company, they seemed to accept me readily enough, despite my quiet, reserved manner. During basic training when the objective was to mould recruits into identical 'tin soldiers', anyone who was an individualist or who was in any way different was subjected to a lot of stick. Yet once a man had joined his regiment and been allotted to a company, there were so many strange characters around that one more arriving was of no concern to anyone! Certainly, the tin soldiers that the basic training instructors had striven to produce were nowhere to be seen. At least, that's how it was in a rifle company in Malaya.

At this time, I was privileged to know a man who was surely the greatest individualist or odd bod in that or any other regiment. I refer to the one and only Joe Costello. Joe, then 32 years old, was a huge, brawny fellow with magnificent bushy ginger moustaches, an inexhaustible spirit and constant good humour. After running away from home at the age of 14 to join the Merchant Navy, Joe had become a tramp prior to the 1939–45 war. He told me that he had tramped all round Jamaica as well as many parts of England and that he never wore socks, not even in the army. In those pre-war days, Joe had been a Communist Party activist, but now ugly scars marked the spot on his hand where he'd had a hammer and sickle tattoo rather inexpertly removed.

One time when one of the lads in the company mentioned his home town, Joe asked him which street he lived in.

136

'King Street,' the lad replied. 'King Street?' Joe exclaimed. 'I've knocked on every door in that street!'

Joe had served in the 2/4th Battalion, KOYLI, during the Second World War. North Africa and Italy were two of the campaigns that I recall him mentioning. The only mail Joe ever received was – as Bill Downs put it – 'from the brothel bints in Penang'. He loved beer and loved life and was in every way a remarkable character.

The State Mental Home, Tanjong Rambutan, proved to be a happy location for me and, I am sure, for the other members of 'C' Company, but it was not so happy for the inmates. Shortly before dinner on Sunday night, 18 June, I saw some Malay warders enter a cell block which housed male lunatics. The most terrible pandemonium followed while the warders forcibly stripped the patients and threw their clothes out of the door. Batches of fresh clothing were then brought from a truck outside and a tremendous struggle ensued as the warders now attempted to dress the inmates. During this process, one of the lunatics escaped through the open door and ran naked across the grass, pursued by angry warders. Eventually, the man was caught and brought back by a warder, who gave him repeated punches between the shoulder blades. (I employed the term 'warders' in my journal because that is how these people appeared to me. No doubt they were, in fact, nurses.)

That same night, while we were eating dinner in the cell-block that was used as the company dining hall, we saw a wardress enter a block opposite containing female patients. For some reason, she beat one of them to the ground with a bamboo sweeping-brush and then continued to rain blows upon the unfortunate woman as she lay on the floor. At first, there were a few shouts from the lads around me of: 'Go it, girl!' but soon, the general cry turned to: 'Leave her alone, you black bastard!'

The following morning, I noticed some brush-beating going on in the male cells. Some treatment! Many of the patients were really demented and regularly howled and wailed throughout the hours of darkness.

137

Late on that Sunday night, the 18th, a party arrived back in camp after a night out in Ipoh. Johnny Watson – a former regimental policeman who boxed for the battalion – was mad-drunk and began thumping anyone who got in his way. All who tried to calm him down were called 'bastards', including the CSM. Eventually, Major Murray – also drunk – appeared on the scene and called out in kindly tones: 'Johnny – come on, now. Settle down.'

'Fuck off, Murray, you old bastard!' was Johnny's immediate response. He then ran off to the other side of the compound, where he suddenly quietened down and was escorted to the guardroom.

We all thought that he would be sent up for court martial. However, when he was summoned to appear on Company Commander's Orders the following morning, the major merely sentenced him to ten days' close arrest.

My journal records that I was enjoying my life as a company signaller; taking transmissions on the '62' set, charging wireless batteries and lying on my *charpoy* (bed) when there was nothing to do, which was quite often. At such times nobody bothered us; nor were we required to polish our brasses or even our boots. The contrast to life in HQ Company amazed and delighted me. However, I was very anxious to be sent out on a jungle operation and do some real soldiering.

At last, an ambush patrol was scheduled for Wednesday the 21st. I could not wait to get started. Then, for no stated reason, the patrol was suddenly cancelled. Arthur was amused when I clearly showed my disappointment. 'Don't flap, Jock,' he said with a grin. 'It's all very well being an eager beaver, but operations will come along soon enough, believe me!'

That night I joined a score of others who were going on a 'gigolo trip' into Ipoh. We left camp at 6.45 p.m., travelling in a 3-ton truck escorted by an armoured scout car. Although most of us wore civvy shirts and slacks, we all journeyed armed with our personal weapons. The Bren guns that we took were fitted with the 100-round drum magazines that were now being used on all the battalion's transport. We drove to Ipoh and called first at Tac HQ in Ashby Road Camp to deposit the scout car, then continued into the town in the 3-tonner. After stopping outside the Jubilee Cabaret, two chaps obligingly agreed to remain guarding the truck and our weapons while the rest of us dispersed to our various entertainments.

Although Arthur Greenacre and Bill Downs were both among the party, I didn't know what their night's enjoyment might involve or whether they'd want me to tag along, so I slipped away quietly on my own. After a short stroll around, I had a good meal and a Carlsberg lager in the Café Metropole. Afterwards, I went to the Rex cinema to see John Wayne in *The Fighting Kentuckian*. Some of our lads were sitting near the back of the stalls, so I joined them. There were two attractive Chinese girls sitting in front of us. Ginger Thompson kept pulling their hair, so that they eventually had to move to different seats. After the show we met up with the others outside the Jubilee at 11.15 as previously arranged.

On returning to Ashby Road Camp, CSM Allen and Serjeants Bell and Hutchinson suddenly announced that they had decided to stay late in town and that the scout car should therefore remain behind at their disposal. They warned us that as we would have no armoured escort, we would need to keep our eyes skinned. The whole thing sounded very improper to me. Anyway, we took an extra Bren on the 3-tonner and then started back for our company base at Tanjong Rambutan.

Our driver had consumed quite a few Tiger beers and was apparently in a bit of a sweat, due to our lack of escort. He really put his foot down and the truck simply tore along. The road was narrow and winding and passed through quite a few likely ambush spots. It was a pretty dark night and, to top it all, the truck's lights seemed to be fading. The driver continued to accelerate recklessly. At one point, we were heading straight for a *basha* but managed to skid round the bend in the road just in time. We carried on a little further;

139

then – crash! bang! – off the road we went, bumping down a gradual bank, with all of us thrown on our backs. It was truly fortunate that this had not occurred on one of the many parts of the road that were bordered by steep banks or when we had crossed a bridge over a river.

We all scrambled out of the truck and, under orders from Arthur and Bill, took up firing positions on both sides of the lonely stretch of road. We were, in fact, quite close to the spot where the 'D' Company patrol had been ambushed and annihilated less than two weeks before. Our driver had bumped his head and was carried unconscious out of the cab. When he came to, he insisted that he was capable of driving again and poured irate scorn on protests that this might not be wise.

With some difficulty we managed to manoeuvre the truck back up onto the road. Then we all climbed back on board, feeling more than a little dubious about our future safety. However, when we set off again, the driver seemed to be taking it steadier. In a short while, we slowed down as we came to a bend in the road and after turning the bend, the truck suddenly stopped. The driver was once more carried out of the cab. He'd dropped unconscious over the wheel but Arthur, sitting beside him, had speedily applied the brake. Private Knight said that he used to drive in Civvy Street, so he took over the wheel and drove us slowly but safely back to the asylum. While the driver was being carried to his billet, someone ran to get the Medical Officer. It had been some trip!

The following day, we learned that four policemen had been shot in Ipoh the previous night.

That evening, to my considerable joy, the company was assembled in the dining hall and briefed for a battalion operation that was to take place next day. Captain Haddon told us that the police had obtained information that 40 bandits were presently located in an area to the south of Dead Man's Gully, Ampang, where the 'D' Company patrol had been ambushed. It was intended that 'A', 'B' and 'C' Companies should surround the area and lie in ambush

140

along possible escape routes. The Royal Air Force would launch air strikes against likely locations of enemy camps. Then 'D' Company would advance through the area, while the other companies waited to ambush any bandits that were driven out. Three signallers would be required. Arthur would be with Company HQ, Bill with 9 Platoon and I with 8 Platoon.

At last! My first active operation! It all sounded very promising. I felt immensely excited as I hastened back to the Signals tent. There, my primary task was to clean my rifle and check my bandolier of ammunition in readiness for the action which I was sure was now imminent.

At 9.30 a.m. on Friday, 23 June, we duly set out, wearing full jungle kit and battle order. Motor transport conveyed us to a location somewhere past Ipoh, where we debussed. Accompanying us on this operation were a police guide, a police interpreter and six Dyak trackers.

The Dyaks (as we called them) were, in fact, Ibans from Sarawak – descendants of headhunting tribes – who had been recruited into the Civil Liaison Corps and allocated to army units as trackers. Their bodies were covered with blue tribal tattoos and their stretched ear lobes were pierced with large holes. Some of them had long black hair gathered in a bun at the back, and others wore bangles of human hair around their wrists and displayed locks of hair dangling from the hilts of their long knives – practically swords. Initially, I felt very wary of Dyaks, supposing that they were all eagerly awaiting an opportunity to chop off someone's head. After a while, however, I learned to accept them as just part of the team.

After leaving the road, we marched well spread out along a track for about 3 miles. It was mostly open country. Any expanse that was particularly exposed was covered by a Bren group while the rest of us crossed in sections. Eventually, we came to a river which marked the boundary of the area that our company was to cover. As we began to cross the river, walking in file along a narrow log, the RAF arrived upon the scene. Flights of Tempests and Brigands

141

flew in low towards the jungle area beyond the river, firing their rockets and cannons. It was a grand sight! We watched the flights of planes swoop overhead, one after another, white streams of smoke whisking back from their wings before the rockets flew forward to explode in the jungle ahead. Soon, the noise of the bombardment increased as the Bugle Platoon, from Tac HQ, began shelling the area with 3-inch mortars. The 4th Hussars then joined in with their 2-pounder guns and someone opened up somewhere with a Bren.

By the time the air strike was completed, we had all crossed the river. The company now took up ambush positions in the scrub on the hill slope beyond, spreading out in our sections over an extensive area and facing down towards the river. I began to set up my wireless, slinging my 90 feet of wire aerial as high as I could between two trees. Then Captain Haddon approached me and told me to take my aerial down as we were moving on. I had just completed this task when Captain Haddon returned and told me to put the aerial up again as we were staying where we were.

I erected my aerial once more, a little further up the slope this time, being eaten alive by red ants from the trees while doing so. On testing my set, I found that the calibration was faulty and that I was therefore unable to tune in to the battalion frequency. When I reported this to Captain Haddon, he instructed me to take my aerial down and set it up again on top of the hill. So I dismantled my aerial, packed up my wireless and, with customary difficulty, hoisted the weighty apparatus onto my back.

Being unused to carrying the '68' set in addition to my rifle, ammo and other signalling gear and equipment, I had grown pretty tired during the earlier march to the river. My remaining energy had then been expended on twice erecting and dismantling the aerial wire. Now, as I started up the hill with my back bowed beneath its burden, I found that I was close to exhaustion. It took me all my time to keep on my feet as I staggered up the slope. Finally, drenched in perspiration and weak at the knees, I managed to reach the top. I literally dropped flat on my face and just lay there, gasping for breath and listening to the pounding of my heart.

Very aware of the dryness in my mouth and throat, I pulled my aluminium water bottle from the webbing container on my hip. To my chagrin, I found that the cap had become cross-threaded and resisted all my efforts to unscrew it. In a desperate rage, I smashed the cap against a rock until I dented it beyond repair and it dropped off. Then, I gratefully quenched my thirst.

I knew that it would be useless to mount my aerial again as the set was definitely faulty. Anyway, I was just too tired. When Captain Haddon came up the slope a moment later, I explained my first conclusion to him though not my second. After a little hesitation, he told me to pack up my set and report to my ambush position.

Upon descending the hill, I took my place in the ambush line next to the platoon serjeant, sitting amongst the shrubbery on the slope and watching the track below which ran along adjacent to the river bank. At that moment I felt rather dejected. The conditions of sheer exhaustion and raging thirst which I had just experienced had completely dispelled my earlier feelings of delight and excitement upon witnessing the air strike. This, added to rekindled memories of the tough jungle march to Kroh under CSM Taylor, now caused me to question in my mind whether I really wanted to spend month after month in successive states of exhaustion, soaked in sweat and mud and feasted upon by all manner of insects. It seemed to me that rear echelon signallers in the paradise of Penang Island, doing clean and mainly sedentary duties, were to be envied. Perhaps I should apply for employment in HQ, I considered, and be back there safe and sound, drinking ice-cold minerals in the NAAFI and going to the pictures in town with cousin John?

This idea seemed immensely attractive until I suddenly remembered the night in Kroh, near the end of my jungle training, when I had finally sought out CSM Taylor to tell him of my decision that I wanted to do some proper soldiering while in Malaya. Then, in my mind, I addressed myself with two simple sentences – What did you expect war would be like? It's bound to be hard!

I was merely stating the obvious, but doing so ended the matter there and then. I finally realised and accepted that if I wanted to be a real soldier, I would have to consider exhaustion and discomfort as part of the game. I had now been in the army for ten months and that number of months would pass again before my resolve would once more come into question.

This seemingly final resolution sent my spirits soaring. I felt very content as I sat on that hill slope, clutching my loaded rifle and looking down through the trees and shrubs towards the track, along which I fervently hoped would soon come figures in khaki drill uniforms with red stars on their caps. Little did I care that I had been unable to establish radio contact. I fully intended to perform my duties as a company signaller to the best of my ability but, first and foremost, I was resolved to be 'a rifleman' at every opportunity.

I looked to my left now, to where the platoon serjeant sat quite close by with his Sten gun resting across his right thigh. Serjeant Hutchinson was a tall, strongly built man, good natured and quite soft spoken.

'Do you usually get much on these ambush operations?' I asked him quietly.

'No.' He shook his head. 'Not usually.'

I later learned that Serjeant Hutchinson had personally bagged a bandit in March 1949. (See Chapter Five).

Despite his negative response to my question, I remained hopeful that the enemy would oblige me by walking into our ambush. As hour succeeded hour, however, my hopes began to recede. At intervals during our long wait, our section detained 13 suspects who came along the track below our positions. They were brought in easily enough with calls of: *Mara sini!* (Come here!), reinforced by weapons pointed at them, and motioned to squat in the bushes out of sight. The suspects – presumably local labourers –

appeared to be quite innocent except for two young Chinese men and a teenage girl.

When this trio were spotted by the river and called in, the girl immediately put up her parasol, then laid it in the grass. They then crouched behind the parasol and appeared to hide something at the river's edge before walking over to our positions in the shrubbery of the hill slope. Serjeant Hutchinson ordered one of the Chinese men to go back and bring whatever it was that they had hidden and said to a rifleman, Private 'Ches' Allen: 'Keep him covered. If he makes a run for it, shoot him!'

While Ches took and maintained a careful aim, the Chinese walked slowly back to the river's edge, then returned with the girl's parasol. Serjeant Hutchinson spoke sharply to the man in Malay, sending him back once more. This time, he returned with a large knotted cloth sheet, containing a large amount of rice. We could now be fairly confident that we had detained three enemy food suppliers.

By 5 p.m., much to my disappointment, no armed bandits had come our way, so 8 Platoon assembled from the section positions and we set off along the track with our suspects. The company rendezvoused at a small kampong (village) where we handed over our suspects to the police for detention or clearance. We then marched on until we reached the road where our transport picked us up. We arrived back in camp about 7 p.m.

I later heard that a soldier in 'B' Company had spotted a bandit running away, fired at him with his rifle and missed. In their sweep through the area, 'D' Company had found two deserted camps. Apparently, eight camps altogether were located during this battalion operation and some documents and equipment were recovered from them.

The following night, the company was briefed for another operation. This time, 'C' Company was to comb the area upon which the previous day's air strike had been made and 'D' Company would search a large hill feature beyond. Arthur was to be signaller with Company HQ, while Bill and I went together with 8 Platoon.

145

On Sunday morning, the 25th, we were once more taken by trucks along the same route and deposited at the track that we had followed on the previous operation. We were again accompanied by several Dyaks, two policemen and also one Sakai guide. As we were waiting to march off, Serjeant Hutchinson asked one of the Dyaks what he would do to the bandits if we caught any. The Dyak replied that he would cut off their heads and burn them so that they shrank. He smiled and picked up a pebble to indicate the size. I wondered what he meant by 'burn'? His way of describing some kind of intense heat process, I supposed. When questioned about a small glass phial that was suspended from a string around his neck, the Dyak told us that it contained a magic potion which would prevent him from being killed.

We moved off in sections, with one section covering the movements of another through fairly open country. Eventually, we turned off down a slope to the river at a point a little to the west of where we'd laid our ambush last time. We then waded the river and halted on the jungle slope opposite.

Matchets were now busily employed to clear an area of undergrowth for a base camp. Then, as the men of 8 Platoon began to construct *bashas* and defensive positions for the Bren guns, Bill and I went off to put up our aerial, stretching it across the river between two trees. When we returned, we found two Dyaks in the process of building a shelter with our poncho capes and groundsheets. 'Just the job!' Bill exclaimed. 'They're building us a *basha*.' However, we soon realised that they were constructing a dwelling for themselves. So we grabbed back our two ponchos, leaving them the groundsheets, and arranged to 'kip in' with a Bren gunner and his number two, enlarging their *basha* to accommodate four.

Patrols were sent out that afternoon but all returned to base with nothing to report. In the early evening, Bill tuned in our '68' set to receive a news broadcast from Radio Malaya. Reception was extremely poor, but we heard something about Russian tanks crossing a border and later heard mention of Indo-China. We therefore concluded that the announcer was reporting that Soviet forces had invaded French Indo-China in support of the Viet Minh rebels. Captain Haddon commented brightly to Major Murray: 'Must be war then, sir!'

'Looks like it,' the Major replied with little apparent interest.

A young soldier called Reeves then protested to Captain Haddon: 'Oh, don't say that, sir!'

'Why not?' Captain Haddon retorted. 'I could just do with a nice war to liven things up a bit! Couldn't you?'

'Well, I wouldn't mind,' Reeves replied dubiously. 'But I'd like to go home first, sir.'

I'm sure he spoke for all of us.

That evening, there was a heavy downpour of rain. I spent an hour on 'stag' (sentry duty) under a poncho cape, watching the level of the river rising alarmingly. All of our *bashas* were swamped and we thought that our camp was going to be flooded out, but fortunately, the rain stopped after darkness fell and the river level gradually receded.

Next day, Monday the 26th, patrols went out again. This time, seven bandit camps were found but all of them had been abandoned for some time. A sack of rice and a few utensils were recovered and the camps burned by the patrols. In the evening, as we sat in groups, eating the 'all-in' stew concocted from our tinned compo rations, Captain Haddon asked one of the Dyaks whether he would eat a bandit if we killed one. Without hesitation, the Dyak replied that he intended to eat the first bandit that he killed but only if he killed him. He couldn't eat a man that someone else had killed, he explained.

Shortly after that, a sentry leapt up from behind his Bren gun, exclaiming fearfully that a bootlace snake had been winding its way straight towards him. A couple of the lads chopped away nearby undergrowth with their matchets but the deadly little snake had gone.

On these first two days, the signallers, mortar men, medical orderlies and a few others were left behind to guard the base while the remainder went out on patrol. I was rather disgruntled about this and even more dismayed when told that this was normal procedure. At night, everyone did a two-hour stag, sitting alone behind a Bren gun in the dark. The jungle was very silent during the day but came alive at night with a cacophony of weird and scary noises in the surrounding trees and bushes.

At my own request on the morning of Tuesday the 27th, I went out on patrol with 8 Platoon as a rifleman. We crossed the river and climbed to the top of a hill. Here, we split into two sections, led by Captain Haddon and Serjeant Hutchinson, which then set out in different directions in search of tracks to follow. I was with Captain Haddon. We marched for quite a distance, climbing up and down hills, having to chop our way through the jungle as we went, and wading up to our waists through some swamp areas. Twice we had to change direction due to some strange insects which stung our scouts painfully. I suggested to Captain Haddon that this must be a bandit secret weapon! This remark seemed to amuse him considerably and he repeated it to the major later.

Finding no tracks or signs of the enemy, we eventually turned back and descended to the river, where we rendez-voused with Serjeant Hutchinson's section. From there, we followed the river until we reached our base.

Meanwhile, 9 Platoon had found another deserted bandit camp. In the vicinity, however, one of the platoon's Bren gunners had seen a bandit running away. Instead of opening fire, the lad had turned and said to Serjeant 'Taggy' Bell: 'Serjeant, there's a Chinaman just gone down there!' The platoon pursued the bandit for a while but saw no more of him. Taggy mercilessly made fun of the Bren gunner for the rest of the day.

After tiffen, we dismantled our camp and marched back along the now familiar track to the road where our transport awaited us. When we had returned to our company location at Tanjong Rambutan, the Medical Officer gave us an FFI

148

(free from infection) medical inspection. I was dismayed when it was discovered that I had ringworm on my foot and knee and tinea round my crutch. As always, Arthur told me not to flap and that nearly everyone developed skin infections sooner or later.

Also after our return from the operation, we learned the true facts about the news report that we had picked up from Radio Malaya on Sunday, 25 June. Communist North Korea had invaded the West-aligned South Korea. The North Korean Army was well-equipped with Soviet tanks and armaments. This explained our mistaken interpretation of the poorly heard report. I remember that my first reaction was to say to Arthur: 'Korea? Where's that?'

Within a week, the first American troops would be rushed to Korea, under the banner of the United Nations, in an effort to halt the invasion. By the end of August, the 1st Middlesex Regiment and 1st Argyll and Sutherland Highlanders, stationed in Hong Kong, would be the first British troops to join the United Nations forces in Korea. These two battalions were brought up to strength with volunteers from the other four infantry regiments of the Hong Kong garrison. Among the volunteers were some of the lads from my draft who had gone to the KSLI.

From that time on, we followed the news reports from Korea with considerable interest. And, I understand, so did our enemies in the jungle, who were greatly heartened by the initial Communist victories there.

Meanwhile, we had our own little war to contend with. On Saturday morning, 1 July, we were briefed for another 'duffy' (operation). The police were positive that there were 40 bandits encamped in an area adjoining the Kuala Kangsar road. The bandits had been seen 15 days previously by an Indian who was bathing in a river, and only two days ago, bandits had burned a bus on the road. We were told that police informers were also working on definite reports that there were 100 bandits in an area on the opposite side of the road, but for the present we weren't interested in them. This caused Stan Swalwell to remark later: 'If we meet those hundred bandits, we'll tell them to fuck off! We're not looking for them!'

That afternoon, 8 Platoon was scheduled to depart to search one sector of the designated area, and 9 Platoon would leave the following day to comb another sector. Bill Downs and I were again going with 8 Platoon, while Dennis Westwood would be signaller with 9 Platoon. I was so confident that the enemy could not continue to be elusive to me that I bet Dennis a dollar that 8 Platoon would make contact with bandits this time. Dennis readily accepted the bet.

Bill and I assembled with 8 Platoon at 2.30 p.m. During the 'standing load', a rifleman livened us all up by putting a shot through the verandah roof. It rained pretty hard during the truck journey to the Kuala Kangsar road and by the time we debussed, we were soaked through.

We set off across some sparsely wooded country until we came to a railway track, which we followed for a short distance. After turning off from the railway, we crossed a river, found a main track and proceeded along it, passing through a couple of small kampongs. It was fairly flat country and with Bill and me taking turns at carrying the '68' set, the march wasn't too fatiguing. Eventually, we arrived at a tin mine, where Captain Haddon decided we should stay the night.

Bill asked one of our Dyaks if he would climb a palm tree to put up our aerial. After the Dyak had made a couple of hopeless attempts, Bill climbed the tree himself with far more agility than the jungle dweller had displayed!

An English-speaking Malay from the tin mine staff seemed eager to talk to us. Captain Haddon asked him if he knew the Celestial Cabaret in Ipoh and if he'd danced with any of the girls there. The Malay looked puzzled and then asked: 'Do you want one tonight?'

Before Captain Haddon could reply, Bill quipped: 'Tell him I'll have one, sir!'

Later, the mine's Chinese manager offered Captain Haddon one of the Chinese women workers for the night; which offer, of course, the captain declined to accept.

We slept that night beneath a long, sloping attap roof. Each man had to do two-and-a-half hours' stag. Towards ten o'clock, two of the sentries reported hearing small-arms fire from the direction of the Kanathan rubber estate. Serjeant Hutchinson confirmed their reports. After considering his options, Captain Haddon decided that it would not be wise for us to proceed over there in the darkness and risk being shot up, either by the enemy or by Malay special constables. So sentries were doubled and the rest of us settled down again to sleep.

The next morning, Sunday the 2nd, we moved into a police post that was established in a fenced compound adjoining the mine. Bill and I set up our wireless there, with good reception. Eager to be included in any action, I once more asked and received permission to go out on patrol as a rifleman.

The patrol's route first lay through a wooded area, proceeding along the top of a pipeline in order to avoid some marshes. After carrying the '68' set the previous day, it felt great to be travelling light, with only my rifle, bandolier of ammo, bayonet, water bottle and a tin of *makan* (corned beef) to carry. In addition to rifles and Sten guns, the patrol's armaments included two Bren guns and a 2-inch mortar. The NCOs also carried grenades.

After crossing a hill, we climbed a very steep slope to the top of a second hill, from where we had an excellent view of the surrounding country. Here we split up into four groups to look for tracks. The group that I was with followed a stream until we reached a waterfall which dropped a couple of hundred feet. The stream had very steep banks but it was traversed by a log, just above the waterfall. Private Smithson looked at the log dubiously and remarked: 'My name's not Tarzan!' Nevertheless, we all crossed the log safely. At the other side, we found a track through the thick *ulu* (jungle), which we followed for a short way. Then we returned to rendezvous with the rest of the platoon on the hilltop, beside an old Malay *basha*.

Captain Haddon decided that the platoon should follow up the track that our group had found. As we were about to set off, several explosions reverberated in our ears. We turned to see clouds of smoke belching from a nearby hill, with five Lincoln bombers, accompanied by Brigands and Tempests, swooping over it. Some of the aircraft now banked and flew straight towards our hill.

'Take cover!' yelled Captain Haddon.

We quickly dived for whatever cover we could find. Luckily, the planes flew over our hill without strafing it and then turned back towards their original objective. After firing their rockets into the hill's summit, the planes flew in low over the treetops, with machine guns blazing. We later learned that this had been one of the biggest air strikes ever mounted in Malaya and that 'A' Company had been following it up. I couldn't help wondering what might have happened had we decided to reconnoitre up that hill instead of the one that we had chosen.

After setting off back to once more cross the log above the waterfall, we could still hear the bombardment continuing. We carried on along the track, our eyes searching the jungle on both sides of it, but found nothing. Eventually, we returned to the *basha* on the hilltop, ate a frugal tiffen, then made the return journey to the tin mine, taking a different route to lessen the risk of ambush.

When we got back, Captain Haddon said to me: 'Well, Scurr, that's two patrols. Third time lucky, they say!'

'I hope so, sir,' I replied, thinking then of the dollar I was going to have to pay to Dennis Westwood for not having been 'lucky' this time!

After a brew of char, we started back towards the Kuala Kangsar road. I was very tired after patrolling earlier through some pretty rugged terrain and now had the set on my back. By the time we reached the road and our waiting transport, I was very much on my last legs, slowly tottering the final hundred yards. Nonetheless, the fact that I reached the trucks without collapsing gave me a considerable feeling of satisfaction.

Back in base at Tanjong Rambutan, we had another FFI after 'conner'. This time, it was confirmed that I had ring-worm on my knee and foot, tinea on both legs and round my crotch, foot-rot between the toes of both feet and large blisters on the sole of my right foot. After treating my various skin diseases with the appropriate ointments, the medical orderly completely wound my right foot with a bandage and I was 'excused boots' for three days.

Despite these ailments, I was very content with my life in 'C' Company at that time. Company funds had provided a gramophone, some amplifiers and a small selection of records, all placed in the care of the Signals detachment. Through the amplifiers, we used to broadcast music in the evenings to the company's quarters, either from the wireless or from the gramophone. I really used to enjoy sitting with a bottle of Tiger and a tin of cigarettes, listening to the music and the amiable chatter of my companions. The Signals' favourite records were of Teresa Brewer singing 'Music, Music, Music' and Al Jolson singing 'Sonny-Boy.'

On Friday night, the 7th, we were briefed for an operation. The 'grif' (information) was that a Chinese male had been buying 5 katty of pork (0.75 katty = 1 lb) from a shop in Tanjong Rambutan every day for five days and had been seen taking the pork into a certain area between Tanjong Rambutan and Ipoh. The police had picked the man up but he wouldn't talk, except to insist that the meat was for his family. Therefore, 'C' Company was going to search the specified area on a one-day operation. Arthur and I would be going with Company HQ and Bill with 8 Platoon.

Reveille was at 1.15 a.m. on Saturday the 8th and we departed at 2.30. Even at that hour, the lunatics were awake and clinging to the wire mesh of their cells, some of them wailing and screaming hideously.

After our transport had dropped us near a tin mine, we advanced along the road in the darkness, 8 Platoon taking the lead, with 9 Platoon following behind. I was acting as number two scout for Company HQ in the rear. We halted at a bridge for a while. Then, on moving off once more, 9 Platoon and Company HQ turned off along a track to the left of the road. After proceeding for about 200 yards, Major Murray suddenly realised that we'd lost contact with 8 Platoon – which had, in fact, turned off onto another track earlier. The major railed against 9 Platoon's leading scout, calling him 'a blockhead', and then led us all back to the road. A man was sent to look for 8 Platoon and soon arrived back with Captain Haddon. After the two officers had conferred, everyone set off again in exactly the same directions as had originally been taken.

We each had to keep fairly close to the man in front so as not to lose contact in the darkness. Four chaps did get lost at this stage but found their way safely back to Tanjong Rambutan about five hours later. Every time we passed a kampong, all the village dogs barked like fury. Eventually, we left what had been fairly open country and entered some bushland, stumbling down tracks, for the greater part through tall *lallang* (elephant grass), until we reached a stream about 5 a.m. Here we crouched down and waited until daylight.

At dawn, we continued our march for quite some time before halting once more at the foot of a hill beside some banana trees. Major Murray now turned to his tall and hefty batman and said: 'Cut me down a bunch of bananas.'

'They're not ripe, sir,' the batman, known as 'Lofty', dutifully pointed out.

'I don't care if they're ripe or not!' the major snapped. 'Cut me down a bunch!'

With that, Lofty drew his matchet, chopped away a bunch of bananas from the nearest tree and handed it to the major. 'Here you are, sir,' he said politely.

Major Murray peeled one of the bananas and then hurled the bunch to the ground. 'These bananas aren't ripe!' he protested to his bemused batman. 'What are you trying to do? Poison me or something?'

We had three Malay police guides with us. One was

armed with an automatic rifle, another with a double-barrelled shotgun and the third with a single-barrelled shotgun. Major Murray now decided that we'd gone the wrong way and called the police guides 'stupid cunts'. CSM Allen smiled at me and said quietly: 'He's lost, so he's blaming it on the guides.'

After a slight delay, we began to climb the hill before us. It was a pretty stiff climb. At the top we found some trenches and clearings among the trees where *bashas* had obviously been situated. This base certainly hadn't been used for some time and was probably originally constructed by the Communists working with Force 136 during the war.

Arthur and I put up our aerial here and set up the wireless. After a short rest, 9 Platoon departed to patrol another designated area. Four of us from Company HQ were then sent down the hill to get water for char. When we reached the bottom, we had to cut our way through the brush to reach the river. After filling our 'brew cans', we had quite a struggle trying to climb back up the hill without spilling the water. It was really hard work.

Once we had brewed up and eaten tiffen, we set out to patrol in the general direction of our transport rendezvous. The men of the company carried no packs on this one-day operation but, of course, the signallers had to carry their sets and corresponding gear. Our route now lay up and down hills through thick jungle. Keeping on one's feet while carrying a '68' set on a steep jungle slope was not an easy task. Arthur carried the set for a while, then I did, then Scaife, the medical orderly, very kindly took a turn. Even with this swopping of the load, the march was very tiring.

After a couple of hours, to our surprise and great annoyance, we found ourselves once more at the foot of the hill from which we had started two hours before! Major Murray now decided to take the direct route back, following the track by which we had come that morning. After a while, we reached a river with a waterfall cascading into it. The major called a halt, then suddenly stripped off his equipment and his shirt and leaped into the river. Muttering: 'Oh, dear! Oh, dear!' he submerged himself beneath the water a couple of times and then climbed out.

When we resumed our march, we met up with 9 Platoon at a kampong and finally reached the road where 8 Platoon awaited us. No one had seen any sign of an enemy. Half an hour later, at 5 p.m., our transport arrived and brought us back to camp.

The following morning, Sunday the 9th, when I was taking a transmission on the '62' set, I heard a report from 'B' Company that some bandits had walked down a track straight into a section ambush the previous night. The section had opened fire prematurely, however, and the bandits had got away unharmed.

In an ambush situation, troops lying in a line of concealed positions on high ground above the track were supposed to hold their fire until as many as possible of the enemy's main body had moved into the killing zone. This would normally be determined when the leading man of the main body reached the number one stop – the last soldier in the ambush line, normally armed with a Bren gun. When the number one stop opened fire, the rest of the line would follow suit.

On this occasion, I heard later, a young soldier had got excited upon sighting the enemy and fired immediately. The remainder of the section then had no choice but to open fire also as the bandits rapidly disappeared from view. There was, of course, much criticism of the young soldier's action, but the jungle at night was frightening at the best of times, even without an armed enemy suddenly looming into sight!

The hours of darkness contained many perils for soldiers in Malaya. On the night following 'B' Company's abortive ambush, there was a tragic accident in 'D' Company. Second Lieutenant Pyemont had recently arrived from Blighty and was in the jungle on his very first operation. That night, Sunday, 9 July, he apparently decided to check that the sentry was awake. When a dark figure carrying a torch suddenly appeared on the track, the sentry opened fire. I was told that when the bullet struck him in the chest, Second

Lieutenant Pyemont cried out: 'My God! You've killed me!' then keeled over dead.

A tragedy for the young officer and for the sentry. Anyone who had ever been alone on stag in the hooting, shrieking, jungle night could feel nothing but sympathy for the sentry's predicament when confronted by an unexpected human presence. As it happens, the sentry did not appear to be perturbed.

There had been persistent rumours over recent weeks of a big operation coming up, to be followed by two months of rest and retraining in Penang. The rumours seemed to be well founded, as evidenced by the fact that the Royal Marine Commandos were in the process of taking over our battalion locations. Then, on the morning of Wednesday the 12th, our Signals tent was taken down and we were moved into one of the cell blocks. All of our signalling equipment was then transported to Penang, except for the wireless sets that we would require on the coming duffy.

Also gone to Penang was signaller Dennis Westwood on the first leg of his journey home and demob. I was sorry to see him go; he was a great lad! Captain Haddon had also departed temporarily for a spell of leave in Hong Kong, and 8 Platoon was now commanded by the newly arrived, fresh from Sandhurst, Second Lieutenant John Crisp.

My last journal entry written in Tanjong Rambutan, dated Wednesday, 12 July, stated: 'This afternoon, we all had a great laugh. Corporal Orum was walking along the verandah when a rat, up in the rafters, pissed on his hair!'

10

Operation 'Acorn' – Lenggong
July 1950

Operation 'Acorn' was to take place in the Lenggong area of Upper Perak and was scheduled to last for 14 days. The battalion would be operating on both sides of the Kuala Kangsar–Grik road, where the bandits had effected six ambushes in the previous two months. Troops of 40 Commando, Royal Marines, and the 2nd Battalion, Malay Regiment, would also be involved in the operation.

At 'C' Company's base in Tanjong Rambutan on Thursday, 13 July, we packed all our belongings in our kitbags, which were then taken off to Penang. It had been intended that I should be 8 Platoon's signaller on this operation. However, on testing our '68' sets, it was found that the wireless I would be taking was 'dis' (not functioning), so it had been decided that I would now accompany Arthur with Company HQ while Bill would go with 9 Platoon. The length and scale of the coming operation raised my hopes enormously. Surely with 14 days at our disposal we must bring the enemy to battle, I convinced myself.

That night, we slept in our jungle kit and departed in trucks early in the following morning of Friday, 14 July. The journey north was long and wearisome. We reached Lenggong Police Station about noon. Tac HQ was camped in tents adjacent to the station.

After a short halt, we carried on along the narrow, winding road until we met a marine convoy coming the other way. One of their trucks was in a ditch. The Malay driver of the 3-tonner that I was travelling in, while trying to drive around another marine vehicle, put our truck down the bank on the other side of the road. Fortunately, the bank was not very steep. As we all jumped out of the truck, a shot rang out. Everyone started to dive for cover. However, we soon discovered that one of the marines had discharged his rifle accidentally.

We managed to push our truck back onto the road and our convoy continued on its way until it reached a police post where we were supposed to find transport to take us across the Sungei (River) Perak. The sampans were there but there were no boatmen, so we proceeded further up the road. Eventually, we halted at a spot where we located one sampan, manned by two Chinese: one to punt and one to paddle. With this one sampan, the company crossed the Sungei Perak, eight men at a time. We were warned to take off our packs and equipment and sit very still as sampans overturned very easily. However, there were no mishaps and we were all borne safely across the river.

From this east bank, we set out through *lallang* and open country along the edge of the jungle. Arthur was carrying the '68' set, while I humped the smaller '88' set plus the signals gear and our personal kit, all packed in several satchels suspended from round my neck on webbing straps. Weighed down in this ill-conceived manner, my strength was rapidly drained. The sun was extremely hot without any shade and I soon felt that I was on the verge of collapsing.

Second Lieutenant Wride noticed me staggering and asked me quietly: 'Are you OK, Scurr?'

'I'm all right, sir,' I replied. I wasn't 'all right', of course, but I managed to keep going until we reached a Chinese squatter area, where we halted and 'bivvied down' (bivouacked). As I was unrolling my poncho cape to make a *basha*, Major Murray approached me.

'Was the heat a bit much for you, Scurr?' he asked in kindly tones.

'I think so, sir,' I answered awkwardly.

'Don't worry,' he said. 'You'll get used to it in time.'

I could only hope that he was right. Although my medical

category was Grade 1 fit – as it had to be for the infantry – I was aware that I wasn't a physically robust person. However, I was determined that I would stay on my feet, no matter how exhausted I became. Basic training had taught me that I could do this, I considered. For a moment I thought of my training platoon officer, Mr Waite, 'the blond bastard'. I still hated him but I felt grateful to him just the same!

It rained that evening. This seemed to bring leeches out in force. As I lay resting in my *basha*, I had to burn one of the creatures off my neck with a cigarette and two more from my arm.

That night, I did a two-and-a-half-hour spell on stag, sitting on a log behind a Bren gun which was mounted upon a bigger log, facing down the slope towards the river. After I had sat for about an hour in total darkness, listening to the flow of the river below and the myriad of night noises of animals, birds and insects, I suddenly became aware of something moving in the bushes about 4 yards to my right.

In an instant I crouched down, facing right, and pointed my rifle in the direction of the sound, thumbing the safety catch forward. In the process of crouching, I noticed that my knees literally knocked together and my heart was hammering in my chest. Once I was in position, though, I was aware that I was scared but under control. It was a strange, almost pleasurable feeling – terror without panic. Whatever was before me continued to move in the bushes, making the branches swish and the leaves rustle. Was it a bandit? Was it a tiger?

I could see nothing in the pitch-dark and did not consider it wise to flash my torch. So I held my rifle firmly forward, index finger on trigger, and told myself to wait. As soon as I felt something touch the muzzle, I would fire, I decided. The rustling sounds continued in the same spot. Whatever it was did not appear to be going anywhere. I therefore felt that the cause of my acute anxiety was more likely to be an animal than a man. Of course, I couldn't be sure. The perspiration was running down my forehead but I still felt in control. I waited. The noise continued. I remained still and listened intently. The rustling carried on for easily half an hour and then just ceased as abruptly as it had begun. I nonetheless continued to crouch with my rifle pointed in that same direction for the remaining hour of my sentry-go.

Early next morning, while doing another period of stag in daylight, I enjoyed watching a monkey climbing along a fallen tree nearby. I had no doubt, however, that my visitor of the night before had been something considerably heavier than a monkey.

After breakfast, the company moved on into the jungle. I had strapped the '88' set and my several satchels of gear together into the form of a backpack. Although still very heavy and bulky, my load was now borne more comfortably than the day before. Around midday, we came upon an old Force 136 camp in a clearing at the top of a hill and the major decided to make a base there. Old soldiers in the company remembered this place as 'Bully-beef Ridge' from the first Lenggong operation in April 1948, before the Emergency officially began. The whole site was infested with ants and other insects and leeches were also pretty common.

During the afternoon, we heard an explosion quite a distance away. A patrol that went out discovered a deserted bandit camp but found no clues as to the cause of the explosion.

That night, as Arthur and I were lying in our *basha*, trying to ignore the swarms of mosquitoes and get some sleep, Major Murray and the new Second Lieutenant Crisp sat on a log outside and gradually got drunk on the major's whisky. The session culminated in an argument between them regarding the weight of the major's pack.

'My pack seems to get heavier every day,' Major Murray asserted. 'I'm sure it's heavier than you are.'

'I don't think so, sir,' Mr Crisp replied.

'Well, I'm sure it is,' Major Murray insisted. 'Look! You get across my shoulder and I'll lift you up. Then, we'll soon see.'

Sounds of the major grunting as he took the strain were followed by the thud of Mr Crisp hitting the ground.

'You nearly did a somersault there,' Major Murray declared enthusiastically. 'See if you can do a somersault. I can. Watch this!'

A succession of thudding noises followed amidst general utterances of hilarity. Throughout this time, within our *basha*, Arthur and I were finding it increasingly difficult to contain our amusement. Just after 1 a.m., the disturbance ceased and the two officers moved off, presumably to sleep. A few minutes later, a rotted tree fell to the ground, just brushing our *basha* and landing across the log upon which the drunken pair had been sitting.

The following day, Sunday the 16th, we worked hard with matchets and chainsaws, chopping away undergrowth and felling trees in order to create a sufficiently large clearing for the next day's airdrop of supplies. While I was doing my spell on stag, sitting behind a Bren gun on the hill slope, a large tree suddenly crashed down, hitting the ground right beside me. When felled upon the ridge, it had gone down in an unexpected direction. Some of the lads came looking for me and were relieved to find that I was not lying beneath the fallen trunk. I was equally relieved and promptly removed myself and the Bren to another position further down the slope.

An airdrop to the whole battalion took place next morning, Monday the 17th. Around 10 a.m. we heard the distant drone of an aircraft. Fluorescent nylon panels had been spread out in the centre of the clearing and damp leaves were now piled upon the fire to create signal smoke. Arthur made wireless contact with the pilot of the plane, who seemed to be having difficulty in locating our dropping zone. There was a tall and stout tree in the middle of the clearing that we had been unable to fell.

Major Murray now said to Arthur: 'Corporal Greenacre, tell the pilot that they should try to avoid dropping the supplies on the tree in the middle of our DZ.'

162

Arthur dutifully relayed this message and the pilot immediately replied: 'I can't even see your bloody DZ – never mind the thing in the middle!'

Two smoke canisters were now added to the fire, so that a thick column of smoke rose into the sky. A few minutes later, a Dakota flew low over the clearing, then turned to cross it again. The first crates of rations were pushed out of the plane, silk parachutes opened out and the crates glided gracefully to earth. The first couple of crates landed safely, one of them crashing through the branches of the large tree. Then, as had been feared might happen, a parachute became caught on one of the high branches of the tree and its crate of rations remained suspended in its harness. The remainder of the crates parachuted into the scrub around the clearing but were soon recovered.

Earlier that morning, 9 Platoon had departed to spend a couple of days patrolling on its own. As the airdrop ended, 8 Platoon set out on a day patrol. I accompanied this patrol, carrying the '88' set in case we became hopelessly lost. In that event, I would be able to establish contact with any Auster spotter plane that was sent out to look for us.

We made our way upriver for some distance, then turned off into the jungle and followed several tracks, to no avail. After a short halt for tiffen, Mr Crisp studied his map but didn't seem to have a clue where we were. So, after the NCOs and even the privates had all given their opinions on the subject, it was decided that we should head back to camp. Soon after we had started, our two scouts ran into a swarm of hornets and were both badly stung. We seemed to walk for miles in what Joe Costello (the former tramp) assured me was entirely the wrong direction. Eventually, we ended up on the river beneath the squatter area where the company had camped on the first night of the operation, and followed the river back to base from there.

The following morning, Tuesday the 18th, Major Murray ordered Arthur and me to build a better *basha*, making it more stable and roomier. His intention was to rest in our

163

basha during the day and sleep outside in his hammock at night. When he took up residence that first morning, I was standing outside with nothing in particular to do.

'Do you want to come into your house, Scurr?' the major called from inside the new *basha*. 'Because if you do, you'll be most welcome.'

Rather reluctantly, I crawled in beneath the overhead poncho and sat upon the groundsheet beside him.

'You're a National Serviceman, are you, Scurr?' the major asked me genially.

'Yes, sir,' I answered.

'Are you enjoying the army?'

'Well – not really, sir.'

'Why not?' His tone became less cordial.

I hesitated for a moment, trying to think of an answer that wouldn't offend him, and finally said: 'Well, it's quite a hard life, sir.'

'It's not hard!' the major declared caustically. 'It's not hard at all!'

I knew that there was no future in this conversation, so I remained silent. The major glared at me.

'Well, don't sit about in here, doing nothing!' he snapped. 'Go and see if Corporal Greenacre needs any assistance operating the wireless!'

I made a hasty departure, resolved to stay clear of the *basha* whenever Major Murray was in it in future.

Patrols found three abandoned camps that day, and 9 Platoon returned to the company base in the evening. Arthur and I had rather a disturbed night. First of all, we had considerable difficulty in burning a leech off Arthur's penis in the darkness! Then, heavy rain in the early morning nearly swamped us out of our new and 'better' *basha*.

We were glad to see the sun rise so that we could dry out our kit. Patrols were sent out again that morning but found no signs of the enemy. My only excitement was being stung by a hornet when I hit it, thinking it was a fly.

On the wireless net that day, Wednesday the 19th, I

heard that a patrol of 'B' Company had found a camp for 60 to 100 men and that between 10 and 20 bandits had fled from the camp half an hour before the patrol's arrival. Coffee and tapioca were still cooking on the fires and supplies and mail had been left behind. I was considerably encouraged by this news. The enemy were definitely in the area – if we could only find them!

That afternoon, attempts were made to bring down the crate of rations that was suspended by its parachute in the tree. Five mags of Bren and about ten rounds from a rifle were all fired at the tree branch without, however, any success.

I woke up early next morning to feel and hear a mosquito rattling around inside the orifice of my ear. It was obviously in a panic, and so was I! I hastily searched for a torch and shone it into my ear, hoping to draw the insect out towards the light. I was greatly relieved to feel the mosquito crawling out and quickly scooped it away with my finger.

Shortly after daylight on Thursday the 20th, we packed up our camp and continued on our way. While on the move, we heard the explosions of an air strike that was being made in support of one of the other companies. Our route lay alternately through open country and jungle. It was a long, hot and very fatiguing march. About 1 p.m., we halted on a hill beside an old burned-out police post to have tiffen. We were weary and scorched by the hot sun and had long since emptied our water bottles. The only water available for making tea was rainwater that had accumulated in some large earthen storage jars that stood outside the charred wooden structure. There was green scum on the surface of the water. However, we were so desperately thirsty that we scooped the scum off and then filled our brew cans. The resulting tea tasted fine and apparently did us no harm.

From here, the two platoons set out in different directions to make their own camps. Company HQ moved on for a few hundred yards until we reached a schoolhouse on top of another hill, just above a squatter area. Here we made our base. Our police guides obtained beer, minerals and fruit for us from the squatters' village below, all of which were much appreciated.

Just after dark, dogs began barking down at the village. Major Murray went down with the police guides to check if any strangers had arrived, while the rest of us stood by to rush down there if necessary. However, the major soon returned, saying that nothing was amiss.

On the morning of Friday the 21st, we had another airdrop, with some of the parachuted crates of rations just missing the schoolhouse roof. Shortly after, 8 and 9 Platoons returned to collect their rations. We had numerous tins of 'buckshee' biscuits that we had no wish to carry with us, so the major decided to issue them out to the Chinese squatters. Through a police interpreter, spokesmen for the squatters gave an assurance that they would not give the biscuits to the Communists as they were all strong supporters of the KMT (Kuomintang – Chiang Kai-shek's Chinese Nationalists).

Later, I heard on the wireless net that 100 bandits were reported to have crossed the western boundary of 'A' Company's area and that the Marine Commandos were going to lay ambushes around their supposed route.

At midnight, I was on prowler guard with Private Frank Keenan. Frank – a Bren gunner in 8 Platoon – was very pally with Arthur and was always pleasant company. As we strolled round the summit of the hill, we suddenly heard a rustling in the long grass and scrub about 10 yards down the slope. We both stopped and pointed our rifles in the general direction of the sound. Whatever it was crept nearer.

'There's definitely something there,' said Frank. 'Shall we fetch Corporal Greenacre?'

'OK,' I replied. 'I'll cover it. You get Corporal Greenacre.'

Frank hurried off to the schoolhouse and summoned Arthur, who was Guard Commander. Arthur ran out, soon followed by Major Murray. By this time, the rustling in the long grass was continuing to draw closer and Frank and I had raised our rifles to our shoulders, with safety catches forward and fingers on triggers, ready to fire at any moment.

'Don't panic! Don't panic!' warned the major, swaying back and forward as he spoke.

Now, nearly all of Company HQ had turned out and lined up behind us with weapons at the ready.

'I'm going down to have a look,' Major Murray announced. 'So don't shoot me.'

As always at that time of night, the major was fairly drunk. He staggered downhill, rifle in hand, and shone his torch into the scrub. Whatever was there scuttled away. The major returned, saying that all he had seen was something brown. We suspected that it was probably a wild pig but, of course, we couldn't be certain.

Next morning, Saturday the 22nd, it was found that two of our chaps were too sick to continue with the operation. One had piles and the other had severe jungle sores on his legs. Major Murray decided to send them back to Tac HQ at Lenggong.

'Follow the track back the way we came,' the major instructed them. 'D'you think you can find your way back to the river?'

'I think so, sir,' said one of them.

'Good,' said the major. 'Now keep your eyes open. If you spot any bandits, don't try to fight them. Hide in the jungle till they've gone. When you reach the river, try to find someone to take you across in a sampan. All right?'

'Yes, sir.' The men nodded, looking a little uncertain. It all sounded very vague to me and exceedingly dangerous. I considered that sending them in alone like that was an awesome responsibility for the major to take. Fortunately, as we later discovered, the two men did reach Tac HQ safely.

The company moved on again that morning into continuous jungle terrain, with 8 Platoon leading and 9 Platoon in the rear of Company HQ. Our route lay up the Sungei Soh (River Soh). The jungle on both sides was very dense and there were no tracks along the banks, so we waded up the river most of the time. The rocks on the river bed were very slippery, and for a while we were wading up to our waists. After a short break, Arthur and I somehow found ourselves marching with the rear section of 8 Platoon.

Towards midday, the column was suddenly halted and word was passed back to take off our packs and go forward with our weapons at the ready – quietly!

'Can you let me past, Jock?' said 'Pongo' Kennedy, behind me. 'I'm supposed to be his number two,' he added, nodding towards Frank Keenan, the Bren gunner, who was just ahead of Arthur and me.

'There's maybe going to be a scrap, eh?' I said hopefully to Pongo as he eased himself past me in the rocky water.

'Looks like it,' he replied positively.

I felt very excited. This was it, I was sure! At that moment, I had a sudden memory of school companions who had been inclined to mock me because of my shy manner and lack of prowess on the sports field. I then became happily aware that I was now wading up a jungle river, clutching a loaded rifle, as I approached an imminent armed encounter with Chinese bandits. If they could only see me now – I thought to myself – this must be more manly than playing football!

We moved forward, slowly and cautiously clambering over rocks, ducking beneath tree branches and wading through varying depths of water. Suddenly, I saw some *bashas* ahead along the left bank – bandit *bashas*. However, to my bitter disappointment there was no sign of any occupants. The men of 8 Platoon were in the process of searching the tracks round about, but there was clearly no battle.

I soon learned that upon sighting the camp, 8 Platoon's leading scout had seen a bandit crouching at the river's edge. Before the scout could fire, however, the bandit had disappeared into the *ulu*. There were four small *bashas* with lean-to attap roofs which could not have accommodated more than 20 men. Soon, 8 Platoon returned, having found no further signs of the enemy; that is, all except Serjeant

Hutchinson, who apparently had run off on his own in pursuit of the fleeing bandit. After half an hour, the serjeant also returned without success.

We went back for our packs, and then moved up the river again until we turned off up a track to the summit of a hill. Here we found an old and fairly large Force 136 camp with some structures of *bashas* remaining. We made base here and the two platoons later went out on patrol, 8 Platoon locating another abandoned bandit camp.

Major Murray retired to his hammock in the afternoon, complaining of having a fever and a high temperature, which he let everybody know about. For example he gave an order to CSM Allen: 'Serjeant Major! Will you tell the men not to chop the trees with their matchets? I need peace and quiet. I've got a temperature of a hundred and two!'

Patrols went out again next day. The major sat by the wireless all day, driving Arthur and me crazy, constantly complaining about his illness. At the evening wireless transmission, he informed the Intelligence Officer that if he wasn't any better by the following day he'd have to be evacuated. Our hopes were high!

The next morning, Monday the 24th, having announced that his temperature had now risen to 103, the major set off back to Lenggong with – I noted – an escort of ten men (unlike the two sick privates that he'd sent back unescorted). The escort arrived back late in the afternoon with an officer from 'A' Company, Lieutenant Hutton, who had been appointed to take over temporary command of the company.

Just before dusk, Second Lieutenant Wride chatted to Arthur and me for a while. I ventured to mention that it was nice and peaceful now that the major had gone.

Mr Wride responded: 'Well, my attitude to the major is that he had a very difficult time during the war, so I'm prepared to excuse his various idiosyncrasies.'

'What's he like in the mess, sir?' Arthur enquired.

'At breakfast, he's bloody! Quite unapproachable,' Mr Wride stated. 'By lunchtime, he's just starting to come to life and be a bit more human.' Mr Wride then smiled as he continued: 'But at dinner, he's absolutely marvellous company. He can be quite charming and he's so interesting when he tells all his stories about the war. I could listen to him for hours!'

Listening to this assessment, I began to feel a little repentant. Perhaps 'the Mad Major' had some good points, but I was still glad he was gone!

Early the following morning, a party set off down the Sungei Soh to receive an airdrop in a specified clearing. Bill Downs had developed a bad case of dysentery and was passing blood. Consequently, Arthur went with the airdrop party, taking Bill's '68' set. Then, when the remainder of the company followed down the river, I carried Arthur's set. We made camp near the DZ, and I had the aerial erected and a *basha* built by the time the airdrop party arrived back with the supplies.

'C' Company had, in fact, patrolled its area pretty thoroughly. The CO now issued us fresh orders by wireless, saying that he had a job for us on the other side of the Sungei Perak. So we dismantled our newly built *bashas* and as soon as our patrols came in, set off at a pretty fast pace through fairly open country.

I was quite tired, but suddenly strangely contented. I watched the file of jungle-green-clad men marching ahead of me, holding weapons at the ready and slightly bowed beneath the burden of their packs. To the rhythm of the soft padding of our jungle boots, I began to sing silently within my mind 'The longest mile is the last mile home'. Happily, I thought to myself: This is the life for me!

Arriving at a kampong by the Sungei Perak just before nightfall, we made our camp on the river bank. Beer was obtainable in the kampong and the company drunks made the most of it, singing loudly until after midnight. Lying awake, listening to the usual variety of regimental and obscene songs – 'Now they sent us off to Constance to see what we could do . . .', 'We are the KOYLI . . .', 'Mary in the garden sifting rice . . .', 'I took my girl on a cycling tour . . .', 'Oh, Deolali sahib . . .', etc. – I found that for the first time since before my call-up I was entertaining thoughts of signing on as a regular. This is the life! I thought once more.

We crossed the Sungei Perak next morning, Wednesday the 26th. This time, there were two sampans to transport us. When it was my turn to cross, our sampan ran aground on a sandbank in the middle of the river. However, the two boatmen managed to set the vessel afloat again without capsizing and we were soon safely across.

When the company had all crossed the river, we moved on up to the road where the CO, Lieutenant Colonel 'Winger' Brown, was waiting. As each of us passed him, the colonel said quietly: 'Well done!' It was simple, sincere and much appreciated – certainly by me.

Still suffering badly from dysentery, Bill left us here to be taken into Tac HQ and, from there, to the British Military Hospital at Kamunting. Motor transport took the rest of us north. I travelled in 'A' Company's armoured vehicle, known as a 'battle-waggon'. It was hot and stifling like being enclosed in a coffin, I considered. When the convoy finally stopped at a kampong, I was really thankful to get out into the open air.

Once the company was assembled, we set off through the rubber, then through open country and eventually made base at a kampong on the edge of the jungle. Patrols went out that afternoon and again the following morning when 8 Platoon found an abandoned camp and tracks leading north. Tac HQ informed us on the wireless net that another unit would be following up 8 Platoon's find.

In the afternoon, we moved back to a school near the road. Arthur had a strain in his stomach and wasn't feeling too good. Now that the operation was coming to an end, we were all pretty weary and looking forward to withdrawing to Penang as though we were going on leave. That night, we didn't even bother to build *bashas* but merely kipped down beneath the stars. Fortunately, it didn't rain.

The following morning, Friday, 28 July, we gladly

marched to the road, where transport picked us up and carried us 'home' to Prai, arriving there at about 5 p.m. It began to rain as we crossed to Penang Island in the ferry and we were soon soaked through. However, we didn't mind at all. When Glugor Barracks – now renamed Minden Barracks by the KOYLI – came in sight, we all gave a loud cheer.

Our trucks turned into the camp entrance and approached the guardroom, which stood to the left of the road. Dirty, dishevelled, and worn out after 14 days of jungle-bashing, the men of 'C' Company broke into song:

> I'm all right! You're all right!
> I'll be up your flue tonight! . . .

Three regimental policemen in immaculate uniforms stood on the guardroom verandah and stared at us from cold, impassive faces. Looking back at them, I was conscious of two disparate emotions: an instinctive fear of RPs and the unjust contempt which rifle company personnel tended to feel towards 'rear echelon wallahs'.

The trucks conveyed us to barrack blocks on the far side of the camp known as 'the company lines'. Here the four rifle companies would be accommodated for the next two months of rest and retraining. Arthur and I now got our kit together and made our way over to the Signals *basha* in HQ Company block, where we secured beds for ourselves and were greeted by many old friends.

Tom Joy informed me that following the reports, a week before, of large enemy movement across 'A' Company's western boundary, units of the Marine Commandos and Malay Regiment had surrounded 100 bandits near Lenggong and laid ambushes along possible escape routes. However, during the night, the entire enemy force had slipped away through the jungle undetected.

So the big operation had ended without any bandits being killed or captured. This statement might make it appear that the whole thing had been a colossal waste of time and energy. Nothing could be further from the truth. Prior to Operation 'Acorn', there had been regular weekly ambushes on the Lenggong–Grik road. The operation brought this to an end and curtailed other terrorist activity in the area. Our extensive sweeps through the region had put both large and small concentrations of the enemy on the run and located many of their camps. Operation 'Acorn' had not been a failure.

At this time, I was just beginning to realise something that I would eventually know for sure. Constant patrolling, with or without actual contact, meant harassment of the enemy; flushing him from his havens or forcing him to lie low, and disrupting his vital food supplies. The many 'no contact' operations throughout the arduous Malayan campaign contributed to the final victory as surely as did the minority of forays that resulted in kills or captures. It must also be true to say that when contacts were achieved, they were the product of all the sweat and toil of all the patrols that had combed the area over the preceding weeks or months and not just of the one patrol that struck lucky. Indeed, I do not believe that there was ever such a thing as a wasted operation in Malaya.

11

Rest and Retraining – Minden Barracks, Penang August–September 1950

During the two months of rest and retraining, my journal records numerous trips into Georgetown with my cousin John, sometimes accompanied by Chas Schaverien and occasionally by Johnny Ainsworth or Ken Phipps, a friend of cousin John's who had originally been on the QM's staff before transferring to 'A' Company. The pattern of these trips was always the same; a visit to the cinema – invariably to see an adventure film – followed by a meal at either the Broadway Café or the Chinese Town Hall NAAFI. Sometimes, we would go shopping. Nylon stockings were still scarce in Britain at that time and were a popular present to send home.

Arthur Greenacre was taken into hospital a few days after our arrival in Penang, due to his persistent stomach complaint. Happily, he soon recovered, as did Bill Downs from his dysentery. As for Major Murray, it transpired that he was seriously ill with scrub typhus – a jungle disease which often proved fatal. Fortunately, he would completely recover by the time the battalion retraining period was over.

Tuesday, 1 August, was Minden Day, celebrated every year by the KOYLI in commemoration of the regiment's first battle honour, won at the Battle of Minden on 1 August 1759. In the morning, the whole battalion paraded on the sports field, with every man wearing a white rose above the KOYLI bugle badge on his green beret. First of all, we were addressed by the CO, who told us about the glory that

174

our regiment had won in the battle and about our regimental motto, '*Cede Nullis*' (Yield to None), which he declared might be a good motto for the British Empire in those troubled times. Then the CO took the salute as the battalion marched past, led by the band and bugles playing our regimental march, 'With Jockey to the Fair'. It was the first battalion parade since the beginning of the Emergency in June 1948 and most of the men present hadn't drilled for months. We may not have been particularly smart that morning but we nonetheless marched proudly.

Minden Day tiffen was described in my journal as 'a slap-up conner'. In fact, our menu comprised: crème of tomato soup; roast pork and apple sauce, stuffing balls, roast and creamed potatoes and green peas; fruit jelly and trifle with cream; plus cheese and biscuits, fresh fruit and minerals. A bottle of Tiger beer per man was supplied by the battalion PRI (President of the Regimental Institute) and a bottle of Carlsberg for each man was donated by the East Asiatic Company (Importers). The band played dance music throughout the meal and Corporal Jock McClung of the Signal Platoon gave us a performance of his version of Highland dancing.

In the afternoon, there was a soccer match, in which the battalion team drew with the 4th Hussars, 2–2. After the match, a representative party from the 2nd Battalion, Coldstream Guards, presented a silver bugle to the CO. Like the gift from the Scots Guards two months before, this bugle was given in appreciation of KOYLI hospitality. The band and bugles then sounded retreat, thus performing the final official ceremony of Minden Day, 1950.

From then on, battalion retraining began in earnest, with drill parades and senior and junior NCOs' cadres, and with the rifle companies concentrating on shooting practice and patrol and ambush techniques. Before commenting on Signal Platoon training and other activities of this period, I shall describe an interesting extra duty that I had to undertake at this time and the events which led up to it.

Just after reveille on Saturday, 5 August, I was detailed

by Corporal McClung to go on an escort duty with a lance corporal of the regimental police. We left barracks at 7.30 a.m. and after crossing in the ferry to Prai, we travelled by train south to Taiping. Once there, we proceeded to the British Military Hospital to pick up a prisoner who had deserted from 'D' Company six weeks before.

When we entered the indicated hospital ward, we found the prisoner – whom I shall call Private Harper – seated upon his bed, awaiting our arrival.

'Hi, Harper!' the RP lance corporal greeted him genially.

Harper gave us both a broad smile and seemed genuinely pleased to see us. Before making the return journey, we took him to a not very clean little café called the Melahti. A young Malay woman who served us became very excited when she saw our cap badges. The lance corporal told me that she had been the sweetheart of the 2nd Battalion when that unit had been stationed at Taiping in 1947–48. We bought Harper a meal and a bottle of Tiger, very aware that it would be some time before he would be able to dine in a café again.

As we ate, Harper told us the story of his desertion, brief details of which I jotted down in my journal the following day. However, I am able to present a far fuller account here, due to the fact that 40 years later, while still working on this book, I came face to face with 'Harper' at a KOYLI Malaya Veterans' Reunion in Wakefield. This was his story.

On Sunday, 25 June 1950, the battalion PRI serjeant – in the process of touring the rifle companies to collect the financial proceeds of the company canteens – arrived at 'D' Company base, Ashby Road Camp, Ipoh, quite late in the day. Not wishing to continue his journey after dark because of the risks involved, he decided to stay the night with 'D' Company. For safekeeping, the serjeant deposited the PRI funds collected, to the sum of 2,200 Malayan dollars (£282 – a fair amount of money in 1950), in a strongbox in the armoury.

Now it so happened that this strongbox was in the charge of Private Harper, who had secured himself a cushy number

176

in the armoury, having done his share of jungle-bashing in 10 Platoon. Harper immediately approached his pal – whom I shall call Lance Corporal Ennis – and assured him that if there was ever an opportunity for them to get together with their two lady penfriends in Australia, this must be it!

Ennis agreed. So that night, they took the money and proceeded into Ipoh, wearing civilian clothing as though going for a night on the town. They then caught the late-night train down to Kuala Lumpur, where they transferred to the Singapore train. As a precaution, they got off this train at Seremban, in Johore, and took a taxi to Johore-Bahru. Here they rested for a while, had a meal and bought some items of clothing, before hiring another taxi to take them across the causeway into Singapore.

At the far end of the causeway, the taxi was stopped by two Sikh policemen, who asked the two soldiers to produce their pay books. It was their ill fortune that Ennis had left his behind. The policemen insisted that Ennis would have to return to his camp and get his pay book before they could proceed into Singapore. To avoid any suspicion, the two friends readily accepted this, turned the taxi round and went back to Johore-Bahru.

After buying a newspaper, they went into a café. Harper studied the shipping lines and noticed that certain ships called in at Port Swettenham. Resolved to try their luck there, they set off in another taxi and arrived at Port Swettenham late that night. They booked into a small hotel and the following morning, after scouting around, moved to another hotel near the docks.

Ill fortune continued to thwart them. No Australia-bound ship passed through. After 19 or 20 days' absence from their unit, with Ennis growing increasingly jittery, Harper finally agreed that they should give themselves up. They took a taxi into Kuala Lumpur and then decided to have a final fling before surrendering. First of all, they enjoyed a meal and a drink and then went to a dance hall. As the end of their spree drew near, Harper asked the dance-band leader if he would kindly play the tune 'Time on My Hands' and extravagantly tipped him ten dollars. After listening to this lovely, wistful melody, they left the dance hall and ordered a trishaw wallah to take them to the military police.

Proceeding down a road, they spotted a military police jeep coming the other way. After flagging the MP driver down, they explained to him who they were. The MP heaved a sigh of relief and informed them that they had been reported seen in various parts of Malaya, even on the Siamese border. Then the MP drove them to a nearby RASC camp, where they were detained while awaiting an escort from the KOYLI. This escort duly arrived two days later and took the two prisoners back to Glugor (Minden) Barracks, Penang.

After being charged accordingly, subject to a court martial, Harper and Ennis underwent a period of close arrest in the battalion guardroom. During this time, Harper suffered an outbreak of jungle sores on both of his legs and was therefore sent to Taiping Military Hospital for treatment. Here he met up with a marine commando who had a few dollars on him and who, after about a week, suggested to Harper that the pair of them should slip out of the hospital and enjoy themselves. This they did. However, upon their return to the hospital, they discovered that their absence had been reported, and they were duly paraded before an RAMC colonel. This officer roundly rebuked Harper, awarded him 28 days' stoppage of pay and subsequently informed the KOYLI that he could be 'collected'. Accordingly, the regimental police lance corporal and I had travelled to Taiping on Saturday, 5 August, and picked Harper up. I can now continue the account from the entry in my journal.

After our meal and drinks at the Melahti café, we now proceeded to the railway station. The lance corporal left Harper and me seated upon two facing benches while he went off to get our travel warrants cleared. I suddenly felt very sleepy and my head began to nod.

Harper grinned. 'Why don't you get your head down,

178

Jock?' he suggested. 'Go on – have a kip! I'm not going to run away.'

'No.' I shook my head. 'I'd better not.'

The next thing I knew was when I felt a hefty thump upon my shoulder. I opened my eyes to see the lance corporal standing over me and on the opposite bench, my prisoner calmly sitting with my rifle resting across his knees!

We then boarded our train and delivered Harper to the guardroom in Minden Barracks at about 10.30 p.m.

Forty years later, 'Harper' told me that he had to wait approximately three months for his court martial. He was subsequently sentenced to 15 months' detention in Ipoh Military Prison, obtaining seven months' remission for good behaviour. Upon returning to the battalion after completing his sentence, the adjutant asked him if he'd like to go home on the next boat. Harper, however, replied that he wished to remain to complete his tour and sail home with his friends in a few weeks' time. He was then posted to 'C' Company.

There was a strange sequel to the story that I have just related. The regimental police lance corporal i/c escort (whom I have intentionally not named) himself deserted, several months later, and went to live with his Eurasian girlfriend in Georgetown. Although the military police were called in, they could find no trace of him. To the best of my knowledge he was never heard of again.

During rest and retraining, early morning parades became regular activities. On Wednesday and Saturday mornings, we had respectively RSM's and adjutant's drill parades. Other mornings, we paraded 15 minutes after reveille for PT, which sometimes consisted of doing normal physical jerks but frequently meant being employed on pitching tents, shifting furniture or picking up waste paper. Barrack room inspections, drilling to the biting commands of RSM Tanner and being sought out for fatigue duties by Bugle Major Bert Harbisher or Corporal 'Bummer' Young (fulfilling the role of HQ Company Orderly Serjeant) was all rather reminiscent of basic training days, though certainly not so oppressive.

In the middle of August, I spent the better part of two weeks firing on the range at Ayer Hitam with a party from HQ, attached to 'A' Company. One day while waiting to take my place on the firing line, I was approached by Serjeant Howgego, known as 'Bamboo John', who had assisted with my draft's jungle training five months before.

'Hello, Scurr,' he greeted me brightly. 'How are you getting on? D'you like the army a bit better now you're settled in?'

'I like it out on the mainland with the rifle company,' I replied. 'But I don't like it in HQ.'

Serjeant Howgego's amiable manner immediately vanished. 'I know why you don't like it in HQ,' he stated in harsh, hostile tones. 'It's because you have to do some work! I know what it's like in the rifle companies. You're skiving all the time, lying about on your beds! That's why you like it out there!'

I started to tell him that humping heavy loads up and down jungle-covered hills wasn't my idea of skiving, but he turned abruptly and walked away before I could say more than a couple of words. I felt rather upset and bewildered by his sudden change of attitude. It seemed to me that to like being in the field with a rifle company should be regarded as commendable by an old soldier.

I completed my firing-range course on Sunday the 20th, classifying first class on the Bren gun but only second class on the rifle. For whatever reason, I still had not regained the rifle shooting standard of my army cadet days.

A REME inspection of the battalion's weapons was also completed about this time. The findings were that 26 Brens, 30 Stens and 150 rifles were declared 'beyond local repair'. Such were the arms we'd been carrying on operations! Of course, everything deteriorated in the jungle.

Following range classification, I was employed for a period as operator to Brigade in the wireless tower. This suited me fine as it kept me out of the reaches of Bert

Harbisher and Bummer Young. While in Penang, I continued to be treated for the foot-rot and tinea that I had acquired in the *ulu*.

At the beginning of September, we learned that the British government had announced that all conscripts would have to serve an extra six months, apparently because of the Korean War. This meant that my presumed six months of remaining service were now doubled up to a full year. This did not please me at all and my displeasure was not lessened by the supposed compensation of an extra 21 shillings (£1.05) a week pay during the final six months.

Drill, PT, fatigues and the general bull and regimentation of life in HQ did not render me well disposed towards the army at that time. On Sunday, 3 September, I noted in my journal: 'About a month ago, I had crazy notions of signing on as a regular, but I think and hope that I've now got these ideas out of my mind.'

However, there were also good times. On Tuesday the 19th, in the company of about 20 others from HQ, I went on a trip along the coast in a motor launch. We were dropped off at a small island off the southern tip of Penang called Pulau Rimau (Tiger Island) at about 10 a.m. There was a lovely little beach surrounded by palm trees, and we swam and explored the uninhabited island at our leisure. Chas Schaverien and I found a disused lighthouse. The view from there of the island and the sea was really gorgeous. After we'd consumed our tiffen of corned beef *banjos* (sandwiches) and lemonade, the launch returned for us at 1.30 p.m. and took us back. It had been a grand morning's break.

Thursday the 21st was Battalion Sports Day; not something that I would normally be interested in attending. However, we were all eventually rounded up and paraded on the sports field to hear an address by the C.-in-C. Far East Land Forces, General Sir John Harding, KCB, CBE, DSO, MC. He told us: 'I'm very pleased that I dropped in on you on Sports Day. For Sports Day is a family occasion. A regiment is a family.' He then went on to congratulate

181

Lieutenant Colonel Brown on the splendid way he had organised and led the battalion. The CO made a brief reply to the effect that everything that had been attributed to him was really a credit to everyone in the battalion.

Although today I can appreciate the value of sport in the army and also would fully endorse Sir John's statement that a regiment is a family, the hostility and resentment that remained within me at that time towards some aspects of army life caused me to write in my journal: 'There's only half the family in the fucking clink and the other half doubling about like cunts on fatigues and early morning parades! Mummy's cooking is fuck-all like it, and our uncles address us by nasty names!'

With the whole battalion in barracks, there were, in fact, a considerable number of men under close arrest or on 'jankers' (confined to barracks) at that time, but not, of course, 'half the family'.

The following Saturday afternoon, the 23rd, I and several others from HQ were put on tent-striking fatigues as a punishment for not attending the start of the Battalion Sports Day proceedings. There had been nothing on Company Detail to indicate that we should. However, Corporal Bummer Young claimed that he had told us to attend. 'Like hell he did!' I commented in my journal.

On Tuesday the 26th, the nine members of my signals training cadre were reassembled, along with three other signallers, to sit a classification exam. Presiding was a Royal Signals officer from 2 Squadron, Malaya Signals Regiment, who had come up specially from Taiping. The exam lasted all day and everyone passed except a lad called Hodson (who was later promoted!). Our results averaged 78 per cent, which showed a pretty high standard. Consequently, I was now officially classified as a regimental signaller.

During our rest and retraining period, our Signals Officer, Captain Saltonstall, had left for home, where he had secured a place in Staff College. This left Serjeant Haley in command of the Signal Platoon. Serjeant Cook was unfortunately hospitalised, having burned himself in an accident, and Jock McClung was now promoted to serjeant. There were other changes at that time. Headquarters Company Commander Major 'Porky' Gowans was due to go home; his place was taken by Major Doyle. Also, Serjeant Major Jennings replaced Potts as HQ's CSM.

I spent the final week in Penang doing odd jobs such as laying telephone lines, in addition to the usual early morning and afternoon fatigues. I was very glad that rest and retraining was coming to an end. Cousin John and I had seen some good films during our trips into Georgetown, including classic favourites such as *The Black Swan* and *The Sea Hawk*. However, I'd had enough of the regimentation and bull of barrack life and was itching to get back to the *ulu* and hopefully meet some bandits.

On Thursday afternoon, 28 September, all Signals and MT (Motor Transport) personnel who would be going on detachment to rifle companies were assembled in the dining hall to be addressed by the new Company Commander. He gave us a sincere and straightforward talk regarding the good conduct he expected from HQ Company personnel on the mainland, particularly if we came under fire.

Afterwards, we sorted out the signals kit that we would be taking to our companies. I was again posted to 'C' Company and Chas Schaverien to 'B'. That night, Chas, John and I went down town to do some final shopping and had an excellent farewell meal of curried chicken, washed down by Tiger beer, in the Broadway Café.

I was sad to be leaving my friends but was very eager for the jungle.

12

'C' Company – Kulim
October–November 1950

We reported to our companies on Friday night, 29 September. The following morning about 9 a.m., 'C' Company departed from Minden Barracks in a convoy of several trucks. By 1 p.m., we had arrived at the company's new location – Kulim in South Kedah.

Our camp, which we took over from a company of the 1st Battalion, Worcestershire Regiment, lay just outside the town. The officers' mess, serjeants' mess and company office were all incorporated in an old, derelict, planter's bungalow with dirty-white walls and a wide verandah at the top of the front staircase. In the foundations beneath the bungalow, amongst supporting stone columns, were located the company stores, the combined dining hall and canteen and the living quarters of Company HQ personnel – officers' batmen, MT and Signals. The cookhouse and ablutions sheds were on the far side of the building, while the guard tent was pitched on a grass verge beside the narrow roadway leading up to the camp from the main road to Kulim. The MT park – a square of hard sand – lay between the old bungalow and a raised stretch of grassland upon which 8 and 9 Platoons were accommodated in rows of brown squad tents. Beyond the platoon lines were the tents of a field ambulance detachment, providing us with an excellent MRS (medical reception station).

This time, 'C' Company Signals consisted of Lance Corporal Arthur Greenacre, myself and two new chaps from the latest cadre – Eric Hann and 'Swede' Martin. (Bill

Downs was now NCO i/c 'D' Company Signals detachment.) That first afternoon and most of the following day were spent getting everything shipshape. We first constructed a canvas 'wall' around our quarters to protect us from the elements. Then we erected our aerials and set up the loudspeakers for the camp broadcasting system. Lastly, we organised storage of our signals equipment and our own personal 'bed spaces'; each contained nothing more than a folding iron bed and a wooden kit box.

On my first impression of our new home, I noted in my journal: 'It's a pretty poor show compared to Tanjong Rambutan; still, it's not too bad.' However, this opinion did not long prevail. Kulim, in fact, became my favourite location and the three final months of 1950 – which I call my 'first Kulim period' – provided my most satisfying time in Malaya. It was a time when I was at my best, both physically and mentally; when I was sure of myself and the men around me; and when I was still eager and full of hope. All of my training was now over, as was my initiation in jungle operations. I no longer felt a 'new boy', but started my time at Kulim with the confidence of being an established, and experienced, member of 'C' Company.

The Company Commander, Major Murray, had fully recovered from his scrub typhus and hadn't changed a bit. Also very much the same were Captain Haddon (second in command) and Second Lieutenant Wride, commanding 9 Platoon. On the other hand, 8 Platoon's Commander, Second Lieutenant John Crisp, altered considerably in my estimation at this time.

During the Lenggong duffy, I had regarded the recently arrived Mr Crisp as an amiable, easy going, average second lieutenant. However, in Kulim, he acquired a certain charisma in my eyes, due to his obvious eagerness to make contact with the enemy. Wiry-haired, stocky and tough, Mr Crisp tended to force the pace when on patrol. Consequently, the men of his platoon soon nicknamed him 'Killer' Crisp. Even so, I would say that – as officers go – he was fairly popular. As far as I was concerned, I grew to revere him to the extent that I remember one day saying to his batman, Reg Allen: 'I'd follow Mr Crisp anywhere!'

Arthur Greenacre remained his usual, likeable, unflappable self, always keeping everything firmly under control in his own quiet way. As always, the first thing to be pinned on the wall above his bed was a photograph of his girlfriend – a lovely Welsh nurse called Dilys. The two new signallers, Eric Hann and 'Swede' Martin, fitted in with us very well. Eric was a former electrician's mate from Twickenham and had some amusing, if dogmatic, views on women, religion and other matters. He and I had some quite heated though essentially friendly arguments and quickly became really good mates. Swede, a Somerset lad with a strong county accent, was very slow at learning to take wireless transmissions; for a while he refused in near panic to even try. We didn't really care, though, as he was such amusing company, keeping us in howls of laughter with his yarns about his former life in Yeovil and his comments on daily happenings in the company.

During the retraining period, Joe Costello, the former tramp, had left 'C' Company – indeed, with three others had left the KOYLI – having volunteered for a new airborne unit that was just being formed: the Malayan Scouts. The purpose of this unit was to operate in the deep jungle of the central mountain ranges and counter the influence and control of the Communists upon the aboriginal tribes – Temiar, Semai and others – universally, if incorrectly, known to the troops at that time as 'Sakai'. (In May 1952, the Malayan Scouts would become the 22nd Regiment, Special Air Service.)

McAllister and Swalwell, my two one-time companions in Holding Company, Bordon, had both been promoted – McAllister to full corporal and Stan Swalwell to lance corporal. Frank Keenan, mentioned earlier as a Bren gunner in 8 Platoon, had also been promoted to lance corporal. The best-known company 'characters' during this period were Privates Clarke, Cooper, George, Lightfoot, Mains,

Meredith, Nolan, Pilgrim and Randle (i.e. best known for getting sloshed in the canteen and singing bawdy songs).

As 'C' Company established its new base at Kulim, the other rifle companies were deployed as follows: 'A' Company at Serdang, 17 miles from Kulim; 'B' Company at Kroh and Klian Intan, and 'D' Company temporarily at Sungei Patani, moving shortly to Pelam Estate. On 4 October, HQ Company, much to its dismay, was transported from Minden Barracks, Penang, to tented accommodation in Airfield Camp, Sungei Patani. Minden Barracks was being loaned to the 1st Battalion, Suffolk Regiment, for two months' rest and retraining.

Kulim was quite a good base for recreation. From camp into town was only a short walk and my journal records fairly frequent evening visits with friends, either to go to one of the two small cinemas or to have a meal and a drink at the only café in town that was not declared out of bounds to troops. I believe there was also a brothel in Kulim but at that time I was still a 'good boy' and did not attend such places! In addition, we enjoyed weekly film shows in camp, provided by the mobile AKC (Army Kinema Corporation) who screened films in the open space in front of the verandah of the officers' mess. Other ranks, seated on rows of forms below the verandah and often drinking bottles of Tiger, tended to liven up the entertainment by shouting out their appreciation of the physical attributes of the film actresses.

During my first Kulim period, I did more than my share of duffies, due to the fact that I was keen (an eager beaver) and was inclined to volunteer out of turn, particularly when Mr Crisp's 8 Platoon was going out. My first operation, however, was with 9 Platoon. In a three-day search in an area known as the Kulim triangle, we saw no bandits but did find considerable evidence of their activity: an entire hill of rubber trees slashed and rendered less productive; groups of deserted *bashas* from which the former occupants had fled, leaving all of their belongings behind; and a kampong where the inhabitants informed us that a party of 30 bandits had stolen their identity cards a month before. This was a regular Communist practice, as was helping themselves to the food and money of the local people they claimed to be 'liberating'.

During those early days at Kulim, I heard tales from Major Murray's new batman – a pleasant lad called Merry – about the major frequently being found on his hands and knees in the officers' mess, playing with his toy jeep, and of the cat staggering helplessly about after the major had laced its milk with whisky! One morning, Arthur went up to the company office with a message and was greeted by Major Murray, who was seated behind his desk.

'Corporal Greenacre, come and play with my new toy!'

For a moment, Arthur wondered if he was being invited to wind up the toy jeep for action, but it turned out that the Major had bought himself a tape recorder – a luxury possessed by only a few in those days.

Major Murray handed Arthur a microphone. 'Speak into that,' he said, smiling mischievously.

Arthur dutifully spoke a few words: 'Hello, this is Corporal Greenacre speaking.'

'You're going to get a surprise in a minute,' the major said excitedly as he wound the tape back.

Arthur managed to produce a suitably astonished response to the sound of his own voice on the tape and made the major very happy. After that, well-known drunken songsters in the company were summoned to have their vulgar – to say the least – party pieces recorded. Subsequently, in the evenings, we could hear these ditties being played in the mess, sometimes to entertain visiting planters and their wives.

Although we were officially only permitted to play gramophone records in the evenings, broadcasting them around the camp through our loudspeaker system, there was an exception to this rule. Major Murray was most impressed by a record we had of Mary Martin singing 'I Want to Get Married'. Consequently, it became quite common for the Company Clerk to come down to the Signals billet at any time during the day and announce: 'The major says he wants to get married!' We would then put the record on quite happily, because we liked it too. Arthur's favourite record, and mine, was 'I'll Remember April', performed by a male singer whose name I cannot recall. We would each make a point of playing it when the other was doing his turn on guard duty.

Early on Saturday morning, 7 October, 8 Platoon set out on a one-day operation without any briefing of any kind beforehand. I went as signaller and took Eric Hann – by now a good pal – with me. We were accompanied by an English police officer and half a dozen Malay and Chinese policemen. The area of the operation turned out to be quite a distance away. Our transport finally dropped us off past Serdang – 'A' Company's location. As on the previous duffy, the terrain was nearly all rubber but thankfully was pretty flat.

Well spread out, we followed a track through the rubber trees until we came to a small group of *bashas*. The police entered one of them and brought out a young Chinese male, clad in white shirt and shorts, whom they identified as a known bandit. It was then that Eric and I first noticed a peculiar-looking Malay in our party who was wearing worn olive-green shirt and slacks, an old jungle hat with the brim pulled down and dark glasses. He was lurking furtively behind a tree and was obviously an informer.

The bandit was questioned for a couple of minutes by the police, who endeavoured to persuade him to take us to his camp, no doubt offering him immunity from prosecution and perhaps a financial inducement. He then led us rather slowly over the countryside for a while until we halted on a down slope. Immediately, we took up all-round defence positions. The informer, at the rear of the column, hurriedly took cover behind a tree, looking around him, obviously scared stiff. For a moment he removed his dark glasses, but quickly replaced them and turned his back when the police brought the bandit back up the slope.

189

'Look at that slimy bastard!' Eric said to me, nodding towards the informer. 'I could shoot him myself!'

Insofar as you can go by appearances, I must say that the Malay did impress me as being the type who would inform for the substantial financial reward rather than from patriotic duty.

It was obvious that the bandit had no intention of leading us anywhere, so we returned to the group of *bashas*. Most of the platoon now started back towards the road, taking the prisoner with them. Serjeant Hutchinson, Eric, myself and about four others remained behind and made our way down to a couple of other *bashas* where half a dozen of our lads and a Chinese detective had been left to keep watch. Another bandit was reported to be living here but was not at home, so the plan was that we should conceal ourselves in or around the *bashas* and wait for him.

Serjeant Hutchinson, the detective, Eric and I entered the bandit's house. His mother, a middle-aged Chinese woman who probably looked older than she was, sat silently in the corner and did not react in any way to our presence. I was just about to set up the wireless when Eric said: 'Here he is now.'

'Who?' I asked.

'The bandit.'

'Where?'

'There!'

I now saw that he meant a young Chinese who had simply strolled in and was pleasantly and unconcernedly handing round cigarettes to us all.

'That's not the fucking bandit!' I exclaimed in utter disbelief.

'It fucking is!' Eric correctly insisted.

Evidently quite unnoticed, the bandit had ridden down the track on his bike. The Chinese detective now produced a photograph and confirmed that he was our man. His mother did not look at all perturbed about her son's arrest. She followed us to the door and stood there without saying a word as we led him away up the track. When we caught

190

up with the rest of the platoon, they said that he hadn't passed them earlier. This suggests that he probably spotted them first and hid in the rubber until they had passed; then pedalled on happily down home, only to find us waiting for him.

We soon reached the road. The two bandits, looking quite happy and contented, were taken away one at a time in a police car. Mr Crisp phoned from the police station for our transport, which arrived after a two-hour wait.

The two Chinese bandits had, I understood, been 'on leave' from their camp in the jungle when they had the bad luck to be seen by the informer. Their ill fortune did not end there. A week or so later, Mr Wride went down to the police station to ascertain how the interrogation of the prisoners was progressing. Upon his return, he commented that the two were 'nearer dead than alive'.

When I think about it now, I naturally feel some human sympathy for them, but I have to be honest and say that I do not recall having any such feelings at the time. They were 'the enemy' and that was that. The Communist terrorists had carried out many hideous atrocities against people of all races in Malaya, including their fellow Chinese, in order to establish their dominion and extract contributions of food and money. They had also mown down members of our 'family' (the regiment) in various ambushes. It was not a time for viewing the enemy with sympathy.

Apart from that, I was not really shocked by their treatment because, during the Second World War – even though I was young and generally innocent – I had always presumed that the British must have tortured prisoners in order to obtain vital information, the same as the Germans and Japanese did. To believe otherwise had seemed to me quite ludicrous.

In the early hours of Monday the 9th, I was awakened by the feeling of an insect crawling into my ear. After breakfast, I went to see the Medical Officer. He looked in my ear but said there was nothing there. However, I could still feel the insect moving around inside. In the afternoon, much to

191

my relief I felt it crawling out. I immediately seized it, and finding it to be a much-hated red ant, put it to death by fire!

Two mornings later, following an FFI inspection by the MO, I had to report sick with tinea of the foot and commenced the required daily treatment. Later in the morning, a public relations officer visited the company. When he entered the Signals billet, I was in the process of unofficially contacting Chas Schaverien at 'B' Company by Morse. He photographed me sitting in front of the '62' set, wearing my headphones, then noted down details of my service in Malaya to send with the photograph to the *Edinburgh Evening Dispatch*. I was young enough to be quite thrilled at the thought of being featured in my home-town newspaper.

Halfway through the interview, the PRO was suddenly called up to the company office to answer a phone call. When he returned ten minutes later, his formerly jovial face was red with anger. 'The bastards have shot my elephant!' he exclaimed.

'Who've shot your elephant, sir?' I enquired.

'Why, the bandits, of course!' he fumed. 'The bloody swines!'

He then regained his composure and continued with the interview completely calm and attentive. At the time, I found his outburst rather amusing, but I suppose I shouldn't have, as he would naturally be upset by the loss of his elephant.

On the night of Friday the 13th, bandits burned down a planter's house on one of the local estates. Although 9 Platoon happened to be patrolling in the proximity, the bandits made their escape without being spotted.

Because of the condition of my feet, I was under MO's orders not to go out on operations for a week. During this time, Arthur, Eric and Swede all went out on duffies. I was very restless and depressed while confined to camp and commented in my journal: 'If I don't get out on another op soon, I'll just about go cuckoo!' However, the MO soon expressed satisfaction with the improvement of my feet, and although I had to continue with treatment for a while, he responded favourably to my plea that I should be allowed to return to jungle-bashing.

Accordingly, on Tuesday night, the 17th, Eric and I attended a platoon briefing for a one-day operation. 'A' Company was going to attack a known bandit camp the following day, with enemy strength estimated at 200 plus. Elements of the Marines and Hussars and a platoon of 'C' Company would be acting as 'stops' on likely escape routes around the area. As my account of this operation is rather critical of someone I liked and therefore do not wish to identify, I shall not specify which platoon of 'C' Company was involved.

We set out at 5.30 next morning, Wednesday the 18th. Just after daylight, we arrived at Selama, where we found a party from Tac HQ positioned at the roadside. Sitting in an armoured scout car was Lance Corporal Bragg of the Signal Platoon, who would be acting as wireless control of the operation. Here the platoon was divided into two groups. Eric went with the Platoon Commander's group and I was assigned to the second group, led by someone I shall refer to only as 'the senior NCO'.

After continuing for a short way in trucks, our group debussed and advanced up a track which soon led us into jungle country. Arriving at a couple of *bashas*, we shang-haied a Chinese to lead us to the spot where it was intended we should lay our ambush. The track we followed was well-cleared but pretty muddy. Our starting point was suppos-edly only half a mile from our destination. Consequently, after we'd marched a few miles, the senior NCO halted us on a slope and consulted his map. He then screamed at the Chinese: 'If you're leading us the wrong way, I'll blow your bastard head off!'

We then carried on. From time to time, some Malays led their 'shit-buffaloes' (as we called them) up or down the track. They were using the water buffaloes to haul logs down to the river. Every time one of these enormous, horned beasts passed, it would sniff at us suspiciously, then

193

try to bolt, causing us brave British soldiers to make a mad dive off the track. The senior NCO now persuaded one of the Malays to guide us and sent the Chinese back.

Eventually, we stopped on a track where there was jungle on one side and rubber on the other. I set up my wireless in the rubber while the rest of the group sprawled out around the track, not in any recognisable ambush formation. At 2 p.m., I managed to contact control, having heard nothing up till then. A voice at the other end identified himself in code as the Battalion Intelligence Officer. He told me that I was the only station that control had managed to contact, apart from 'A' Company. Then he informed me that 'A' Company had, in fact, located the known bandit camp and found it occupied. He asked our exact location and how much rations we had with us. I requested that he hold and ran to the senior NCO.

The senior NCO listened to my excited report with a frowning expression on his face. Then he exclaimed: 'Oh, bollocks to that! He'll make us stay out overnight. Tell him you can't read him.'

'But "A" Company might need help,' I stated, taken aback. 'Anyway, I've already reported his signals as clear.'

'Look, Jock!' he snapped sullenly. 'Just tell him you can't hear him!' He turned away to indicate that the conversation was ended.

I returned to my wireless and donned my headset once more. After giving my call sign, I asked for a report of signals. The Intelligence Officer's voice came through clearly: 'Hello, Fox George Zebra Three Baker. Receiving you loud and clear. Over.'

Feeling absolutely wretched, I replied that he was very faint and asked if he could repeat. The IO answered that he was receiving me loud and clear and could I state our location and rations as requested.

I now replied: 'Hello, Fox George Zebra Three Baker. You are fading – fading. Over.'

When the IO then repeated his message in clear but very

exasperated tones, I pretended not to hear at all and began calling for a report of signals. Ignoring his immediate, frantic response, I then called again for signals, disregarded his reply and closed down.

I felt like an accomplice in a crime. Dejectedly, I wondered how 'A' Company was faring. It now began to pour with rain from a dark, cloudy sky which exactly reflected my mood. After we'd sat for another hour wrapped in our poncho capes, we marched off, constantly lashed by the rain, until we reached the road. Our transport arrived there at 4.30 p.m. and took us into Selama, where Tac HQ was still positioned.

As I stood in the back of the now stationary 3-ton truck, I heard a voice call: 'Scurr!' I looked round and saw that I was being summoned by Major Murray, who was standing at the roadside, accompanied by the CO, Lieutenant Colonel Brown, and the Intelligence Officer, Captain Davis. I swiftly climbed down from the truck and approached the trio, feeling very guilty. I halted with my rifle held at shoulder arms and saluted.

'What happened, Signaller?' Captain Davis enquired. 'Why couldn't you hear me? I could hear you clearly enough.'

'I heard you OK at first, sir, but then reception began to fade,' I lied anxiously.

'Well, I was shouting loud enough!' he protested. To my great relief he pursued the matter no further. Instead, he told me that all KOYLI patrols had now come in but that the Marines and Hussars were still out. Therefore, he wanted 'C' Company to take over wireless control of the operation and maintain a listening watch.

After the Intelligence Officer had given me all the necessary instructions, I returned to the truck. I glanced towards the senior NCO, who was sitting in the cab. He looked back at me blankly and I climbed up into the rear of the vehicle. I considered that Captain Davis seemed to have accepted my story but I still felt pretty awful about the incident. The senior NCO was a popular personality whom I had always liked, but I knew that the resentment that I now felt towards him would take a while to subside.

On returning to 'C' Company's base at Kulim, I was relieved to hear from Arthur that 'A' Company had not been left to do battle, unaided, against the estimated minimum of 200 bandits. As so often happened in these situations, everything had gone wrong. Eventually, the following facts emerged.

After 3 Platoon, 'A' Company, had silently crept through the jungle to within 25 yards of the enemy camp, they could clearly see four armed bandits – three men and one woman – moving around in one of the *bashas*. However, Lieutenant Sibbald ordered his men to hold their fire in the hope that more bandits would show up. As the soldiers continued to lie in supposedly concealed positions, they suddenly realised that they could no longer see any of the four people in the *basha*. When they advanced into the camp, they found that the bandits had completely disappeared, leaving a revolver, some packs and a quantity of food, clothing and documents behind.

The moral of this tale would appear to have been: Four birds in the hand are worth two hundred in the bush!

The following morning, Swede Martin informed me that the major wanted me. I proceeded upstairs to the company office with mild trepidation. From behind his desk, Major Murray looked up at me through his habitual dark glasses.

'Now, Scurr,' he said. 'Do you play golf?'

'No, sir,' I replied.

'What?'

'No, I don't play, sir.'

'Oh!' The major looked perplexed and stared down at his desk for a moment. Then he asked: 'What's this about you writing a book?'

'Well, I'm hoping to write a book about Malaya one day,' I explained.

'Oh!' He looked at me very directly. 'Will I be in it?'

I hesitated. At that time, I was intending to create a novel

196

based upon my experiences and presumed that it would very likely contain a fictitious 'mad major', but I did not consider it wise to say so.

'I don't know who'll be in it, sir,' I said cautiously.

'I hope you're taking notes,' he responded keenly.

'Oh yes, sir, I am,' I replied.

'Good.' He nodded. 'All right. That's all.'

That night, I went into town with Phil Cox (former 'X' Cadre companion in Bordon, now Company Pay Clerk) and Yong, our Chinese Civil Liaison Officer. Yong was very friendly with Phil and one or two others from the company, all of whom he had introduced to his wife in Kulim. On this occasion, Yong was very insistent that he wanted to see some weird film about spacemen, so I told Phil to go with him and then went alone to the other cinema to see a new Errol Flynn western called *Montana*.

Serjeant Hutchinson left us to go home just prior to my next duffy with 8 Platoon. This left the platoon without a serjeant, a situation which continued for a few months. In the meantime, a former NCO of the Durham Light Infantry who had joined the company during retraining, Corporal Hudspeth, seemed to rise to ascendancy. Due to the pockmarks on his cheeks and jaw, Hudspeth was unkindly nicknamed 'Cave-face' by the men. Although perhaps a little abrupt in manner and not always too bright, Hudspeth was a good organiser and I rather liked him.

On Monday night, 23 October, 8 Platoon was briefed by Mr Crisp for an operation on which Eric and I would be going together. An informer was going to lead us to a place where the bandits were being supplied with food. It sounded quite promising. Present at the briefing were several young chaps from a new draft for whom this would be their first operation.

We left at 6.15 on Tuesday morning, the 24th. Our transport dropped us on a pretty wide track in the Anak Kulim area. Eric and I marched with the rear section, taking turns at carrying the '68' set. Accompanying the platoon were an English police officer and a Malay jungle squad.

We eventually halted in some sparse woodlands and took off our packs. Four riflemen, Eric and myself, under the command of an NCO, were left to guard the packs – much to my disgust – while the rest pushed on. The NCO was a very nice chap whom I had known for some time but – for reasons which will soon become evident – I do not intend to name him but will refer to him throughout as 'the lance corporal.'

To minimise the spreading of the news that troops were in the area, we stopped and detained several Malays and Chinese who came along the track. Then, at about 1 p.m., there was a sudden rattle of firing in the hills further up the track and we knew that the platoon had hit something.

We now allowed the detained women to return to their homes, and also one of the men. Soon, this man came back with all of his family, carrying their belongings, which didn't amount to more than a few bundles. He began to load these belongings in a basket on the back of a bicycle that he had left with us. We asked where he was going and understood from his gesticulations that the shooting had scared them, so they were leaving their home. For the time being, we decided to hold them and indicated that they should squat down, which they did without a murmur. They were soon joined by another rubber-tapper family, who came along the track with their hands up and their eyes wide with fear. The children were very small but seemed to react to the unease of their parents. It was very sad to see them standing on the muddy track with their little hands high above their heads and their frightened eyes darting uncertainly between us and their parents. However, when we smiled at them and indicated that they should drop their hands, their faces relaxed into broad grins and the family quickly squatted in the grass beside the track, all looking very relieved.

The lance corporal then did a bit of doctoring with his 'J' pack. First of all, one of the mothers showed him a cut on her child's arm and the lance corporal put some iodine on it. Then the other mother came forward and indicated that

198

one of her children had a stomach upset, for which 'Doctor' Lance Corporal prescribed and supplied an appropriate pill.

During all of this time, we were all wondering what the platoon had encountered. It had sounded like a heavy, though short, exchange of fire. We wondered if there had been any casualties. I felt very aggrieved that I had been left behind and the lance corporal felt the same.

'I could punch Crisp on the nose for leaving me here,' he declared. 'Another opportunity missed. I'd give anything to kill a bandit!'

An hour or so later, the platoon returned. We soon learned that as our chaps had been ascending a hill, they saw four bandits running away. Immediately, Mr Crisp, the police officer, Ginger Thompson, his mate Smith and one or two others up front all blazed away at the fleeing bandits with their carbines and Sten guns. One of the bandits stumbled as though he had been hit. He also dropped his revolver, and his tracks, from there, looked as though he'd dragged his foot. Some of our chaps said that the bandits fired a short burst back but Mr Crisp wasn't certain. The platoon then found a small camp for about 15 men cleverly concealed on the side of the hill. In addition to the revolver, some packs, clothing (including some for a woman), food-stuffs and documents were recovered.

Eric and I now set up our wireless and got through to Kulim pretty clearly. I felt quite delighted, transmitting the message to Arthur: 'Shots exchanged with figures four bandits. I say again. Shots exchanged with figures four bandits . . .'

After we had eaten our conner, we once more shouldered our loads and all moved on in the direction of the bandit camp. We proceeded up a narrow, boulder-strewn valley. The trees and shrubs on both sides seemed to be full of dark shadows and everything was exceptionally still and quiet. There was something really malevolent about that valley.

Even as that thought was forming in my mind, Eric said

199

to me quietly: 'I don't like this place, Jock. It gives me the creeps!'

Mr Crisp now called a halt and announced that we would lay four night ambushes in the area: one on the main track that we had just ascended; one at the bandit camp; one at some *bashas* nearby that the bandits were probably also using; and one at a *basha* on the ridge where a woman and some small children lived. Aware of the lance corporal's disappointment at being left out of the earlier excitement, Mr Crisp said to him: 'All right, Corporal ... I'll let you have your choice of ambush position.'

'The camp!' the lance corporal exclaimed eagerly.

So, it was settled. Corporal Hudspeth and the lance corporal's section headed for the camp, while the two remaining sections were allocated the *bashas* and the main track for ambush. Mr Crisp said that he would take the single *basha* on the ridge and that Eric and I and Yong, the CLO, should go with him. The Chinese woman who resided in this *basha* claimed that she knew nothing of the bandit camp a couple of hundred yards away. However, she had stacks of rice and quite a bit of cash and was obviously a food supplier. The police officer and his jungle squad now departed, taking the arrested woman and her children with them.

By nightfall, everyone was in position at the four ambush locations. Mr Crisp, Yong, Eric and I kipped inside the *basha* on the hard floor, each taking turns on stag, seated on the doorstep, ready to alert the others at any sight or sound of the enemy. At intervals during the night, the eerie and unusual silence which seemed to pervade that valley was disturbed by the sudden explosions of two hand-grenades, two or three bursts of Sten gun fire and a couple of rifle shots. The noise made by the grenades exploding was terribly loud and seemed to resound throughout the valley. At the various times of these detonations and shootings, we all stood to, crouching outside the *basha* and peering into the pitch-darkness around us with our weapons held at the ready. There was obviously some kind of sporadic activity at one or more of the other positions. Beyond that, we had no notion of what might be happening.

Next morning, Wednesday the 25th, the platoon rendez-voused at our position. First to arrive were the men from the ambush position covering the main track. One of them was a Bren gunner, 'Matt' Busby, who had lately been growing very friendly towards Eric and me. Looking rather weary, Matt shook his head as he approached us. 'This trigger-happy new draft!' he complained. He then went on to tell us that one of the new lads had fired his Sten at shadows and another had similarly fired his rifle twice. The latter had been running to and fro all night, saying that he could see bandits all around them. Lance Corporal Frank Keenan was in line next to this young soldier. Frank asked him what he was shooting at. The lad replied that he could see bandits down below them but Frank was unable to see anyone.

Soon after my chat with Matt, a party arrived from the position at the bandit camp. I was quickly aware that all of them seemed to be strained and talking in hushed tones. Unable to contain my curiosity, I approached a rifleman called 'Ches' Allen and said to him: 'Listen! What's all this about?'

Ches said to me quietly: 'Come over here and I'll tell you.' After we'd moved a little way up the hill slope, he then told me: 'It's Don Hicks. He was shot last night at the camp.' He then named 'the lance corporal' as the man who'd done the shooting.

Don Hicks was a very nice, quiet sort of lad who was well liked by everyone who knew him.

I bit my lip. 'Is he badly hurt?' I asked.

'He's dead,' Ches replied.

I felt quite shaken but listened intently as Ches explained that bandits, flashing torches, had been seen moving from tree to tree around the ambush position at the camp and that grenades had been thrown at them. The lance corporal had then spotted or heard someone apparently coming up the track towards him in the darkness and had opened fire with his Sten gun. That 'someone' had been Hicks.

After receiving this sad news, I returned down the slope and saw the lance corporal sitting alone on a slab of rock. His eyes were very red and he looked utterly miserable. We all felt very sorry for him, as well as for Hicks.

Shortly after that, Eric and I set up our wireless on the hill slope out of earshot of the others. I made contact with Kulim and passed Mr Crisp's message to Arthur: 'Private Hicks killed by own troops during the night. Over.'

Arthur's voice sounded shocked as he replied: 'I read back – Private Hicks killed by own troops during the night. Is this correct? Over.'

I confirmed that it was. Arthur requested that I hold and shortly, Major Murray came on the air and asked to speak to Mr Crisp. When Mr Crisp had given brief details of the incident, the major said: 'This is a terrible thing! Make sure it doesn't happen again! Over.'

Mr Crisp looked at me and shook his head in disgust. We then arranged for transport to be sent to collect Hicks' body. After the transmission was completed, Mr Crisp handed me back his headphones and quoted the Major's words contemptuously: 'Make sure it doesn't happen again!' I had to agree that it was a very thoughtless remark.

Meanwhile, Lance Corporals Keenan and Short and one other had gone up the hill to the camp and carried Hicks' body down to the main track. Then, after breakfast, Corporal Hudspeth, Frank Keenan and a small party carrying Hicks' body on an improvised stretcher set out to meet the transport. A couple of patrols also went out from our position on the ridge. The lance corporal, looking very strained and drawn, quietly insisted that he wished to go out on patrol as normal.

The valley now seemed even more sinister than it had the day before. Hicks' death must have had a bad effect on our nerves as we found ourselves jumping at the slightest sound.

While awaiting the return of the patrols, those of us remaining were sitting around for the most part in glum silence.

Looking at our faces prompted Corporal Huddleston to exclaim: 'Cheer up, you blokes, for God's sake! Accidents happen. You're all sitting there looking as though the world had come to an end!'

Well, it had come to an end for Don Hicks. It just didn't seem fair. We didn't like it one bit.

After tiffen, the platoon moved back down the valley to the spot where we had guarded the packs on the previous day, and made base in a large, deserted *basha* nearby. Towards dusk, Mr Crisp left with one section to lay another ambush at the bandit camp. The remainder of us all kipped down inside the *basha*, with stag positions at the two opposite windows. It seemed a good idea to keep close together and hopefully avoid accidents, but as someone pointed out to me, a couple of grenades through the windows could have finished off the lot of us.

In the morning, Thursday the 26th, Mr Crisp's section returned, having had an eventless night. Some patrols went out for a short while – I went with one of them – but nothing was found other than a camp that was about two years old. After tiffen, we all set off back to the road at a fast pace. Contrary to normal practice, everyone made plenty of noise, as we had been told over the wireless that an 'A' Company patrol was on its way in through the same area and we didn't want to risk having a scrap with them. In fact, we met the 'A' Company patrol just before we reached the road. The transport that was bringing some of our company back from Hicks' funeral at Taiping cemetery picked us up and took us back to camp.

When I entered the Signals billet, Arthur asked me: 'What happened then, Jock?'

I explained briefly that the lance corporal had accidentally shot Hicks.

'Yes,' said Arthur, 'but what about the boot lace?'

'What boot lace?' I asked.

'Well, they're all saying that there was a boot lace tied round Hicks' neck.'

This was news to me but I was soon to hear it mentioned again. When the patrol had been dismissed, we had all been told to report back to Corporal Hudspeth for an ammo check. I now took my bandolier of ammunition and walked over to 8 Platoon's lines. As I entered Corporal Hudspeth's tent, Mr Crisp was just inside the flap, on the point of leaving. I heard Mr Crisp say: 'And what about the boot lace?'

Hudspeth answered grimly: 'It was still round his neck.'

This was the beginning of a controversy which for me and numerous others was never satisfactorily resolved. It now seemed that either before or after Hicks had been accidentally shot, he may also have been strangled. There were numerous theories as to how this could have occurred, including one put to Second Lieutenant Wride by an officer of the Malayan Police to the effect that Hicks had been murdered by another British soldier! This preposterous suggestion can, however, be discounted, as can the more feasible theory – favoured by Matt Busby and myself at the time – that Hicks had been overpowered and strangled by bandits who then 'walked' the body in front of them as a shield, hoping to get close enough to the section's positions to lob in grenades.

Following our return from the operation, a board of enquiry into the death was held with Major Doyle – at that time HQ Company Commander – as chairman. The autopsy revealed that death was due to a gunshot wound to the chest. A bullet had deflected from a bone in Hicks' right shoulder, passed down through his lung and lodged in his heart. A length of thin cord – generally referred to as a 'boot lace' – had been knotted and drawn tightly round Hicks' neck, causing a groove in his flesh but not breaking the skin. The boot lace had been tightly drawn just before or just after death, but it was not possible to determine which, and it had not caused asphyxiation. It was also found that a bone in the neck had been fractured with no apparent indication of cause.

A witness at the enquiry stated that Hicks' shirt had been buttoned up to the neck and the collar turned up. Therefore, it was suggested that Hicks may have tied the boot lace round the closed collar in order to exclude insects. Then, as he moved up the track or when he was shot, the lace may have got caught in something which pulled it tight around his neck. While it cannot be ruled out beyond all possible doubt, this explanation appears to me highly unlikely, even absurd. Although our theories varied, most of us remained convinced that something sinister had happened to Hicks prior to being shot.

Many months later, Lieutenant Green of 'D' Company, quite unprompted, said to me: 'I'd like to know what happened to that chap in "C" Company.' I was unable to give Mr Green a definite answer to his question at that time, nor can I supply one now. However, combining the information that I noted in my journal in 1950 with that gleaned from official records and from correspondence with John Crisp and Frank Keenan in 1990, I feel able to present a brief account of what seems to me most likely to have occurred.

When Corporal Hudspeth and the lance corporal had laid their ambush at the bandit camp at dusk on that Tuesday, 24 October, for some reason Privates Hicks and Powell had been allotted a position forward of the rest of the section. Late into the night, an unknown number of bandits approached the camp and, over a considerable period, endeavoured to draw the section's fire by flashing torches and making tapping sounds on the tree trunks. Eventually, Corporal Hudspeth responded by throwing two hand-grenades. It is possible that these grenades exploded fairly close to where Hicks and Powell were positioned and that this prompted Hicks to move. Whatever the reason, Hicks left – or was separated from – Powell and disappeared into the darkness. Going up the track, it seems likely he was set upon by a bandit, who looped a boot lace (or similar length of cord) around his neck and drew the knot tight. Being a hefty lad, Hicks possibly managed to pull away from his assailant. At that moment, the lance corporal became aware of movement on the track and, thinking that the bandits were going to rush the section's positions, opened fire with his Sten gun, discharging two bursts which struck Hicks in the knee and shoulder. As previously explained, a bullet deflected from a bone and pierced his heart.

The disbelief and horror experienced by the lance corporal when he discovered lying on the track, not the body of an enemy, but that of Don Hicks, can be imagined. At that time, it was supposed only that Hicks had been shot. The following morning, Mr Crisp wished to get the body away quickly and did not look at it closely. However, when Corporal Hudspeth, Frank Keenan and a small party were given the job of carrying the body down the main track to meet transport from Kulim, they noticed a thin length of cord, which they described as a jungle boot lace, knotted tightly round the dead man's neck. Next day, when the platoon returned to Kulim camp from the operation, Mr Wride promptly asked Mr Crisp about the cord around Hicks' neck. This was the first that Mr Crisp had heard of it, just as I learned of it for the first time when questioned by Arthur Greenacre.

I have not mentioned Don Hicks earlier in this book, simply because he was someone I merely saw around but never got to know personally. The lance corporal who shot him, on the other hand, I knew quite well. Always pleasant and with a ready smile, he was a first-rate chap and a good NCO. It took him a while to get over the tragedy but he eventually pulled through.

Hicks' death really brought home to me that we weren't playing a game but were, in fact, in a situation of constantly lurking danger. From that time on, I was more wary on operations during the hours of darkness, tending to regularly glance over my shoulder when on stag. Eric told me that the incident had the same effect upon him.

A new serjeant now arrived in the company to replace the departed Serjeant Hutchinson, namely Serjeant Baddeley, formerly the Battalion Provost Serjeant. Regrettably, he remained with us but a few days.

On Wednesday afternoon, 1 November, a soldier was preparing a Bren gun inside the arms *kote* (armoury) for going on a motor convoy escort duty. The Bren was accidentally discharged, sending a shot through the arms *kote* door. Unfortunately, Serjeant Baddeley was standing just outside the door at the time and the bullet struck him in the thigh. When I, along with others, rushed outside on hearing the shot, Serjeant Baddeley was lying on his back with an arc of blood squirting up in the air from the hole in his thigh. Someone gave him a cigarette while another man ran shouting for the MO. After emergency treatment, the serjeant was rushed off to Taiping Military Hospital.

Three weeks later, on Tuesday the 21st, Serjeant Baddeley died. He was buried in Taiping cemetery the following day.

On Saturday, 4 November, an Indian barber visited the company. He was much in demand and continued to work well into the night, plying his trade in the canteen. Well-oiled on Tiger beer, Private Roy 'Nobby' Clarke – a tall, good-looking Canadian – requested that the barber should cut off all of his hair and shave his head until he was completely bald. On seeing this carried out, several other drunks eagerly demanded the same treatment, one after another, much to the barber's consternation. Rather original was Private Bob Lightfoot, who instructed the barber to leave a scalp-lock across the top of his otherwise shorn head in the style of a Mohawk Indian! The bald-pated drunks seemed to think the whole thing was hilarious – which it was. They then provided themselves and the rest of us with further entertainment by tearing up each other's shirts.

When these chaps woke up sober next morning and looked in the mirror, they were far from pleased and all came to breakfast wearing their jungle hats. Later that day, Serjeant Thomas of 'A' Company paid a visit to our camp.

While standing in the MT park, he heard a voice call: 'Look what we caught out in the jungle, Fred!' Turning his head, Serjeant Thomas was surprised and amused to see Serjeant Taggy Bell emerge from an adjacent tent, pulling on a rope which turned out to be around the neck of a big, brawny figure, clad only in a loin-cloth (towel), with a Mohawk scalp-lock standing up like a brush on top of his shaved head!

On Wednesday morning, 8 November, I attended a briefing for an operation. 8 Platoon was going to return to an area of the Bongsu Forest Reserve where it had recently found a small, abandoned camp. The platoon was then going to search for a track nearby that it was believed might be used by food suppliers en route to a larger camp, and ambush the track that night.

We left at 1.30 p.m. and were eventually dropped off by our transport at a track which we followed through pretty open country to the edge of the jungle. Mr Crisp then took out a small patrol to reconnoitre. After his return, Mr Crisp led the whole platoon to a track into the jungle that his patrol had found. It was a well-cleared track with large ferns forming a natural archway overhead. When we reached a point where another track led off to the left, Mr Crisp decided that we should lay our ambush here, along the edge of the main track with the number one stop – a Bren gun – covering the track junction.

The platoon was divided into groups of three. I was with a Sten gunner and the medical orderly. Each of us took a turn at staying awake and watching the track, doing two hours on and four off. As always, the screaming of monkeys and other jungle noises made the pitch-darkness more frightening. However, my main headache was the medical orderly. He kept hearing things – such as our own lads moving in the next position in the line! – and repeatedly woke me up to report it. Even when I was doing stag and he was supposed to be sleeping, he kept grabbing my knee and declaring in considerable alarm that there was someone coming up the track. I continually tried to reassure him and told him to relax and go to sleep – all to no avail. The poor chap was one of the RAMC personnel from the MRS who did not normally go out in the jungle.

After an otherwise eventless night, we moved on up the track at first light. We halted for a short while, during which I endeavoured to set up my wireless in a hopeless tangle of jungle. I ended up with Steve, our Tamil Civil Liaison Officer, holding a branch up in the air with the near end of the wire aerial tied to it. Even so, I managed to get through to Kulim with comparatively clear reception. Mr Crisp decided against having breakfast and when I'd finished taking down my aerial, feeling pretty weary, I found the rest of the platoon with packs on backs, waiting to move on.

Our route lay through dense and difficult country, crossing numerous hills. With my set on my back, I found the march very fatiguing. Eventually, we arrived out of the jungle into rubber, which terminated at a river. We waded this river up to our knees and carried on through open *lallang*, passing a couple of tin mines, and finally reached Karangan on the main road, where we halted. And was I glad!

We brewed up while waiting for our transport, which duly arrived about noon and took us back to camp. At this time, I was being treated for a small amount of tinea round the crotch but was pleased to find that my foot-rot had completely gone.

On Friday morning, the 10th, half of 8 Platoon was rushed out to a spot on the road to Pelam Estate where bandits had been reported. It seemed that an estate manager had ridden his motorbike through a bandit ambush just before our battalion MO was due to drive up that stretch of road. Our lads soon returned, however, having found no further signs of the enemy.

During this period at Kulim, I was rostered for guard duty approximately one night in eight. To lessen the frequency of guard duties for NCOs, signallers were performing the function of i/c reliefs, which entailed remaining

209

awake in the guard tent and waking up the members of the guard when it was their turn to go on stag.

On the night of Saturday the 11th, I found myself once more on guard. Just after 2.30 a.m., I was sitting quietly at the table in the guard tent when I became aware of a figure standing in the darkness outside. Then I heard Major Murray's voice calling the Guard Commander: 'Corporal!'

'Corporal Huddleston's asleep, sir,' I called out.

'Who's that?' the major asked hazily, obviously drunk as always.

'Private Scurr, sir,' I answered.

'Oh.' Major Murray stumbled into the tent. I could hardly believe it was real. There was the major at half-past two in the morning, staggering around in his pyjamas with a bag of golf clubs slung over his shoulder! He just stood before me now, swaying to and fro and focusing his eyes upon me. 'Oh, it's you, Scurr,' he said, slurring the words. He seemed about to say something else, then suddenly turned and staggered outside, his golf clubs clacking together as he did so.

'Good night, sir,' I called after him.

'What?' He hesitated. 'Oh – good night.'

I watched the major disappear into the darkness, heading back towards the officers' mess, and heaved a sigh of relief that his visit had been brief. At that time, I gave him little credit for being a war hero, an experienced pilot and a fine pianist with a great love for music. I only saw him as a nutter with an alcohol problem whose proximity always made me feel uncomfortable.

The following Wednesday, the 15th, I made a brief trip to HQ Company at Sungei Patani to collect a new '68' set. Cousin John, I found, had been promoted to lance corporal and still seemed content with his lot in the QMs. When Corporal Bummer Young saw me, he asked me two questions: 'What company are you from?' and 'Are you staying the night?' – meaning that if I was, I'd be put on guard! I was happy to tell him that I would shortly be making the return journey to Kulim.

Malaya during the years 1947–51, the 2nd/1st KOYLI upheld the long established
utation of the British Light Infantry rifleman.

nmunist terrorists were ruthless, cruel and murderous, yet those who surrendered
were captured could prove to be intelligent and even amiable. (Imperial War
seum)

The principal enemy was always the jungle – dense, humid, debilitating and emana
decay and an aura of lurking death.

Men of 11 Platoon, 'D' Company, prior to the highly successful action at Karan
on 11 January 1949. Five of the seven combatants are shown here. Standing – 1st
Corporal Battersby; 3rd left, Rowbottom; 4th left, Abernathy; 1st right, Serje
Chadwick. Crouching – 2nd right, Paris.

Company being conveyed by train to Alor Star in July 1949, a few days before
bushing opium smugglers on the Thai border.

YLI wives and other civilian and service personnel in Western Road cemetery,
nang, attending the funeral of four 'B' Company soldiers who were killed in an
bush on the Kroh–Klian Intan road on 3 December 1949.

Elephants used to carry supplies for 'C' Company during a jungle operation in Up Perak, 9–23 December 1949.

The author bound for Malaya aboard the troopship *Devonshire* in February 1950.

...yout of jungle equipment, medications, rations and weaponry. Shown in the ...reground are the .303 Lee Enfield No.5 rifle, the Australian 9-mm Owen sub-...chine gun and the American .30 M2 automatic carbine. (Imperial War Museum)

... Company soldiers firing a salute in Batu Gajah cemetery on 11 June 1950 at the ...eral of six men killed in an ambush at Ampang the previous day. Brothers-in-arms ...the 4th Hussars can be seen (centre) waiting to lay wreaths.

Charles 'Chas' Schaverien – a close friend of the author's in the Signal Platoon – w posted to 'B' Company at Batu Gajah in June 1950 but joined the author in ' Company at Serdang eight months later.

Serjeant Ken Hutchinson of 8 Platoon in his ambush position in the jungle on June 1950, during the author's first active operation.

orporal Arthur Greenacre (left) and the author at 'C' Company's operational base
mp on 26 June 1950.

e Costello, a former tramp and a great character, poses with his Bren gun at the
ate Mental Home, Tanjong Rambutan, in June 1950. Joe later served with the
alayan Scouts (SAS).

Author's view of 'C' Company's march up the Sungei Soh on 22 July 1950, shor before locating a bandit camp. Arthur Greenacre, carrying his No.68 wireless set, preceded by Bren gunner Frank Keenan.

'A' Company parading on the sports field at Minden Barracks, Penang, on 1 Augu 1950 – Minden Day. Serjeant Fred Thomas (front, facing right) and Second Lieute ant Peter Sibbald (foremost officer – eventually to become a major general) had bo assisted with training the author's draft.

cond Lieutenants David Wride (left) and John Crisp, with Major Murray's car, in e entrance to 'C' Company's base at Kulim in October 1950.

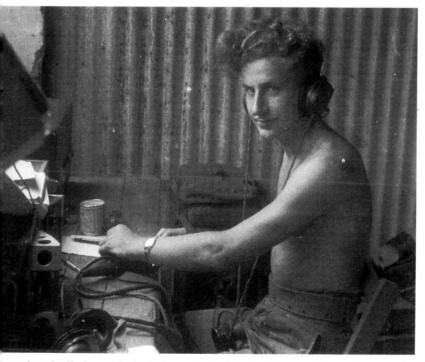

e author, badly in need of a haircut, in the Signals billet at Kulim, photographed a public relations officer on 11 October 1950.

Men of 8 Platoon waiting for transport after carrying the body of Donald Hicks
the road from the ambush position at Anak Kulim on 25 October 1950. Seated fro
right – Corporal Hudspeth, Frank Keenan and Joe Short.

John Kitchen – the author's cousin – with pet monkey 'Jacko' at Battalion H
Sungei Patani, in November 1950.

Platoon soldiers (left to right) Stan Swalwell, Brodie, Matt Busby and Steve – a
[T]amil Civil Liaison Officer – in the Bongsu Forest Reserve, late in 1950. (Imperial
[W]ar Museum)

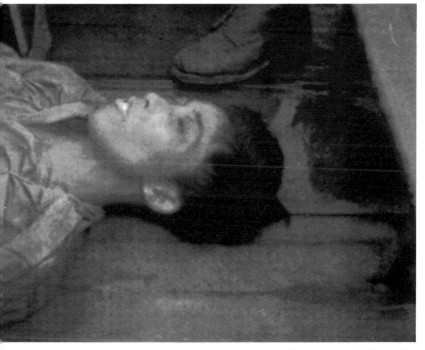

[C]ommunist bandit killed by 8 Platoon in an action near Junjong on 23 November
[19]50. He was a young man, much like ourselves.

8 Platoon departing for Junjong on 27 November 1950 to investigate an alleged wh
flag of surrender. The author, with crossed kukris insignia on his sleeve, is imme
ately followed by Ginger Thompson, Leading Scout.

Major Murray (crouching right) and Arthur Greenacre (shirtless) with Malay
Police officers on the padang (green) at Bukit Mertajam, in wireless contact with t
author who was climbing the adjacent mountain with a police jungle squad on
November 1950.

Bren gunner Donald 'Matt' Busby – a close pal of the author's – fondly displaying a coloured portrait of his sweetheart, Enid, at Kulim in December 1950.

board HMS *Hart* bound for Sungei Perlis on 15 December 1950. Author at foot stairway, looking towards the camera, with Allan Knight to his left. Arthur eenacre and Ray 'Hank' Hancock are seated together, second and third from right.

Men of 9 Platoon burning the *bashas* of a bandit camp during an operation in Gunong Inas Forest Reserve on 14 January 1951.

Lance Corporal Jim Whitehead of 'B' Company (previously of 'A') – a very popu
soldier in the battalion – who was killed in action at Pelam Estate on 26 January 1⁹
during an attack on a bandit camp.

e author at Serdang, after returning from a patrol in March 1951. He is wearing
uthorised ammunition pouches on his belt with an issued 1944 pattern pouch
g on his left hip, and has fitted a personal adaptation to his rifle sling.

ate Charles Walker (left) with two others from 'B' Company. Charlie had served
the author during basic and jungle training, and was tragically killed in an
ush at Kejai on 20 May 1951.

Signaller Eric Hann and the author became good friends in 'C' Company towards end of 1950 and were reunited in 'D' Company at Kulim in June 1951. Eric is se here with pet dog, 'Spunker'.

In July 1951, the 1st KOYLI completed its last patrols of the jungles and rubl estates of North Malaya, and the following month sailed for home, leaving comrades buried in Malayan soil. (Imperial War Museum)

13

*The Bongsu Forest Reserve
17–19 November 1950*

The jungle which the British Army patrolled in Malaya had been in existence for a hundred million years and ranked amongst the toughest terrains to traverse in the entire world.

It has been claimed that the strain, enervation, tension and depression of military operations in the Malayan jungle were so severe that some young soldiers committed suicide while others 'just died'. I have to say that I personally never knew of any such cases. However, I did observe men who seemed to be close to breaking point and eventually I appeared to approach that vicinity myself, as will be related in due course.

The simple, matter-of-fact entries in my journal tend to understate the many physical hardships and mental stresses experienced on jungle operations. Phrases such as 'I found the march very fatiguing', or 'I was absolutely all in' do not adequately convey the gruelling rigours that I and my fellow soldiers had to endure.

Within two months of my return from Malaya, I wrote an account of a jungle trek while the details were still fresh in my memory. This description was constructed from my recollections of a particular operation in the Bongsu Forest Reserve which took place at the time that we have now reached in my story. In order to present the reader with a more vivid picture of a soldier's life in the jungle, I shall here integrate that detailed account with my journal's description of the operation.

On the morning of Friday, 17 November, I once more set out with 8 Platoon to comb an area in the west of the Bongsu for the suspected large camp of the Communists' 8th (Kedah) Regiment. Transport dropped us off at a small kampong, from where we first searched an expanse of rubber in Merah Estate. We eventually paused amongst the rubber trees at the foot of a hill slope while Second Lieutenant 'Killer' Crisp studied his map.

The fringes of the Bongsu were visible at the top of the slope. With a wave of his hand, Mr Crisp indicated to the two scouts, Privates Thompson and Smith, that they should carry on straight up. On reaching the top, the scouts followed the jungle edge along the ridge for a short way until they came to a gap in the thick scrub which indicated the beginning of a track. They pointed this out to Mr Crisp and entered the Bongsu. In single file and holding our weapons at the ready, the rest of us followed.

Overhead the dense, matted foliage shut out the sun and the sky while the jungle seemed to close round us as though swallowing us up. With every step, our boots sank into the compressed and rotting leaf mould underfoot. The atmosphere was damp and decaying and small rustlings in the undergrowth were all that disturbed the vast silence. All around us in the deep gloom lay a rugged miscellany of dull shades of green and brown, formed by the interwoven tangle of giant, vine-covered tree trunks up to 200 feet in height, sturdy young saplings and large clumps of attap palms and thorn scrub. The trees and undergrowth were visibly crawling with numerous varieties of ants, beetles and insects of every description.

The track that we were following was well enough cleared to confirm previous passage of human beings. Only occasionally did Ginger Thompson, the leading scout, have to draw his matchet to chop away an obstructing branch or trailing vine. On reaching the other side of the hill, we made a gradual descent. As I neared the bottom I could see the men ahead of me already starting to climb the next hill.

This slope turned out to be exceptionally steep. I scrambled up as best I could, grasping branches and roots to heave myself upwards. The sweat ran from my pores, soaking my shirt and slacks more and more as the climb continued. My shoulders and back ached beneath the 40-odd pounds of my '68' set, augmented by the weight of my other loaded gear, while the shoulder-straps of the harness dug painfully into my flesh. I was, of course, further weighed down by my rifle, ammunition and standard infantry equipment. In total, my burden weighed about 64 pounds.

Reaching the top, the scouts and Mr Crisp walked slowly up the slight rise of the ridge to regain their breath and then increased the pace again. As always, this meant that when those of us who were in the rear section were approaching the summit, we had no choice but to keep going without slackening our speed in order not to lose contact with those in front.

The descent from this hill proved as steep and difficult as the ascent had been. I carefully selected my footholds and with every step down, my wireless jolted heavily on my back. At some points, I would lower myself so far while clinging to a sapling, then let go and slither swiftly down, halting my momentum by catching hold of the next tree.

Gaining the foot of this hill brought no respite to our labours. We followed the track straight up through the thick bracken of the slope opposite. My knees were now growing decidedly weak from the prolonged climbing and my lungs gasped for breath as I struggled on upwards, using anything I could grasp to pull myself up, even putting my trust in clumps of grass to support my weight. Perspiration running into my eyes made them sting and blurred my vision. Then, to my great relief the summit was finally conquered and the 'packs off' signal was passed back along the line.

I leaned my '68' set against a moss-covered tree and eased the carrying straps off my shoulders. I then lowered the set to the ground and flopped down beside it. All along the track, the men of the platoon were sprawled on their backs, breathing hard but otherwise silent. After a few minutes, I sat up and leaned my back against a tree. I glanced at the little beads of perspiration standing out all over my forearms. My shirt and slacks were soaking wet and visibly steaming, and the uncomfortable sensation of streams of sweat running down my chest and back made me want to pull my clothes away from my body.

After unscrewing the cap of my water bottle, I drank three mouthfuls, resisting the temptation to take more. Just then, a small, brown, worm-like creature crawling up my left jungle boot caught my eye. I picked up a piece of twig and knocked the leech off my boot. Then I dealt similarly with another one crawling up my thigh. I noticed that other men along the track had also become leech-conscious, brushing their small assailants off their boots and clothing or burning them off with lighted cigarettes if they were firmly dug into flesh and already sucking blood or otherwise clinging on with their suckers.

All too soon the platoon formed up and moved on again. For some time we followed the ridge, brushing aside the long, drooping fronds of the attap palms. Sudden crashing sounds in the overhead foliage high to our right announced the rapid passage of half a dozen little grey monkeys, leaping from tree to tree. Our route continued downhill, then up a more gradual slope of bracken and rhododendron scrub, down the other side and then straight up a hill that seemed steeper than ever. With my lungs heaving painfully, my leg muscles aching and my knees wobbling as though about to collapse beneath me, I was dismayed to see that above me, men were still climbing with no sign of the top.

The other men, particularly the Bren gunners, were also heavily laden. Each man's pack contained several tins of 'C' rations in addition to his personal gear. On succeeding days, as the rations were used up, these packs would grow lighter. My burden, however – the '68' set and gear – always weighed the same. It was customary on operations for riflemen periodically to give the signaller a break by carrying his set for a while, particularly on later days when their packs were light. Although I sometimes received offers of

214

this nature, I always refused them (during this period) and insisted on carrying the '68' set myself at all times. This might appear quite mad – and probably was – but to me it had become a matter of pride and of proving something to myself.

It may seem hard to understand, but at this time I derived a strange satisfaction out of struggling on, weighed down in a state of sheer exhaustion and even teetering on the verge of collapse. In accord with the ancient Christian ethic of redemption through suffering, I believed that withstanding this continual, gruelling punishment would more than adequately compensate for every time I had given a poor performance on the sports field during my schooldays, every time my shy manner had given rise to mockery and every time I had dreaded bullies as a child. I believed that in the jungle I was being cleansed of all my previous failures to 'measure up' and that afterwards I would be able to return home with my head held high, completely redeemed, and that people would respect me for what I'd been through.

I was 19 years old and very naive, but that is what I truly believed at that time.

On 'jelly' legs, I at last reached the top of the hill and followed on down the other side. I could hear the gurgle of a swirling river below. Staggering down through the gigantic fronds of nipah palms which overhung the river's muddy bank, I was grateful to find that Mr Crisp had decided to halt here for tiffen.

Corporal 'Cave-face' Hudspeth now addressed us: 'All right. Packs off, yous blokes. Anybody in Number One Section with cheese or cake in your packs, get it out. We're not having a brew-up' – he was interrupted here by a few quiet moans – 'and don't start whining, yous blokes! We haven't got time for a brew. Mr Crisp wants to push on as soon as we can. So you'll drink water and like it!'

Our NCOs posted sentries and urged the rest of us to spread out along the bank so as not to present a bunched-up target for any enemy that might appear. We were each handed out small portions of cheese and cake, which we ate ravenously, washing them down with mouthfuls of water from our water bottles.

Lance Corporal Frank Keenan, whom I'd known since I'd joined the company at Tanjong Rambutan, was sitting on a rock next to me. 'Killer really loves those bloody hills,' he said to me. 'We're all knackered! You'd think the bastard could at least let us have a brew-up.'

'Yes,' I agreed. 'I can tell you one thing, Frank – if he had to carry my set, he'd soon slow the pace down a bit.'

In fact, I really respected Mr Crisp and I'm sure Frank did too, but I suppose that grumbling just made us feel better. After our frugal meal, we refilled our water bottles from the river. I always used to faithfully insert my issued sterilisation tablets, although I had the impression that most of the lads didn't bother.

The word soon came to put our equipment on and form up. Mr Crisp ordered the scouts to proceed upstream. The river water was knee-deep and felt very cold at first, but it had a refreshing effect upon our hot, sweating bodies and tired feet. Every so often we had to clamber over slippery granite boulders, while the moss-covered slabs below the surface proved a menace. Tripping and slipping under pressure from the strong current, one or two of the men fell headlong into the water and emerged with arms scraped and bleeding from the sharp-edged rocks. In addition to concentrating upon keeping our feet, we were ever aware that in the river we made a clear target for ambush. Consequently, we warily eyed the river banks for any signs of movement or disturbed foliage.

After a while, the scouts spotted a track on the right bank and Mr Crisp indicated that they should follow it. As I emerged from the river to become once more submerged in a tangle of trees and scrub, I was not surprised to see that our route again proceeded uphill. The jungle grew thicker as we progressed and the scouts frequently had to employ their matchets to chop through branches and linea creepers which barred our way.

216

At the foot of the second hill since leaving the river, my shoulder brushed against a rotted dead tree, dislodging upon myself a shower of vicious red ants. A series of stinging pains on my arms and neck was followed by more on my chest and back as my assailants crawled beneath my shirt and employed their pincers for all they were worth. I endeavoured to brush them off and beat myself about the body in a frenzy from the repeated anguishing bites. I hurried on, still being bitten and aware that men behind me were also now under attack.

My attention was soon diverted to the difficulties of our next climb. Owing to the density of the jungle, we found it necessary to continually squeeze between tree trunks and duck beneath low-hanging branches and festoons of rattan creepers as we ascended. The jagged thorns of trailing vines whisked the hats from our heads, ripped the sleeves of our shirts and raised little red beads of blood on our forearms where the barbs had hooked into our flesh. At the top, we found ourselves pushing our way through thick, rough ferns of our own height which bruised and scratched us as we passed.

We descended the other side of this hill and began to climb the next one. As I staggered and stumbled upwards, I could hear the agonised gasps of my winded lungs as I gulped down mouthfuls of the stale jungle air. The salt from the sweat that soaked my entire body stung my eyes and in the many cuts on my arms. I swore madly when, crawling beneath a low branch, my wireless set was caught upon it. I tugged violently and uselessly to free it. Then the man behind eased my set beneath the branch and I was able to continue upwards through the green tangle of scrub.

As I neared the crest, I began to falter in my steps and found myself briefly leaning against the trees as I passed them, trying to gain some respite from my pain and weariness. Desperately, I thought to myself: If Killer doesn't stop for a rest at the top of this hill, it'll be just impossible for me to go any further! However, there was no halt at the top and I kept going just the same.

217

On these operations, I learned that the limit to human endurance was far beyond my previous supposition. However much I told myself that my strength was completely drained, somehow I could always manage to keep one foot plodding in front of the other. Sometimes I found myself wickedly hoping that someone else would collapse so that we would be forced to stop. In fact, the number of occasions when men did collapse from heat exhaustion were surprisingly few.

Halfway up the next slope, after clambering weakly over a fallen tree-trunk, I was suddenly aware that the man in front of me was giving the 'packs off' signal. I managed to lower my set to the ground and sprawled out on my back at the side of the track. My heart was hammering and my chest continued to heave rapidly as I tried to regain my breath. At that moment, the habitual musty stench of decaying vegetation was quite nauseating. On both sides of me, the other men lay silent in their utter exhaustion. Continuous exertion in that stifling jungle oven had sapped every ounce of our energy.

As my breathing gradually slowed, I seemed to sink into a semi-coma. It was an utterly weak, light-headed, almost blissful sensation. Just to lie there on my back seemed like Heaven. I wished that I could lie like that for ever. I wished that my heart would simply stop beating so that I could just die and not have to get up on my feet again. That would solve everything as I no longer had the strength to stand up, let alone march.

After a few minutes, my thoughts grew more rational and I knew that somehow I would manage to stand up – and march! I sat up wearily and took four mouthfuls of water. I always drank as little as possible on the march because I had found that the more I drank, the more I wanted. In any case, water consumed with no guarantee of a refill was something I dreaded. I always needed the assurance that there was water left in my bottle if I needed it.

Further up the track, I saw a man with his head tilted back as he emptied the last contents of his water bottle down his throat. I thought to myself how foolish he was and that if he asked me for a drink from my bottle later, I would refuse him. We all started with full bottles. It was up to each man to conserve the precious liquid or do without. Even comradeship has its limit!

I now discovered a leech firmly dug into my left forearm. I lit a cigarette and pressed the burning tip onto the creature's back. It was several seconds before the leech released its hold, curled up and rolled off onto the ground. I applied pressure upon its bloated body with a twig until the skin burst and I saw my own red blood flow out of it. The little dark spot on my arm was bleeding freely, so I dabbed the wound with my handkerchief. Actually, I had disciplined myself never to smoke on operations but carried cigarettes and matches in my waterproof pouch merely as a means of 'de-leeching'.

Another bloodsucker was crawling up towards the top of my right jungle boot. It clung on all the firmer when I tried to brush it off with the twig. So I stopped and waited. Gradually, the narrow tip of the leech's body began to reach forward, feeling its way. The tip carefully came to rest and the remainder of the body arched up in a forward movement. Then, as the sucker at the rear released its hold to complete the step, I swiped with my twig and knocked the creature several feet away into the mouldering leaves. It wriggled there for a moment and then began to wend its way straight back towards me. I now picked the leech up on my twig and this time hurled it a good distance away into the brush. Though leeches were undoubtedly a curse – and in large numbers could be dangerous – there were times when I found them quite diverting. I certainly never hated them the way I did mosquitoes.

When we resumed our march, the pace slackened a little. We had all had more than enough, even sturdy Mr Crisp. Clambering and tripping over a profusion of entwined tree roots, our aching and blistered feet plodded on to the summit of the hill, took us gingerly down the reverse slope and were then gratefully cooled in the process of wading another river. On gaining the opposite bank, we followed the track a short way up the slope. Then, to our immense relief, Mr Crisp decided to make camp.

Packs were gladly discarded and, in many cases, shirts. We then set about chopping away the undergrowth with our matchets and soon cleared a considerable area. The men split into twos or threes to build bivouacs. Frameworks were constructed from chopped-down saplings or by merely stretching a bedding line (length of rope) between two trees, over which poncho capes were draped and secured with either string or jungle vine. On this occasion, I built a 'lean-to' *basha* with Mr Crisp, whose batman was absent due to sickness.

Once accommodation was organised, the men of the platoon handed in their tins of 'C' rations to Corporal Hudspeth, who began sorting the tins into piles for the number of meals that would be required during our stay at this patrolling base. Two men were making a fireplace with the aid of an entrenching tool and several large stones. Number Two Section was sent to chop wood for the fire while the men of Number One Section collected the brew cans and, careful to take their weapons with them, went down to the river for water.

Feeling very content as always that I had managed once more to stay on my admittedly tender feet during the arduous march, I slung my wire aerial across the clearing between two trees and set up my wireless for the next evening transmission. It was always a gamble as to whether the radio waves would be able to surmount the barrier of the jungle hills. However, at 5.30 p.m., I successfully tuned in to the battalion frequency, netted in on control's signal and waited patiently for 'A' and 'B' Company patrols to make their reports. When it was 'C' Company's turn, I transmitted my SITREP (situation report) back to Kulim without any trouble. The SITREP merely contained the coded map reference of our location – as near as Mr Crisp could figure it! – with NFTR (nothing further to report).

Corporal Hudspeth cooked our conner and supervised the ladling out with considerable efficiency. With my enamel plate of canned steak and kidney pudding, potatoes and peas in one hand and my aluminium mug of tea in the other, I sat down beside Busby, Number One Section's Bren gunner, and Brodie, his number two on the gun. Matt Busby had become a good friend of mine and often came over to the Signals billet in the evenings to chat to me and smoke my cigarettes. He was a strong, handsome and lively lad from Helston in Cornwall who kept a large coloured photograph of his girlfriend, Enid, beside his bed and who told quite a few tales of previous lustful exploits with other young ladies.

Ginger Thompson, the former Durham miner, also came over to join the group. 'Join the army and see the world!' he exclaimed as he squatted down. 'By the left! When I gang home from this lot, I won't even sail on a ferry boat!'

Brodie asked him: 'Where's your mate, Smithy?'

'He's on stag, poor sod!' Ginger replied. He then turned to me. 'Listen, Jock! How come thoo's nearly always out with us? Does thoo volunteer?'

'No.' I shook my head.

'Well, I heard thoo does,' Ginger insisted. 'Thoo must be bloody mad, ganging out in all this shit when thoo doesn't have to.'

'Jock likes it,' Matt Busby interposed. 'He's thinking of signing on.'

'No, I'm not,' I protested. 'Well, I might some day. But I want to try Civvy Street first.'

'You'll be in for a shock in Civvy Street,' said Matt. 'All you ever did there was go to school, go to the cadets and go to the pictures. You've never had a job. You've never had a woman. You know fuck-all about anything!'

Before I could respond to Matt's scornful but fairly accurate statement, Ginger cut in. 'What? Has thoo never had a woman, Jock? What's thee been doing with theeself all thee life?'

221

I felt my face redden and in order to divert the focus away from myself, asked Ginger: 'How's "wor lass" getting on, Ginger? Have you heard from her lately?'

'Aw, that's all finished,' Ginger replied. 'Didn't I tell thee, Jock? The little cow was knocking about with some bloke and he babbied her!'

After we had eaten, Corporal Hudspeth assembled the platoon in a semicircle round him.

'Right! Listen in, yous blokes,' he announced. 'This is tonight's guard list. So open your lugs and I'll read out what times yous are on. Listen for who's on after yous and if yous don't know where he's sleeping, find out!' He read from the list in his hand, slowly and clearly, and then asked: 'Right! Now has that sunk into your thick skulls?'

Ginger Thompson immediately spoke up. 'I notice thoo's got me and Smithy on late stags again,' he commented sourly.

'If yous are on late stags, that's your bloody bad luck!' Hudspeth snapped.

'Ay, righto,' said Ginger. 'Funny how we're unlucky every bastard time!'

Mr Crisp now stepped forward. He was stockily built, had dark, wiry hair and for some reason always reminded me of Mickey Mouse.

'All right, cut that out!' he said calmly but firmly. 'We don't want any bickering. We have enough to contend with, without that. OK – rum up!'

We quickly scattered to get our mugs and then formed an eager queue to receive our nightly rum ration, carefully measured by Mr Crisp. Those that did not want any were very popular with their friends.

This duty done, Mr Crisp said finally: 'You can dismiss now. But keep quiet. I don't mind you talking in whispers as long as you keep it that way. And remember – no lights. Cover your cigarettes with your hands.'

As always in Malaya, the daylight faded into complete darkness within 15 minutes. Having put on our jungle pullovers, as it was liable to grow chilly later on in the night,

222

Mr Crisp and I crawled into our lean-to *basha* and settled down. We had to be ready for any emergency so did not even remove our boots. I kept my rifle by my side with one leg through the sling so that it could not be removed by an intruder without wakening me. My ammunition pouch served as a pillow. This was not quite as uncomfortable as it sounds, as the pouch did not contain ammunition but my towel wrapped around my washing kit. My ammunition was carried in small, unauthorised pouches, which I wore clipped on to the front of my belt.

After we had stretched out, Mr Crisp asked: 'D'you want a fag, Scurr?'

'No thanks, sir,' I answered. 'I never smoke on patrol. It's supposed to be bad for your wind.'

'Maybe so,' he said dubiously. 'But it's the first thing I think about.'

He lit a cigarette, shielding the flare of the match as best he could. Somehow, we started talking briefly about school examinations. I cannot recall the details of the conversation other than my impression that Mr Crisp hadn't done too well in his exams, which prompted him to comment: 'I don't like brainy people. They've got a disease!' Then, he added: 'You're quite clever, aren't you, Scurr?'

'Oh, I'm not too clever, sir,' I earnestly assured him. 'I failed in maths.'

I heard Mr Crisp give a quiet chuckle. He seemed quite at ease but I was not. I was very conscious of the barrier of rank between us. At that time and later, I often sensed that he would have been happy to chat to me man-to-man but I always remained constrained by the fact that he was an officer and I was a private. When I think about it now, it seems rather sad, yet I can't help feeling that – in the army – that is how things should be. Class barriers undoubtedly help to maintain discipline.

On this occasion, we were both too weary for prolonged conversation anyway. However, sleeping was not an easy matter. With the night had come the inevitable swarms of mosquitoes, mercilessly biting our exposed faces and hands and even striking through our clothing. To call these insects a menace would be a gross understatement. I hated the little bastards with an all-consuming passion! What annoyed me most was the way mosquitoes always seemed to go for my ears. I would lie listening to a high-pitched buzzing growing louder and would often scoop the insect away just as it was entering my earhole. The risk of malarial infection was, fortunately, considerably reduced by our taking a daily Paludrine pill. However, the continuous and painful bites raised small red lumps which were apt to grow aggravatingly itchy. I had tried army-issue anti-mosquito oil, only to find that the mossies loved it!

As I lay there that night, I compared my plight to someone trying to sleep while tormentors repeatedly jabbed him with pins. Eventually though, lying on my right side with my jungle hat over my exposed left cheek and ear, I did manage to fall asleep.

'Jock! Jock!' A hand shook my shoulder vigorously. 'Come on. It's your turn for stag.'

'Oh – OK,' I mumbled. I reluctantly came awake, convinced that I had only just closed my eyes. I pulled on my jungle hat and crawled out of the *basha*. Ches Allen awaited me, with his torch, partially covered by his hand, shining on the ground. Everything seemed unfamiliar in the dark. I followed Ches blindly, tripping over bivouac strings and tree stumps, still half asleep. Eventually, we reached the Bren gun, which was pointing down the track towards the river.

Ches handed me the torch, the luminous watch and the guard list. 'OK?' he asked quietly.

'OK,' I whispered. Shielding the glare beneath the palm of my hand, I shone the torch on the ground to assist Ches on his route back to his bivouac, then switched it off.

Feeling very alone in the almost total darkness, I sat down upon the ammunition pouches behind the Bren gun. I shivered a little and crossed my arms to try to get warmer. The roar of the river's current below sounded very loud and from somewhere in the night all around me came the constant cacophony of the jungle chorus. Crickets, cicadas, grasshoppers and tree frogs discordantly chirped, whirred and croaked in competition with the harsh chatter of monkeys, the deep wailing of gibbons and the strident screeching of hornbills. Intermittently, tree trunks groaned eerily as they swayed in the night breeze.

Large shadows loomed darkly about me and the trees and bushes shook from time to time when the wind or some prowling creature stirred them. I had thankfully long since learned that the 'glowing eyes' which sometimes appeared amongst the foliage did not indicate the presence of wild beasts but were, in fact, merely fireflies. Nonetheless, I was fully aware that the Malayan jungle was inhabited by tigers, leopards, elephants, rhinos, crocodiles, bears, wild pigs, an exceedingly dangerous breed of wild ox called a seladang, and several species of lizards, snakes, deer and monkeys. These animals normally gave human intruders into their domain a wide berth – but there were exceptions.

On a recent patrol, Corporal McAllister had been walking up a jungle track when he suddenly came face to face with a tiger. In a state of mutual panic, both Mac and the tiger had turned and run for their lives in opposite directions! As I recalled this encounter, I found myself pondering on the possibilities of being stalked at that very moment by either a tiger or a bandit. Chillingly, I concluded that the second possibility frightened me far more than the first.

I had once asked Ginger Thompson, whom I considered to be a brave type, if he felt scared when he was on night stag in the jungle. He readily admitted that he was and said that anyone who claimed that he wasn't scared was a liar! Well, I certainly wasn't a brave type but I was pleased to find that I controlled my fear well when I was on night stag. Never once did I open fire at 'walking trees', as some men were prone to do.

Roll on two ruddy hours! I thought with a sigh. My eyes were becoming more accustomed to the dark now and I could distinguish more easily the trees and shrubs that surrounded the track. Every so often, I glanced in a complete circle around me to ensure that there was nobody creeping up on me from behind. Hardly likely, I tried to reassure myself, but no harm in making sure!

A hideous scream from just across the river made me start. Probably a monkey, I told myself hopefully. I began to relax a little and to while away the time I silently ran some of my favourite songs through my mind, particularly those that reminded me of home. Memories of holidays with cousin John and of my last years at school flooded back to me, making me long to be home again. I remembered, then, the 1949 school concert in Edinburgh's Usher Hall when we had performed Mozart's *Magic Flute*. There had been one lyric about 'the childish fear of death' . . .

A loud swish and crash followed by rustling on the track just a few yards in front of me, brought me harshly back to the present.

My God! What was that?

My hand flew to the cocking-handle of the Bren and gripped it tightly. My heart was thumping rapidly as I listened for any further sounds that might indicate someone creeping or rushing forward. Watching intently for any visible signs of movement, I kept my eyes shifting around all the time, knowing that if I focused my gaze upon any bush or shadow for any length of time, it was bound to move.

After several tense but thankfully eventless moments, I breathed freely once more. Must have been a falling branch or a rotted tree keeling over, I told myself. I glanced at the luminous dial of the watch. Only 20 minutes had gone by. Another hour and 40 minutes to go!

I wondered how close the enemy were? It was certain that their 8th Regiment had camps in the Bongsu. Information indicated that there was a big camp somewhere in this region. However, without specific information on exact location, finding a bandit camp in the dense jungle was like looking for a needle in a haystack. It was perfectly possible that we could have passed by a camp at only a few yards' distance during that day's march without being aware of our narrowly missed opportunity. I wondered if the big

226

camp would ever be found and if I would be present when it was.

When my two hours of guard duty had finally passed, I gratefully sought out my relief and retired to my *basha*. Soon afterwards, it began to rain quite heavily. Despite this, I was so tired that I sank rapidly into sleep, unaware of the extent to which the rainfall was penetrating the overhead poncho and thoroughly wetting Mr Crisp and me and most of our kit.

The platoon was astir soon after daylight and washed in the river by sections under the protection of posted sentries. Breakfast of porridge, sausage and bacon (all from tins) was hungrily devoured. The medical orderly issued out Paludrine pills to be washed down with tea. His next task was to hold a sick parade, anointing the tinea rashes, ringworm, jungle sores and foot-rot of more than a third of the platoon.

Mr Crisp decided to take Number One Section on an all-day patrol, leaving Number Two Section to guard the base. I volunteered to go with the patrol and was immediately saddled with the small but quite weighty '88' set, which I reluctantly hooked onto my belt.

Corporal McAllister now addressed us: 'All right, form up! One up the breech, riflemen!'

I levered a round into the breech of my rifle, applied the safety catch and took my place in the line, eager to get started.

Ginger Thompson turned to Mr Crisp and complained: 'Why can't we stay in camp, sir, and let Number Two Section gang out for a change? Number One gets all the dirt!'

Mr Crisp smiled. 'Move off, Thompson,' he ordered quietly.

Ginger led the way followed by his mate, 'Smithy'. We climbed to the ridge of purple-flowered rhododendron which overlooked our camp, moving more easily than we had the previous day, having no heavy loads strapped upon our backs. Our route continued down the reverse slope of that hill and up through the attap of the slope opposite.

227

The jungle grew more dense as we proceeded. Ginger and Smithy drew their matchets and began to chop away vines and shrubs that were overgrowing the track. Following in file, the rest of us picked our way carefully, ducking beneath overhanging linea creepers and low branches. Occasionally, the patrol would come to an abrupt halt while Ginger hacked at some tough, obstructing creeper, cursing quietly at every stroke. Here and there, a fallen tree would lie across our path. Sometimes, the width of the prostrate trunk would be so great that we'd have to help one another climb over. We also assisted each other to pull free from the thorned vines which persistently hooked into our shirts or our arms.

Eventually, the undergrowth thinned out as we filed down a comparatively gradual slope. At the foot, we turned into a narrow valley which was formed around the bed of a dried-up stream. Mr Crisp glanced continually up the slopes on either side and soon indicated a track up the hill to our right to Ginger. The climb was precipitous and took us through a dense thicket of bamboo. We constantly had to squeeze our bodies between the wiry, tubular bamboo shoots as we struggled upwards. Despite being free of heavy burdens, we reached the top dripping in sweat and breathing hard.

We continued to search through this hilly region, watching in vain for footprints, recently broken foliage or other signs of human passage. One slope that we climbed through clumps of attap palms and criss-crossed lengths of rattan creeper seemed endless and was so steep that we kept missing our footing and slithering back down several feet. When we finally reached the summit, Mr Crisp consulted his map, calmly announced that we were lost and suggested that we stop for tiffen.

Gratefully, we flopped to the ground, cautiously assuaged our thirsts and began ridding ourselves of the leeches that we had collected. I found two clamped onto my neck, busily drinking my blood, and got Matt Busby to burn them off with his cigarette. Others that I discovered on my slacks and boots I was able to vanquish unaided. Portions of cheese, cake and a little salmon were now handed out and we all settled down to eat.

On this occasion, Matt told me something appertaining to jungle operations that I found very interesting. He said: 'D'you know what really gets on my nerves? It's the constant anticlimax. You come upon a bandit camp, only to find that the birds have flown. Or you go out, acting on information that turns out to be either out of date or completely false. You get all keyed up and ready for a fight, then find there's nobody to fight. There again, every time you go out on a duffy you never know whether a fight might be sprung upon you unexpectedly. It's not the things that happen out here that get me down. It's the things that don't happen and the things that might happen.'

'I suppose that makes sense,' I replied. 'But in your case, Matt, I'd say you sometimes get over-anxious because you want to get back to Enid in one piece.'

Matt's girlfriend was in a resident girls' college, training to be a teacher. They corresponded continuously and she seemed to be habitually on his mind.

'That may be right, Jock,' Matt said with a slight shrug. 'Perhaps you're lucky not having that kind of a problem.'

'Maybe,' I agreed. 'But I certainly hope I can get that kind of a problem when I get home.'

Although during my teens I had been in love from afar, I had no conception in my total innocence of what becoming really involved in 'that kind of a problem' can do to a person. I simply believed that when I went home, fate would present me with a beautiful young lady like my favourite movie goddess, Maureen O'Hara, and we would float off together on pink clouds festooned with roses. (After my return home, I did find my 'Maureen O'Hara', but when I floated off I did so alone, on clouds that had faded to far more sombre hues.)

After tiffen, we walked up and down the same track half a dozen times, looking for a suitable direct route back to base. Just as we found a way down the long, steep slope, a wind suddenly arose as if from nowhere, shaking the trees and bushes.

Oh-oh, I thought, here it comes!

Sure enough, the rain began; first of all in large, isolated drops and then gradually growing heavier. To begin with, the dense overhead foliage sheltered us to a certain extent but this protection did not long prevail. With a loud roar, the rainfall suddenly increased until it was coming down in a solid torrent of tropical fury. Within a minute we were soaked to the skin, our drenched clothing hanging heavily and uncomfortably cold upon our bodies.

Swift, heavy drops thudded noisily on the crown of my jungle hat, the brim of which kept filling up and overflowing, while streams of water ran continuously off the barrel of my rifle. I shivered from the touch of my soaking shirt upon my skin. It was a miserable feeling.

The rain turned the ground to mud beneath our feet as we clambered down the slope. Scores of leeches, revelling in the wet mire, swarmed to feed off our blood. We brushed them off as best we could and kept going. Squelching and slithering and sometimes sinking ankle-deep in the thick slime, from which we extracted our boots with considerable difficulty, we miraculously found ourselves at the river.

From here, we waded downstream, with the rain continuing to lash us mercilessly. Streaks of lightning flashed around us, followed by loud, rolling claps of thunder. When the rain eventually stopped, the electrical storm did not abate. We continued to follow the river, wading knee-deep, until we finally reached our base camp.

Weary and bedraggled, we surveyed our sagging, swamped *bashas* with dismay. Inside, we found every article of kit soaking wet, as the rain had simply swept through our bivouacs in torrents. We emptied out the large pools of water that were weighing down the overhead poncho capes and straightened up the sapling frameworks. Mr Crisp gave me a routine SITREP to radio to the company base. I knew that contact with Kulim was impossible in the electrical storm but I went through the motions of tuning and calling, only to receive loud, distorted cracklings through the headphones in reply.

At about 6 p.m., heavy rain began to fall again. Corporal Hudspeth and Lance Corporals Keenan and Short struggled to light a fire with the damp wood at their disposal. Over the fireplace, they erected a groundsheet shelter, under which they crouched, stripped to the waist, and fanned up the flame which they had finally managed to kindle, shielding it with their bodies from the lashing rain. Maintaining their patience with constant oaths, they gradually built the fire up and put the brew cans on to boil.

Eventually, Corporal Hudspeth yelled triumphantly: 'Conner up! Hurry up, yous blokes, for God's sake!'

The rest of us made a swift dash from the shelter of our *bashas* and queued up in the pouring rain as the three 'cooks' ladled out the stew and tea as fast as they could. We then hastened back to our bivouacs with the contents of our plates or mess tins swimming in rainwater.

As it grew dark, our rum ration was especially welcome. The storm still raged and, indeed, continued throughout the night. Like everyone else in the platoon, Mr Crisp and I got little sleep that night. Rain swept into our *basha* at the sides and dripped through leaks in the overhead poncho cape. Even worse, a continual flow of water cascaded down the hill and over the groundsheet upon which we were lying. The chill of the night added to our soaking-wet discomfort and we shivered as we squirmed in muddy pools of water which seemed to grow constantly larger around us. Rain always brought out mosquitoes in force and that night was no exception. The damnable insects attacked us with merciless persistence until we could have screamed.

Every so often, the night would light up as lightning flashed from the sky and the peels of thunder which followed seemed to shake the whole jungle. Miserably cold in my watery 'bed' and jumping from the continual bites of the mosquitoes, I nonetheless managed to fall asleep sometime after midnight.

At 3 a.m., I was awoken to take my turn on stag. I took

up position behind the Bren gun under the shelter of the outermost bivouac. I felt very drowsy and shook with cold. The usual scary chatter of the night was either absent or rendered completely inaudible by the ceaseless roar and patter of the rainfall. I peered out into the darkness, too miserable to care who might approach. No fears sought me out. My soaking-wet discomfort and the relentless, whining, biting mosquitoes held my complete attention.

We were glad to see the mist-shrouded dawn of Sunday, 19 November. The rain had stopped an hour or so earlier and we were thankful that the sun would soon grow hot and dry out our clothing. When Corporal Hudspeth called: 'Conner up!' we queued up with eager enthusiasm as a good hot breakfast was just what we needed to warm our chilled bodies and raise up our spirits. However, we were all soon completely dismayed to find ladled into our mess tins what appeared to be just hot, greasy water with a few minute scraps of bacon floating on the top.

'What the fuck's this swill?' Ginger Thompson enquired on behalf of all of us.

'Bacon soup,' Corporal Hudspeth replied.

'Bacon soup?' repeated half a dozen incredulous voices.

'By the left!' Ginger exclaimed after taking a spoonful. 'I've had some queer meals on duffies but never anything like this!'

'It tastes like water someone's used for washing up greasy dishes,' Smithy said, managing to laugh.

'For God's sake!' Brodie complained. 'What did you have to make this for?'

'Well, there was only a couple of tins of bacon left,' Hudspeth protested hotly. 'I had to do something with it.'

'Well, thoo didn't have to make soup out of it!' Ginger retorted.

'If that's how yous blokes appreciate my cooking,' Hudspeth growled at Ginger, 'maybe you and Smith would like to do it from now on and see if yous can do any better!'

Mr Crisp now intervened with just a wisp of a smile on his face. 'All right! Cut it out, all of you!' he snapped.

'When you've finished your breakfast, strike your bivvies and pack up ready to go.'

Breakfast was already over as far as most of us were concerned. We dismantled our *bashas*, separating the components of the structures and casting them in different directions into the brush. The purpose was to leave as little visible evidence of our campsite as possible. Empty 'C' ration tins and other items of litter were all buried and the 'fireplace' covered over with leaves.

When we commenced our return journey, the marching pace was set as fast as the thickness of the jungle would allow. Nearly all tinned rations having been consumed, everyone other than myself was now marching with only a light load on his back. Consequently, I had no choice but to drive myself on under considerable strain so as not to lose contact with the man in front of me. With few breaks, we continued up and down the inevitable hills, at one time ascending through thorn bushes while being eaten alive by midges and sandflies. I somehow managed to keep up, even though I eventually found myself gasping for breath and reeling like a drunk. By now, I had come to expect and accept being in a state of exhaustion and to regard it as just part of the game of being a soldier.

After leaving the jungle, we stopped for a rest by some *bashas*. I gladly sank to the ground, eased my arms out of the '68' set's harness and stretched out on the grass, feeling too weary even to take a much-needed drink of water. Soon, however, I began to recover my strength, prudently assuaged my thirst and then set up my wireless. I made quite clear contact with our camp at Kulim and arranged for transport to collect us.

Tiffen consisted of a small portion of corned beef per man – all that remained of our rations. We then continued our march through the rubber. It began to rain again but we no longer cared. We were on our way home.

Arriving at the kampong from which we had departed two days before, we squatted down to await our transport. A rather noisy group of Malay villagers gathered round us excitedly when they spotted a tortoise trying to escape from Brodie's pack. Brodie had found the tortoise in the jungle the previous day and decided to keep it as a pet. Soon, our transport came and carried a wet, weary but very happy bunch of lads back to camp.

When I stripped off my stinking, sweat-and-mud-stained clothing back in the Signals billet, I shook showers of water and leeches from inside my jungle boots and discovered several blood-smeared bites on different parts of my body. During this duffy, we had been constantly brushing or burning leeches from our flesh, boots and clothing, and some of the chaps had an exceptional number of bites. My feet were painfully tender as I walked in plimsolls to the ablution sheds for a welcome cold shower. The prospect of having a clean body, eating a good dinner, drinking at least one Tiger beer and sleeping between sheets on a bed was sheer bliss.

Poor Brodie had little time to enjoy the antics of his pet tortoise as he was almost immediately hospitalised with an attack of malaria.

14

Kulim and Sungei Perlis
November–December 1950

As I continued into the second half of what I call my 'first Kulim period', I was still generally contented with my life in 'C' Company. I had good friends around me and now considered myself to be an experienced jungle soldier who was managing to cope with the various stresses and strains surprisingly well. Of course, I had still not been given the opportunity of personally participating in an armed encounter with the enemy, but I remained confident that this final test could not be far away.

In fact, while 8 Platoon had been toiling through the Bongsu to no apparent avail, other members of the company had experienced some brief excitement. On Friday, 17 November, a day patrol in the Junjong region led by Captain Haddon came upon a *basha* from which was heard the sounds of human laughter. As the patrol approached to investigate, three bandits – one male and two females – hurried out of the *basha* and made a run for it. Captain Haddon and a few others immediately opened fire but all three of the enemy escaped, apparently unharmed.

Shortly afterwards, Private Knight was on stag nearby when he spotted a Chinese male coming along the track towards him. At the same time, the Chinese also saw Knight and quickly turned and ran. Knight instantly fired at the running figure with his Sten, but the gun jammed after discharging only four rounds. However, the man's belt somehow fell to the ground and the patrol found, attached to the belt, a wallet containing a grenade, several documents and other items.

After Arthur had told me these details upon my return from the Bongsu, Allan Knight came into the billet and told me the whole story again. He was greatly excited and obviously delighted with his experience – though not with his Sten!

Since our posting to Kulim, the battalion had been issued with quite a number of Australian 9-mm Owen sub-machine guns and American .30 M2 automatic carbines. The Owen was more accurate and had a higher rate of fire than the generally unreliable Sten gun, so most of our NCOs and scouts had traded in their Stens for Owen guns, despite the fact that the latter were heavier to carry. Platoon officers and serjeants had mostly adopted the light M2 carbines.

On Monday night, the 20th, we were advised of a company operation that was to take place the following day. A bandit who had surrendered to the police was going to lead 8 Platoon to the camp from which he had deserted; 9 Platoon and Company HQ would lay ambushes at likely escape routes in the area and two police jungle squads were also going to act as 'stops'. I was to be signaller with 8 Platoon. Arthur told me that Mr Crisp had specifically asked for me – which pleased me no end!

At 8 Platoon's briefing in the dining hall/canteen, Mr Crisp explained his plan: 'If we find the camp, Number One Section will go straight in. Number Two Section will try to work round the flank and move in from there. Then Number Two Section will take up defensive positions in the camp while Number One Section pursues the fleeing bandits. Now, we mustn't overlook the possibility that this bandit might be leading us into an ambush. So keep your eyes open at all times.'

At this point, Corporal Hudspeth spoke up: 'If we do run into an ambush, the bloke nearest to the bandit shoots him. OK?'

We all murmured approval and Mr Crisp didn't raise any objection, so I presumed that this proposal had been adopted as part of the plan. All things considered, I entertained high hopes for this operation.

Reveille was at 4.15 the following morning and 8 Platoon left in trucks at about 6 a.m. We first picked up an English police officer, two Malay constables and the surrendered bandit at Kulim Police Station, then our transport dropped us all off just outside the town as it became daylight.

We moved along a flat track through the rubber until we reached more hilly country where the going became a little harder. As we marched up a gradual track round the side of a hill slope, Lance Corporal Short, at the head of Number Two Section, suddenly shouted out: 'Get down! Quick!'

The whole platoon dived as one man onto the adjacent bank, safety catches were thumbed forward on rifles and the click of sub-machine gun bolts sounded all along the line. I was sure that this was it! I felt excited but in control. I awaited the whine of ambushers' bullets and peered up the hill through the long grass, considering in which direction to fire back if I couldn't spot a target.

No fire came. A rubber tapper – whom Lance Corporal Short had spotted crouching behind a tree – ran out with his hands up, chattering loudly in alarm. We stood up and wiped the sweat from our brows. The rubber tapper grinned anxiously, keeping his hands in the air.

We moved on once more, up and down hills, until we halted while Mr Crisp and the section commanders had a confab. Then Corporal Hudspeth briefed Number Two Section:

'Right! Now the bandits are just over there.' He nodded to his rear. 'We've to go straight into the *bashas*, and Number One Section's going to work round the side. Now it's rough country and hellish thick. So keep your eyes and lugs open!'

These instructions appeared to reverse the original plan. No matter. We moved off silently and cautiously with safety catches half-forward. For a moment I had a mental image of lead projectiles smashing into my skull, either killing me, blinding me or leaving me insane. I found these prospects

237

quite alarming and immediately banished such thoughts from my mind. If this was it – and I was sure it was – I wanted to do it well.

We crossed the summit and descended a hillside track. As yet, there was no sign of a camp. We carried on through some bracken and waded across a small stream. The signal was now passed back that there were three *bashas* ahead and our bandit guide, in the custody of the two Malay constables, was sent to the rear of the column.

This was it! I eased my safety catch fully to the 'off' position and held my rifle at the ready. Crouched tensely forward, we ascended the short slope to the ridge. Suddenly, I saw them. Three *bashas* just below us – with the men of Number One Section calmly taking off their packs.

'I was so disappointed I could have wept!' was the comment in my journal. We searched around the large wooden *bashas*. There were some women and children staying there but it was obvious that bandits hadn't been there recently. Matt Busby told me that Mr Crisp had drawn a grenade from his belt before crossing the ridge. Presumably, Number One Section had not worked round the side as per the second plan but had gone straight in as per the first!

Five men were left here while the bandit now led the rest of us to an announced second camp. As we crossed another hill, we noticed Communist stars carved on some of the trees. Then we halted on the reverse slope where the bandit claimed that his comrades had previously pitched tents. This was the 'second camp'. There was nothing to be seen.

Mr Crisp took a Bren group and searched the surrounding country, to no avail. We all then returned to the three *bashas*, where we had tiffen and I set up my wireless. I duly made contact with Arthur, who was with Company HQ in the vicinity of Junjong. Major Murray then came on the air and asked to speak to Mr Crisp. He reported that Company HQ had found 40 pounds of rice hidden in a hole amongst the rubber and instructed Mr Crisp to send out a patrol to check the area between our two positions. I remained on listening watch, making contact with Arthur every half-hour.

Our patrol returned at about 3.30 p.m., having found nothing. We then set off at a brisk pace, which we kept up all the way back to the company base at Kulim. I later noted in my journal: 'I thoroughly enjoyed this duffy. It was very exciting and I was certain we were going to come to grips until the big anti-climax. This time, I slung one ammo pouch on the left of my belt with bayonet attached, balanced by my water bottle slung on my right. I found this just the job!'

I have included this quote, word for word, as evidence of the unquestionable enthusiasm that I felt during this period for soldiering in Malaya. Of course, following upon my previous gruelling trek through the Bongsu jungle, it is not really surprising that I 'thoroughly enjoyed' a less exacting march through a rubber estate. Having said that, I normally preferred forays into the jungle to patrolling through rubber, despite the added hardships and discomforts. The jungle seemed more of an adventure.

The following day, Wednesday the 22nd, half of 8 Platoon went out again to ambush the spot in the Junjong area where Major Murray had found the 40 pounds of rice. This time, my mate Eric Hann went along as signaller. The account of this operation which follows is compiled from statements of participants that I noted down in my journal at the time and from further information received in correspondence, during 1990, with John Crisp and Frank Keenan.

On reaching the intended ambush location, Mr Crisp discovered that the 40 pounds of rice had already been taken, presumably by bandits. However, after searching through the area, another stash of rice was found. So the platoon established a base in a deserted rubber tapper's *basha* nearby. Leaving Corporal McAllister, Private Freddy Mains and Eric behind in the *basha*, Mr Crisp then set out with the remainder to lay a night ambush near the spot where the rice was hidden.

After considerable difficulty in finding a suitable location,

239

the ambush party finally took up positions above and below a bend in a track which wound round the side of a hill. It was now dusk, and hardly had the men settled down when the number one stop – a Geordie – passed the word that two armed bandits were coming along the track, possibly followed by others. Mr Crisp warned the party to hold their fire. However, just as the bandits reached a large rock which jutted out onto the track, the Geordie was unable to maintain his nerve and opened fire. As a result, the bandits swiftly took evasive action, heading off through the rubber above the track and then firing down upon the ambush party. Lance Corporal Frank Keenan and one of the two men with him below the track instantly returned fire at the muzzle flashes among the trees up the slope. At that moment, the Tamil Civil Liaison Officer, called Steve, suddenly jumped to his feet on the upper side of the track and was narrowly missed by a burst of fire from Frank Keenan's Owen gun.

The bandits had successfully made their escape through the rubber. 'That's it,' Mr Crisp said gloomily. 'The ambush is ruined. We might as well go back.'

Meanwhile, the three men left at the *basha* had heard the shooting and had taken up defensive positions. Soon, they heard sounds of someone running down the track towards the *basha* and crouched down with weapons at the ready. The door burst open and a Chinese male rushed in, panting for breath, and got the surprise of his life when he found that he was confronted by the gun muzzles of waiting British soldiers. Just then, there came the sounds of more people approaching the *basha*. Corporal McAllister ordered his men to get ready and keep the Chinese covered. The lads all hastily crouched down again, but to their relief they discovered that the approaching persons were, in fact, Mr Crisp and his ambush party.

Mr Crisp and Steve, the CLO, took the Chinese into a small adjoining room and interrogated him for a while without success. An offer from the Dyak tracker to make the man talk was resolutely turned down by Mr Crisp.

During the remainder of the night, Mr Crisp, Steve, Frank Keenan and Stan Swalwell took turns at guarding the prisoner.

At daylight the following morning, Thursday, 23 November, arrangements were made by wireless for the Chinese to be brought in to our base in Kulim. I witnessed his arrival, prior to his being handed over to the police. He was soon identified as being none other than the man that Private Allan Knight had fired at when his Sten gun jammed during Captain Haddon's patrol on 17 November, previously described. In the prisoner's pocket was a letter which, when translated, proved to be a report of that day's events in which the captured Chinese claimed that he had thrown a grenade at the British sentry (Knight) which had failed to explode. Allan Knight was really gleeful when he learned that a grenade had been thrown at him!

Meanwhile, the men of 8 Platoon were following up the ambush incident of the previous night. Leaving Corporal McAllister, Eric and two others at the *basha* with the wireless and packs, Mr Crisp set out with a patrol of 13 men. After searching for a while, the Dyak picked up the tracks of the bandits who had evaded the ambush party and led the patrol in pursuit. Half-an-hour later, the uphill trail left the rubber and continued into jungle. Here, the Dyak pointed out footprints which he declared were very fresh.

Mr Crisp then – to everyone's surprise – produced a bandit cap, placed it upon his head and walked boldly up the track. The rest of the patrol cautiously followed behind him. Suddenly, two bandit sentries – one armed with a Thompson sub-machine gun – leapt up from the bushes just ahead and fired a couple of bursts across the front of the patrol, without scoring any hits. The patrol had automatically dived into cover except for Mr Crisp, who remained on his feet, shooting back at the enemy with his M2 carbine. To Mr Crisp's great dismay, his weapon soon jammed, and when he tried to rectify this, the base of his magazine fell off and all the contained ammunition spilled upon the ground.

241

As the two bandits turned and ran, Mr Crisp yelled: 'Come on! Get into the bastards!' He then commandeered the Bren gun, rushed forward and opened fire at the two running bandits. However, the pair were now well ahead and soon made their escape.

Frank Keenan, who had been bringing up the rear of the patrol when the shooting began, now asked the three men in front of him: 'Where's Mr Crisp?' They said that he'd gone on, so Frank took the lead and hastened forward. Unwittingly heading at right-angles to the direction taken by Mr Crisp, Frank suddenly sighted a large group of bandits who were just turning a bend in the track ahead. Along with the men behind him, he immediately hit the deck. Frank then lobbed a grenade at the enemy before him, but in his excitement, he'd forgotten to pull the pin! Nonetheless, the bandits fled for their lives, perhaps assuming that there was a far larger party behind them than there really was.

Meanwhile, Mr Crisp, followed by four others, was continuing down the hill. He soon came to an open patch of *lallang* and in the valley below, at a distance of nearly two hundred yards, he could see about 15 uniformed bandits throwing off their packs and fleeing. Mr Crisp promptly fired several bursts from his Bren gun and saw one of the enemy fall.

This was, of course, the same group of bandits that Frank Keenan's party had previously bumped into. Guided by the gunfire, Frank reached the high ground, to find Mr Crisp, Lance Corporal Stan Swalwell, the Bren gunner who was known in 8 Platoon as 'the bible-thumper', the CLO and the Dyak all behind a large fallen tree, firing downhill at the bandits below.

Mr Crisp looked up and said: 'Good, Corporal Keenan! I'm glad you're here!' He then pointed down the slope to where a bandit lay shot and wounded. At the same time, the Dyak tugged at Frank's sleeve and indicated all the bandits who were running across the fairly open ground trying to gain the protection of the jungle on the other side of the valley. Frank immediately opened fire with his Owen gun, aware that he and the others with sub-machine guns were at a grave disadvantage at that long range. The Dyak was much better placed with his rifle but he wasn't a practised shot.

At this point, some of the bandits decided to try to reach their downed comrade and carry him off. Mr Crisp placed the Bren gun resting upon the bible-thumper's shoulders and kept these bandits pinned down and away from the wounded man with a steady stream of fire. The hot, expended cartridge cases were cascading down the bible-thumper's back as the Bren gun continued to rake the area. Finally, the bandits gave up the struggle and withdrew. Everything was suddenly very quiet.

Mr Crisp now took Frank Keenan's Owen gun and five of his magazines and handed Frank his pistol. The bible-thumper, once more manning his Bren gun, and the Dyak were left with Frank to provide covering fire if required, while Mr Crisp led the rest of the patrol down the hill to check the area below. On approaching the fallen bandit, who had been seriously wounded by the Bren gun bullets which had penetrated his back, the patrol was very aware of the risk of grenades being thrown or detonated as they drew near. Mr Crisp decided to take no chances and fired a burst from his Owen which struck the bandit in and around his groin and finished him off.

Strewn around the ground were several discarded packs and other items of equipment and clothing, some of which were bloodstained. This pointed to the likelihood that other fleeing bandits had been wounded by the patrol's fire; an indication which was later confirmed. There was no further sign of the enemy. The battle was over.

Mr Crisp then called Frank and his two men down from their covering position and the patrol ate tiffen, with Freddy Mains sitting on the corpse. After the meal, Mr Crisp took a small party down to the camp which the bandits had abandoned when the shooting had first commenced. The camp lay just beyond the spot where Frank and his men had encountered the enemy group at the bend in the track. It had apparently accommodated about 30 men but was now completely deserted. Consequently, Mr Crisp's party soon returned.

The patrol now cut down a stout sapling, and after binding together the wrists and ankles of the dead bandit, slung him on it in order to carry him back. Enemy dead always had to be delivered to the police for identification. Earlier in the Emergency, it had been considered sufficient to bring back the head and hands, but this practice was stopped after official complaints. If a patrol was deep in the jungle, carrying back a dead body was a slow, arduous and – in that heat – nauseating procedure. But it had to be done.

Thus bearing their slain enemy and also the abandoned packs – which were later found to contain many documents that would be of interest to the police – the patrol did not retrace its steps to the platoon base but marched off on the shortest route to the road.

In the meantime, back at the base *basha* Corporal McAllister and his three men had no idea of what had transpired. That afternoon, while I was taking a routine transmission on the '62' set in our Signals billet at Kulim, Eric contacted me, saying that Corporal McAllister wanted to speak to Major Murray. I quickly summoned the major from the company office and handed him a headset.

McAllister told him: 'Mr Crisp hasn't returned, sir, and we're wondering what to do if he doesn't get back before dark. The men are beginning to get a bit jumpy, sir.'

The major replied: 'Try to stay calm and all keep close together. I repeat – keep close together. We'll stay in contact and keep you advised.'

Soon after that, Mr Crisp telephoned the major and reported that they'd found a camp for 30 bandits and had killed one. Transport was immediately despatched to pick them up and brought the triumphant patrol into camp at 5 p.m. At that same time, Arthur was able to make wireless contact with Eric to arrange a transport pick-up of Corporal McAllister's now much relieved little band.

The entire company turned out to watch as Mr Crisp's returned patrol lined up in the MT park and unloaded their weapons. Major Murray shook the obviously delighted Mr Crisp by the hand, then gave a brief 'well done' speech to the others.

When the patrol was dismissed, the rest of us gathered round the 3-ton truck to see the dead bandit who was lying on the truck 'floor', still roped to the sapling. He was a young Chinese, clad in khaki drill shirt and slacks with puttees wound unevenly round his calves, and wearing black canvas and rubber ankle boots. Blood soaked the perforated cloth around his groin and formed a pool between his legs and there was another pool of blood by the small of his back. A chunk of flesh had been knocked out of his right forearm and the face of his wristwatch was smashed. His eyes and lips were half-open and there was some kind of froth at the corner of his mouth. His skin had turned a deep yellow colour and there was a faint but unmistakable sickly-sweet odour emanating from him.

The expression on his face was completely vacant. I thought to myself that he certainly looked dead. Life, the vital factor that had been in him a short while before, had gone out of him and left this empty, rather meaningless carcass which still had a man's shape though the man himself was no longer there. This was, in fact, the first dead person that I had ever seen. In the past, I had sometimes worried about how I might react to seeing a badly shot-up human body. In the event, I felt perfectly all right and seemed to experience a rather morbid fascination.

Major Murray instructed Serjeant Bell to prepare the body for display to the people of Kulim. 'Taggy' Bell then summoned two toughies from 9 Platoon, Privates Goff and Jarman, who transferred the body to the back of a 15-hundredweight and tied it in an upright position to the truck's framework with a rope beneath the arms and round the neck. Finally, on the major's instructions, Serjeant Bell slung the dead bandit's Lee-Enfield Mark III rifle around his neck to show that he'd been armed. Several recovered bandit packs were also loaded into the truck.

Most of the company were still assembled in the MT park, watching these preparations, which prompted considerable hilarity. I was suddenly surprised to see our new Medical Officer – a Scottish, National Service second lieutenant of the RAMC – jump up into the truck. Presumably from professional interest, he unbuttoned the dead man's trousers and tentatively prodded the lacerated genitals with his fingertips. I could see the dangling shreds of pink flesh where parts of the scrotum and testicles had been shot away.

Just then, Taggy Bell turned and yelled to the major: 'The doctor's examining him to see if he's dead, sir!'

Everyone howled with laughter at this remark. We were all in very high spirits. Suddenly, it seemed as though all the months of unrewarded slogging through the jungle had been worthwhile after all. The company's morale had unquestionably soared as a result of this one success.

When all was ready, Major Murray and Mr Crisp climbed into the major's jeep and drove out of camp, followed by the 15-hundredweight with the body bouncing stiffly in the back. The intention was to drive round the town, exhibiting the dead terrorist, and then deposit the body and packs at Kulim Police Station. It all seems rather barbaric when I remember it now but I had no such thoughts at the time.

My principal concern that evening was that fate had dealt me a cruel rebuff. On one of the rare occasions that I had not gone out as 8 Platoon's signaller, the platoon had fought an action. It just did not seem fair! I suppose I may have taken some comfort from the fact that I was not the only one who had been left out. Corporal Hudspeth, Ginger Thompson, Matt Busby, Brodie, Smith and some others all missed that particular operation. I believe that it had been previously scheduled that they should all go into HQ for a dental check-up. Nonetheless, we were all happy about the platoon's success.

Mr Crisp was undoubtedly the hero of the hour. Upon relating his account of the action to me, Steve, the CLO, concluded: 'I tell you, that officer is a very brave man. The number of times the bandits fired at him! Yet he paid no attention and kept going forward until he got his man.'

A bandit who surrendered five months later disclosed that he had been in the camp at the time of 8 Platoon's attack. He had known the man who was killed and he said that four other bandits had been wounded, one of whom still walked with a limp.

Late in the evening of that triumphant day, the company was visited by the CO, Lieutenant Colonel Brown, who was shortly going home. He gave us a farewell speech which was simple, straightforward and sincere and introduced his successor, Lieutenant Colonel J.C. Preston, DSO, who seemed very nice.

At 2.30 p.m. the next day, Friday the 24th, I left camp with 8 Platoon to follow up any signs that we might find of the 30 bandits. Arthur went with 9 Platoon on the same mission, only in a different direction. Although we discovered tracks of five men and a dropped Japanese round of ammunition, and later a small but deserted camp, none of these finds proved fruitful, so we returned the following day. During this time, Mr Crisp seemed edgy and irritable, which I had never observed him to be on an operation before (and never did again). I felt that he was badly in need of rest but managed to stop myself from saying so.

Arriving back in camp at about 5.30 p.m., I found that 9 Platoon had not yet returned. However, Serjeant Bell telephoned late in the evening to say that he and his patrol had got lost and had made their way to the road. Transport was then sent to bring them in. This meant that seven chaps, including Arthur, were left out at the platoon base which had been established the night before. I managed to make wireless contact with Arthur and arranged transport for the next morning. At Major Murray's insistence, it was planned that I should give Arthur a call at 1 a.m. to check that all was well, even though wireless contact at that time of night was normally impossible.

I dutifully sat up until one in the morning, fine-tuned the '62' set to the battalion frequency and began to transmit Arthur's call sign. As I had expected, night-time interference and atmospherics were all that were audible. I nonetheless persisted for 15 minutes, then switched off the set and the light, climbed into bed and gratefully sank into a sound sleep.

A quarter of an hour later, I was aroused to consciousness by a hand vigorously shaking my shoulder. Opening my eyes with a start, I could just discern a large figure bending over me in the darkness. Then I heard the major's drunken voice: 'Scurr! Wake up, Scurr! You've got to call Corporal Greenacre.'

'I already have, sir,' I replied sleepily. 'But I couldn't get through. There was too much interference.'

'Try again,' he said.

'But there's no point,' I protested. 'Contact just isn't possible, sir. Anyway, it's after one-thirty. Corporal Greenacre won't be listening now.'

'You don't know that,' the major insisted in slurred tones. 'Give him another call!'

Suppressing my inner wrath, I climbed out of bed, switched on the light and the '62' set and put on the headphones. I called the patrol's call sign again and again, hearing only a discordant jumble of radio signals and atmospheric cracklings in reply. Major Murray stood over me, swaying back and forward. 'Keep trying,' he demanded. I continued making the calls.

Eventually, the major said: 'I don't think there can be anyone listening. What's the point of us calling them if they're not going to listen?'

'You're absolutely right, sir,' I said wearily.

The major turned to go, hesitated and then said: 'Well, goodnight, Scurr.'

248

'Goodnight, sir.' I switched everything off and most gladly returned to bed once more.

During the battalion's first transmission of Sunday the 26th, I made contact with Arthur and received his message that they were about to depart for the transport rendezvous, with nothing further to report. I took the written message up to the company office. Major Murray glanced at the message form, then picked up a bulky news journal from his desk.

'I thought you might like this, Scurr,' he said. 'It's a Scottish journal that I have sent to me every month. I'll keep it for you from now on.' He smiled. 'News from the homeland, eh?'

I took the journal from his hand. 'Thank you very much, sir,' I said. 'That's very nice of you.'

I returned to the Signals billet feeling very confused. One moment he was driving me round the bend and the next he was being kind and considerate towards me! He was certainly aptly nicknamed 'the Mad Major', I considered.

Information received from the police indicated that the enemy documents captured recently by 8 Platoon had revealed that morale was very low in the Communist units that were operating in our area. The numbers of 'C' Company and police patrols which were forever probing the jungles and rubber estates made it both difficult and hazardous for these units to undertake terrorist activities or even to obtain food supplies. This proved the point that I made in an earlier chapter that constant patrolling, even without contact, was still harassing the enemy and contributing very positively towards his final defeat.

At the same time, reports were received that a large white flag had been hoisted on a hill near the camp where the bandit was killed, in full sight of the road. At 10 a.m. on Monday the 27th, I gladly accompanied the men of 8 Platoon as they set out to investigate the matter.

We left our transport at a spot past Junjong and marched off up a track, followed by a police jungle squad. A white object was visible up on a hill ahead of us but it was impossible to say at that distance whether or not it was a flag. We considered it rather unlikely that some bandits had decided to surrender in a group, so we kept well spread out in case it was a carefully planned ambush.

Further up the track – whether by plan or opportunism – a platoon of bandits had, in fact, taken up ambush positions. Concealed on a slight rise which overlooked a stretch of track where there was a sheer drop on the other side, our enemies were silently waiting. Present was a Chinese terrorist who surrendered to the police five months later and subsequently told the story.

The Chinese described how two military scouts came into view along the track. The bandits all raised their weapons to firing positions with excited anticipation of the whole patrol marching on into the killing zone. Then, to their dismay, the British officer, who was close behind the scouts and only 20 yards from the end man of the ambush line, held up his hand and the members of the patrol promptly squatted down in the grass along the side of the track.

After waiting for a while under quite unbearable tension, the bandits gladly raised their weapons once more as the British soldiers stood up, ready to move on. For a moment, though, the soldiers did not move. Their officer was studying his map. Then the officer addressed the two scouts and pointed to his right. The bandits now watched in helpless consternation as the patrol filed off to its right along another track, disappearing from view amongst the trees and shrubbery. Purely by chance, an apparently perfect ambush had been thwarted.

(I cannot say with certainty that this narrow escape from ambush occurred at the exact time that I have presented it. The terrorist – whom we nicknamed 'George VI' – surrendered in April 1951. Shortly after, he told the story of the foiled ambush to Lieutenant Green of 'D' Company who retold it to me three months later. George VI had not given a precise date but had merely stated that the incident had occurred in the Junjong area around that time. Checking through my journal, everything appeared to point to the operation currently being described. Whether, in fact, it did happen then or earlier or later, the story remains a valid example of the lurking dangers that we constantly faced.)

Naturally cautious but nonetheless oblivious to any watching eyes, we proceeded on our way. As we mounted a hill through the rubber, the leading section suddenly chased after some rubber tappers. For some reason, an elderly Chinese and his son were detained; perhaps they were not in possession of identity cards. The Malay constables from the jungle squad were none too gentle with the old man when he protested.

We then carried on to a *basha* at the top of the hill where I set up my wireless. The white object could not be seen from here. It seemed likely that we had taken a wrong turning. No one could remember exactly in which direction the white 'flag' had been. As it began to rain, a couple of patrols went out. They returned about 3 p.m., having found nothing. The old man was now released but his son was brought with us when we set off back down a track towards Junjong to meet our transport.

When we drove off in our trucks, we could again see the white object in the distance. An Auster aircraft was scheduled to fly over the hill the following day, but – to the best of my knowledge – nothing was discovered. Perhaps it had, indeed, been a white flag, placed there for a purpose and then later removed. We'll never know.

Two days later, on Wednesday the 29th, reveille for me was at 4.30 a.m. An hour after that, still feeling sleepy, I travelled in the armoured scout car, manning the Bren gun, to Bukit Mertajam Police Station. On arrival, I dismounted from the scout car, and the driver then handed me down my rifle and my '68' set.

Waiting for me by the roadside as the day began to dawn was a young English police officer. To my surprise, he shook hands with me and introduced himself as follows:

'Hello! I'm Lieutenant Wilton. Now that means fuck-all!

You don't have to call me "sir" or anything like that.' He hesitated for a moment and then added: 'But I think you'd better call the DO [District Officer] "sir".'

He took me into a small room within the station where half a dozen police officers were seated round a table, each with a map spread out in front of him.

Lieutenant Wilton introduced me: 'This is our wireless chappie, sir.'

I saluted the DO, who was seated at the head of the table, and snapped out: 'Good morning, sir!'

The DO very cordially invited me to sit down and handed me a map. I felt as though I had been strangely elevated above my rank of private soldier! The DO then continued with his briefing. A party of 14 bandits was known to be living in a cave on Bukit Mertajam – a jungle-covered mountain 5,000 feet high. Our battalion mortars were going to bomb the mountain. Then, four police jungle squads would advance up the slopes to search for the hideout or for any bandits that had been flushed out.

After the briefing, I moved off with the DO, three English lieutenants and two of the squads. We passed through the town (named after the mountain) and began to climb the lower slopes of the 'Bukit'. It was pretty steep and the pace was very fast. As a result, I soon felt more than a little tired and my steps began to slow. One of the lieutenants – a tall, sturdy man – hastened back to me.

'Look!' he exclaimed curtly. 'Can't you go any faster?'

'Not with this on my back, I can't!' I replied loudly and firmly, indicating my wireless.

'Here!' he snapped impatiently. 'Give it to me!'

I hoisted the '68' set onto his back and he started off up the slope. Less than 20 yards further on, a halt was called. The lieutenant came back down and placed the set gingerly at my feet.

'I say!' he said, looking very shamefaced. 'I'm frightfully sorry! I had no idea it was so heavy.'

'Yes, it is quite heavy,' I replied, trying to sound casual and unconcerned.

'I do hope you'll accept my apology,' he continued earnestly.

I couldn't believe this! An officer apologising to me? 'Of course,' I said. 'It's quite OK.'

I now set up the wireless and made contact with Arthur, who was with Major Murray and the Mortar Platoon – in fact, the battalion buglers – on the *padang* (green) between the base of the mountain and the town. The 3-inch mortars commenced firing at 7 a.m. Some of the Malay constables grew very alarmed and began to burrow into the ground. Firing continued for a full hour. The last few bombs fell dangerously close to our position and a couple of pieces of shrapnel whirred into the ground amongst the squad below me. I made a hurried call to Arthur to urge an immediate ceasefire. (Later, I learned that the buglers/mortarmen had fired 130 bombs and claimed that 3 were reported to have fallen short of their target.)

The bombardment was now completed. We continued with the ascent through the jungle and it proved a steep, difficult and arduous climb. The tall lieutenant assigned a constable to carry my set for a while. The Malay glared at me with eyes smouldering with hate and resentment, which I considered most unfair, seeing that it hadn't been my idea! After we'd climbed a hundred yards or so, he was completely out of breath and seemed absolutely bushed, so I took the set back from him and continued to bear my burden upwards through the green tangle of scrub. We eventually completed the 5,000 feet to the summit and, hacking a way through thousands of dry ferns, found the trig point – merely a tripod of three poles tied together at the top.

From here, we had a wonderful view of the surrounding country and even of Penang Island. Also, the air was lovely; really cool and fresh. I was able to contact Arthur now, using only a rod aerial – QSA 5/5 (receiving and sending 'loud and clear') – and gave him the message: 'Everest conquered.' But there had been neither sight nor sound of an enemy.

At about 10.30 a.m., we moved a short distance down from the summit. Two ambush parties took up positions for half-an-hour; then we continued down the mountain. We heard some firing over to our right. An officer up front signalled to us to take cover, which we promptly did. However, it was soon realised that the sounds of firing were being carried to us from a range at a nearby quarry.

Around noon, we made contact with two other squads who had been in ambush positions. No bandits had been sighted, so we proceeded round the side of the mountain until we reached an old *basha*. Here, I set up the wireless again. We brewed some coffee and ate our haversack rations. Mine consisted of some sandwiches that Arthur had personally prepared in the cookhouse that morning. To my dismay, I found that the 'sandwiches' had nothing in them! Rain lashed down on us while we ate but fortunately stopped a short while after.

Orders now came, via the wireless, to return to the police station. At 2 p.m., we continued round the mountainside, progressing slowly through the dense bush, and eventually began to wend our way downhill. We passed an old, burned-out bandit camp as the rain began again, finally reached the *padang* at the foot and marched on through the town to the police station. To my delight, all of the police officers specially came over to me to thank me and to say goodbye.

I returned to Kulim in the scout car, with Arthur travelling behind in a police jeep. Back in camp, Major Murray asked me how I had got on.

'Fine, sir,' I answered. 'Those police officers are really nice blokes.'

'Not like some officers you know, eh?' the major retorted.

'Oh well, sir,' I mumbled, embarrassed.

The major laughed and walked away.

On the whole, I was very satisfied with my day. When Arthur had told me the previous evening that I would be operating with a police unit, I had not been at all happy. However, it had proved to be an interesting and mainly enjoyable experience. The officers were great and the con-

254

stables in the squads were generally all right, though perhaps inclined to be a bit stupid. They did not march with weapons held at the ready as we always did, and some even had Sten guns slung on their backs without magazines loaded. All very dodgy if the enemy were suddenly encountered!

It also pleased me to realise that I was one of the few soldiers in the KOYLI who could claim to have climbed Bukit Mertajam.

Two days before, I had received an unhappy surprise on returning from the Junjong operation to find that Serjeant Stan Haley (Signals Serjeant) had arrived with Private Harry Marsh to replace Eric Hann, who, rather inexplicably, was to be sent to 'A' Company. Eric and I were both pretty upset by this development as we had become really good mates. I complained to Stan Haley about it but Stan was quite adamant that the arrangement must stand. Now, upon returning from Bukit Mertajam, I found that Eric had left earlier in the day. Actually, Harry Marsh was a cheery little regular soldier with whom I always got on very well, but I knew that I was really going to miss my 'mucker' Eric.

At this time, I was interested to learn that the bandit captured by 8 Platoon on 22 November had stated that he had seen Mr Crisp on four previous occasions and that he recognised several other members of the platoon. I had often felt that bandits hiding in the jungle might be observing our movements, even though we did not see them.

Late on Thursday night, 30 November, four bandits were reported to have approached our camp in the vicinity of the MRS (Medical Reception Station). In the ensuing alert, the Guard Commander, Corporal Hudspeth, fired a shot from his Sten at our own sentry. We had been told that when the Marines were garrisoning the Kulim camp, bandits had stolen some medical supplies from the MRS one night. Presumably, they were attempting a similar raid on this occasion but this time fled empty-handed.

The following night, Friday, 1 December, there was a tragedy in 'A' Company. Upon return from a football match, a soldier had sat down upon his bed in a squad tent. While manipulating his rifle bolt, he accidentally shot his mate, a lad called Gregory, who was seated on the adjacent bed. The poor chap who fired the shot was distressed to the point of madness and had to be kept under strict surveillance. An ambulance and escort vehicle were rushed from our company base to Serdang to bring Private Gregory to our MRS, but unfortunately he died before reaching Kulim.

During a nine-day operation around Alor Star in North Kedah, 12 Platoon, 'D' Company, captured two suspected enemy agents on Friday the 8th. One of the agents was persuaded to lead the patrol to a bandit camp but at the end of the trek undertaken, nothing was found. An angered Dyak tracker then threatened the agent, who consequently became frightened and made a run for it, only to be shot in the back by the Dyak.

On that same Friday afternoon, 8 December, our Signals detachment at Kulim was reinforced by two chaps who were required for a coming, and apparently secret, operation. One was a new Signals NCO – though an 'old soldier' – from the latest draft, Corporal Spires. The other was an old pal of Arthur's, Ray Hancock, known always as 'Hank'. He was a handsome, rather wild character who had gained quite a reputation at Tac HQ, Sungei Patani, for assuming the role of Dracula when drunk!

That very night, Arthur and Hank went drinking down town. On arriving back at lights out, Hank first pushed down the walls of the dhobi wallah's tent and caused quite a disturbance, before hastily retiring to the Signals billet. Arthur tried to persuade him to quieten down and go to bed but Hank just wouldn't co-operate. When Arthur said genially to Swede Martin that he hoped he would sleep well, Hank commented loudly: 'Why shouldn't he sleep well? He's got sheets and a pillow and a mattress; of course he'll sleep well!'

At this point, CSM Allen shouted from the serjeants' mess immediately above our billet: 'Keep quiet down there!'

'Who's that?' Hank called out.

'I'll give you who's that! Keep bloody quiet!' CSM Allen responded. He then shouted over to the guard tent: 'Guard Commander! Take the names of the men making a noise down here!'

Corporal McAllister now entered our billet a little hesitantly and said: 'The serjeant major says I've to take some names.'

'Names?' Hank queried. 'What does he want names for? There are names of mountains – of rivers – '

'Keep quiet!' McAllister replied and quickly withdrew.

Hank now lowered his voice a little but was far from subdued. 'Arthur,' he said now. 'Do you know who I am?'

'Who?' Arthur enquired.

'I'm Dracula!' Hank announced.

'No!?' Arthur feigned amazement.

'I am!' Hank stated emphatically. 'If I say I'm Dracula, I am Dracula. I was Dracula at Sungei Patani, so I can be Dracula here. D'you see these teeth? They're my eye-teeth. They're sharp. And d'you know what they do?'

'What?'

'They bite!'

'OK,' said Arthur. 'Now you go to bed.'

'You don't believe I'm Dracula, do you?' Hank said, peeved. 'But I am! Do you want me to prove it? What do you want me to do?'

'I want you to kill Superman,' Arthur spoofed.

'Impossible!' Hank replied. 'There's no such person. I'm the only one who could be. I have the strength of a thousand men.' He paused, looked out into the darkness and then turned back towards Arthur before continuing: 'Tonight's the night! I can feel it! Can't you see him over there? He wants me to go with him. Don't let me go, Arthur! Hit me on the head – do anything – but don't let me go!'

'OK, I won't,' Arthur said wearily. 'Now let's get some sleep.'

'A razor!' Hank exclaimed, sitting on his bed. 'I must

have a razor – to shave with! Ha! Ha! Ha!' He took the blade from his razor. 'Arthur, have you ever had your blood sucked?'

Arthur now said firmly: 'If you don't be quiet, Hank, I'll put you in the nick myself!'

This seemed to finally calm Hank down. 'I've been in the nick before,' he said quietly. 'I can go in again.'

However, he chose instead to get into bed and go to sleep. I felt greatly relieved. Although to the best of my knowledge Hank had never actually sucked anyone's blood, there could always have been a first time!

Before breakfast next morning, CSM Allen came into our billet and informed me that I had to appear on Company Commander's Orders for pushing in the dhobi wallah's tent the night before. I immediately protested my innocence but the CSM assured me that the dhobi wallah had identified me, saying that the culprit had been 'the signaller with the moustache'. Hank then owned up to the fact that he had been responsible.

It turned out that as the dhobi wallah's tent was collapsing around him, he had spotted Hank and remembered him as a signaller who had served previously with the company. Fortunately for Hank, the major only gave him a reprimand for his drunken conduct.

On Saturday, 16 December, Battalion Headquarters happily returned to Minden Barracks in Penang. The personnel of Tac HQ remained at Sungei Patani, though moving from Airfield Camp to 'Mandalay Lines' – home of the 6th Gurkha Rifles Training Wing.

Shortly after this move, 'D' Company spent three days in Penang, co-operating with HQ Company and the police in a screening operation on the island which, in fact, netted five wanted Communists.

During the first two weeks of December, we heard many rumours concerning a big duffy that was shortly to take place. Those in the know were sworn to secrecy, but the whispers suggested that 500 bandits were concentrated on an island somewhere off the Malayan coast, that they had

Japanese officers who were fugitives from the war, that their supreme commander was an East European Communist, that 'C' Company had been selected to assault the island because there were fewer married men in 'C' than in any of the other companies, and that we would soon be embarking on a ship for our secret destination.

I thought that it all sounded highly unlikely but when, one morning, we were mustered for issue of life jackets, toggle ropes and extra bandoliers of ammunition, I began to think again.

Then, on Friday the 15th, the CO himself arrived at Kulim to brief us. The past rumours were shown to have been far-fetched but the details given to us by Colonel Preston were still pretty spectacular. Informers had declared that 300 to 500 bandits were concentrated in the Wang Raja Valley, some way up the Sungei (River) Perlis and just below the Siamese border. The valley was 800 yards long, 400 wide and surrounded by sheer cliffs. 'C' Company would be transported up the coast in a Royal Navy frigate, HMS *Hart*, to the mouth of the Sungei Perlis, from where we'd be taken by launches up the river under cover of darkness. When daylight came, there would be an air strike to seal the bandits within the valley. 'C' Company would then advance upon the objective.

Accompanying us would be the OSPC (Officer Supervising Police Circle) of Perlis, two informer-guides, a police interpreter and also men from the Bugle Platoon, armed with flame-throwers and gas guns as the valley was said to contain many caves in which the bandits were dwelling. The duffy was to be known as Operation 'Ricebag'.

It sounded very promising. I was aware of an acute feeling of shared excitement and expectancy as we made our final preparations. Corporal Spires, Arthur, Swede, Hank and I were all going, taking three '68' sets between us. Harry Marsh would be remaining behind.

We left Kulim at 3.30 p.m. and were taken in trucks to Butterworth. From there, we were conveyed out to the waiting frigate in motor launches. Already on board were

259

our Signals Serjeant, Stan Haley, and Corporal Ivor Lewis who would be operating Tactical Control.

At the first opportunity, I had a confidential chat with Stan Haley regarding my Signals friend, Chas Schaverien. I'd heard a story that Chas had 'gone off his head' while serving with 'B' Company. Stan reassured me that it was not quite that bad. There had, however, been an incident which resulted in Chas throwing a bayonet at another signaller. Consequently, Chas had been brought in to HQ, Penang, for a rest from the pressures of the jungle.

At 10 p.m., HMS *Hart* sailed northwards in heavy rain. The ship was completely blacked out and we were instructed not to smoke. We had no choice but to sleep on the deck as best we could, wrapped in our ponchos.

Around 3 a.m. on Saturday the 16th, we were roused from our fitful slumbers to find ourselves 3 miles off the mouth of the Sungei Perlis. We stumbled below for a quick breakfast and then assembled on deck in full kit while two large police launches came alongside. The CO looked on silently as Major Murray, in his customary drunken state, was supported up from below and carried onto one of the launches. As we began to clamber over the side, I heard one of the sailors at the ship's rail say: 'Good luck, boys!' Once we were all safely aboard, the two launches set out towards the mouth of the river and the dark outline of HMS *Hart* rapidly faded out of sight behind us. In the mouth of the Sungei Perlis, the leading launch became stuck on a mud bank for a while but finally pulled free after guidance from a local Malay fisherman.

The day dawned at about 6 a.m. as we sailed on up the river. Shortly afterwards, the launches pulled into the bank on our right and we leapt ashore. Unfortunately, one poor chap strained his back when he jumped and had to be lifted back on board the launch. Once ashore, we immediately sank up to our knees in thick, black swamp. After emerging from this, we proceeded in file along a narrow, slippery path through the paddy fields. In addition to my wireless and other normal gear, I was very aware of the weight of my extra 50 rounds of ammo. Ahead of us, we could see a high, steep hill, beyond which we presumed that the enemy-held valley was located.

We hadn't gone far before six Tempest fighter planes zoomed overhead and swooped on the objective, pouring rockets into it. We halted behind a low hill feature and quickly laid out air panels to mark our position. As we did so, the Tempests pulled out and six Lincoln heavy bombers roared in. The Lincolns plastered the objective, I was told, with 30 tons of high explosive. As each stick of 1,000-pound bombs hit the ground, the banana trees shook around us and our clothing billowed out from our bodies with the blast, even at that distance. Enormous clouds of smoke and dust arose over the high hill ahead. Then, the bombers flew off and the Tempests, having loaded up again at Butterworth Air Station, returned, fired another batch of rockets and then opened up with their machine guns. I noticed that the flashes from the machine guns firing were visible a few seconds before the crackling sounds reached us.

Corporal Spires had now set up his wireless and was working back to our Tactical Control on board the ship. As the RAF completed its bombardment, an Auster aircraft flew over, spotting. Then it was the Navy's turn. HMS *Hart* opened fire with her 4-inch guns from the mouth of the river. We could hear the roar of the guns, the whistling as the shells flew over our heads and the explosions as they hit the objective.

Now, all firing ceased and 8 and 9 Platoons began to advance up the steep hill towards the valley. Company HQ – which included all the signallers – followed shortly afterwards. After wading through a few muddy pools, we halted beside a couple of *bashas* in a coconut grove. There were no sounds of battle from the valley ahead, so the major took a small party up there.

We soon learned that no bandits had been found in the bomb-blasted valley and that there were no signs of any bandits having been there in recent months. The informers now claimed that the valley where the 300 to 500 bandits were located was one of the same name about five hours' march over the border into Siam! I couldn't believe it. What a bloody fiasco!

The CO arrived on the scene in the early afternoon to confer with Major Murray and the OSPC. The men of Company HQ set about building *bashas* as it started to rain. Hank, Swede and I built a lean-to which was really pathetic. The rain came pouring in and the whole structure began to sag. We were helpless with laughter as we contemplated our hopeless handiwork. We then constructed a more stable edifice with the 'roof' sloping both ways, which kept us reasonably dry.

Patrols returned that evening, having searched the whole area of the valley. Only one thing of interest had occurred. The two informers, scouting ahead of 9 Platoon, had crossed the border and seen two armed bandits hacking at a tree. Both the informers and the bandits had immediately fled in opposite directions.

At 6 p.m., a small delegation of Thai police officers came down the river in a launch, concerned by the heavy bombardment of territory so close to the border and anxious to know our intentions. However, they soon departed back up-river, apparently reassured by the OSPC. It was forbidden for British Army units to cross the border in pursuit of the enemy, but there was some cross-border co-operation between Malay and Thai police forces.

Shortly after this visit, a Malay jungle squad that had been in a blocking position to the east of the Wang Raja Valley arrived at our base. Hodson and Headon were attached to the jungle squad as signallers and were happy to join us for a brew-up. While we were assembled round the fire – seven signallers plus a few others from Company HQ – enjoying our mugs of hot char, Hodson suddenly asked me: 'Have you been writing any more books, Jock?'

'I'm writing a story at the moment about a highwayman,' I replied, feeling rather self-conscious as all eyes around the fire suddenly focused upon me.

Hodson turned to CSM Allen, standing next to him, and

262

said loudly: 'D'you know what I don't like about his books? In the one I read, there's this pirate captain captures this Spanish *bibi* [woman]. She asks him to come to her, tha knows. So he taks' off all her clothes – and then Jock goes on to the next chapter!'

The serjeant major grinned and the other lads all laughed. I was really embarrassed, especially as Hodson's imagination was running away with him. The chapter had, in fact, ended without any of the lady's clothes being removed!

Next morning, Sunday the 17th, patrols went out again. Apart from doing stags, my only activity was to form part of an escort for Captain Davis, the Battalion Intelligence Officer, and his party, who were returning to the river after holding another conference with Major Murray and the OSPC. There were four of us in the escort. Our secondary – or perhaps it was our primary – mission was to bring back a bottle of whisky for the major!

The patrols returned to base after an eventless day and we were pleased to learn that the 'crowns and pips' had finally accepted that the operation was a failure and that we would be returning to Kulim the next day. As a military operation, 'Ricebag' had been successfully executed. It was just that the enemy was inconveniently in another country!

That night was spent in comparative comfort compared to the previous one when we'd been bitten mercilessly all night by mosquitoes.

We set off at 9.30 the following morning and, after another muddy march, were taken downriver by police launches to Kuala Perlis. After a welcome drink of Tiger beer in a café, we boarded our motor transport and commenced the long journey back by road, arriving in Kulim at about 5.30 p.m.

The anticipation and early stages of Operation 'Ricebag' had been very exciting – but what an anticlimax!

In the early hours of Friday the 22nd, my friend in 8 Platoon, Matt Busby, was asleep in his squad tent. Suddenly, he woke up to perceive a figure hovering beside his bed. He saw the blur of two hands and a face coming at him out of the darkness, but when he tried to move he found that he was paralysed with fear. Unable to utter a sound, he desperately tried to clap his hands in order to rouse his sleeping companions but his arms were frozen at his sides.

At last, he managed to yell out: 'Come on, boys! Come on! Come on, boys! Come on!'

The others in the tent jumped from their beds and switched on the light to find Matt almost in hysterics. The members of the guard, alerted by his cries, turned out and searched the entire camp area. But there was no sign of any intruder. In the meantime, poor Matt had dissolved into tears.

Matt was a physically strong and – in my estimation – brave type of person who did not seem the kind to go to pieces. When I discussed this occurrence with him later that morning, I reminded him of what he had said to me in the Bongsu, a month previously, about the wearing effects upon the nerves of constant anticlimax and never knowing what might happen. Matt replied that he believed that there was a connection; yet he swore to me that he had been wide awake when he saw the figure and was convinced that he had seen a ghost.

On Christmas Eve a newly arrived draft was sent out to patrol around the Junjong area for three days. Mr Wride was in command and Harry Marsh went along as signaller, accompanied by a few volunteers from the rest of the company. In addition to being extra training for the new draft, the primary purpose was to have a force of sober soldiers held in readiness in case an emergency occurred during the Christmas period.

That evening, Arthur, Hank, Swede and I went down to Kulim and had a drink together in the 'in bounds' café, which was very enjoyable and made a good start to the festivities.

Next morning, being Christmas Day, a mock football match was played on the football field downtown: officers and senior NCOs versus the men. Hank and I bought a Tiger each from the café before going to watch it. The teams wore fancy dress. CSM Allen's costume consisted of two teapot lids tied over his otherwise bare chest, and a dishcloth for a sarong. Poor Arthur was so drunk he didn't know what he was doing. He was supposed to be playing for the men but spent most of his time wandering up and down the field in his pyjamas, smiling. Once or twice he confiscated the ball and brought the game to a complete stop! It was really all most amusing. Very pistols and smoke grenades livened up the action, as did the water wagon which drove onto the field, squirting everyone in sight.

When we returned to camp, Corporal Spires gave me a severe dressing-down for having gone to see the match when I was supposed to be duty signaller, taking the wireless transmissions. I suppose that he was absolutely in the right but I didn't think much of his Christmas spirit and told him so in irate terms. Needless to say, it ended with Corporal Spires threatening disciplinary action, so I had to shut up. For the next couple of days there was a strained 'atmosphere' and we just didn't speak to each other. Then one night we began to exchange joking remarks about the loud moaning of a drunken soldier, and after that, friendly relations were restored.

Christmas dinner was a great success. There were four bottles of beer per man supplied by 'Charlie' – the company's civilian contractor, and Mr Forbes, Manager of Bukit Mertajam Estate, the East Asiatic Company and Malayan Breweries. The cooks provided an excellent meal, comprising tomato soup; roast chicken with sage stuffing, roast and creamed potatoes, cauliflower and peas; Christmas pudding with white rum sauce; fruit cocktail and cream; and coffee and minerals. The Battalion Quartermaster, Major Stevenson, his wife and his daughter dropped in out of the blue and assisted the officers and serjeants in serving the meal.

When we were finally being provided with coffee, Allan Knight, who was seated next to me, looked up at Mrs Stevenson and asked her very seriously: 'Will you kiss me?'

Mrs Stevenson kindly obliged, and immediately other chaps round about began clamouring for a kiss also. With-

265

out hesitation, Mrs Stevenson turned to her plump daughter and said: 'We'd better organise this properly, Margaret. Come on! We'll stand on those two tables over there and they can queue up.'

So, mother and daughter duly stood on top of two tables, side by side, in the centre of the dining hall, while most of the men present eagerly formed two queues, awaiting their turn to climb up on one of the tables and receive a kiss from the lady of their choice. Hank queued up twice and told me that he enjoyed the mother best. I didn't join either queue. Even after four beers, the prospect did not appeal to me in that 'conveyor-belt' situation. However, considering the pleasure that it obviously gave to so many, I felt that the two ladies should have been officially commended for gallant conduct 'above and beyond the call of duty'! Actually, the last time I saw Margaret – later that afternoon – she was running, squealing, from the dining hall with Roy Clarke and a couple of other 'old' soldiers in hot pursuit!

That night, Hank and I went downtown. After Hank had made two phone calls, one after another, to his 'bint' in Penang (who I believe was a nurse) we proceeded to the café, where we sat for hours, eating steaks – which Hank insisted should be served without vegetables – drinking Tiger and talking. Although Hank joked a lot in his usual way, the trend of the conversation was, on the whole, serious. We talked very openly about ourselves and some very personal happenings in our lives. It seemed to me that in our inmost thoughts we had much in common. Hank came across that night as someone with a carefree – even mad – manner but who felt very deeply about things within his own heart. I evidently enjoyed it all immensely as I noted in my journal the following day: 'I think this was the most enjoyable evening I've had since I came to Malaya.'

The café owner eventually boarded up and kept glancing at the clock, but it was 1.30 a.m. before we finally left the café and strolled, half-drunk, back to camp. Arriving at our destination 15 minutes later, the Guard Commander told us to go quietly to bed. We had omitted to book out and both

Mr Crisp and the CSM had commented on the fact that we were absent. However, there were no repercussions.

By Boxing Day, things began to get out of hand and, in fact, downright ugly. Prolonged drinking was having its effect. Some of the men became mad-drunk and three were put under close arrest for assault. One of the drunks challenged Corporal Paddy Quinn to a fight, but Paddy – in my opinion rightly – refused to be provoked into a drunken brawl. Hank staggered into the Signals billet halfway through the afternoon, wild-eyed and smouldering with potential violence, but Arthur managed to calm him down. Johnny, the cook – a big fellow prone to outbursts of temper at the best of times – displayed an irrational dislike for the major's present batman, Merry, and repeatedly accosted him with insults and threats. A small, good-natured lad, Merry protested: 'I haven't done anything to you, Johnny!' When Johnny responded by lunging violently towards him, Merry had no choice but to flee and take refuge in the officers' mess. Worst of all, on that Tuesday night, some of the drunks seized a cat, held it down on a table and chopped its head off with a matchet.

For many of us, therefore, the return to normal duties on Wednesday, 27 December, was welcomed with great relief. After tiffen, Swede Martin and I accompanied 8 Platoon into the Bongsu to search an area where the police suspected there was a bandit camp. Our transport took us up a very bumpy path through the rubber.

After debussing, we marched on into the jungle of the Bongsu and eventually crossed a river. On the other side, we cleared an area of undergrowth and built our bivouacs. It was dark by the time that our camp was completed and conner was served.

In the middle of the night, the sudden loud report of a Bren gun firing aroused us all from our slumber and sent us reaching for our weapons. However, it turned out to be merely a certain private (whom I shall not name) on guard who was an expert at shooting 'walking trees'!

Next day, patrols went out, leaving a few of us in base.

Around 11 a.m., there came a clear and unexpected crackling sound in the bracken nearby. We immediately stood to in defensive positions with weapons at the ready. The tree-shooting private went into an obvious state of funk, white-faced and trembling. A couple of the old soldiers made sneering, critical comments. I felt sorry for the lad, who, after all, couldn't help the way he was. As it turned out, nothing further occurred though the source of the noise remained a mystery.

Two more patrols went out the next morning, all to no avail. There had been no sign of the suspected enemy camp. After tiffen, we packed up and returned through pouring rain to the bumpy path in the rubber where our transport collected us. Upon arrival at Kulim, we learned that two more reported camps had presented themselves for investigation.

Consequently, on the following day, Saturday the 30th, both 8 and 9 Platoons were sent out. Arthur went with 9 and I with 8 Platoon. During the two-day operation, we found a small abandoned camp containing some food supplies, while 9 Platoon discovered nothing more than a months-old campsite.

Upon our return, Arthur and I were surprised to find that Hank had made a sudden departure. After being in the Signal Platoon for three years, Hank had been transferred to 'A' Company to serve his last few weeks in Malaya as a rifleman. He had known nothing about the transfer until it had suddenly appeared on Battalion Orders. Arthur was very angry about it and I had to agree that someone somewhere had treated his old pal very badly.

15

Kulim and Serdang
January–February 1951

So, 1950 had come to an end. If I had been rather unhappy in the early months, the satisfaction that I derived from the rest of the year more than compensated for this. Like every other National Serviceman, I constantly longed for the day when I would sail for home. 'Roll on the boat!' was every-one's favourite expression. Indeed, it was just as often quoted by regulars as by NS men. Even so, I was convinced – rightly or wrongly – that I was soldiering as well as most men in the company and better than some. I had also proved to myself that even if I couldn't kick a football through a goal-mouth, I could march for miles with a heavy load on my back through some of the toughest jungle terrain in the world and stay on my feet. Despite any misgivings that I might still have had about army life, I cannot stress too strongly the happiness that these two factors gave me at that time.

If 1950 had been a good year for me, it had not been good for Malaya. During that 12-month period, there had been 4,739 recorded terrorist incidents in Malaya – more than three times the number of incidents in the previous year – and 983 'contacts' had been made by units of the security forces. In the course of these events, 648 bandits, 393 members of the security forces and 646 civilians had been killed. In the year just commencing – 1951 – numbers of terrorist incidents and contacts would rise to 6,082 and 1,911 respectively, while fatalities would total 1,078 bandits, 504 members of the security forces and 533 civilians.

There was a higher level of terrorist activity in the south of the country, particularly in the states of Johore, Selangor and Pahang. Consequently, although units operating in the south had their share of 'no contact' patrols, the likelihood of contact and of achieving a high score of kills was greater for them than it was for units in the north of the country. Our battalion had a tough assignment, just the same, and had suffered comparatively heavy casualties in some pretty nasty ambushes during the past two-and-a-half years.

As 1951 began, the area for which we were operationally responsible in the states of Kedah, Perlis and Province Wellesley extended for more than 9,000 square miles. While 'C' Company remained in Kulim, 'A' Company left Serdang early in January and moved to Kuala Nerang in North Kedah. At the same time, 'D' Company relieved 'B' at Kroh and 'B' Company moved briefly to Pelam Estate before settling in Lubok Segintah near Sungei Patani.

To assist in patrolling this enormous area, the battalion had recently been considerably reinforced. Large drafts arriving from Britain, totalling just over 300 men, had enabled the rifle companies to each form a third platoon. For 'C' Company, this meant the re-creation of 7 Platoon, constituted by the 46 men of the new draft that had arrived in December. Unfortunately, 7 was never a happy platoon and – in my opinion – the time of its formation marked a definite decline in the general 'cosiness' of the company. The principal reason for this was the man who took command of 7 Platoon – Serjeant 'Pedlar' Palmer. Now, Pedlar was tough and efficient, and I'm sure would have been worth four average men in a battle situation. I suppose that he was just the kind of NCO that the army needed. However, his critical and pugnacious manner made him very unpopular with his men, as did his tendency to constantly drive them hard on patrol.

There was some general re-allocation of personnel at this time. Corporal Huddleston and Lance Corporal Short were transferred from 8 Platoon to 9. Lance Corporals Frank Keenan and Stan Swalwell were both promoted to full

270

corporal, while Corporals 'Cave-face' Hudspeth and Paddy Quinn would both soon be leaving for Penang to study for the 2nd Class Certificate of Education. Corporal McAllister shortly departed for Kuala Lumpur with a couple of others to participate in the annual boxing tournaments.

On the morning of Monday, 1 January, Corporal Spires – who had joined us specifically for Operation 'Ricebag' – returned to HQ Company in Penang, leaving Corporal Arthur Greenacre, Swede Martin, Harry Marsh and myself as 'C' Company Signals detachment.

At 7.15 a.m. on Wednesday the 3rd, a party of bandits ambushed a police truck on the road from Pelam. The police drove through the ambush with a few wounded, and soon afterwards the bandits halted and burned an estate lorry. As soon as news of the incident was received, 9 Platoon rushed out. Harry Marsh and I went along, taking one '68' set between us.

We knew that firing had still been going on half an hour before we left and we were consequently very hopeful of contact as we proceeded rapidly along the road to Pelam. Suddenly, our vehicles speeded round a bend in the road into clouds of smoke.

'Have your weapons ready, lads!' warned Lance Corporal Short.

Our convoy pulled up beside the estate lorry, which was a charred wreck and still burning. We leapt from the trucks and spread out along the grass banks on both sides of the road. The bandits had gone but not long ago. Sounds of small-arms fire could be heard some distance away to our right. Our Dyak quickly picked up the bandits' tracks and we set off through the rubber at a brisk pace.

Eventually, we met some rubber tappers, who told us that the bandits had passed them only ten minutes before. We turned and doubled in extended order over a slight rise, then resumed patrol formation once more, still moving at the double as we followed the fresh tracks. Leaping over streams and ditches, we hurried on for well over 400 yards. This was very fatiguing, especially for me with the set on my back. At last, we halted. Second Lieutenant Wride, in a state of considerable excitement, ordered 'packs off', detailed a small party to remain with the packs and told me to set up my wireless.

Lance Corporal Short asked me: 'Are you staying behind, Jock?'

'Unfortunately, yes!' I replied angrily, slamming my set down on the ground hard enough to shatter every valve in it, and then added: 'Every bastard time!'

'The signaller wants to come with us, sir.' Joe Short made the plea to Mr Wride, but the latter replied:

'Well, I'm sorry but somebody's got to stay behind!'

The Dyak was now gesticulating wildly and Mr Wride promptly set off again at a run, leading the bulk of the platoon in hot pursuit. As Harry and I were putting up our aerial, we heard more sounds of firing. However, it was too distant to be our boys. (We later learned that the bandits had brushed with a police patrol while making their escape.) After tuning in to the battalion net, I made wireless contact with signaller Ron Stringer, who was now at the scene of the ambush with a 'D' Company patrol. Soon after that, Corporal Quinn returned with a small party and told us that the platoon had been unsuccessful in locating the enemy.

We now moved on to Karangan, where Mr Wride and the rest of the platoon were waiting. From there, we all marched back to the scene of the ambush. On the way, a rifleman collapsed from heat exhaustion. I set up my wireless at the roadside and called for transport, and we were all brought safely back to camp soon after 3 p.m. Despite the disappointing outcome, it had been quite an exciting day.

On Thursday the 4th, I travelled into Penang with the ration truck in order to bring back some required Signals equipment. Minden Barracks looked as nice as ever and I was told that life was pretty cushy there at that time. I had a good chat with cousin John and with my Signals friend Chas Schaverien, who was currently employed in the wireless tower. I suggested to Chas that he might like to come to 'C' Company as a replacement for Harry Marsh, who would shortly be going home. When we consequently presented ourselves in the Signals Office, Serjeant Stan Haley immediately said to Chas: 'I know what you've come for. You want to go back with him.'

We confirmed that this was so and Stan promised to arrange it when the time came. I then happily collected the Signals gear from the stores and reported to 'C' Company's truck at the QM's. As well as the rations, we brought back a new weapon to the company: a De Lisle silent carbine, designed for knocking off sentries in the jungle without alerting the rest of the enemy camp. An opportunity to try it out would have been much appreciated!

At about 6.30 p.m. on Saturday the 8th, I was hastily alerted to don my jungle kit, and promptly left camp with 9 Platoon, having received no information as to where we were going or why. We stopped on the road near Junjong, debussed and followed a track for a few hundred yards, before halting on the approach to a kampong. Here, we waited in the rapidly growing darkness.

As Mr Wride was about to walk past me on the track, I quietly hailed him. 'Excuse me, sir,' I said, a little exasperated. 'But would you mind telling me what we're supposed to be doing? I mean, is there any grif?'

'Right,' Mr Wride replied. 'The grif is that the bandits have burned down two kampongs further down the road this afternoon. This kampong would appear to be the next one in line.' He paused. 'I always like to brief everyone before an operation but on this occasion there just wasn't time. I apologise for that.'

Mr Wride was a tall, fine-looking chap who had that something about him which enabled him to command respect and obedience without ever requiring to be belligerent or even raise his voice. As a schoolboy and action-film fan, I had naively imagined that all British Army officers would be like that!

We now continued into the kampong, where Mr Wride allotted the platoon to positions of all-round defence. I set up my wireless on the verandah of a *basha* and had a hell of a job putting up my aerial in the dark. After a brew-up, we all settled down in our positions. To while away the time I listened to musical broadcasts from Radio Malaya until midnight, feeling very content with my lot. At 1 a.m., I received a call from Arthur in Kulim. We established contact-QSA 5/1–2; meaning that I could hear him clearly while he was receiving me faintly. This was really quite remarkable for that time of night.

Up until then, the whole platoon had remained awake in defence positions. However, nothing had occurred, so sentries were posted and the rest of us went to sleep. Soon after daylight, we had breakfast and then marched back to the main road, where our transport was awaiting us. I took considerable satisfaction in supposing that our presence the previous night may well have saved that Malay village from being burned down and, indeed, might have shifted the bandits out of the vicinity.

Tuesday, 9 January, heralded the commencement of a new phase of my army service: 9 Platoon was sent on detachment to 'A' Company's former base at Serdang, with Harry Marsh and me detailed as the detachment's signallers. During the morning, 8 Platoon patrolled the road in the Terap region as an anti-ambush precaution. However, 9 Platoon's convoy arrived safely at Serdang just as the rear party of 'A' Company was departing.

The base at Serdang was pretty primitive, with undependable water and electricity supplies. The old planter's bungalow – with Platoon HQ upstairs and the combined dining hall and canteen downstairs – was fairly dilapidated. The men of the platoon were accommodated in squad tents beyond the MT park. Surrounding the camp on all sides were rubber trees and more rubber trees. The village of Serdang had been declared out of bounds, so we would be permanently confined to barracks except when we went out on operations. It would be fair to describe Serdang as rather a bleak outstation in every way.

Our first task was to get the place shipshape. Harry and I

established our '62' set upstairs in the platoon office, and erected our aerial as well as our loudspeakers for broadcasting music around the camp, as at Kulim. Our beds were located in a corner section of the platoon office. Mr Wride, Serjeant 'Taggy' Bell and Albert Green, Mr Wride's batman, all had rooms on the upstairs floor. Although there was a frequent lack of water in the pipes, we were deluged with rainwater through the leaking roof and windows every time it rained. Despite everything, my journal entry described our quarters as a 'really nice billet'.

My friend Matt Busby had been seconded from 8 Platoon to manage the PRI canteen in Serdang, as Private Eathorne did (at some profit, it was said!) in Kulim. Matt was billeted downstairs amongst his store of drinks and foodstuffs. Separated from Brodie and other pals of his old platoon, Matt relied heavily on me for company and we became very close friends during this period. I even corresponded briefly with his girlfriend, Enid, regarding some personal problem that Matt was concerned about. Enid eventually fixed me up with a penfriend from her young ladies teachers' training college, with whom I exchanged very friendly letters for the duration of my remaining time in Malaya.

Our first operation from this new location was a foray into the Gunong Inas Forest Reserve on Sunday the 14th. Information had been received about a camp to which it was believed that several parties of bandits had retreated recently. Accompanied by a police officer, his jungle squad and an informer, we cautiously approached the indicated site of the camp. Suddenly, a shot rang out – but it transpired that Mr Wride had pressed the trigger of his Owen gun accidentally! Without delay we scrambled swiftly up a short slope into the bandit camp, only to find that it was deserted.

There were two attap *bashas* which would accommodate about 15 men. They had been built at least a month before but there were signs of more recent occupation. We recovered a few medical supplies, then set fire to the *bashas*. In the meantime, a far larger fire had mysteriously started in

275

the vegetation around the approach track through the valley below us. We were unable to see anything through the thick scrub, but the roar and crackling sounded very loud and close, as though the flames were spreading up the hill towards us.

We promptly departed in the opposite direction and, after wading through some swamps, came to a stretch of burned-out *lallang* which was still alight and smoking in some places. From here, we undertook a long and fatiguing march along a main track until we reached a small kampong, where we stayed the night.

Next morning, we returned safely to Serdang, only to find that the camp's electricity and water supplies had both ceased to function. Consequently, we were unable to wash off the mud and sweat from our bodies until the following day.

At 7 p.m. on Tuesday the 16th, the Serdang police reported to Mr Wride that an outburst of small-arms fire had been heard nearby. When Mr Wride came through to the Signals billet, I believed him to say to me: 'Scurr, get some estate on the phone and ask if there's any shooting going on there.'

With that, he departed and I duly dialled the operator at Serdang telephone exchange. 'Give me some estate, please,' I requested. 'Any estate.'

'Any estate?' the Malay operator queried.

'Yes, any estate,' I answered. 'It doesn't matter which one as long as it's a rubber estate.'

First of all, I was connected to an estate where the recipient of my call answered in Cantonese. So I asked the operator to try another. This time, an English voice informed me that there was no trouble on his estate. A third call received the same reply.

At that point, Mr Wride returned and I understood him to ask me: 'Have you got some estate yet, Scurr?'

'I've phoned three so far,' I replied, thinking that I'd done rather well.

276

'You've phoned three?' Mr Wride asked in perplexed tones. 'What d'you mean?'

'Well, you asked me to phone some estate,' I explained, equally disconcerted.

'No!' Mr Wride exclaimed. 'I said to phone Somme Estate!'

We didn't laugh about it until later. After getting Somme Estate on the line, Mr Wride spoke to the English manager, who said that his special constables had opened fire in the darkness but he was unable to say whether their targets had been real or imaginary. Mr Wride wasn't keen to take the platoon out there as the AKC van had just arrived in camp to give us a film show.

'I don't want to turn my chaps out at this time of night if it's just a case of a few jittery SCs firing at shadows,' he told the manager.

'I quite understand,' came the cool reply.

'But if anything further develops, ring us immediately,' Mr Wride added.

I was then detailed to sit by the phone while everyone else went to watch the films. However, as no phone call came during the next hour and a half, Mr Wride sent his batman to bring me to watch the second feature.

During this period, I was on very friendly terms with Second Lieutenant David Wride. I suppose being at that outstation with no other officers for company would leave him rather isolated. Consequently, he tended to stroll into the Signals billet quite regularly and would chat to me about life at Sandhurst 'where bullshit was bullshit', his home in Farnborough, his girlfriend and the films that he liked. His favourites, I was pleased to hear, were *The Four Feathers* and *Northwest Passage*. His father was a lieutenant colonel and his young brother, Norman, was also in Malaya at that time. Norman was a lieutenant in the Malayan Police. Although stationed in another region, he had visited his brother at our camp in Kulim. While on patrol, Mr Wride would sometimes call me 'Jock' but he always reverted to

277

calling me 'Scurr' when we were once more back in base. At no time, however, did I address him as anything other than 'Mr Wride' or 'Sir', no matter how friendly the chat.

There was one operation at that time when I 'bivvied' with Mr Wride and his batman, Albert Green. Despite a downpour of heavy rain, the bulky and almost constantly humorous Serjeant 'Taggy' Bell was organising the cooking with his customary efficiency and culinary magic. Taggy could do wonders with a few tins of compo rations plus some rice and curry powder. When he now yelled: 'Conner up!' Albert and I both expressed dismay at the idea of venturing forth from the shelter of our *basha* into the rainstorm. To our surprise, Mr Wride promptly grabbed our mess tins and mugs and dashed out through the deluge. Shortly after, soaked through and bedraggled, he returned with our meals, still hot if somewhat waterlogged. It wasn't very often that an officer would act as 'batman' to two privates!

This occurred during a four-day duffy of almost continuous rainstorms, from which we drove back along flooded roads on Monday, 22 January. At that date, there were nine men hospitalised in the Kulim MRS with malaria. Upon returning from the operation just described, Corporal Huddleston discovered that he was feverish. It also happened that the weekly ration truck had arrived at our camp from Kulim that afternoon but had omitted to bring the normal supplies of tea and sugar with the other foodstuffs. Consequently, Mr Wride gave me the following message to transmit by wireless to Kulim: 'CORPORAL HUDDLESTON HAS HIGH TEMPERATURE. PLEASE SEND AMBULANCE. ALSO TEA AND SUGAR.'

As was frequently the case during an evening transmission, there was considerable atmospheric interference. Swede Martin, operating the '62' set at Kulim, asked me twice to repeat the message, which I did. Swede told me later that he eventually took the following written message to Major Murray: 'CORPORAL HUDDLESTON HAS MY LITERATURE. PLEASE SEND AMBULANCE WITH TEA AND SUGAR.' The major immediately demanded clarification! Swede came back on set and asked me to repeat the message once more. This time he received the details correctly. The ambulance duly arrived, bringing our tea and sugar rations, and took Corporal Huddleston back to Kulim, where malaria was instantly diagnosed. Fortunately, Corporal Huddleston made a speedy recovery and was able to leave for Penang at the end of the month, before taking his boat to Blighty.

My Signals friend, Chas Schaverien, had now been posted to 'C' Company, but for the time being was stationed at Kulim. I was nonetheless cheered by the thought that he would soon be joining me.

Having close friends to share the hardships and the good times was one of the assets of soldiering in Malaya, but it could also bring pain. Lance Corporal Jim Whitehead was a tall ex-miner from Barnsley with a droll sense of humour. In October 1950 he had transferred from 'A' to 'B' Company, where he was once more reunited in 6 Platoon with Private Gerry Sweeney, an old mate from basic training four years previously.

In January 1951 'B' Company was based on a rubber estate at Lubok Segintah, South Kedah. Early in the morning of the 26th of that month, the two friends were in their tent, preparing to go out on patrol. Gerry noticed that Jim was strangely quiet, so he said to him: 'Are we fit, then?'

Instead of his customary wry remark about the purpose of the patrol, Jim replied: 'No. I am bloody fed up with this game! I'll be glad to get on the boat home.'

Neither Gerry nor their other mate, Corporal Bill Lyness, had ever seen Jim like this before. Jim had only one more month to serve in Malaya, which now seemed just as well.

Under the command of Major Sutcliffe, 4 and 6 Platoons commenced their patrol through Pelam Estate, with 4 Platoon leading. After a few miles there was a short break; then 6 Platoon prepared to take the lead. As Lance Corporal Gordon Hill, leading scout, moved up to the front, he passed Jim Whitehead, who was sitting at the side of the track. Jim had emptied his magazine and, holding out the bullets in his hand, he said to Gordon: 'Look, Gord, a handful of death!'

Gordon Hill took the lead, with his pal, Private Arthur Bills, following as second scout. They soon entered secondary jungle, which they had to chop their way through, and eventually came to an area where trees had been chopped down. There appeared to be no one there, but tools had been left lying on the ground. Continuing along the edge of the clearing, they came across a track that ended abruptly. This seemed to indicate one of the bandits' tricks, which was to go in different directions and break the track in order to conceal their position. Their suspicions were increased when they spotted a fountain pen on the ground at this spot. The two scouts summoned Second Lieutenant Harrison and showed him their finds, but he ordered them to continue through the jungle.

After 6 Platoon had turned down the hill and reached the bottom, they were once more among rubber trees. Major Sutcliffe, just ahead of 4 Platoon, now looked up and spotted Communists in their khaki drill uniforms at the top of the adjacent slope. Shouting an order, he launched the two platoons in an assault up the hill. This brought a fusillade of enemy fire from the high ridge. Hastening to get to cover, Gordon Hill saw Jim Whitehead fall and realised he had been hit. Once under cover, the two platoons returned fire up the slope. An EY rifleman discharged a grenade, which hit a tree and exploded above the men of 6 Platoon, showering them with shrapnel and injuring one man in the foot.

Major Sutcliffe now urged his men forward as the bandits appeared to be withdrawing. But there was a rearguard that remained upon a knoll on the ridge, maintaining a determined fire upon the troops below. Gordon Hill and Arthur Bills began to work their way round one side of the knoll, hoping to cut off the enemy's escape, but the bandits must have fled out the other side, where one Chinese – later revealed to be an officer – was still continuously firing from the knoll.

On that other side, three soldiers were making good progress. One was Serjeant 'Geordie' Dee, a big, bluff character whom I remembered well from my draft's jungle training days. The second was a fairly small and stocky lad, Private 'Judo' Roberts, so nicknamed as a result of his often stated devotion to that sport. The third was Private 'Dinger' Bell, a slim and studious-looking signaller who was quite new to operations, and who had swiftly discarded his '68' set upon coming under fire. Once this trio had succeeded in flanking the lone bandit's position, Dinger Bell and Judo Roberts opened fire with their rifles. A well-aimed shot from the latter hit the bandit in the head and brought him down. Geordie Dee then ran forward and finished the Chinese off with a burst from his M2 carbine.

Meanwhile, Gerry Sweeney and Corporal 'Lofty' Watts had advanced around the base of the hill and then up the flank where the firing hadn't been so heavy. As they neared the crest, all sounds of gunfire suddenly ceased. Then, as the two made their way to the centre of the hill, one of the lads there called out : 'Hey Gerry, your mate's been hit!'

Gerry hastened down below the crest and found Jim Whitehead lying on his back. He could not see a mark on him, so he took off his pack to put beneath his friend's head, saying: 'You'll be all right, Jim. We'll soon get you fixed up.' But then when he put his hand under Jim's head he realised to his horror that part of the back of the head had been blown away. The bullet must have entered his mouth and gone straight through. Gerry's mind flashed back to Jim's strange mood early that morning and wondered if it had resulted from a premonition.

When Gordon Hill and Arthur Bills also arrived upon the scene, they saw that Corporal Bill Lyness was standing solemnly over Jim's body and had placed his hat over his face. Like others around them, they stood there for a moment completely numbed.

Well sited on the knoll was a camp that had been occupied by 60 bandits. Documents, foodstuffs and 11 packs were recovered from the camp. Some days later, 6 Platoon was patrolling in the same area when they came upon a swampy clearing in the jungle. There were four recently killed bandits in the swamp who could have been left there following 'B' Company's attack. However, there was no way of knowing for sure, so 'B' Company were unable to take credit for these kills and the police were summoned to collect the bodies.

Jim Whitehead was well-known and liked in the battalion and his loss was mourned by men from all companies who attended his funeral in Penang cemetery.

On hearing the details of this action, I felt very envious of Dinger Bell. It seemed to me most unfair that he should have been granted this experience so early in his service as a signaller, while I had participated in numerous operations without having had the opportunity to fire my rifle at the enemy!

A few days after this skirmish, 6 Platoon, 'B' Company, was rushed to prevent further trouble in the Junon area, following a rather bloody incident. Apparently, Malays in this district, heartily sick of Chinese squatters giving aid to the local bandits, had attacked the squatters' shanties and chopped up the inhabitants with their parangs, killing quite a few of them. The men of 6 Platoon did all they could to patch up the wounded. One elderly Chinese man was found sitting in a chair with his face sliced away and hanging forward from the rest of his head, right down to his jaw. While awaiting more expert medical aid, the platoon officer lifted the face and pressed it back into place, hoping this might help. The platoon discovered a camp near the squatter area from which the bandits had bolted just a few hours prior to its arrival.

On Wednesday the 31st, my fellow signaller Harry Marsh left Serdang to go home and was replaced three days later by my friend Chas Schaverien. That same day, Saturday, 3 February, Mr Wride left us, having been temporarily seconded to HQ in Penang in order to train a new draft from Blighty.

16

Serdang and Kulim
February–April 1951

On Wednesday morning, 7 February, 9 Platoon departed
for Kulim and 8 Platoon arrived to take over detachment
duty at Serdang.

During the ensuing period, my relationship with Second
Lieutenant John Crisp was friendly but fairly formal. Somehow, I was inclined to be slightly tense in Mr Crisp's
company and ever aware of the fact that he was an officer
and I a private soldier. I had been able to forget the
difference in rank and relax with David Wride but was
never able to do so with John Crisp. Initially, I sensed that
he was quite keen to be on friendly terms with me. However, I was unable to surmount the rank barrier and
although he always treated me pleasantly, we normally only
spoke in the line of duty. I suspect that my reticence was
mainly due to the fact that I continued to revere Mr Crisp
as a hero figure.

Visits by a local planter and his daughter and by police
officers from the neighbourhood happily provided some
social relief for Mr Crisp. The platoon now had a serjeant,
by name of Dignan, who had been transferred to 'C'
Company from the recently formed Mortar Platoon in HQ.
Serjeant Dignan was a small, stout, likeable fellow Scot. He
always treated me well, as he did everyone else as far as I
know. One night, when the planter and his daughter came
to watch an AKC film show at Mr Crisp's invitation, Serjeant Dignan was drunk and apparently manifested his
'love' for the young lady. The following morning, Mr Crisp

phoned the planter, offering profuse apologies and giving assurances that such an incident would never happen again.

Matt Busby remained in his post as 'canteen wallah' and we continued to be very good friends at this time. Fortunately, Matt also got on well with my Signals mate, Chas Schaverien. Chas was a small, dark-haired chap who was well educated and generally cheerful, though inclined to be introverted – to a lesser extent than myself, I should add! We took turns at going out on patrol as signaller, and whoever remained in camp was always pleased to see the other's return.

Much has been said about the especially close friendships formed by soldiers, particularly when they are depending upon one another in difficult and dangerous circumstances. I can only confirm that there was indeed something 'special' about the bonds of comradeship which I experienced in the army, even with men from different social backgrounds with whom I may have had little in common in Civvy Street. Wearing the same uniform and sharing the same regimentation, petty injustices, hazards, ordeals, discomforts and revelries seemed to nurture a friendship and affection which were not normally expressed but which were deeply felt. Among good friends remembered over the years, army mates remain unique.

During my time in Serdang, my consumption of Tiger beer increased and drinking, in fact, became a regular nightly activity. Two large bottles of the potent brew were enough to make me very happy, while three tended to render me uncharacteristically boastful or even argumentative. The only time when it was my steadfast rule never to consume alcohol was on the night preceding an operation. It seemed to me that jungle-bashing was hard enough without starting out with a hangover. Even with this precaution, however, it is probable that drinking had an unbeneficial effect upon my general physical condition. Jungle marches seemed harder than ever to endure. At this time, I also began to have periods when I grew rather morose. It may not just have been drink, of course, that caused these things. Perhaps all the months of bearing a heavy load on jungle trails, with all the tension involved, was beginning to take its toll.

On the other hand, it cannot be denied that the pleasure I derived from drinking Tiger beer in the company of my mates was considerable. As we were confined to camp during off-duty hours, having a drink was really the only thing there was to look forward to. Also, when tramping through the jungle, sweltering in the damp heat and close to exhaustion, the prospect of an ice-cold Tiger beer when I returned to camp was a tantalising inspiration to keep plodding on.

By now, I had ceased to welcome the agonies of jungle marches as a means of 'absolution' for my boyhood and adolescent inadequacies. I was content that I had already paid my 'penance' in full and believed that I had, in fact, 'redeemed' myself a hundred times over. Carrying my '68' set and other gear up and down jungle-covered hills was something that I now viewed quite sensibly as hard, gruelling toil which was taking a lot out of me.

Even so, I still found myself regularly volunteering to go out on duffies for which a signaller was not required, such as one-day local patrols or night ambushes. I continued to live in hope of viewing the enemy through my rifle sights, one fine day.

On Thursday evening, 22 February, news reached us that a soldier in 'B' Company, Private Fee, had been grievously injured while diving into the Muda river in Central Kedah. He later died in Penang General Hospital and was buried in Penang cemetery on Wednesday, 21 February.

Late on Saturday afternoon, the 24th, Major Murray arrived in Serdang to confer with Mr Crisp. After a while, I was called through to the verandah where the major and Mr Crisp were seated in basket chairs, having a drink.

'Now, Scurr,' the major said, looking up at me with a warm smile. 'How would you like to come back to Kulim? You've been stuck out here for quite a while now.'

I hesitated for a moment. Although Kulim was a much

preferred location, my friend Chas had only recently arrived in Serdang; we had long wished to serve together on the same outstation. Also, 8 Platoon had always been my favourite.

'I'd rather stay here, sir,' I replied.

'I can't tempt you to come back?' the major asked in a kindly tone. 'After all, the bright lights of Kulim are far away and the brighter lights of Penang are even further.'

'No, sir,' I said. 'I'm quite happy here.'

Major Murray turned to Mr Crisp and said: 'You must be taking good care of him.'

'I must be,' Mr Crisp agreed, with a grin.

As always, I was relieved to be dismissed. Even though he was being kind and considerate towards me, I still felt an inner dread that the major might suddenly switch to being 'difficult'.

On Sunday evening, the 25th, we were briefed for a company operation to be launched in the Bongsu Forest Reserve. The plan seemed good. Because of the locations of recent road ambushes of police and civilian vehicles, Intelligence considered that the bandits had established their camps in the north and west of the Bongsu. Therefore, following an air strike, seven 'C' Company patrols and two police jungle squads were going to probe these areas. At the same time, 1,000 auxiliary police were going to lay ambushes across the region which extended between the north and west target areas. Chas was detailed to operate a set for Captain Haddon's patrol and left for Kulim that evening.

Next morning, Monday the 26th, we left camp at 6.45 and debussed from our transport about half an hour later at Terap. From here, we marched some way along a track and then halted. Within the next hour, some Brigands and Lincolns flew overhead. We heard their bombs exploding shortly after, although we were unable to see anything. When the bombing stopped, we pushed on into the Bongsu, encountering quite a lot of mud and water at first. All the

286

time, we travelled pretty steadily uphill through thick jungle and the going was very hard.

Eventually, we came upon the remains of what Mr Crisp and the Dyak estimated to be a four-day-old camp. This was quite near the location of another camp that 8 Platoon had burned down a few months before. Fearing lest there might be bandits again using the old camp, Mr Crisp ordered 'packs off' and detailed four chaps to remain behind.

Serjeant Dignan asked me: 'Are you staying behind, Jock?'

'Not on your life!' I answered. 'I was left behind once before!'

'So was I, Jock!' interjected Private Reeves meaningfully. Although I knew men who readily stated, no doubt very wisely, that on no account did they wish to meet any bandits, most of the lads were keen to 'have a go'.

Mr Crisp led us cautiously up the slope to where the camp was situated on the hilltop. The charred structures of several large *bashas* encircled an open clearing on the edge of which stood two bamboo seats, similar in design to park benches in Blighty. However, it was immediately obvious that the camp was quite unoccupied, so we dejectedly returned for our packs.

Serjeant Dignan's section now left us to patrol another area and the rest of us moved back up to the camp, where I set up my wireless. Mr Crisp took out a small patrol while the remainder of us 'reconditioned' one of the large, charred *bashas* with ponchos. All 14 of us kipped side by side in that *basha* for the night. The CLO and the Dyak had constructed a small *basha* of their own nearby. Consequently, we only required one post for night stag.

Mr Crisp took out an all-day patrol on the following day. I spent my time taking wireless transmissions, doing stags, brewing up, etc. Water was a bind here as it had to be carted up in brew cans from the river, which lay at the foot of the steep slope.

Next morning, Wednesday the 28th, we packed up and set off to patrol on a roundabout route back to the road. As nearly all rations had been eaten, leaving packs practically empty, Mr Crisp set a fairly fast pace, irrespective of the 50 pounds still on my back. We descended to the river and waded up it for a short way until we reached a slope that we had climbed two days before, while on our way to the camp. On seeing the footprints in the mud that had been left by our own jungle boots, Mr Crisp immediately conjured up a party of bandits and led us rapidly up the slope, despite protests from the scouts that we were following our own tracks! We halted at the top of the hill after an agonising climb, and Mr Crisp at last realised his mistake.

'Well, I just can't understand how this happened,' he said rather sheepishly. 'I'm sorry, chaps.'

'You're not half as sorry as we are, sir!' I could not resist commenting.

After descending the slope once more, we climbed the opposite one. That was just the beginning. For the following three-and-a-half hours, we continued to climb hill after hill, scrambling beneath creepers and through dense undergrowth until all were near exhaustion. With my '68' set and other gear weighing heavily upon my back, I felt more on the verge of collapse than I had ever done before. Later, I wrote in my journal: 'I became so weak I almost wept.'

Immediately behind me was Private Reeves, who, observing my faltering condition, twice offered to relieve me of my load within half-an-hour, but both times I refused. Then, after climbing with slow steps to the top of yet another hill, tottering and stumbling all the way and straining my lungs to gasp in breath, I suddenly felt Reeves' hands grasp the harness of my '68' set.

'Jock, for God's sake!' he exclaimed. 'Let me take it!'

Silently, I allowed Reeves to ease the set's harness from my shoulders. I found it very disheartening to thus break my long-maintained tradition of never letting anyone in the company carry my set for me. However, at that moment it seemed to me that I really had no choice, given the state of

288

near-collapse that I had reached. Despite this, I felt that I had accepted a breaking-point and was far from happy about it.

As we made our way down the reverse slope, Reeves' pack felt so light that I hardly knew I had it on. Strangely, from then on, we kept on the flat nearly all the time. Although hopelessly lost, we eventually struck a good track, with pig-traps dug at intervals along it, which led us – much to our delight – out of the jungle and into the rubber. We now descended to a river where we brewed up. Feeling in a bit of a daze, I summoned what energy remained to erect my aerial, tune in my wireless and request transport. After tiffen, we continued our march to the road, where our transport collected us and took us back to Serdang.

When Chas returned from Kulim, he told me that, in the Bongsu, Captain Haddon had stepped on one of the RAF's bombs which had failed to explode when dropped. Fortunately, neither did the bomb explode when trodden on! I also learned that none of the other patrols had achieved any more success in finding the enemy's occupied camps than we'd had. After what was undoubtedly one of the worst day's marches I'd ever been subjected to, I was far from delighted when I found that I had to spend that night on guard duty!

At the beginning of March, Mr Crisp took most of the platoon out on an operation with Chas as signaller. Lance Corporal Scott was left in charge and those of us remaining in camp had a pretty cushy time. One of my favourite pleasures, that weekend, was watching a troupe of large black apes leaping around among the rubber trees just beyond our camp's perimeter fence. On Sunday night, 4 March, however, I observed another display that was far from entertaining.

Just after 6 p.m., a storeman was sitting quietly on his bed, showing a couple of the lads photographs in his album. Suddenly, he went berserk. For no apparent reason, he began knocking down the plank walls of the stores with his bare fists and breaking the planks across his knee. Then he began slinging heavy equipment about as though it were a feather-weight; all the time growling like a wild animal.

The dozen of us who had been left in camp watched in bewilderment and increasing alarm. Our main worry was that he might start throwing the stored grenades and mortar bombs around. So, while someone tried to attract the storeman's attention, another person would run in behind him, snatch a case of grenades or bombs and run out at the other side of the half-demolished shed. Thus, over a short period, all of the explosive items were safely removed.

The storeman continued to wreck his abode for about three hours. Every so often, he seemed to weaken and would break into tears. Then he'd summon new strength and would start again, smashing down the remains of the walls and hurling equipment about. Few dared go near him. He was quite a big chap and seemed suddenly endowed with superhuman strength. Pilgrim, the cook, bravely approached him and offered him a fag. The storeman responded by growling and savagely lashing out, so that Pilgrim had to rapidly withdraw.

Our principal medical orderly at Serdang was Private Edney, RAMC. Lean and bespectacled, Edney was an 'old soldier' who always claimed to have been present at any Second World War battle that anyone cared to mention. Though he had an awful voice, the lads used to encourage him to sing in the canteen at night, calling him 'Nelson Edney'! Recognising the situation as being a medical problem, he felt that it was his responsibility to resolve it.

'We've got to overpower him before he does any more damage,' he announced. 'So I want some volunteers to rush him.'

Everyone remained silent.

'Come on!' Edney urged, eyeing would-be hard cases. 'Where's all me toughies?'

The 'toughies' responded by saying: 'Bollocks to that!' and other such comments.

Edney now shook his head and, completely alone, crept up behind the storeman and leapt on his back. With a roar, the storeman threw Edney off onto the ground. Undaunted, Edney tried two more times with the same result. Fortunately, each time that the storeman cast Edney away he seemed to lose interest in his assailant and returned to smashing up objects. Just the same, Edney was truly brave.

Lance Corporal Scott, after rather a long delay, phoned Major Murray at Kulim. The major then contacted the Serdang police. Eventually, a police van drove up and the OCPD (Officer Commanding Police District) got out, accompanied by a couple of Malay constables. When the storeman once more sank to his knees during one of his recurrent weak spells, the OCPD hit him over the head with a baton, knocking him unconscious. The storeman was then put in a straightjacket, taken in the van to the police station and later transported to the British Military Hospital at Taiping.

When Mr Crisp returned from patrol the following morning, he was greatly surprised to find the stores almost entirely demolished.

On Thursday morning, the 8th, Serjeant Dignan took out what was intended to be a one-day patrol and I went with it as a rifleman. Transport took us into Anak Kulim Estate, where a day or so before, 9 Platoon had found a *basha* – unoccupied, at that time – containing three large sacks of rice. Private Derrick Ross, from 9 Platoon, was going to lead us to this *basha* and we were to detain anyone who we found there.

The sun seemed exceptionally hot as we followed a track through the rubber. We crossed a couple of hills and rivers and eventually arrived around 11 a.m. at a large, tin-roofed *basha* which was situated on a slight rise at the foot of a hill. The *basha* was deserted, although the warm ashes in the fireplace indicated that a meal had been cooked there that morning. There was plenty of clothing lying around, mostly of a Chinese woman and child, and freshly dhobied items of clothing were hanging stiffly on a line. The three large sacks of rice were still up in the loft.

We settled down to eat our haversack rations, have a

291

brew-up and wait to see if the occupants would return. By about 3.30 p.m., no one had turned up, so Serjeant Dignan picked out eight of us to remain, comprising the Bren group and mostly chaps with sub-machine guns. He selected me – much to my satisfaction – and made me change weapons with Bramhall so that I had a Sten. Two other riflemen chosen had to make similar exchanges. Then, he sent the remainder of the patrol back to meet our transport, with orders to hold the trucks for an hour and if we didn't show up by then, to return to camp and send transport again at 7.30 next morning.

Serjeant Dignan, Reeves and I carried out a short reconnaissance around the top of the hill but found nothing. Evening arrived and still there was no sign of any occupants. Attempts to catch a chicken proved fruitless, so we partook of a frugal meal, consisting of a small bowl of boiled rice and an equally small bowl of coffee per man. Then we settled down for the night, hoping that either the missing occupants or a party of bandit customers for the rice would approach under cover of darkness.

We did stag in pairs, sitting outside the door of the *basha* with personal weapons plus the Bren gun. My first spell was from 7 till 9 p.m. About eight o'clock, two large dogs that had been hanging about nearby – apparently belonging to the occupants – began to bark, suggesting that someone was coming down the hill. Everyone immediately stood to, with weapons at the ready. Serjeant Dignan ordered me forward to the corner of the *basha*, facing towards the approach track. I took up position and waited expectantly with my finger on the trigger of my Sten, peering into the darkness. The dogs continued to bark. I felt tense yet remarkably calm. We waited. No one appeared. The dogs ceased barking. If someone had been coming, obviously the dogs had warned them off.

The remainder of my stag was eventless, as was my second spell from 3 till 4 a.m. The stone floor of the *basha* was rather cold and hard but I didn't sleep too badly between stags – apart from when I was disturbed by Derrick

Ross, vehemently complaining that I was lying across his 'bed'.

We rose at 7.15 a.m., somewhat later than we had intended, and hurried at a fair pace back to our transport rendezvous. Arriving there about 8 a.m., we found the trucks and their escorts patiently waiting. We now returned to Serdang for a most welcome breakfast, not having had a proper meal for 24 hours.

After my return, Chas told me that Major Murray had come to see Mr Crisp the previous day and had brought a Scottish journal for me. (A month before, he had sent me one with the ration truck.) Chas was inside the stationary scout car, tinkering with the '19' wireless set, when the major arrived and overheard him ask Mr Crisp: 'Where's Scurr?'

'Scurr's gone out with the patrol as a rifleman,' Mr Crisp replied. 'He volunteered.'

'Very good,' the major said. 'He's a good chap, Scurr.'

'Yes, he is,' Mr Crisp agreed.

When Chas told me this I felt really elated. After all the adverse opinions that the army seemed to have of me during my training days, it was nice to know that at last (to quote from my Cadet Discharge Certificate) I had 'gained the esteem of my officers'.

Mr Crisp took out another patrol to ambush the *basha* with the rice over the weekend, while the rest of us took it easy in camp. However, our repose did not last. At 8.45 on Sunday night, the 11th, the police phoned from Selama to say that a nearby post was under heavy attack and asking for our help. While Serjeant Dignan phoned hurriedly through to Kulim to inform Major Murray, I ran downstairs to the canteen shouting: 'Everybody get dressed! Everybody get dressed for going out! There's a battle on at Selama!'

There was one mad rush. Apart from about four members of the guard, everyone in camp, cooks included, scrambled into their jungle kit, loaded their weapons and dived onto the trucks. We were soon speeding along the road,

293

hastened by a call from Serjeant Dignan in the 15-hundred-weight: 'Tell them to get cracking in front! Get a move on!'

This was passed on to our driver in the 3-tonner and then to the scout car in front, and the speed was increased even more. We were soon on a very bumpy, uneven stretch of road, raising a hell of a dust and with bods nearly thrown off the trucks as we sped along. At Selama North, we picked up a few police and then continued at full speed. Malay special constables and kampong guards, armed with shotguns, were stood to at all posts along the road. At last reaching Selama South, we carried on to Sungei Bayor, where we halted and debussed.

Several police squads were standing by and we were soon informed that a kampong just down the track had been attacked. However, everything was now quiet and it appeared that the bandits had withdrawn. A police squad had gone down to check, so we waited for a while. To my great disappointment there was no further bandit activity. After Serjeant Dignan had phoned Kulim to make a brief report to the major, we returned to Serdang, arriving in camp just after 11 p.m.

As I retired to bed that night, I could hardly believe that contact with the enemy had eluded me once more. I had been so sure during our rushed drive to Selama that I was at last heading for an armed encounter. My recurring depression began to descend upon me once more. I was beginning to lose hope.

Mr Crisp's patrol returned the next day, still without success. That night, Chas, Matt and I drank three Tigers apiece in the Signals billet, ending up with a rousing sing-song of regimental ditties, such as:

We are the KOYLI,
We'll kill the enemy by and by,
Every man of the regiment
Is ready to do or die! . . .

All feelings of depression were now vanquished. Good old Tiger! This is the life! I thought. Perhaps on the next duffy, my luck will change!

The next duffy soon came round. At a briefing on Friday night, the 16th, Mr Crisp informed us that the recent swoop on the north and west of the Bongsu appeared to have driven the bandits out as there had been no further terrorist incidents in these localities. Consequently, the same tactics were now to be employed on the other side of the road in the Anak Kulim–Junjong area, where 7 and 9 Platoons were going to operate to the north of our zone and APs (auxiliary police) would be strung out in ambush again, covering gaps and likely escape routes.

During a long and exhausting march from Terap the following day, through rough and hilly country, I was once more absolutely bushed. So, upon receiving an offer from Private Powell, I swopped my set for his pack. A few hundred yards further on, we halted at a kampong and made base. Powell, Reeves and I built a *basha* for the three of us and spent a comparatively comfortable night.

Next day, Sunday the 18th, it bucketed down and our *bashas* became badly flooded. I was unable to make wireless contact due, as I later learned, to a sudden shortage of batteries at both Kulim and Serdang. Sitting in a puddle in my *basha*, looking out at the lashing rain, I felt miserable and sullen and disinclined to bother with anything or anybody. The following day, I was very glad to return to camp and noted in my journal: 'During this op, I just sat on my rear-quarters doing absolutely fuck-all and thoroughly cheesed. I'm afraid my keenness has now worn off.'

Upon my return, Chas told me that Arthur Greenacre had been taken into Taiping BMH with a fever, which proved to be malaria, and that Lance Corporal Charlie Battams had been sent from HQ to act as temporary 'Pronto' (i/c Signals) at Kulim. I wondered if this had been the cause of the shortage of wireless batteries!

By the following morning, I'd cheered up considerably.

While conversing in our billet I remarked to Chas: 'Thank God the government put on the extra six months! If National Service had remained at eighteen months, I'd have been discharged on the twenty-eighth of February and I'd probably be working in an office or something ghastly like that by now.'

Chas shook his head. 'You're mad, Jock!' he said. 'Don't you want to go home?'

'Oh, yes,' I answered. 'I'm really looking forward to going home and to my demob leave but I'm dreading what comes after that.' ·

'Isn't there any civvy job you fancy?' Chas asked.

'No,' I replied. 'I wouldn't mind being a commercial artist in a brassiere factory but nothing else appeals!'

We both laughed. But in fact, there was no civilian job that interested me; yet I still had strong reservations about signing on in the regular army. The thought of regimental bullshit and manoeuvres in Germany – the battalion's next posting – did not inspire me at all. In truth, I preferred just not to think about it and to live in hope that somehow my dilemma would miraculously sort itself out when the time came.

I seemed to be back to my old self by Thursday the 22nd when I volunteered for a night ambush that was to be laid in the Sungei Ular area, where bandits had fired on a police post the previous night. There were two ambush parties of just five men each which were to cover two likely tracks in the area. I was with Mr Crisp's party. We took up position amongst shrubbery, overlooking a narrow track, under a full moon. Mr Crisp was number one stop and detailed me to be number two. As this meant that he trusted me not to open fire until as many bandits as possible had entered the killing zone, I was rather pleased. Armed with an Owen sub-machine gun, I squatted amongst thick fern bushes but had a good view of the track below. I longed for the moonlight to reveal a file of khaki-clad figures advancing along the track. Yet again, the night passed and the bandits did not oblige me.

296

Towards the end of March, I learned that Yong, the Chinese Civil Liaison Officer with the company at Kulim, had been put in 'the clink'. Yong was quite a friendly young chap. Phil Cox, the Company Pay Clerk, used to go to the cinema with him and had also been to his home in Kulim to meet Yong's wife, as had one or two others in the company.

Apparently, Yong went to see Major Murray one day, very distressed because the police had arrested his sister, accusing her of working with the Communists. Yong maintained that this was ridiculous and asked Major Murray if he could do anything about it. So the major phoned the police, who said that they'd look into the matter. A couple of days later, a police van drove into the Kulim camp and the police took Yong away. Not only had they confirmed that his sister was a Communist agent, but in looking again at the case, they'd discovered that Yong was one as well!

On Thursday afternoon, the 29th, we were briefed for an operation that was planned for that night. The grif seemed pretty good. In the Ayer Puteh area there was an old man who lived in an isolated *basha*. Bandits were forcing the old man to supply them with food, and his daughter had reported the matter to a local kampong guard. It was believed that a camp for 15 men lay only a few hundred yards beyond the *basha* and that a small attap *basha* nearby was used as a sentry post. Sometimes, bandits even slept in the old man's *basha*.

The plan was that we would set out that night in order to be in position by first light next morning. Number One Section would then search the *basha*, secure the sentry post and move on to attack the camp, while Number Two Section would work its way round to the rear of the location and act as a stop. Mr Crisp would be i/c Number One Section and Serdang's OCPD would be i/c Number Two. A signaller was not required but once more I volunteered to go along.

We departed in our transport at 10 p.m. In addition to the OCPD, we were accompanied by two Malay SCs and two kampong guards to act as guides. I was allocated to

297

Number Two Section and on this occasion was armed with a Sten gun and a grenade.

After debussing, we proceeded in complete darkness along a track which led into Ayer Puteh Estate. I often wondered if I was still behind the person who was supposed to be in front of me and could only judge my direction by the soft tread of jungle boots ahead. Private Hindmarsh, who was immediately behind me, clung to my Sten sling in order to keep contact. Later, when we encountered hilly country, I followed suit by holding on to the water bottle carrier on the belt of the chap in front of me. Indeed, the whole column soon similarly linked up to avoid losing contact. The guides must have known the track like the palms of their hands as we marched at a fast pace through the pitch-darkness with hardly a moment's hesitation. At one point, as we waded a river, Hindmarsh flapped a bit when he temporarily lost hold of my sling. We also crossed a couple of streams by walking along logs that we couldn't see. Miraculously, nobody fell off.

Eventually, we reached a steep hill, which we climbed blindly on a rough track. Near the top, as the time approached 12.30, it was whispered back that we were going to rest here until the moon rose. We lay back across the track and soon fell asleep. At 4 a.m., we were awakened. The moon had now come up, so we moved on once more, far more easily in the moonlight, of course. Nearly an hour later, we halted again and were told that we were within a hundred yards or so of the enemy's sentry post. Crouching silently in the undergrowth, we awaited the dawn.

Just before first light, two Chinese rubber tappers – one male and one female – with lamps strapped to their heads, suddenly appeared behind us and began tapping the rubber trees. When the police approached them, the woman began to shout in alarmed tones and when frantically told to hush up, continued to utter a string of remarks in her Hokkien dialect, all at the top of her voice. She had thereby given warning of our presence to anyone in the vicinity and I could not help thinking that this was precisely her intention.

It is more than likely that she was, in fact, an undercover 'sentry'.

There was now no time to lose. The OCPD addressed Number Two Section: 'Now, at the top of this valley there's a *basha* and to the left, a sentry post. Somewhere beyond there's supposed to be a camp for fifteen men. Mr Crisp's going straight up to the *basha* and we're going up this hill to the right. If there's anything there we'll get it.'

As Number One Section moved off up the valley, we climbed the adjacent hill slope. At the top, the OCPD split us up into three parties and directed us towards possible escape routes. After my party had pushed through some thick clumps of fern bushes, we met up with men from Number One Section advancing up the hill towards us.

It was too late. The bandits had gone and so had the old man. There were five male rubber tappers at the *basha*, all of whom had identity cards and seemed on the surface to be legitimate. They said that they knew nothing of the whereabouts of the old man.

After all parties had rendezvoused at the *basha*, we had a rest and a brew-up and then marched back. On the way, a dog ran from a *basha*, barking, as dogs often did. One of our kampong guards whipped his shotgun from his shoulder and shot the poor beast in the face. On arriving at the road, we found our transport waiting for us. Now very weary, we were brought back to camp by 10.30 a.m.

There was to be only a short rest for me, however. At five that evening, I had to pull on my jungle kit again and report to Kulim in the scout car. Once there, I was informed by the major that I would be going out with a Malayan Police jungle squad the following day as part of a combined police and 'C' Company operation in the Junjong area. That night, I slept fully clothed on a bare mattress in the Signals billet, not too happy about the prospect ahead of me.

At 7.30 next morning, Saturday the 31st, I climbed into a police Land Rover that had been sent to bring me to Jungle Squad HQ at Sungei Bakap in Province Wellesley. As we started off, the Malay driver said to me: 'We go by Bukit

Mertajam, Johnny. Junjong road very dangerous. Get shot.'
I hastened to agree with his decision. I didn't mind taking normal chances but I'd no wish to commit suicide. People were killed regularly on the Junjong road, and a police Land Rover without any escort would be asking for it.

Accordingly, we took the long detour via Bukit Mertajam to Sungei Bakap. On arrival at Jungle Squad HQ, I was shown to the OCPD's quarters. The OCPD was a stout man in his late thirties; unfortunately, I do not recall his name. He seemed pleased to see me, if only to have someone new to talk to.

'I had to go into the town late last night,' he told me wearily. 'A Chinese had his throat cut. Mustn't have co-operated with the Communists. Things like that are always happening.'

Two police lieutenants soon arrived for their briefing. The OCPD introduced me: 'This is Mr Scurr of the KOYLI.'

One of the lieutenants – a handsome, dark-haired man – smiled and said: 'Yes, I remember him. We met on Bukit Mertajam.' He was referring to the occasion when I climbed the mountain with the police squads the previous November. I felt rather pleased that he remembered me.

On this operation, the police would be searching a Communist hotbed area in three groups. I would accompany the OCPD. As we talked, we heard planes flying overhead and then the explosions of bombs and rockets as the three planned air strikes upon likely targets in the Relau Forest Reserve began. We could only hope that the strikes might panic some bandits into leaving their lair and coming our way.

After the lieutenants had left to organise their squads, a Malay constable came in, holding his stomach with a pained expression on his face. He claimed that he was too sick to go on the operation. The OCPD told him firmly that he would have to go, so no more argument. After the constable had dejectedly shuffled out with head bowed, I asked the OCPD: 'How d'you know he's not genuinely ill?'

'For all I know, he might be,' the OCPD replied. 'But if I let one off, they'd all be in here!'

At 10 a.m., the OCPD was ready to go. With a squad of about 20 men, consisting of two Sikhs and the remainder Malays, we set out in police *gharries* (trucks), which shortly dropped us off in a rubber estate. We were met here by the Chinese estate manager, who said that one of his tappers knew where there was a camp containing 300 bandits. This did not sound to me like a suitable task for 20 men to tackle! Also, recalling tales that I'd heard about Malay constables bolting and leaving their European officer to fight alone made me even more dubious. However, off we went. It was very hot and our march over some fairly open and very hilly country left me utterly drained of strength. As on a couple of other occasions in recent weeks, I found myself dreaming of how nice it would be if I could obtain a transfer to a cushy number in Penang.

We halted at noon and I set up my wireless while the OCPD carried on with six men to look for the tapper who had the info about the bandit camp. My '68' set was one that had been supplied to me in Kulim after being brought there from HQ the day before. The netting dial didn't function satisfactorily, so that I was unable to get through. When the OCPD returned an hour later, he told me that the tapper was not at his house and that the people there had refused to give any information as to his whereabouts.

After a brew-up, we set off back the way we had come as, lured on by the prospect of 300 bandits, we had marched quite far into 9 Platoon's operational area. When we arrived back at our starting point, we followed another track through some paddy and open country and then began to climb some hills. However, the OCPD now decided to call it a day, so we returned a little way to an unoccupied *basha*, where we made base.

I once more set up my wireless. This time, I could receive perfectly but was still unable to send. The net was about three megacycles out of calibration and I was unable to make contact on any of the evening transmissions.

At dusk, the OCPD and I bathed in the river; a rare thing for me to do on a duffy! Most of the jungle squad kipped down outside the *basha*. The OCPD and I were accommodated inside, as were the two turbanned and bearded Sikh members of the squad, one of whom was a sergeant, the other a Bren gunner. The sergeant was armed with a Browning automatic 12-gauge shotgun which loaded with five cartridges. He had served in three Malayan states, the OCPD informed me, and had personally killed five bandits. From tinned meat and vegetables, the two Sikhs cooked us a meal, which they served up with rice, curry, chillies and spices. It was absolutely delicious, and I was pleased to find that this treatment continued throughout the operation.

Next morning, Sunday, 1 April, I was still unable to make wireless contact and knew that I never would with that set. We left about 8.30 and soon began to climb a steep slope of *lallang* – part of the Relau hill ranges – just as the sun began to grow stronger. It was some climb! We rested halfway up, then conquered the second half of the hill and collapsed in the shade of the jungle fringe.

After a fairly long rest, we entered the jungle and followed the ridge for a while. The Sikh sergeant led the way, cutting a path where necessary with an 18-inch sword-bayonet. (Strangely, no parangs or matchets were carried by the jungle squad.) Then, we began a steep descent and at the foot of the slope entered a vast, never-ending stretch of swampland extensively covered with thick ferns. The sergeant continued to hack a way through the ferns for us. We were wading up to our thighs in the swamp, frequently clambering over fallen tree-trunks. At one point, the OCPD fell backwards off a log and got thoroughly soaked, much to his disgust and my hidden amusement.

Soon, we were forced to rest again. I was nearly all-in, carrying my useless '68' set, and everyone else was equally bushed. As we rested, seated on logs or damp mounds, the two Sikhs began questioning the OCPD about me. They were very interested in soldiers, the OCPD explained to me, apparently embarrassed. The Sikhs wanted to know if I was married and how much extra pay I received for carrying the wireless set. When the OCPD translated my reply – that I didn't get any extra pay – they both shook their heads and absolutely refused to believe it. The sergeant then said that he wanted to go to the Korean War but the OCPD told him that this was quite out of the question.

I had the impression that the OCPD was only now being accepted. He'd had a tough time following in the footsteps of his immediate predecessor, who had been killed while leading an attack upon an enemy camp and, I gathered, was greatly lamented by the two Sikhs and others in the squad.

It seemed to us that the swamp water that we were following would develop into a river. Surprisingly soon after we resumed our march, we crawled out into some rubber and there, sure enough, a river was flowing. After following a track along the river bank for a short while, we came to some deserted labourers' lines – the former inhabitants had been resettled – and decided to make base there. The labourers' lines were long, wooden sheds which were divided into partitioned living-compartments.

About 4 p.m., the OCPD and I went on a short patrol, taking only one section, but hadn't gone far when it started to pour with rain. We returned to base absolutely drenched, to find the men of the other section lazing around minus their equipment and, in some cases, minus their jungle-green uniforms. As a result, the OCPD fiercely reprimanded them for not being dressed and equipped in case of an emergency. The funny thing was that he and I were almost identically caught napping shortly afterwards.

Just before dusk, the two of us were in a compartment in the lines, clad only in towels, having hung up our wet shirts and slacks to dry out. We had just stepped outside to talk to the Sikh sergeant when suddenly, a Malay constable rushed up to us calling: '*Tuan! Tuan!*' (Sir) and excitedly babbling something that I was unable to understand.

As I observed others around us making a mad rush for

their weapons, the OCPD hastily explained to me: 'Two bandits coming down the track! Could be scouts for a larger party!'

We hurriedly pulled on our wet clothing and boots, and I flapped for a moment when I couldn't find my rifle. Then, sloppily dressed but fully armed, we hastened down to the other end of the lines. Everyone there was standing to in defence positions and, I noted, the Sikh sergeant had commandeered the Bren gun. It seemed that the two bandits had turned and made a run for it back up the track upon spotting our sentry, who apparently had been too taken aback to open fire.

The OCPD issued a brief order to the sergeant in Malay and then said to me: 'Right! Let's go!'

We both then dashed up the hill. Nearing the top, I could just make out the tree line in the growing darkness and wondered with some trepidation if the enemy might be lying in wait for us there, ready to mow us down. Glancing briefly over my shoulder, I saw that four constables were following – about a hundred yards to the rear! We reached the top, panting hard. There was no sign of anyone. Cautiously, we advanced into the trees and began to search round the top of the hill but it was soon too dark to continue.

'We'll have to go back, I'm afraid,' the OCPD told me. 'For God's sake, let's be careful though! I'm sure the sergeant thinks he's Humphrey Bogart with that Bren gun. He's just itching to use it!'

I have to confess that upon hearing this warning, I allowed the OCPD to lead the way downhill without hesitation. He kept calling loudly that it was us who were coming and we consequently reached the lines safely.

At the OCPD's suggestion, we then bathed briefly in the river. On returning to our billet, he said to me: 'I say! D'you think we should have a plan in case these blighters attack during the night?'

A night attack upon an army patrol was extremely rare

304

but I knew that the bandits were more prone to attacking police units, who certainly suffered comparatively heavy casualties. So I agreed that it would be a good idea to have a defence plan. Consequently, the OCPD called in the Sikh sergeant and arranged that in the event of an attack, our force would be deployed in two sections – one at each end of the lines – with the OCPD in command of one section and me in command of the other with the sergeant as my second in command. I felt quite flattered that firstly, the OCPD was prepared to trust me in a command situation and secondly, that the Sikh sergeant readily accepted that he would be under my orders.

The OCPD and I then settled down for the night, sleeping on top of tables in adjoining compartments. I must say that I lay awake for a while with a distinct feeling of not being safe. However, I eventually dropped off and the night passed without incident.

After breakfast on Monday the 2nd, a short patrol was sent out. Upon its return, we started our march back, soon arriving on the main Sungei Siputeh–Junjong track. It was flat country all the way but was a long, hot and tiring trek just the same. We arrived at Junjong Police Station at 1 p.m., and after phoning for transport, the OCPD and I sat down in the station and each consumed two bottles of orange squash with ice. In our tired, thirsty and sweat-soaked condition, that orange squash seemed like the nectar of paradise!

Our transport soon came and took us back to Sungei Bakap. I had a very nice meal in the OCPD's quarters, consisting of steak, egg and chips and coffee. The OCPD told me that one of his predecessors had been killed in that very room when a terrorist had slung a grenade through the window. He also spoke of the happy times he had known in the Colonial Police in Tanganyika. He had volunteered to transfer to Malaya but now he wished that he was back in East Africa, where the climate and the lifestyle had been so marvellous, he said. After the meal, the OCPD thanked me very genuinely for my company during the three days and then summoned a Land Rover, which brought me back to Kulim, again via Bukit Mertajam.

Transport arrived in Kulim camp shortly after I did, conveying 9 Platoon back from the operation and then taking me on to Serdang. On the way, I recalled my feelings of considerable reluctance, four days earlier, when told that I would be going out with the police jungle squad. Now, I reflected that it had been an experience that I wouldn't have missed for the world! (It would be several years before I came to realise that the Federation of Malaya Police Force had borne the brunt of the fighting in Malaya, killing far more Communist terrorists than the British Army did and sustaining far greater casualties in the process.)

Two days after my return from Sungei Bakap, a tragedy occurred which was deeply felt by the officers and men of 'C' Company. As previously stated, Second Lieutenant David Wride's young brother Norman was a lieutenant in the Malayan Police. At the beginning of April, Norman was temporarily transferred to the Kulim district, which was good news for his brother. However, on Wednesday morning, the 4th, Lieutenant Norman Wride and two Malay constables were driving in a Land Rover through Dublin Estate. The vehicle was ambushed by a party of 70 to 100 bandits and all three of the occupants were killed. I was told that they were all badly shot up at close range and that Norman Wride received a heavy burst of fire from a Bren gun through his head.

As soon as the news reached Kulim, 7 and 9 Platoons went out in pursuit of the gang. Mr Wride had wanted to go out with his men but Major Murray had insisted that he remain in camp. The following morning, Thursday the 5th, at Serdang, we were briefed to the effect that we would be setting out that day to search an area in the north of Pelam Estate where bandits were reported to have been seen.

We left at 12.30 p.m. It was a long truck journey up to Pelam Estate. After debussing, we crossed a bridge, trudged through a stretch of sand along the river bank and then turned off towards some *lallang*-covered hills, which we proceeded to climb. There was no shade from the burning sun, which made the march very disagreeable. We came to a track, which we followed for a considerable distance until we reached a couple of *bashas*. However, there was no water here, so we moved on through some thick *lallang* and ferns and eventually halted again on a hill slope.

Mr Crisp and Ginger Thompson went ahead to look for a suitable base and returned an hour later, just as it began to rain heavily. We now set off downhill into some marshy terrain and sparse jungle, finally climbing a slight rise through a clump of rubber. Here, there remained the dilapidated structure of an old *basha*. Soaked through and with the rain still lashing down upon us, we set about bivouacking around the wooden remains. I kipped in with Mr Crisp and his batman, Mirfield. We spent a pretty uncomfortable night, sleeping in our wet clothes.

Next day, two patrols went out, but owing to midday rain, both returned drenched about 2 p.m. Mirfield and I constructed a new *basha* under Mr Crisp's direction. However, when the downpour was resumed that evening, our supposedly improved *basha* got flooded out. We changed the underneath poncho during a lull but the deluge soon started again and continued on and off throughout the night. As a result, we once more lay soaking wet in puddles of water, trying to sleep as best we could. The habitual plague of biting mosquitoes did not make sleeping any easier.

As we were packing up after breakfast the following morning, Saturday the 7th, Mr Crisp narrowly avoided a large scorpion which he disturbed amongst his gear in our *basha* and quickly crushed it with the butt of his carbine. When we commenced the return march, we found that the rivers and swamps around our base had swollen enormously with the rain. At the foot of the hill, we splashed in up to our thighs and then waded for over a hundred yards through flooded swampland. We had to pick our way carefully, as one moment we'd be up to our knees and the next we'd suddenly sink up to our waists.

After leaving this swamp, we turned off to our right into a patch of *lallang*, only to plunge into more swamp at the other side, once more waist-deep. We waded slowly for another hundred yards or so until we reached a point where the swollen swamp had apparently merged with a river. Cautiously, we crossed the river by walking along a sub-merged but stably fixed log and then stepped into yet more swamp. Some of the lads now began to flap at the sight of some large buffalo leeches in the murky waters around us. The swamp widened out here. We waded through the last stretch, then climbed out into a clump of jungle trees and undergrowth.

There was now a welcome halt, during which we quickly busied ourselves burning the large leeches from our bodies. While resting, Lance Corporal Sandy Cooper spotted a snake wending its way towards him and killed it with a well-aimed slash of his matchet. When we moved on again, we soon left the jungle and followed a main track through the rubber until we reached a kampong with Pelam Estate Office adjacent to it. I'd made wireless contact with Kulim that morning and arranged for transport to pick us up here at 1 p.m. It was then only 11.30 a.m., so Mr Crisp phoned Serdang to hurry the transport up. The result was that trucks from Serdang collected us around 12.30 and we drove off down the road out of Pelam Estate and met head-on with transport from Kulim also on the way to pick us up!

On my return, I was pleased to hear that Arthur was now out of dock (hospital), fully recovered, and was now once more i/c Signals at Kulim.

The following afternoon, Sunday the 8th, Mr Crisp informed Chas and me that our detachment would be withdrawn to Kulim on Tuesday coming with a view to the approaching shuffle of company locations. He told us that 'C' Company would be moving to Kroh, the location near the Siamese border which we recalled from jungle training days. Chas and I both felt that this was bad news, and said so.

'You won't get any bandits up there, sir,' I said glumly.

'Well, why are we going there?' Mr Crisp responded crossly.

Why, indeed? I wondered. It was, of course, possible to meet bandits up there, as men from 'B' Company had found to their cost when ambushed on the Kroh–Klian Intan road in December 1949, but the likelihood of patrol contact was minimal. Still, someone had to protect the area and it was our turn.

On Monday the 9th at 2.30 p.m., Chas and I sent our final transmission from Serdang and closed down our wireless station. It was quite a sad moment for me. Although I had by far preferred my time in Kulim, the wireless station of the Serdang detachment had been very much my baby as I'd organised it from the start and was, in effect, 'Pronto' (in charge). We busied ourselves for the rest of the afternoon dismantling our aerials and loudspeakers and packing up our kit.

The following morning, we said goodbye to our billet, where we'd had some good chats and laughs over numerous Tiger beers, and the entire detachment then boarded the waiting trucks and returned to the company at Kulim. Matt Busby's employment as 'canteen wallah' now terminated, and for better or worse he would be resuming normal duties in 8 Platoon.

Once more accommodated in the Signals billet in Kulim with Arthur, Chas, Swede Martin and a new signaller called Hitchman, I heard the latest news. During an operation which had begun the previous Sunday, north of the Gurun–Jeniang road, 4 Platoon, 'B' Company, had spotted four bandits on the run and – it was believed – had wounded one of them.

Another police officer and two constables were ambushed and killed that Tuesday night, 10 April, in the same area that Norman Wride had been killed and, it seemed, by the same party of bandits. On Wednesday morning, the 11th, 7 and 8 Platoons were warned to stand ready for going out that day. Major Murray sent for Arthur to arrange for allocation of signallers and commenced by saying: 'Now, let's see. What signallers and sets have we got? There's Scurr and Schaverien with their violins. You know why I say that, don't you, Corporal?'

'No, sir,' Arthur replied.

'Well, they never get their hair cut!' the major chided.

Originally, it was arranged that Hitchman and I would go out with 8 Platoon and Chas would go with 7 Platoon. Rations for 48 hours were issued to both platoons. Then, 7 Platoon had its rations withdrawn and was stood down. As we had never been on a duffy together, Chas swopped places with Hitchman so that he could accompany me. Shortly, some policemen arrived in camp with a surrendered bandit whom they had dressed as an SC (special constable).

At 8 Platoon's briefing, Mr Crisp told us that this bandit had deserted from a camp in the Bongsu two days before and had been shot at as he ran away. The camp had been permanently occupied by 60 bandits for the past year and the two recent ambushes, and many previous ones, had been carried out by gangs operating from this camp. The SEP (surrendered enemy personnel) – for some strange reason nicknamed 'George VI' – was going to lead us to the camp. (This was the surrendered bandit, mentioned in Chapter 14, who later told the story of our narrow escape from ambush.)

We left just before noon and after debussing, marched through the rubber in three sections. Chas and I were with Number Two Section. After initially doubling back on our tracks, we climbed a hill in pouring rain to the edge of the Bongsu. Here, we stopped to eat our haversack rations, then entered the jungle by a track that the bandit indicated was his unit's main operational track. Consequently, we were warned to keep our eyes peeled in case we met a party on its way out.

After about an hour's march along this track, we suddenly had a signal passed back to take cover off the trail. Our scouts and their guide had seen two bandits disappearing into the bush on the other side of the river. Number One Section hastened after the pair but saw no more of them.

310

When signalled to proceed, we moved on across the river and up the hill on the other side. Then we descended to the river again and waded up it slowly and cautiously for a couple of hours, ever aware of the possibility of ambush. Eventually, we turned off up a slope and halted on the ridge. The signal for 'packs off' was gladly obeyed.

The enemy's sentry posts, we were told, were located on the reverse slope of this hill and the camp itself was on the next ridge. Mr Crisp divided the platoon into two groups: one to attack the camp and the other to lie in ambush on the flank. He wanted to be sure of wireless contact, he said, so signallers had to remain in the rear. Observing my angry reaction to this, he then conceded that one signaller could go with the ambush party.

Mr Crisp then led the attack group on towards the camp. Chas and I ignored his instructions and both went with the ambush group under Corporal Barker. We moved a little way down the hill and took up our positions, hoping to bag any bandits who made a run for it in our direction. Corporal Barker – an 'old soldier' who had served in the Second World War – pointed out two sentry posts to me which he said that he could see in the jungle ahead of us. I looked in the directions that he indicated but couldn't see anything – for the simple reason that there was nothing there! He then saw one of the sentries – who wasn't there either – move his arm.

Half an hour passed without any sound of firing. Mr Crisp's group then returned, saying that the occupants of the camp had already fled. Disappointed once more, we collected our packs and moved on up to the next ridge.

As we entered the abandoned camp, the first thing to catch my eye was the cleared, hard-earth, combined parade ground and basketball pitch, complete with flagpole and looped goalposts. Round about this clearing stood several large bashas, well-constructed with bamboo and attap, which had raised sleeping platforms inside. These living quarters could easily have accommodated 100 men. In one *basha*, which was clearly the dining hall, there were rows of bamboo tables and benches. Another small *basha* contained a home-made desk and chair and was obviously the 'company office'. Just outside the camp perimeter, which was prepared for defence with Bren gun pits, was a cookhouse containing brick ovens, adjoined by what appeared to be a miniature firing range.

Before their hasty departure, the bandits had apparently pushed in the attap roofs of some of the *bashas*. They had left quite a few odds-and-ends behind, such as packs, articles of clothing, papers, magazines, torches, batteries, candles, jars of Brylcreem, brew cans, etc. One magazine that I picked up in one of the bashas appertained to a Chinese secondary school in Georgetown, Penang. With its class photographs and general layout, it reminded me of my own school magazine.

It was now after 6 p.m. and growing dark. Chas and I set up our wireless and called Kulim at 7 p.m., 8 p.m. and finally at 1 a.m. The atmospheric interference was terrible. We knew we were wasting our time but persisted in making the calls to please Mr Crisp, as the major had instructed that we must make contact that day. I have to confess that when I made the 1 a.m. call, I did not bother with the wireless but merely sat with my back against a tree, repeating our call sign loud enough for Mr Crisp to hear, if he was awake, and asking for a report of signals. Needless to say, I got no reply!

We kipped quite comfortably in the *bashas* but took the precaution to mount doubly manned sentry posts, ready to give warning if anyone approached. The gang that had carried out the latest ambush had not returned to the camp before George VI had run away, so we hoped that they might do so during our stay. When on stag, we were instructed to listen especially for the signal that the bandits always used before entering the camp, which was to clap hands twice. We watched and listened in vain.

When daylight came, an ambush party was sent out to take up position along the main track, while the remainder of us deployed around the camp. Chas and I made wireless contact with Kulim. Major Murray asked to speak to Mr Crisp and told him that if no enemy appeared by noon, we were to return to base. Noon arrived but no bandits. After tiffen, we packed up to go. We left the camp standing in case the police should wish to try their luck ambushing it.

We moved off on a different route from the way we'd come, following a track along the ridges and completely avoiding the river. After a while, on a down slope, we were signalled to take our packs off and move forward. After descending a short distance, we halted again. Word was whispered back that we had reached another camp that our bandit deserter had stayed in. It seemed that there was no one there, however, as we were now ordered to go back for our packs. When we finally entered the very compact camp, we found that it contained some large, well-built *bashas* that would hold about 60 men. However, it had not been used for about a fortnight.

After a rest, we set fire to each *basha* in turn until the whole camp was ablaze. The intense heat soon forced us to withdraw further down the hill. We formed up and set off again, with the fire crackling furiously behind us. After encountering a comparatively small yet steep and tiring hill, we eventually broke out of the Bongsu into the rubber. From here, we followed a long and mainly flat track to the road. After stopping a civvy car, Sandy Cooper and Tait travelled in it to Kulim and soon sent our transport back to collect us.

I noted in my journal that I had really enjoyed this operation, rather like I used to before, during my 'first Kulim period'. It had been much easier marching through the jungle with two signallers. One had carried the '68' set only and the other our kit and wireless gear, swopping our loads at every halt. It was also very satisfying to know that we had, at last, flushed the enemy out of his large base camp in the Bongsu from which he had been inflicting so much damage.

On our arrival back in camp, we found Corporal Bill Downs there as part of 'D' Company advance party. Arthur had left for Kroh that morning with 'C' Company advance party. That evening, Swede, Hitchman, Chas and I busied ourselves packing up all our signals equipment and personal kit, ready for moving north-east the following day.

17

Kroh and Penang
April–May 1951

At 10.30 a.m. on Saturday, 14 April, 'D' Company drove into our camp at Kulim. Grice, Todd and my old mate Eric Hann were the Signals personnel. It was nice to have a chat with them, especially with Eric. The 'D' Company men's first task on arrival was to carry back from the stores to the squad tents and other billets all the beds that we'd been ordered to carry into the stores an hour or so before!

Then, at 1 p.m., having loaded all our equipment and belongings – including pet dogs and chickens – onto our trucks, we embussed and departed. It was a poignant moment. I knew that I'd never forget my time in Kulim.

Our convoy consisted of two armoured scout cars, a civvy car, a jeep and trailer, a 15-hundredweight truck and ten 3-tonners. It was a long and tiring journey. We stopped for a break at a kampong near Baling and then drove up the steep, winding road to Kroh in Upper Perak. After we'd passed the old camp in which I'd completed my jungle training over a year before, we continued up to the new camp that the Marine Commandos had built. Once we had unloaded all of our gear, we carried back to the tents all the beds that the 'D' Company chaps had carried into the stores that morning and began to get settled in.

I had to admit that this was a very nice camp. The squad tents were well laid out and had stone floors. There were clean, efficient showers in the ablution sheds and there was a large, well furnished NAAFI hut. Everything, in fact, was altogether satisfactory. Our Signals tent was situated at the

315

top of a slope, overlooking the rest of the camp, and was very much to my liking as were my companions: Arthur, Swede, Hitchman and Chas.

Despite all these points in its favour, however, I was far from happy with our new location. I was disgruntled with the fact that – unless we had the misfortune to be caught in an ambush on the road – there was practically no possibility of contact with the enemy around Kroh. Except for occasional transit camps, bandits had no need to build camps in this area. All of their base camps lay safely on the other side of the Thai border. From these, they could hop over the border to carry out an ambush or other raid, then slip back again to where our patrols were unable to pursue them. There were so many trails to the border through this vast region of very wild country that the odds against bumping into an enemy group in transit were phenomenal.

On Monday the 16th, only two days after their arrival in Kulim, 11 and 12 Platoons of 'D' Company were led by the SEP, George VI, to a large camp. The Company Commander considered that a direct assault upon the hilltop camp could prove costly in casualties, so he first ordered his 2-inch mortars to bombard the hill. Upon seeing signs of movement on the ridge, the two platoons raked the hill with fire from their Bren guns and then mounted their assault. By the time they reached the camp – which was large enough to accommodate 100 – the estimated 30 occupants had fled.

When I heard this news, I could not help reflecting that if the timing of our move had only been a few days later, 'C' Company would have been given this opportunity and perhaps I might have been there. It just didn't seem fair!

On the night of Wednesday the 18th, I was surprised to be summoned by the Company Clerk to take a phone call from Penang. The caller turned out to be my old pal – now Signals Clerk – Johnny Ainsworth, who gave me splendid news. He'd seen orders regarding our draft, Group 4917, which indicated that our boat to Blighty would be due to sail from Singapore on 8 or 9 July. (In fact, this estimation proved to be three weeks premature.) The idea of going home had always seemed like a far-off dream, but now, on hearing Johnny's news, I began to believe that it really was going to happen.

The following day, Thursday the 19th, it was announced in Company Orders that the 1st Battalion, KSLI (King's Shropshire Light Infantry) would shortly be departing from Hong Kong to join the United Nations Command in Korea. Consequently, volunteers had been requested from the KOYLI to bring the KSLI up to strength. That night, seated round a table in the NAAFI, Matt Busby, Chas and I were discussing this request for volunteers in between joining in the chorus of the latest hit song 'Goodnight, Irene!' When we were halfway through our third bottle of Tiger each, we resolved that we would all put our names down and go together, like the Three Musketeers, to the Korean War.

Just after breakfast next morning, Chas and I were sitting on our beds, feeling a little the worse for wear, when Matt came into the Signals tent.

'Well, I've done it,' he announced cheerily.

'You've done what?' I asked, puzzled.

'Put my name down for Korea,' he said.

I stared at him for a moment until the memory of what we'd decided the previous night emerged from the fog in my mind. 'Oh, bollocks to that!' I muttered at last.

'You said you'd go!' Matt protested hotly.

'Look! I'm "peechy",' I said. 'I've only got three months to do. I've even got my sailing date. Would you go if you only had three months to do?'

'No,' Matt said, more calmly. 'I don't suppose I would. They wouldn't accept you for that short a time anyway.'

Without a word, Chas got up from his bed and walked out. He returned a few minutes later and told us that he'd added his name to the list. Twenty men from the company had so far volunteered, including Mr Crisp.

I was far from happy about the fact that my two friends had put their names down to go to Korea and I had not. In order to qualify I'd have had to sign on and extend my service, and I was not yet prepared to do that. Malaya hadn't exactly been a picnic and I felt that I needed a rest before proceeding to a bigger field of conflict. Also, I'd been looking forward so much to going home soon, despite some feelings of foreboding about my future. I noted in my journal: 'According to how things turn out when I get home, I may sign on for an 18 months' 'K' [Korea] engagement.'

The very next entry complained: 'Now that I'm a 3-star soldier and am on Regular Army pay of £4.12s.9d. (minus 2s.6d. National Insurance) per week, I've received my Income Tax papers!'

At this time, I was amused by the fact that Swede Martin had developed a sudden phobia about the possibility of being bitten by a snake when in bed at night. He therefore adopted the precautionary measure of coating the legs of his bed with rifle-cleaning oil, on the assumption that any snakes which attempted to climb up would instantly slither down again!

On the night of Sunday the 22nd, a patrol of 'B' Company shot an AP (auxiliary policeman) dead when they mistook three APs for bandits. The following day, 11 Platoon, 'D' Company, attacked a small camp, from which six bandits made their escape, leaving a shotgun, ammunition and clothing behind.

The previous Christmas, Serjeant Stan Haley had announced that he was going to arrange a party for the Signal Platoon. Towards the end of April, his plan finally reached fruition and it was agreed that two signallers from each rifle company could attend. When we decided that the fairest option was to draw names out of a hat, Arthur and I were the lucky ones. We were both granted leave passes for four days and drew out extra pay from our savings for the occasion.

Thus, on Thursday, 26 April, Arthur and I travelled to Minden Barracks, Penang, on the ration truck. After we'd had a shower and had changed into our civvy shirts and slacks, we took a bus into Georgetown around noon and went straight to the Broadway Café in Penang Road.

As we mounted the staircase from the street entrance, we could hear 'I Only Have Eyes for You', sung by Al Jolson, being played on the radiogram. I think I'd heard that record practically every time I'd been in the Broadway. Arthur and I sat at a centre table and ordered two Carlsberg lagers, then another two, then another two ... Emily, the slim Chinese waitress, began to get concerned and eventually said to us: 'I don't think you should have any more, because when you get the bill you will say that it is too much, that you did not have that many beers and you will not pay.'

'Look, Emily,' said Arthur. 'You just keep a note of what we have and when you bring us the bill, whatever it is, we'll pay it.'

Emily looked towards me for further reassurance. 'You trust me?' she asked.

'Yes,' I answered. 'We trust you and we'll pay.'

The Carlsbergs kept coming. Arthur talked at some length about his girlfriend, Dilys, and how she regularly visited his mother. Behind us, the radiogram was playing 'Silver Dollar'. Arthur then began to ramble about how nice his Canadian penfriend, Joyce, seemed to be. We continued to order Carlsbergs. The conversation, or at least my perception of it, became more vague. By 6 p.m. or thereabouts, Arthur was sprawled back in his chair, out to the world. I seemed to find this very funny and kept pointing at him and laughing. An American seaman on his way out came up to me and said: 'Why don't you take him back to his ship?' This merely induced a further burst of laughter from me. The American shrugged his shoulders and walked away.

There was a Sumatran waitress in the Broadway called Loh Tow who was very beautiful, though not in any conventional way. She was slightly plump and had a tendency to shuffle around rather lazily in her wooden sandals. Yet her body was very voluptuous and her rather flat-featured, oriental face was nonetheless strikingly attractive – exotic would be the word. She just had that certain something. Male customers in the Broadway couldn't keep their eyes off her and neither could she! Every time she passed a mirror she glanced at her image. However, she was definitely not available to any of the customers. I was told that she had two 'bodyguards' who escorted her home every night when the café closed.

In addition to laughing drunkenly at the sleeping Arthur, I now found myself eyeing Loh Tow and several Chinese prostitutes in the place. The prostitutes, of course, were all smiles, but Loh Tow remained her usual indifferent self. Eventually, I decided to go to the gents. As I staggered down the narrow, spiral staircase, I bumped into a prostitute wearing a tight green dress on her way up. I tried to fondle her but she firmly warded me off and squeezed past me.

Shortly after I had returned to our table, I was suddenly sick upon the floor. A small Chinese waiter hastened over with a pan and brush and very swiftly and efficiently cleaned up. I didn't feel embarrassed or concerned in any way. For some time, I had hardly been aware of what I was doing.

Around 7 p.m., I roused Arthur. We asked Emily for the bill. It came to 23 Malayan dollars (nearly £3 – quite a lot to spend in those days). We paid the bill, descended to the street and took a slow stroll down the brightly lit Penang Road. Suddenly, we realised that we hadn't had anything to eat since six that morning, so we went into the Café de Luxe and ate a substantial supper. Among the records played while we were there were 'China Nights' and 'Silver Dollar'.

Afterwards, we climbed into a trishaw and told the trishaw-wallah just to drive us around. Arthur then said to me: 'Look, Jock, we've got to find somewhere to stay the night. Now, we'll never find anywhere on our own. So the best way is for us to ask the trishaw-wallah to fix us up with two bibies. Then he'll find us a place to stay and we can just ditch the women once we get there. OK?'

I was not sufficiently clear-headed to find any fault with this rather questionable scheme, so Arthur duly made the necessary request to the Chinese pedalling behind our seat. The trishaw-wallah then drove us to an alleyway and disappeared into a hovel. When he returned, he said to us: 'Two

320

nice bibies here. But they want to make themselves pretty and put on their fine clothes before they meet you. I take you first to a hotel and then bring them to you.'

He then drove us to a hotel, where we sat at a small table just inside the entrance. There was no one else there. After the trishaw-wallah had left, Arthur said to me: 'When they arrive, Jock, be really enthusiastic. You're all for them, understand?'

'OK,' I said, beginning to feel decidedly uneasy.

The trishaw-wallah soon returned with two Malay bibies, possibly mother and daughter. They were both finely arrayed in pale green silk garments embroidered with silver, and were wearing a lot of make-up. The young one, in her teens, was very attractive; the old one, not attractive. They sat with us at the table, all smiles.

Looking very pleased with himself, the trishaw-wallah said to us: 'You like them? Very pretty, eh?'

'Very nice!' Arthur replied. 'What d'you think, Jock?'

'Very nice!' I agreed, trying to sound enthusiastic.

'Right!' Arthur now said to the Chinese: 'We like them but we don't want to see them till later on. We want to go to the pictures first.'

The trishaw-wallah explained this to the two bibies in Malay. They looked rather perplexed but nonetheless assented and we parted company. Arthur and I travelled in the trishaw to the Rex cinema. The trishaw-wallah told us that he'd like to see the film as well, so we gave him enough money to pay for a cheap seat and bought ourselves two tickets for the dearer seats. The film that we saw was a mountain-climbing drama called *The White Tower*. If I hadn't been so sleepy as a consequence of the afternoon's drinking session, I think I might have enjoyed it.

After the show, our trishaw-wallah was awaiting us outside the cinema. From here, at Arthur's suggestion, we went to the City Lights Cabaret. I had heard much talk of this place, but this was my first visit. The dance floor was pretty crowded with servicemen and taxi girls. We bought two Tiger beers at the bar and sat at a table for a while, watching the antics on the floor of sloshed soldiers and their provocative, mainly Chinese partners. The rather screeching band played 'Malayan Rose' and 'Silver Dollar'. We seemed to hear the latter everywhere we went.

Our next stop was a small café, where we each had a soft drink. Then, we rendezvoused with the two bibies that we'd met earlier and they followed behind us in another trishaw. We called at three hotels, none of which would accommodate us. At one point, a military police jeep began to tail us; no doubt checking that we did not stop anywhere that was out of bounds. The trishaw-wallah kept pedalling until the MPs lost interest and turned off, and then stopped at another hotel.

This time we struck lucky. The trishaw-wallah led the way upstairs and the two bibies followed silently behind us. On the first floor, we were introduced to the fat, middle-aged Chinese manager, who greeted us very amiably. Arthur and I were allocated a room each. The older Malay bibi motioned to the younger one to go with Arthur, and then she and the trishaw-wallah followed me into my room.

'She sleep with you all night, Johnny,' the trishaw-wallah said to me. 'You pay her twenty dollars.'

The bibi smiled at me, displaying a mouthful of gold teeth. I did not find her at all attractive, nor did I feel ready to sleep with a woman all night when the sum total of my sexual experience was two kisses and holding hands! On top of that, paying the required sum would almost have emptied my wallet.

'Twenty dollars?' I repeated uneasily.

'It is fair,' said the trishaw-wallah. 'You ask your friend.'

I went back onto the landing, where Arthur was still standing with the manager and the young bibi. The trishaw-wallah and the older bibi followed behind me.

'D'you hear that, Arthur?' I said. 'Twenty dollars!'

Arthur looked at me for a moment and then asked: 'And do you not want to pay that?'

'No,' I replied. 'We've still got three more days' leave. I'd only have a few dollars left to see me through.'

Arthur nodded and then said to the trishaw-wallah: 'Too much.'

Twenty dollars was, in fact, the normal price for all night. The trishaw-wallah, looking perturbed, hastily conferred with the two bibies and then asked: 'How much you give?'

Arthur paused thoughtfully and then said: 'Eight.'

The bibies shook their heads disdainfully and without a word began to descend the stairs. Arthur then gave the trishaw-wallah some money which was apparently less than he expected. However, after a heated exchange in Cantonese with the manager, he also departed. The manager now produced the hotel register and entered our names and ranks.

'Regiment?' he next enquired.

'Malayan Scouts,' Arthur replied.

We signed our names and now further saved money by sharing a room, price five dollars. We slept in our shirts on a rather lumpy double bed. It had been a long, tiring and rather unusual day.

Next morning, Friday the 27th, after a negligible breakfast of boiled eggs, we left the hotel and went, first, to an Indian barber shop, where we had a most satisfactory shave, head massage and hairdressing. Our next stop was the bazaar, where we bought new shirts to replace the crumpled ones that we'd slept in the previous night. We then drove around in trishaws for most of the morning. Having considerable hangovers from the day before, we took refreshments in the Green Spot in the form of milk shakes, ice-cream sundaes and ice-cold coffee, all of which went down very nicely.

After eating tiffen in the Broadway, we proceeded down Penang Road to the Café de Luxe, where we began to knock back Carlsbergs once more. We were the only customers in the place and after a while, the Chinese manageress joined us at our table. She asked our names and then said: 'You call me Carmen.' She asked us if we were stationed in Penang. When we replied that we were on the mainland, she looked genuinely concerned and commented: 'Fighting bandits? Terrible!'

Changing the subject, Arthur said: 'I'm surprised it's so quiet in here. This is a really nice café. The layout, the decor, everything is superior to the Broadway, but the Broadway seems to get all the customers.'

'Oh, business isn't so bad,' Carmen said unconvincingly. 'But you should come here more often and bring some of your friends.'

She then produced a pack of cards and the three of us played a simple game which she showed us. Carmen took the game very seriously and scolded me every time I made a mistake. 'No, no, Jock!' she would exclaim. 'You shouldn't have played that card!'

Later, the café's European manager – a fat, middle-aged Dutchman – also joined us at the table and asked Vera, the Chinese waitress, to bring another round of drinks. Unlike Carmen, he had no hesitation in telling us that things were not going well.

'Penang is a bad place for business,' he complained. 'It's a bad place all round!'

'Don't you like Penang?' I asked him.

'No,' he replied sourly. 'It's the gate to Hell!'

I was quite taken aback. For me, the Island of Penang seemed like paradise. 'Will you ever go back to Europe?' I asked now.

'No,' he said, staring at his drink and looking very despondent. 'Never.'

I felt sad at his predicament and wondered if he had some dark secret that prevented him from returning home. However, I didn't feel that I had any right to pry so pursued the matter no further.

After a couple of drinks, they both left us. We drank a few more Carlsbergs until Arthur lolled back into sleep, as he had done the previous day. I just sat there, well sozzled, and kept ogling Vera and winking at her periodically. Vera merely looked back at me without expression; no doubt considering me to be a complete ass!

Approaching 7 p.m., I woke Arthur, suggesting that it was time for conner. Our main dish of lamb chops and vegetables was very nicely cooked and greatly appreciated by both of us. After our meal, we took a ride in a trishaw to the area around the City Lights. We bought two coffees at a street stall and sat with a fat, old and rather decrepit prostitute called Mary, who cackled merrily when Arthur made her an offer of 15 cents! We then took a trishaw back to Penang Road and had a soft drink in the Café de Luxe before finally catching a taxi back to Minden Barracks.

When we entered the Signals *basha* around 9.30 p.m., Corporal Ivor Lewis looked at me with a shocked expression and said: 'What have you been up to, Jock? You look terrible! Your eyes are all red and you've got bags under them.' He then turned to Arthur and said with mock – or was it genuine? – disapproval: 'You've been leading Jock astray!'

Arthur merely grinned and so did I.

On Saturday morning, considerably refreshed by a good night's sleep, Arthur and I travelled by bus to Sandycroft Leave Centre on the north coast. After drinking a Tiger apiece, we went swimming in the sea. The sky was overcast but it was very pleasant just the same. Posing as residents, we had a free meal in the Leave Centre, then bussed into Georgetown where we went to the Odeon cinema to see Robert Taylor in *Devil's Doorway*. During the interval, Lance Corporal Hodson of the Signal Platoon suddenly appeared in the row behind us and said: 'Did you hear about the Gloucesters? They got wiped out in Korea!' (Later, we learned that, in fact, the Gloucester Regiment had been surrounded on a hill above the Imjin River and then overrun by overwhelming numbers of Chinese. Most of the survivors had been taken prisoner.)

After the show, we ate another meal of lamb chops at the Café de Luxe and then returned to barracks, mainly because our money had practically run out.

The following day, Sunday the 29th, was the day of the Signals outing. In addition to Arthur and me from 'C'

Company, there was Kelly and Walters from 'B', Reeves from 'D', Hodson, Lyke and Christer from Tac HQ and, of course, all those not on duty from rear echelon HQ – about 30 of us, all told. Apparently, no one could attend from 'A' Company as all of their signallers were employed on operations that weekend.

At 11 a.m., we left in trucks, which soon dropped us beside a beach at the thirteenth milestone. It was a glorious day with brilliant sunshine. Our Signals Serjeant, Stan Haley, and his Siamese-Australian wife Tilly, had everything organised. Two large containers full of ice were placed on the beach and a good supply of bottled beer was stored in them for later. We all promptly changed into our swimming trunks, swam for a while in the calm, blue sea, then began on the beer.

To our surprise and delight, a truck soon rolled up, bringing Bill Downs, Battams and Grice from 'D' Company. Once they'd been served with beer, they told us that the previous night, four 'D' Company lads and four local people had been wounded by a grenade that had been slung at them in the Queen's Amusement Park in Kulim. The police had managed to apprehend the terrorist responsible. Fortunately, the wounds sustained by Privates Prynn, Osfield, Dowrick and Richardson proved not to be too serious.

We readily consumed a very nice buffet which had been prepared by Cookhouse Serjeant Webb, and washed it down with more beer. About this time, someone spotted old Jim Walters floating far out to sea with a bottle of Tiger in his hand! A rescue party was urgently dispatched to bring him safely back to shore. Then, after more swimming and chatting, the beer was all finally polished off. Just after 5.30 p.m., we set off back into Georgetown, a good time having been had by all.

(Serjeant Jock McClung was no longer with the Signal Platoon, having been transferred to straight duty in 'A' Company.)

Once in town, we all split up, most of the lads going to the Broadway for a further binge. Having very little money

326

left now, I hurried away on my own to the Rex cinema to see *The Pirates of Capri*. Inside, I met cousin John and his friend, Ken Phipps, who was on leave from 'A' Company. After the show, the three of us went to the Boston Café for a cup of coffee prior to returning to camp. I found this quiet evening with John and Ken very pleasant and relaxing after the previous hectic though very memorable days.

On the Monday morning, Arthur and I merely lounged around camp awaiting transport back to Kroh. After tiffen, transport arrived from 'C' Company, bringing in Chas, Knight and Allen, who were all going on leave to Hong Kong. Apparently, this leave had been arranged by Captain Haddon for three men from 'C' Company some time ago. The third man had since gone home, so Knight and Allen had suggested that Chas should take his place. Chas was very excited about going but said that he wished that I was going with him. (Captain Haddon would shortly be leaving 'C' Company to go home, calling at Mysore, India, on the way, to see his brother. From the UK, following leave, he would proceed on secondment to the Sudan Defence Force. Serjeant 'Taggy' Bell was also imminently due to leave the company for home.)

At 6 p.m., Arthur and I commenced our return journey, arriving back at Kroh just before nine. I'd only just sat down on my bed when the tough, much-hated Serjeant 'Pedlar' Palmer of 7 Platoon entered the Signals tent.

'I need a signaller to go out on an op with me tomorrow,' he announced. 'Which one of you is Scurr?'

'Serjeant!' I indicated resignedly.

'Right,' Pedlar said coldly. 'You'll be coming with me. OK?'

'Yes, Serjeant.'

How I wished that I could have said no! During my lengthy sojourn at Serdang, I had been able to avoid operations with the unhappy 7 Platoon. Now, at last, I was caught!

We departed at nine next morning, Tuesday, 1 May. After driving along the Kroh–Klian Intan road, our transport took us through the shanty town of Klian Intan and then down a bumpy track that had been hewn through the jungle. I noticed a monkey climbing a tree to the right of the track and could have sworn that he looked back at me with a pitying expression! We debussed at Kampong Lallang, meeting a Hussars road patrol there, and then set off with a police guide, following a track into the jungle. The track led us along the bank of a wide, muddy river, on the other side of which a troupe of monkeys suddenly crashed their way through the treetops.

Eventually, we halted at a point where Serjeant Palmer declared to our dismay that we'd have to cross the river. Corporal Sharkey decided to test the depth, instantly disappeared below the surface in a whirlpool and had to be dragged out – a very encouraging start! Then the police guide lowered himself into the water further downstream and waded out to an island near the opposite bank with a rope lifeline tied around his waist. Once he had gained the island and the lifeline was secured to a tree, the rest of us began to cross, hanging on to the rope with one hand while holding our weapons above our heads with the other. The yellow, muddy water came up to our chests and the current was pretty strong, with the result that a couple of the lads were swept over and a brew can was lost. From the island, however, it was a comparatively easy wade to the opposite bank and soon the whole platoon was across.

After a short march, we again came to a bend in the river. It had narrowed considerably here, though the current was still strong. We soon found ourselves wading upstream and scrambling over rocks. A short break was called around 1 p.m. for a brew-up and to eat our haversack rations, as well as to rid ourselves of the numerous leeches that we had collected. I found it necessary to burn one of the creatures off the end of my penis. (It was not unknown for a leech to become lodged down the 'pipe' of the male organ. Some men were so fearful of this happening that they wore contraceptive sheaths while on patrol.)

Our march up the river soon continued. Obstacles that

we later encountered included some high rocks that we could only climb with the aid of a rope, and an ipoh tree with roots which measured 4 feet in height and 10 yards in length. It was hard going all the way but, as always, I managed to stay on my feet. Just after 5 p.m., we climbed a hill adjacent to the river and stopped to make camp.

After clearing an area with our matchets, we built our bivvies and then I put up my aerial. My set did not function at first until I discovered that my ATP4 valve was broken and changed it. However, reception was very poor and I was unable to send the routine SITREP of location.

One thing I had to admit was that Serjeant Palmer was well organised in everything that he did. He had two muckers in 7 Platoon – two 'old soldiers', Privates Pendle-bury and Scaife – who were his scouts, who he bivvied with and who appeared to be the only two men in the platoon he had any time for – or who had any time for him! All three of them had volunteered to go to Korea with the KSLI.

As they were cooking the conner, I heard Pedlar say to the other two in contemptuous tones: 'I hope the KSLI are better than this lot. They're like a bunch of bloody school kids!'

When the 'all-in' stew had been served, Pedlar called the Bren gunners and me back to the fire to receive second helpings, presumably because we had extra weight to carry on the march. He also did not put me on the guard roster for that night, supposedly for the same reason.

Next morning, I established good wireless contact and transmitted a routine SITREP to Kroh. After breakfast, we set off again, once more wading upriver, with the water varying in depth from knee to waist. We were again feasted upon by large numbers of leeches and had to brush and burn them off during occasional halts.

At one point, we came to a cascading waterfall which was 20-odd feet in height. The easiest way to reach the top was to climb a rock face on the left side of the fall. As I clambered along a ledge near the top, I reached for a root to pull myself along. The root snapped as I grasped it, causing me to lose my balance and fall backwards. I felt air rushing past me, heard a loud splash and then felt the weight of the set on my back dragging me underwater to the bottom of the river. Two of the lads promptly grasped me under the armpits and hauled me to my feet, and someone found my jungle hat floating on the surface and stuck it on my head. To my credit I'd held on to my rifle throughout. I was then helped back up the rock face to the top of the waterfall without further mishap.

Soon after that, we left the river and climbed a steep hill at a fast pace. I began to feel exhausted and would have fallen behind had we not stopped on the summit for tiffen. As I rested with my back against a tree, Pedlar came over to me and enquired in a dull voice: 'Did you hurt yourself when you fell?'

'No,' I said, shaking my head. 'But I don't suppose it did the set much good.'

He nodded and walked away. I considered that it was good of him to ask, even if he didn't sound interested!

After tiffen, we moved on once more. First we marched downhill a little way, then up again. And from there on, it was upwards, ever upwards. We climbed, often on hands and knees, under thorn vines and through bamboo until we were all cursing Serjeant Palmer good and hard and I was in that state of near-total exhaustion which carrying a '68' set made inevitable. By 3 p.m., I was nearly at a standstill and had to swop my set for the pack of one of the riflemen. However, this chap was soon staggering under the weight and had to hand the set over to another.

Around 4.30 p.m., we heard a prolonged roaring sound, which our police guide said was a wild elephant. Just after that, we broke out of the jungle and sighted the Klian Intan mine. Again I have to admit that Pedlar seemed well able to follow his map and know where he was going. We now made our way through fern bushes on the hilltop until we reached a steep cliff face. The scouts said that there was no way up, but Serjeant Palmer brushed past them. We watched as he carefully edged his way along a ledge on the cliff face and then began to climb. There were muttered comments around me, such as: 'I hope he falls and breaks his bastard neck!' Then, as Pedlar finally reached the top and stood silhouetted against the sky, someone behind me said: 'I wish the bandits would come now. They could pick him off easy up there!'

Now that Serjeant Palmer had shown us the way, we had no choice but to follow on and climb the cliff face, one after another, knowing that if we slipped, we'd had our chips. However, we all safely gained the summit and from there made our way down a steep slope of ferns and rocks until we reached a path round the side of the hill. I took my set back here but felt so utterly spent that I eventually had to be relieved by someone else.

After a while, we arrived at a group of huts next to the tin mine and made our base for the night in a long, empty shed. On checking my wireless, I discovered that the valves were OK but I could nonetheless neither receive nor send. The fault – which was found on my return – proved to be a short inside, caused by my fall into the river.

The following morning, Thursday the 3rd, although we had reached our goal, we moved off again. We climbed a high hill of never-ending earthen steps at a forced pace which inflicted real punishment on my aching leg muscles. Three-quarters of the way up, with my lungs gasping for breath, I was compelled to exchange my set for a near-empty pack. I did not really know any of the lads in 7 Platoon but they were all very good to me throughout the operation. On reaching the top, we continued along a path through the mine and halted on a slope of *lallang*.

Serjeant Palmer now decided to take Number One Section on a patrol from here. The rest of us squatted down in the *lallang* and shivered in drizzling rain for a couple of hours. I was feeling really miserable and despondent. This duffy had definitely been no fun at all. I'd heard of the killing marches enforced by the undoubtedly tough Serjeant Palmer but had always assumed that no one could push men harder than Mr Crisp did. Also, I found the hostile atmosphere in 7 Platoon very disturbing. Although I'd sometimes heard men cursing Mr Crisp, it had never been done with any genuine malice. There seemed to be real hatred in the feelings of some of the men of 7 Platoon towards Pedlar.

I realised then that I had little wish to spend my remaining two months or so in Kroh jungle-bashing in an area where there was practically no chance of contact with the enemy and with a one in three likelihood of being signaller and flayed donkey for Pedlar Palmer. This bleak prospect, plus my memories of my recent brief experience of the bright lights in Penang, made a spell in HQ seem very attractive. I decided there and then to definitely apply for a transfer, but I knew that once I got back to camp I'd change my mind. So I took my message-form pad out of my ammo pouch and wrote the following message to Serjeant Stan Haley: 'TO PRONTO. FROM JOCK. REQUIRE REST FROM JUNGLE WORK. REQUEST EMPLOYMENT AT YOUR LOCATION SOONEST.' I then resolved that without further thought or discussion with Arthur, I would send this message the moment I got back to camp.

When Serjeant Palmer's patrol eventually returned, we formed up and filed back down the hill the way we had come. On reaching the foot of the earthen steps, we carried on to the road, where transport met us at about 4.30 p.m.

As I entered the Signals tent, Hitchman was taking a transmission on the '62' set. I instantly slapped my message to Stan on the table and said: 'Send that!'

Hitchman glanced at the message-form and exclaimed: 'Right, Jock! I'll send this. Let one of those lazy buggers back there come out and do a turn!'

Shortly after, Arthur came into the tent. Hitchman proffered my message-form and asked him: 'What'll I do with this?'

Arthur read the message, shook his head and said rather impatiently: 'Oh, send it in the morning.'

'I've sent it,' Hitchman answered.

'You've sent it?' Arthur hesitated and then said: 'Very well. Stick it in the file.' He then walked over to where I was seated on my bed, taking off my jungle boots. 'What happened then, Jock?' he asked gently.

'Oh, it was fucking awful!' I exclaimed, knowing that this answer was totally inadequate.

I didn't say any more. Arthur turned away and said no more either. I suddenly felt terribly guilty. I felt that I was letting Arthur down, and beyond that, I was betraying my professed ideal of being a soldier. I wondered now if I had done the right thing. But the message had been sent – and that was that.

The following day, I received a message from Serjeant Haley promising that I'd be replaced 'soonest'.

On Monday the 7th, the volunteers for Korea departed to Penang – but not all of them. Applications from Mr Crisp and Serjeant Palmer were not approved. Also rejected were Chas and Matt. National Servicemen with less than six months remaining to serve were not eligible unless they were prepared to sign on for a Short Service engagement. Pendlebury and Scaife, Pedlar's two muckers, were amongst those accepted.

The following night, Lance Corporal Bentham arrived at Kroh to relieve me at a time when I was full of doubts as to the wisdom of my transfer. Bentham told me that he didn't mind being sent to 'C' Company and appeared to be quite genuine about it.

Next morning, Thursday the 10th, I said goodbye to Arthur, Swede and Hitchman and was subsequently loading my kitbags onto the ration truck when Major Murray strode up.

'What's happening here, Scurr?' he enquired. 'Where are you going?'

'I'm going into HQ, sir,' I replied. 'Corporal Bentham is my relief.'

'You're going in for a rest, are you, Scurr?' the major asked.

'Yes, sir.'

333

'Oh, well,' he said. 'I expect you could do with it.'

'Yes, sir,' I said again.

The major walked away. That was the last time I saw him. I'd always found dealing with him a bit of a trial, and yet ... I climbed into the truck, feeling both sad and dubious about my move. I'd been with 'C' Company a long time. Nearly all of my friends were here. It just did not seem right to be leaving. Also, I'd always looked down on 'rear echelon wallahs' and now I was about to become one myself.

After an eventless journey, I arrived once more at Minden Barracks, Penang, found a spare bed in the Signals *basha* and unpacked my kit. Once I was nicely settled in, my previous doubts rapidly disappeared and I felt glad that I had returned to HQ. After all – I told myself – I only had a couple of months to do, so it was quite a relief that I would not be going out on any more operations in the jungle.

This feeling of relief, however, proved to be premature.

18

HQ Company – Penang
May–June 1951

Soon after my arrival in HQ, Lance Corporal Hodson came up to me in the barrack room and said: 'I couldn't believe it when I heard that message you sent. I didn't think you'd ever come in!'

It appeared that I had somewhat tarnished my image but I wasn't unduly concerned. I reassured myself that I'd done my whack in the *ulu* while some chaps in the Signal Platoon had spent nearly all of their time in Penang.

On Friday evening, 11 May, I went into town with cousin John. We had a good conner of curried chicken and rice in the Broadway Café and then went to the Globe cinema to see Joel McCrea in *The Outriders*. It was just like old times.

The following night, I was on guard – again like old times! It was a guard of 12 men, operating from the main guardroom. I did my first stag in the magazine. When I was patrolling alone round the creepy, 'haunted' enclosure, I seemed to be a bit more jumpy than I'd been when performing this duty in the past. I remembered what Matt Busby had said to me once about the wearing effect upon the nerves of climax changing to anticlimax in the jungle. I wondered whether my nerves might have been affected by this or by the many other tensions of operations on the mainland.

On Sunday morning, the 12th, I began work in the wireless tower, maintaining communication with the rifle companies and Tac HQ, as well as with Brigade. This regular employment suited me fine. There was a marvellous view from the wireless tower of the surrounding country, the coast and the ocean. The masses of green palm trees along the shore and the deep blue sea beyond formed a visual composition that was absolutely breathtaking.

Regular features in Minden Barracks at this time were RSM's drill parades before breakfast and a CO's kit inspection every Saturday morning. Due to the latter, Friday afternoons and evenings were devoted to bulling up personal equipment and the barrack room. It all seemed to be aimed at licking HQ Company into shape for the battalion's return to Blighty in August, which would be followed shortly after by a posting to Germany. One day, Private Foster said to me: 'You picked the wrong time to come in here!' I could certainly see what he meant, but I was not convinced that bull was more punishing than staggering up hills with my lungs turning inside out! For the moment I remained reasonably content.

During this period, the nick was kept full up with hard cases from the Korea Draft. The volunteers for Korea – 7 corporals, 6 lance corporals and 78 privates – appeared to incorporate a fair percentage who were a drunken and lawless bunch. I was told that the rifle companies had been glad of the opportunity to unload their hard cases and troublemakers upon the KSLI, prior to our battalion's coming move to Germany. It was even rumoured that in 'D' Company, when the CSM read through the list of volunteers, he went into a particular tent and persuaded the occupants to add their names to the list! When cousin John was doing his stint as Orderly Corporal one morning, he entered the draft's barrack room, to be greeted by a bottle which smashed against the wall just beside his head. Certainly the day of the draft's departure was a great relief to HQ Company. I hasten to add that there were many good chaps among them and all were heroes in my eyes.

While these men were being shipped off to Hong Kong, ultimate destination Korea, there were others whose thoughts were firmly fixed on a boat going in the opposite direction. Private Charlie Walker and Corporal Fred Sparkes of 'B' Company were due to sail home on the troopship *Dilwara* on 24 May. Charlie had been with me in basic training, although he was in a National Service Intake Group (4913) preceding that of the rest of us (4917), and was in fact the Durham lad who had pulled me back into the column when I had attempted to drop out during the 9-mile march at Bordon. Fred had transferred from the King's Royal Rifle Corps, joining our draft for jungle training in March 1950. It was then that he first met Charlie, and when they were both subsequently posted to 5 Platoon, 'B' Company, they formed a close friendship which lasted throughout their service together.

On Sunday, 20 May – four days prior to their sailing date – the two friends set out on their last patrol. Departing from the company base at Lubok Segintah, 5 Platoon marched all day through rubber and overgrown secondary jungle, halting to make base at Kejai, near Baling Estate, around 4 p.m. The day had been long and hot but otherwise uneventful, and Charlie and Fred were in good spirits as they sat on the bamboo verandah of a Malay *basha*, laughing and joking and handing out boiled sweets to some Malay girls. They supposed patrolling was over for the day, but Serjeant Geordie Dee now called for a few men to accompany him up the track to a police post about a mile away. Apparently a rather ill-at-ease Malay had shown up, saying that the police there wished to confer with the military. So Fred and Charlie once more hitched up their equipment.

A patrol of seven men set out up the track with Charlie as leading scout, armed with his De Lisle silent carbine. After three-quarters of a mile, the track led out of the jungle into rubber. Proceeding up a small incline with thick scrub to the right, Charlie suddenly spotted some uniformed figures and dropped to the ground.

'This is the military!' Charlie yelled out.

'Police!' a voice called back.

Charlie now stood up. A sub-machine gun opened up from the scrub and riddled his chest with bullet holes. As Charlie fell dead, the rest of the patrol briefly froze. Then,

337

as a fusillade of fire was unleashed upon them, they dived into cover. To his surprise, a private named Hicks landed on top of a prone Communist bandit and promptly fired two shots into him. Corporal Fred Sparkes had seen his mate Charlie go down, and angrily fired his Owen gun at the smoke from the enemy's weapons, which was all that could be seen of their assailants.

The Bren gunner, Peter Griffiths, took up a firing position behind a tree. He was very aware of the horrendous noise of the gunfire around him and particularly of the bullets which were passing close by him, cracking and banging in a terrifying way. He aimed his Bren to the right towards the enemy fire, letting off five-round bursts. Spotting gunsmoke from behind a tree close in front of him, he fired straight through the trunk. Then the Bren gun's barrel fell off. Forgetting his training, he picked up the barrel by the flash eliminator, burning his left hand, and slammed the barrel back into place.

As the enemy fire began to slacken, Serjeant Geordie Dee shouted: 'Get the Bren up here!'

Peter started to crawl forward, but seeing Geordie on his feet, he got up and ran to him.

Just then, a voice called from the scrub: 'Stop firing! Police!'

'They are not!' Geordie yelled. 'Rapid fire!'

Geordie bent over so that Peter could site the Bren across his shoulder. Peter opened fire at a glimpse of some bandits disappearing over a ridge. Then everything went quiet.

The patrol now examined the immediate area. The bandit positions were heavily blooded in three places, including behind the tree that Peter Griffiths had fired through. Peter picked up his jungle hat with a splinter of tree bark sticking through it. Charlie and the bandit shot by Hicks were both confirmed to be dead. The bandits had taken Charlie's De Lisle silent carbine, after shooting at his hands to release his grip, no doubt damaging the weapon in the process. Fred Sparkes was grief-stricken and totally bewildered that fate could have been so cruel as to strike down his best mate only four days before they were due to sail home together.

Charlie Walker was buried in Penang cemetery the following day, Monday 21 May. Fred Sparkes was corporal i/c pallbearers and Peter Griffiths was the leading bearer.

On Tuesday night, the 22nd, John and I were sitting at a table on the NAAFI verandah, having a drink. RSM Tanner was walking along the road at the foot of the grass slope which ran down from the verandah. He glanced up at us, stopped, hesitated and then called out: 'Corporal Kitchen!'

John immediately hastened down the slope to stand before the RSM, who then asked him: 'What are you doing, drinking with that private, Corporal Kitchen?'

'Well – he's my cousin, sir,' John explained.

'Oh!' said the RSM. 'Well, look, Corporal, you know very well that you shouldn't be drinking in barracks with privates. In future, meet him downtown when you're wearing civvies. Understand?'

'Yes, sir.'

The RSM departed. John came back up to the verandah and finished his drink. After that, however, we were not able to meet in the NAAFI again.

The next morning, I was detailed to attend a messing meeting, which was regularly convened to discuss complaints about cookhouse meals – which never improved as a result! I arrived at the meeting just on time, according to my watch, and ten minutes late, according to the Company Commander's! Consequently, the following morning, Thursday the 24th, I found myself on Company Levee. The stated charge, however, was not that I had been late but that I was 'absent' from the meeting. Serjeant Haley took great pleasure in informing CSM Jennings that I had been in attendance. I waited, all bulled up, on the verandah outside the company office until the Company Commander arrived – three-quarters of an hour late! The Company Commander then had to admit that I had indeed been at the meeting and the charge was dismissed, though I received a sharp warning from the CSM about punctuality.

Chas Schaverien arrived back from his leave in Hong Kong on Wednesday the 30th. He'd had quite an exciting time and had even managed to visit Japan. We were both delighted when Stan Haley said that Chas could remain in HQ for the time being and arranged for his kit to be sent from Kroh with the ration truck the following day. That night, Chas joined John and me in a trip downtown. We saw *Two Flags West* at the Odeon, dined at the Broadway, then – on the way to the bus terminal – suddenly decided to go to the City Lights Cabaret. Chas and I both had a fair amount to drink and were very reluctant to return to camp. John had remained sober, however, and escorted us to a taxi, which deposited us all at the guardroom at about 11.40 p.m.

A kit layout scheduled for Monday, 4 June, was cancelled at the last moment so that we could devote our energies to scrubbing and bulling up barrack rooms in preparation for the following Thursday's visit by the CO of the 1st Battalion, Manchester Regiment. The Manchesters were due to take over our operational area when the KOYLI sailed for home.

That night, Chas and I went downtown and had what my journal simply described as 'a really good night'. After partaking of a fairly expensive chicken meal in the Broadway, washed down by a couple of Tigers apiece, we strolled up Penang Road in a very happy mood. There was a definite feeling of excitement in the air as we moved through the throngs of noisy, leisurely passers-by. As always, my eyes were alert for the dainty and graceful Chinese girls with their slim, curvaceous figures and their smooth and slender thighs tantalisingly revealed by the long splits in their cheongsams. The way they dressed and walked always made them seem to me to be exceptionally feminine and exotic. They were, however, mainly girls from well-to-do Chinese families who would not even look at a British soldier. But what a pleasure it was to look at them!

We soon made our way to the City Lights. (I was highly amused by someone's description of HQ Company as the

'City Light Infantry'!) Once inside, I found the subdued lighting, the rather tawdry decor and the slightly out-of-tune dance music strangely exciting. We knocked back four gin and vermouths each while watching the Chinese taxi girls cavorting on the dance floor. These did not possess the beauty and polish of the girls that we'd seen on Penang Road but they nonetheless exuded a cheap, yet powerful stimulation. There were two girls, clad in flower-patterned pyjama suits, who danced with one another, constantly thrusting their loins together and grinning towards us. I found them rather vulgar and was far more inspired by the sight of other girls dancing with servicemen and holding them very close. I had never learned how to dance – not that that would have been a requirement! – but anyway, we hadn't bought any tickets.

Around 10.30 p.m., we stepped outside, decidedly intoxicated, and climbed into one of the dozen trishaws that zoomed towards us.

It just seemed the thing to do. I turned my head and said to the trishaw-wallah: 'Take us to two bibies, John!' (In dialogue between soldiers and locals in Malaya, everyone was 'John' or 'Johnny'.)

First the trishaw-wallah drove us into the grounds of some hotel, and then for some reason drove out again. After a while, we stopped in a dark side street where we were invited to get out and enter the backyard of a house. There were two Chinese girls here who evaded our initial amorous attentions, saying that girls did not like men when they were drunk. Fair comment! So we got back in the trishaw and continued to another similar hovel where a single Chinese girl was for sale. However, she was very small and very young. I shook my head and said to the trishaw-wallah: 'Too small!' Away we went again.

The trishaw-wallah now said: 'I take you to Siamese bibi.' He pedalled on down dark, narrow streets and eventually stopped again.

We got out of the trishaw at the dingy entrance to a small, low-down hotel. A plump Siamese woman came out, clad in a white blouse and red sarong. On her feet were wooden sandals which clacked noisily as she walked. I placed my right hand on the front of her blouse and then ran the fingers of my left hand through her flowing black hair. I felt immensely excited. The woman's dark, slanting eyes were warm and friendly. She smiled at me and patted my cheek.

'You like me, darling?' she asked.

'Yes,' I said. 'I like you.'

'Come on!' She grasped my arm. 'We go upstairs.'

Chas and I accompanied the woman up a narrow wooden staircase to the first landing. Chas sat down on the stairs and I followed the woman into a bedroom. It was a small room, containing only a bed, a chair and a chest of drawers.

'Five dollars,' the woman said simply.

I handed her the required sum, then watched with mounting excitement as she unbuttoned her blouse and removed it. She next discarded her brassiere and, finally, with a quick movement she unwound the red sarong from her waist and stood before me completely naked.

This was the very first time in my 20 years that I had looked upon 'forbidden fruit'. I have to say that I was most impressed! I surveyed the smooth, creamy flesh of her large, drooping breasts and plump belly with sheer delight. This was surely a good five dollars' worth!

She now held out her arms to me. 'Come on, darling,' she said. 'You take off.'

Upon the bed, she displayed neither surprise nor scorn at my innocent ignorance. 'Come on, darling,' she said softly. 'Come on.' She patiently and tenderly helped me through. At no time did I experience anxiety or embarrassment; I was only aware of the warmth and totality of her embrace. Nor did the effects of alcohol diminish my appreciation of that pleasurable short time. Despite the inevitable limitations of a first sex experience, I was overwhelmed with joy.

As I was preparing to leave, I smiled to her and said: 'Thank you very much.' I was aware that these words were totally inadequate to express the gratitude that I felt towards her. The money I had paid her seemed paltry for what I'd received in return.

She gave me a fond smile, patted my cheek and silently guided me to the door. When I went out onto the landing, I found Chas sprawled face downwards on the staircase, apparently asleep. I pulled him to his feet and, ignoring the fact that the woman was tugging at his sleeve, staggered down the stairs with him and into the waiting trishaw.

As we drove off, Chas said to me: 'Why didn't you want me to go with her, Jock?'

'Well – I thought you'd probably get a dose,' I lied, knowing full well that I just hadn't wanted my mate to go with 'my girl'.

The trishaw-wallah now delivered us to the taxi stand and we finally arrived back in camp as happy as sandboys just before midnight.

In the sober light of the following morning, I gave serious consideration to the previous night's great event. Although not a churchgoer, I had always been a fairly religious lad, so I presumed that I had probably committed some terrible sin. I even prayed for forgiveness. However, I knew that I was not at all repentant. Throughout the day, I kept having warm, delicious memories of the Siamese woman's cream-coloured flesh and of how kindly she had treated me. No – I had no regrets whatsoever.

We continued to scrub out and polish our barrack rooms in preparation for the coming visit of the CO of the Manch-esters. In the meanwhile, CSM Jennings had been posted to 'A' Company and Bert Harbisher, the Bugle Major, had assumed the post of Acting CSM of HQ Company. The consequences were not long in showing. On Wednesday, 6 June, my journal aptly commented: 'Starting from this morning, the stupid bastard is making us do a muster parade every morning on the square!'

On Thursday the 7th, it was my misfortune to be barrack room orderly. I was lying on my *charpoy* (bed) around 10 a.m. when a corporal from the MT Platoon – who, I

343

presumed, was Orderly Corporal – came into the Signals *basha* and said to me: 'Listen! There's an old wog who's supposed to be sweeping the square but he's dead slow. Now I want you to go down there and grip him. D'you understand? Grip him! The CO of the Manchesters will be here in half an hour, and if there's one speck of dirt left on that square, the Bugle Major will have me and I'll have you! Got it? Now, jump to it!'

I leapt up and hastened down to the barrack square, no doubt correctly assuming that the Orderly Corporal had attempted to grip the 'old wog' and had failed. I soon came upon an old Indian sweeping-wallah, turbanned and white-bearded, who was feebly flicking the surface of the square with a bamboo brush. Indicating to him that he should move the brush faster, I exclaimed: *'Jildy! Jildy!'*

The old sweeping-wallah looked at me as though I was mental, nodded his head and then continued with his pathetic efforts exactly as before. Mindful of the Orderly Corporal's warning, I seized the brush from the old man's hand and frantically swept the entire square myself. I then handed the brush back to the sweeping-wallah, who appeared quite unable to comprehend what he'd just seen with his own eyes. When the CO of the Manchesters came round some time later, he hardly looked at the barrack rooms or the square. It had all been a lot of fuss and sweat for nothing!

On Friday the 8th, much to the annoyance of both of us, Chas was sent to Tac HQ in Sungei Patani for permanent employment there. Four days later, Johnny Ainsworth (Signals Clerk) gave me the bad news that our sailing date had now been put back to 1 August.

Every morning on muster parade, Bugle Major Bert Harbisher, MM, BEM, was his usual pig-self. He seemed to have it in for the Signal Platoon. Whenever bods were needed for fatigues or extra duties, he always called on us. It was the same every day. After roll-call and issue of anti-malaria Paludrine pills, Harbisher would bawl: 'Signal Platoon – stand fast! The remainder – to your duties, dismiss!'

Then, as the employed, MT, band and bugles and others all disappeared from the square either to work or skive, Harbisher would check up on what each one of us was doing. Those who weren't on duty in the wireless tower, telephone exchange, Signals Office or stores, were allocated to whatever dirty jobs were going. (It is only fair to point out that Bugle Major Harbisher was always very smart on parade, possessed considerable organisational abilities and had a splendid military record.)

In barracks in the evenings – if I wasn't on guard or going to the AKC with John – I always went to the NAAFI, usually alone now that Chas had gone and John was barred from drinking with me. During the day, I really looked forward to these solitary drinking sessions. I loved to sit at a table on the NAAFI verandah, looking out at the palm trees and savouring every mouthful of ice-cold Tiger beer. Often, I daydreamed about how wonderful it would be when I arrived back home, suntanned, with my FARELF flashes on my sleeve, my medal ribbon on my chest and with tales to tell of carousing in exotic Penang and hunting for bandits in the depths of the Malayan jungle. I'd never actually been in action, of course, but I wouldn't need to admit that. I could always spin a few yarns, I considered, and could allude to a couple of skirmishes as though I had been a participant. After all, it wasn't my fault that action had not come my way. No one had sought it harder than I had done and I'd suffered plenty in the process. So, I reasoned, why should I deny myself the right to bask in a little well-deserved glory?

As more Tiger fired my imagination, I pictured the enthusiastic greetings that I would receive from old school-mates and the beautiful maidens that would swoon at my feet. I couldn't wait to get home!

When I went back to the Signals *basha*, usually well-oiled, I nearly always ended up sitting on Lance Corporal Tom Joy's bed and talking a load of baloney. One day, Tom said to me: 'Are you going to the NAAFI tonight?'

'Yes,' I replied. 'And I'm going to get drunk too!'

'Well, do me a favour,' Tom pleaded. 'When you come back, don't come and talk to me!'

I couldn't blame him really. However, when I returned from the NAAFI that night, I still went straight over to chat to him – much to his dismay!

On Wednesday morning, the 13th, Stan Haley came into the Signals *basha* and told Corporal Bragg that a signaller was needed for 'C' Company. Without hesitation I jumped up from my bed and said: 'I'll go.'

'Oh no, you won't!' Stan exclaimed.

'Why not?' I asked in surprise.

Stan explained: 'When the CO saw the message you sent from Kroh, he wrote me a memo saying that you were a jungle-weary soldier and that you were to have no more *ulu*. So that's final!'

Even though the CO's decision was certainly very considerate and proof of his concern for the men under his command, I was far from pleased. In my journal, I complained to myself that the decision was quite ridiculous. Maybe I had got weary, but I'd never actually collapsed with exhaustion, as had happened to some men in the battalion. I could have carried on at Kroh to the end of my tour if I'd wanted to, I told myself. I have little doubt that this last assumption was correct, although there is no question that I had been finding continual states of near-exhaustion harder to take and presumably was, therefore, jungle-weary.

That afternoon, Chas came in from Tac HQ and departed for 'C' Company the following morning.

On Thursday the 14th, I was issued with BD (battledress), greatcoat and khaki shirts in preparation for my departure to Blighty in just six weeks' time. 'Roll on the boat!' I commented eagerly in my journal.

I received a nice surprise that afternoon when Eric Hann arrived from 'D' Company. That night, we went downtown. First of all, Eric did some shopping and got measured for a civvy suit at Joe Kee's in the bazaar. Then, we dined at the Broadway and knocked back a couple of Tigers each. After

346

that, we went to the City Lights, where we drank gin and vermouth and more Tiger.

The tinny band was playing 'Malayan Rose' when Eric discovered that he had only one dollar and fifteen cents left. Hurriedly I counted my money and found that I had ten dollars.

'Ten dollars,' I said meaningfully. 'We need that, don't we, Eric?'

Eric laughed in a wild, sozzled manner. Then, on searching my pockets, I concluded that I must have lost another ten dollars somewhere. (I may well have spent it on booze!)

'You must have more!' Eric complained now. 'We need another dollar for the taxi back.'

I managed to find another 40 cents.

When we left the City Lights, vaguely intending to walk to a suitable place, a trishaw-wallah immediately offered to take us to 'bibies'. We told him that we couldn't pay him anything but he said that was OK.

'Fuck-all for you!' Eric emphasised as we climbed into the trishaw.

'OK, Johnny,' the trishaw-wallah responded, knowing that he would get his cut from the bibies.

We were driven to a lane off Penang Road, on the opposite side from the police station, and halted outside a dingy hotel. The trishaw-wallah got out and soon brought a bibi from inside the building. She was plump and was dressed in a blouse and sarong.

'I know you!' she exclaimed eagerly, pointing at me. 'You come here before with small friend.'

I couldn't believe my luck! Against all the odds, I'd been brought back to the same Siamese bibi that I'd been with last time! She grabbed my arm and told the trishaw-wallah to take Eric to another address and call back for me later. I gave Eric five dollars and the trishaw drove off.

The woman put her arm round my waist and I was immediately excited by the warmth of her body against mine. 'You shouldn't get drunk, darling,' she scolded me mildly.

347

She took me upstairs to the same bedroom. I paid her the five dollars and once more enjoyed watching her remove her clothing.

While holding her in my arms on the bed, I asked her: 'What's your name?'

'Dolly,' she answered.

'I like you, Dolly,' I said very sincerely. 'How old are you?'

'Forty,' she replied.

'Forty?' I exclaimed. 'My mother's only a few years older than you.'

Dolly smiled. 'I'm twenty-eight,' she said now.

I didn't know what to think. She looked older than 28 to me but certainly a lot less than 40. 'D'you take many men?' I asked her.

'You my first man tonight.'

'You take men often?'

She smiled again. 'No.'

'Then how d'you make money?'

'I work,' she said simply and, I suspect, untruthfully. 'Come on now, darling – before your friend comes back.'

I'd had more to drink than on the previous occasion, but Dolly's patient guidance and stimulation left me, once more, happy and very grateful.

As she watched me clumsily dressing, she said again: 'You should not get drunk, darling. You come back tomorrow night but you not drink.' She took a photograph from a drawer and handed it to me.

'Who's this?' I asked stupidly.

'It's me,' Dolly replied. 'You like it?'

I focused my eyes upon the head-and-shoulders studio portrait. 'Oh yes, Dolly,' I said, quite delighted. 'I'll keep this.'

'You will keep it?' Dolly looked into my eyes. 'You will not give it to any of your friends?'

At the time, I was so naive that I believed that she was happy at the idea of me keeping the photo. It did not occur to me that her probable hope was that I would show her picture around the barracks and gain her more custom!

'I'll put it in my photo-album,' I said, placing the snap in my pay book.

Then she showed me another photograph, this time of a young girl, perhaps in her mid-teens. 'This is my girl,' she told me. 'She goes to school here in Georgetown.'

'Very nice,' I said.

'You come back tomorrow?' she asked.

'No, I'm on duty tomorrow night.' I lied.

'When you come back?'

'Sunday,' I lied again.

'Sunday?' Dolly nodded. 'OK. You come Sunday and you not drink – and I bring my girl for you.'

I was completely astonished by this announcement and my mind seemed to sober up considerably. Could she really mean this? What was her intention? Was it just that she liked me? Or was it, perhaps, that she wished to introduce her daughter to 'the game' with someone who was gentle? Whatever Dolly's motive was, I knew that this was one present that I could never accept.

Fortunately, at that moment, I heard Eric calling from the street below: 'Jock! Jock!'

Dolly went down with me. As I climbed into the trishaw, she said: 'Sunday then, darling – but you not drink!'

I looked at her hard but remained silent. I was pretty sure that I would never see Dolly again, but I knew that I would never forget her. Of course, I was well aware that to regular members of the 'City Light Infantry', going with a prostitute was nothing special – just a bit of fun really. But, even if a whore, Dolly had been my first woman of any description and she'd treated me so very nicely. As I write these words – 40 years later – I still retain fond memories of Dolly. She was certainly a lot more kind to me than some of the women I was to tangle with in later years!

The trishaw-wallah drove Eric and me to the taxi stand. I asked Eric how he'd got on.

'He took me to a Malay bibi,' Eric told me. 'She was fuck-all like it! Anyway, I had to stop in the middle because I heard the MPs outside!'

We took a taxi back and arrived at the camp entrance at about 11.45 p.m. After we'd got out of the taxi, I placed our remaining one dollar and fifty-five cents in the driver's hand and we walked speedily up the road as he began to count it. Very soon, we heard his pleading cries of: 'Hey, Johnny! This not enough! – Johnny! Give me my money, Johnny!' His anguished pleas followed us all the way up to the guardroom. I felt rather sorry for him, but we had to get back to camp and just didn't have any more.

Apparently, after putting on the lights in the Signals *basha* – not allowed after lights out – I then made more noise than Eric considered advisable, loudly making contemptuous remarks about 'rear echelon wallahs'. However, if I woke anyone up, no one complained. Anyway, it had been a great night!

The following morning, Friday the 15th, prior to Eric's scheduled return to Kulim, I went with him to the Signals Office to see Serjeant Haley.

'Stan,' I said very determinedly, 'Ron Stringer will be leaving "D" Company in a week's time to go home. I want to take his place.'

Stan hesitated for a moment. 'But you've only got a month to do!' he finally protested.

'I don't care,' I said. 'I want to go.'

'Well, all right,' Stan replied. 'But if you get killed, don't blame me!'

For whatever reason, there was no mention of the CO's instruction that I should have no more *ulu*. I thanked Stan and left the Signals Office, feeling absolutely delighted that I would not be ending my service in Malaya as a rear echelon wallah. I desperately wanted to serve with a rifle company again and go back into the jungle, no matter how wet and weary I became. Best of all, it would be in Kulim – my favourite location, where everything had seemed to go right for me.

I felt like I'd suddenly been given a new lease of life.

350

19

'D' Company – Kulim
June–July 1951

Before breakfast on Thursday morning, 21 June, HQ Company mustered on the square for RSM's drill parade. The initial inspection resulted in ten chaps being put on Company Levee, most of them charged for not wearing their best boots, even though there had been nothing on Company Detail to suggest that this was required dress. As RSM Tanner moved along the front rank, my heart sank as I heard the charges being made. When he reached me, he instantly snapped: 'Where are your best boots?'

'Packed in my kitbag, sir,' I lied.

'What for?' the RSM queried briskly.

'I'm leaving HQ this morning, sir,' I lied again.

'I see.' The RSM moved on. I inwardly heaved a sigh of relief. I'd got away with it!

Actually, I was leaving HQ that day, but not till the afternoon. I'd had a trip to the cinema and farewell drink with cousin John downtown a few days before. When the time came to go, I shouldered my kitbags and went in search of 'D' Company's ration truck. At the stores, I ran into Ginger Thompson, who had come in on escort to 'C' Company's truck, and told him my destination.

Ginger shook his head. 'Thoo's bloody mad, Jock, ganging out of here when thoo's peechy,' he said. ('Peechy' meant 'near the boat'.) 'And "D" Company, as well. They're unlucky sods, tha knows. They're always bumping into some bugger! Watch out for theeself!'

I was not greatly concerned by Ginger's warning, but I

was a little apprehensive regarding all the stories that I'd heard about the large concentration of hard cases and nutcases in 'D' Company. When I arrived at Kulim that evening, the camp was much the same as I remembered it. The Signals billet was still beneath the raised-up bungalow, but was located at the rear and walled-off with canvas from the other sections of Company HQ. In command of the Signals detachment was my old mate from Ipoh days, Corporal Bill Downs – now nicknamed 'Dickie' Downs after the famous racing driver of that period, but I still called him 'Bill'. The other signallers were my mucker Eric Hann, Ron Stringer – who had been with me during both Jungle Training and Signals Cadre, and Derrick Grice – a really nice lad who never swore. I must say, I was very glad to be back.

'D' Company Commander was Major Harding, who, on brief acquaintance, impressed me as being an intelligent, serious and rather reserved man. The platoon commanders were Lieutenants Green and MacKay and Second Lieutenant Betts. Serjeant Major Potts – who had been with HQ Company when I first came to Malaya – was now 'D' Company's CSM. Also in 'D' Company now as Platoon Serjeant was Jock McClung – who had given me so much help and support during my first days in the Signal Platoon.

Next morning, Friday the 22nd, we had to bull up both ourselves and our billet, due to a visit by the new C.-in-C., FARELF (Commander-in-Chief, Far East Land Forces), Lieutenant General Sir Charles Keightley, KCB, KBE, DSO. When we paraded on the MT park, he gave us a short address about the good work we were doing. After that, he went to lunch with the officers and didn't bother us any more.

I soon lost my previous apprehension about hard cases and nutcases. The chaps in the company were, in the main, an OK bunch of lads. There were, however, a few recognisable nuts around While having a drink on Saturday night, the 23rd, I witnessed a most peculiar game of 'truths and dares'. Contestants who were unable to answer general knowledge questions were subjected to the most bizarre forfeits, such as: drinking a glass of beer into which someone had dipped his penis, having sexual relations with a pin-up picture on the wall and even being urinated upon!

The following night, we had a company concert. The regimental band had come especially from Penang and supplied very enjoyable dance music, while a good buffet was laid on by the cooks, supervised by Serjeant Webb from HQ cookhouse. There were also hilarious performances by various members of the company, including Bill Downs, Corporal Guy (medical orderly) and Private Emery (MT driver), singing songs and telling jokes. The other signallers, Eric, Ron and Derrick, plus two other chaps and myself, all sat round a table with about 30 Tigers on ice in a tin bath. We had quite a jovial time, joining in the singing with great enthusiasm – even when other people had stopped!

At 11.30 p.m., when the concert ended, we retired to the Signals billet, where we continued to sing and argue over nonsensical issues for some time. Eventually, a chap called Gus declared that he was going to 'fill someone in'. I got the impression that he was threatening to set about Ron Stringer and immediately stated my intention to 'fill in' anyone who tried to thump one of my muckers! This was most uncharacteristic of me but Tiger beer had strange effects upon people. Fortunately for me, the situation suddenly switched back to one of amicability, as Gus would have made mincemeat out of me!

Anyway, the night's revelries made a good send-off for Ron Stringer, who left us next morning for Penang to prepare for his boat home. That day I heard that Arthur Greenacre had now left 'C' Company, also to go home. I felt really sorry that I wouldn't have the opportunity to say goodbye to him. Arthur was one of the best!

On Tuesday morning, 26 June, I set out with 11 Platoon and half of 12, under the command of Lieutenant Tim Green, for the Junjong area. There was no specific grif but there was always a fair chance of encountering bandits in the region around Junjong. Despite my wish to return once more into the field, I undertook this first 'D' Company operation with some reluctance, rightly assuming that I would be very much out of condition after the weeks of rear echelon duties and beer-swilling in Penang. Fortunately, the operation did not turn out to be too strenuous, even though it lasted for seven days.

The first two days of patrolling some small hills of over-grown rubber proved fairly uneventful, except when one private was bitten by a scorpion and had to be evacuated.

On the third morning, Thursday the 28th, we crossed some large stretches of paddy fields by rather unstable footpaths, then followed a long, sandy track to a settlement in the Ayer Puteh Estate. The settlement was a fair-sized 'new village' of wooden *bashas*, to which squatters on the jungle fringes had been 'resettled' to prevent them from being preyed upon by bandits in quest of food, funds or recruits. Malay SCs (special constables) guarded the settlement day and night. We made base in a *basha* which was, in fact, the settlement office. A short recce patrol was sent out that afternoon but located no signs of the enemy.

The following day, Friday the 29th, at 9.30 a.m., we received a resupply of rations by road. This transport also brought back the chap who had been bitten by the scorpion and who now appeared to be perfectly fit. Lieutenant Green took out a patrol in the morning and Serjeant Urquhart led another in the afternoon. Both returned with nothing to report.

Every night at dusk and every morning at dawn, Mr Green made us stand to in defensive positions around the *basha*, even though we were in the middle of the settlement, which was surrounded by a barbed-wire fence, guarded by SCs! When it was time to stand down, Mr Green would tiptoe out and give two low, two-note whistles. His men then immediately responded with a chorus of whistles, rendering a complementary bar from 'The Cuckoo Waltz'! I could not contain my laughter every time this happened.

Mr Green was a bit of an oddball, but he was a real gent

and very nice. I liked him. Serjeant Urquhart was big and tough-looking, though he treated everyone civilly enough.

On the Saturday morning, Serjeant Urquhart set out with a patrol to spend 48 hours in the Anak Kulim area, while Mr Green took the remainder out on a local day patrol. On this and succeeding days, the medical orderly, Mr Green's batman and I were the only ones left in base. In the mornings, the three of us always used to go down to the river to wash, by a strange coincidence at the same time that the bibies from the settlement used to bathe! The bibies always kept their sarongs on while in the water, I hasten to add. It was all very pleasant just the same.

The three of us also had the task of cooking all the meals. I wasn't too happy being lumbered with this chore, but it never occurred to me to volunteer to go out on patrol as a rifleman, as I had so often done during my keen days.

There was a woman with very sensual facial features and a shapely body who lived with her husband in an adjoining *basha*. One evening, I saw her leaning against a palm tree with a bare thigh thrust forward from her sarong, very much in an alluring Dorothy Lamour pose. I couldn't take my eyes off her and she knew it. Then she suddenly cleared her throat, leaned her head forward and spat a mouthful of phlegm into the grass at her feet. Dorothy would never have done that! My romantic illusion was instantly and permanently shattered.

Braithwaite, the medical orderly, kept giving her tins of 'C' rations, hoping that this might gain him some recompense. She always accepted the tins with great delight but never showed any sign of warming towards poor Braithwaite!

On Sunday, 1 July, Mr Green took out another patrol, which brought back a small wild pig that had been shot by kampong guards. The pig rendered us some fine pork chops and additional meat for our stew. Late that night over an extra brew of tea, Mr Green, his batman, Braithwaite, a few others and myself discussed bandits and various incidents in which men of the battalion had been involved. After a while, Mr Green said: 'I'd like to know what happened to that chap in "C" Company.' He was, of course, referring to Don Hicks. I mentioned that I had been on that patrol. The others showed considerable interest, so Mr Green suggested that I should tell the story. I gave them a fairly detailed account of the day's events, culminating in the tragedy of Hicks being shot in the ambush position at the bandit camp and the later discovery of a bootlace tied tightly around Hicks' neck. I also put forward the theory that a bandit may have set upon Hicks prior to his being shot. Mr Green confirmed that details told to him by Mr Crisp ran along similar lines.

It was then that Mr Green told the story – described in Chapter 14 – of the foiled ambush of a 'C' Company patrol in the Junjong area which had been related to him by the surrendered bandit 'George VI'.

These discussions continued until a late hour. After all the chat about bandits and violent death, I kipped down feeling a little jumpy, which wasn't helped much by a couple of rats which began to scamper around the room. When I confessed my uneasiness to Braithwaite next morning while we were preparing breakfast, he had no hesitation in telling me that he had felt the same.

That morning, Mr Green took out another patrol and Serjeant Urquhart's patrol returned from Anak Kulim. Someone from the latter party said that they'd had considerable difficulty in restraining their Dyak tracker from shooting rubber tappers. Otherwise, the 48 hours had been eventless.

On the following morning, Tuesday the 3rd, a half-hour march took us to the main track through the rubber, where our transport met us. Although it had lasted for seven days, this was undoubtedly the cushiest duffy I'd ever been on. In some ways, though, it had been quite enjoyable.

Two days after our return, on Thursday the 5th, 12 Platoon was patrolling through the Bongsu. While descending a down slope, the scouts spotted three bandits ahead of them. The leading elements of the platoon instantly charged down the slope, firing as they went, and claimed to have wounded one of the bandits. However, all three of the enemy managed to escape through the thick jungle.

On Sunday night, the 8th, Bill Downs had to rush out with 12 Platoon after the police had been shot up again on the Serdang road. The following morning, 10 and 11 Platoons went out, together with Eric and me, allocated as signallers. Our transport carried us a short distance past Serdang before we debussed. From the road, we moved off through the rubber. Because of the weights on our backs, Eric and I were placed together near the head of the column, along with the two medical orderlies, Braithwaite and Gascoyne. This made sense to me, as when you were marching at the rear, you always seemed to have to make an extra effort to try to keep up.

Eventually, we came to the Relau mountain ranges and began to climb, the dense jungle closing around us. From then on, our path lay upwards most of the way. The hard climbing soon resulted in the usual near-exhausted condition, but we carried on, scrambling up and sliding down. At one point, I slipped off a steep track and crashed several yards down a slope. I cursed wildly as I crawled back up through ferns and thorns to resume my place in the file.

Occasionally, we splashed into a stretch of river and followed it for a short way, which gave us a breather before climbing yet again. Our two officers, Lieutenant Tim Green and Second Lieutenant 'Tiger' Betts, seemed to be pretty well lost towards noon, so we made bivvies on a slight slope by the river. Eric and I had just erected an aerial when I was informed by Mr Green that I would be going on a patrol with Serjeant Urquhart in the afternoon.

After tiffen, the patrol set out. Our objective was to try to find a hill called Bukit Batu Puteh which wasn't marked on the map. Upon this hill, 100 bandits were reported to be regrouping in a camp. There were 14 men in our patrol!

The first thing we had to do was to climb a thousand-foot hill. I was loaded with my '68' set and wireless gear; the

357

others carried nothing on their backs. Also, the fact that I was still tired after the morning's hard march did not help matters much. As we finally neared the top of the hill, all drenched in sweat and panting for breath, I was still on my feet but decidedly tottering. Serjeant Urquhart observed my condition and kindly carried the '68' set for a while.

From the top of this hill we made our way down the other side, soon breaking out of the jungle into rubber. For ages we seemed to be constantly on downhill tracks. When we reached the flat, we passed through a couple of kampongs, checking identity cards and enquiring as to the whereabouts of the mysterious hill. It was all to no avail and finally we were guided to Kampong Sungei Kechil just after 5 p.m.

Serjeant Urquhart decided that we should stay the night here as it was too late to return to our base. We found accommodation in the police post and dined frugally on the biscuits and tea which we'd fortunately brought with us in case of emergency. Wireless conditions were very bad. Consequently, I was only able to get through to Eric long enough to send half of the SITREP. Around 9.30 p.m., I went with Corporal Sid Oakes and a Bren gunner to a cafe in the kampong for a cup of coffee. The coffee was not very good but I was happy that Sid Oakes – who did not know me – had invited me along.

Next morning, Tuesday the 10th, we breakfasted on tea and biscuits, then set off back. Everything went well until we reached the foot of the hills. From there, the way back was a matter of doubt, as Serjeant Urquhart was convinced that our base was not at the spot on the map that our officers had indicated the previous day. After climbing the first long stretch of hill slope, Serjeant Urquhart relieved me of the set. We carried on uphill, constantly changing direction as Serjeant Urquhart and Corporal Oakes puzzled over the map. Eventually, we accidentally stumbled onto the correct route, finding a Sten magazine that one of the lads had lost on the way down the day before.

The Dyak was now put out in front to follow our own

tracks back to base. Sid Oakes took over the set from Serjeant Urquhart until we reached the summit. After a rest here, I hoisted the set on my back once more and we began the descent of the thousand-foot hill, struggling through the jungle until at last we reached the river. Sid now took the set again and we soon thankfully arrived back at base – only to find that all the bivvies had been dismantled and the two platoons were all packed up, ready to move on. We were hardly delighted when we heard that the intended route was the one that we had just covered twice in the last 24 hours!

So, after tiffen, we all began the trek back. Movement was very slow, owing to the fact that a chap who had dislocated his knee had to be carried on a stretcher constructed from saplings and poncho capes. Serjeant Urquhart appointed Private Harvey to be my number two and relieve me of the set when I got tired. However, the dead-slow pace up the thousand-foot hill suited me just fine. On the other hand, the relays of stretcher-bearers had a terrible struggle and constantly changed over. While the bearers were trying to circumvent one difficult obstacle – a fallen tree-trunk – the patient fell off the stretcher and rolled a few feet down the hill. Despite ourselves, some of us couldn't help laughing, but the patient didn't seem very pleased!

All of the Dyaks were now sent out in front to clear the jungle ahead with their parangs. When we were near the top, I still felt able to continue but Harvey said he'd give me a break just the same, so I swopped my set for his pack. Soon, we were on our way down the other side and eventually came out into the rubber once more. I took my set back and we carried on downhill, which was very tiring for feet and legs. The injured chap was now being carried bodily between two men, while his kit and that of his bearers were carried on the stretcher. We had a rest at the first *basha* that we reached and were all served with coffee by the Malay occupants, which was a lovely and most welcome surprise. When we moved off again, however, the cursing stretcher-bearers had soon had enough, so we halted at the foot of the hills and bivvied in the rubber.

'Tiger' Betts was a National Service second lieutenant; a nice enough chap in his own way but inclined to be rash and hasty. When we were queuing up at the fire that evening for 'all-in' stew, the four Dyaks joined the line, mess tins in hand. Upon seeing this, Mr Betts strode up and waved the Dyaks away.

'Off you go!' he exclaimed sharply. 'You have your own rations.'

Sid Oakes immediately intervened. 'They only have their own rice, sir,' he said. 'We always give them some stew to go with it.'

'Oh!' said Tiger. He then beckoned to the scowling, withdrawing Dyaks. 'Righto! Come on! Get your conner!'

The Dyaks disdainfully shook their heads. '*Tidak*' (No), they responded and walked sullenly away.

After the meal, Braithwaite held a sick parade, in which he treated a score of men for foot-rot, tinea and sweat rash. As the last patient limped off, Braithwaite called out: 'Does any other fucker want treatment before I put my kit away?'

To this, Lieutenant Tim Green spoke up in his posh accent: 'Yes! I do – but I'm not a fuckah!'

Eric and I had built a *basha* with the two medical orderlies. It rained a little that night but not enough to wash us out.

Patrols went out next morning to screen the area. One of the patrols took three medically unfit men to the road for evacuation to Kulim: the chap with the dislocated knee, another with a high fever and a third with severe jungle sores on his leg. After tiffen, two other patrols were planned. I asked if I could participate in one as a rifleman and Mr Green granted my request. However, in the event, the patrol did little more than walk along the ridge above the camp and come down the other side.

Mr Green seemed to have a silly spell that evening. He kept creeping up on unsuspecting privates and demanding:

360

'*Quelle heure est-il?*' When his victim looked at him blankly, Mr Green would triumphantly exclaim: 'That's French!' Then he would move on to the next suitable target.

Observing this caper, I casually positioned myself in his general line of approach. Sure enough, he pounced, pointing his finger at me, and snapped out: '*Quelle heure est-il?*'

I glanced at my watch and replied: '*Il est cinq heures et demi.*'

Mr Green stared at me for a moment and then exclaimed in astounded tones: 'You spoke French!'

When I explained to him that I'd studied French at school and then listed my passes (which weren't all that many) in the Scottish Higher Certificate, he seemed very impressed.

'You did a lot better than I bloody well did!' he commented.

For a while that night, the rain really poured down but the consequences were not too severe inside our *basha*. In the early morning of Thursday 12th, I was on stag from 4.30 to 6.30 a.m. As I watched the dawn breaking in vivid yellow streaks over the green palm fronds of the tree line in front of me, I suddenly thought what a beautiful country Malaya was and how sorry I would be to leave it. Of course, I still longed to go home but I couldn't help feeling that once I did, life would never be the same again.

In this wistful mood I completed my stag and returned towards my *basha*. Three figures were huddled around the fire, starting to prepare breakfast. Without thinking, I diverted my steps and crouched beside these others, took out my tin-opener and busied myself opening numerous tins of sausages and bacon. Once the brew cans were on the fire, I continued towards my basha. Eric watched me approach, as he reclined on his stomach beneath the overhead poncho, and I soon realised that he'd been watching me all the time.

'You're mad, Jock Scurr!' he said as I ducked beneath the poncho. 'You're far too bloody keen!'

I grinned. Voluntarily undertaking a cooking chore when just coming off two weary hours of stag would appear to be a strange thing to do, I supposed. Perhaps I'd suddenly felt very much a part of everything and needed to signify it, if only to myself. As I considered this, I realised that I was quite content with my general performance on this duffy. The first two days had been hard going but I hadn't done too badly. I had experienced being a jungle soldier again pretty much the way I'd wanted to, and I was now very glad that I had returned.

After breakfast, we packed up and moved off at 7.30 a.m., arriving at Sungei Kechil just after eight. Our transport promptly met us there and conveyed us, via Sungei Bakap and Junjong, back to Kulim.

Our main pastime in the Signals billet was arguing, usually over some really crazy subject. It was normally everyone against Eric, due to his insistence that all film actresses were prostitutes and other such extreme opinions that he held. Late in the afternoon, Eric and I always filled our tin bathtub with ice obtained from the cookhouse, and placed several bottles of Tiger amongst the ice in readiness for our nightly drinking session. Bill Downs usually drank with Roy Guy, Emery and Ayres. Sometimes we joined them but at others, we just sat and chatted in our corner, always getting hilariously drunk.

On the night of Saturday the 14th, yet another police vehicle was shot up on the Serdang road. An English officer and a Malay constable were both killed; grim news for two more families.

The following morning, Bill, Derrick, Eric and I were all sitting on our beds, having a jovial chat. The three of them had been detailed to go out on a company operation the following day, while I would be remaining in camp. I was just declaring, mockingly: 'When you can sit down and say you've done your last patrol – ' when Mr Green rushed into the billet and said: 'Scurr, get dressed for going out right away!'

'Oh, for fuck's sake!' I exclaimed. The others all laughed. Then I asked: 'What's the grif, sir?'

Mr Green replied: 'The grif is that there are a lot of

362

bandits fucking about on the Junjong road and I intend to put a stop to it!'

With that, he left. As I hurriedly pulled on my jungle kit and equipment, Eric said to me: 'D'you want me to go, Jock? After all, you're peachy.'

It was always considered dangerous to tempt fate when you were near the boat.

'No, I'll be OK,' I replied. 'But thanks all the same, Eric.' I grabbed my '68' set and my rifle and off I went.

Mr Green and Serjeant Urquhart had hastily assembled a patrol from Company HQ – clerks, cooks, storemen and others who would not be going on the next day's company operation. Apparently, it had just been reported that a party of bandits had held up a bus on the Junjong road, and we were going to try to cut them off. We climbed into the waiting trucks and drove on our way.

As we speeded along the road, I pondered over the fact that this would definitely be my last operational chance to make contact with the enemy. Would I finally be lucky? Did I really want to be lucky when I was peachy? On balance, I decided that I did want to be lucky.

Our transport took us to a spot near the Junjong road, where we debussed and set off up a track. Though they were from Company HQ, the chaps did really well as regards keeping properly spaced out and adopting appropriate formations. We marched along the track through the rubber in normal file; then, on coming to a hill, we advanced up it in irregular arrowhead. At the top we had a short rest. Serjeant Urquhart detailed a man to carry my set for a while. However, I wasn't tired so I declined the offer. We now moved on along the ridge and then turned downhill in extended order. At the foot, Ayres was so eager to give me a break that I felt it would be ungrateful not to hand the set over to him.

We continued through the rubber, searching *bashas* on the way. At this point in my story, I would love to be able to present the reader with a grand finale, describing how – on my very last patrol in Malaya – I was confronted by a large concentration of the enemy and in the ensuing pitched battle acquitted myself with honour, etc., as happens in novels and films. Regrettably, real life is never that obliging – at least, not to me! As we proceeded through the rubber and the time went by, it became obvious that the bandit gang had escaped us. (I am, of course, now old enough and wise enough to appreciate that had I on this or any previous occasion found myself in a situation where live rounds were singing past my ears, sowing death and mutilation around me, I might well not have been so keen to experience a second such encounter!)

After halting at another *basha*, I set up my wireless, made clear contact with Kulim and arranged a transport rendezvous. Then I shouldered my set once more and we bashed on. We picked up four men and twenty women – all Tamil workers on Sungei Ular Estate – who didn't have their identity cards with them, and took them all the way to the settlement to be identified. There, our transport awaited us.

On arriving back at Kulim camp about 4 p.m., I found that 9 Platoon, 'C' Company, had come from Kroh to take part in the next day's operation. I was delighted to find Chas Schaverien with them and to have this unexpected opportunity to see him again before I left for home. Chas told me something which I found very amusing. Apparently, during a recent duffy up in the Kroh area, Mr Crisp had – for the first time – taken a turn at carrying the '68' set. When he eventually handed the set back, he breathlessly and fervently exclaimed: 'I'll never curse the signaller again!'

Other news of interest was that, having completed his tour, Corporal Frank Keenan of 8 Platoon had recently sailed for home. I had always liked Frank and, as with Arthur Greenacre, I regretted that I had been unable to say goodbye and wish him well.

On Monday morning, the 16th, all three platoons of 'D' Company, plus 9 Platoon, set out on the operation which was to be concentrated around Junjong. A platoon of 'B' Company would also be taking part. Junjong had always been a Communist hotbed and definitely merited this concerted effort. I was the only signaller left in camp and would fulfil the function of working control of the operational wireless net.

Rather at a loose end that night, I counted back through the pages of my journal and found that I had participated in a total of 42 active service operations. No doubt many people could claim to have done more, and some a lot more, but I was well satisfied with this number. Although I could truthfully say that I had seen bandits both dead and alive, action had always eluded me – sometimes only narrowly – but certainly through no fault of mine. All of my efforts to achieve a contact had yielded only anticlimax and disappointment. Yet, on reflection, it seemed to me that in this constant game of hide-and-seek and frequent close pursuit, with the ever present danger of ambush, I had, in effect, been fighting the enemy all the time. It had been very tough and very scary at times and I may have got weary towards the end, yet I honestly felt that for someone who had never been able to consider himself either physically robust or brave, I had nonetheless come through it all rather well.

During the three days' duration of the operation around Junjong, I sat in front of the '62' set almost constantly throughout daylight hours. One message that I had to relay to the five platoons specified that they should keep their eyes open for 40 naked bandits who were on the run in the operational area! A police patrol had apparently surprised the bandits while they were bathing. However, there was no further sighting of the fleeing nudes, and we later heard that a large number of uniforms had been stolen from Jungle Squad HQ at Sungei Bakap.

Another old mucker, Matt Busby, arrived in Kulim camp on Wednesday night, the 18th, as one of the escort for 'C' Company's transport. All personnel returned from the operation the following morning, and I was able to bid farewell to Chas and Matt before they departed for Kroh. It was hard saying goodbye to such good friends. I would be doing a lot more of that in the very near future. Men have often stated that their army mates were the closest and best friends that they ever had. For 20-year-old 'Jock' Scurr, who'd had very few real friends during his schooldays, there was no question about the validity of this statement.

On Saturday night, the 21st, Eric and I were having our usual drinking session and had knocked back several Tigers when I decided to go out to urinate. Outside the billet, sitting on the backstairs to the officers' mess, Private Ayres was busily vomiting. In the darkness, I slipped in his spew and fell flat on my back. I duly picked myself up and continued on my errand, being too drunk to be greatly concerned by what had occurred. It was only when I returned to the billet and Eric angrily complained when I sat upon his bed, that I realised that I was dripping in spew!

'D' Company held another party the following night. Again we had a dance band, buffet and a buckshee Tiger and Carlsberg per man out of company funds. One item of the entertainment was a dance performed by three of our Dyaks to a weird, monotonous melody sung by one of them. The dance entailed them wildly swinging their long-bladed parangs around, which wasn't too well appreciated by the chaps sitting at the front! Anyway, Eric and I consumed a tubful of Carlsberg on ice between us, which made the entertainment all seem a lot better than it actually was.

Monday, 23 July, was my last day at 'D' Company. At 10 a.m., all the 'peechy-wallahs' of 4917 Group – namely: Ellis, Emery, Hancox, Hill and myself – were summoned to the company office to be interviewed individually by Major Harding. When it was my turn to stand before his desk, Major Harding rightly said that in my case 'C' Company Commander would be better qualified to express appreciation of my service, but he thanked me just the same and wished me the best of luck. He asked me what career I intended to embark upon.

'Probably something in the art line, sir,' I replied vaguely. 'Architecture – something like that.'

In fact, I hadn't a clue what I'd do in civil life. Demob

leave was going to be great, I considered. But after that? I was absolutely dreading it!

Finally, I said goodbye to my Signals pals, Derrick, Bill and my old mate Eric. It was handshakes and smiles all round. Then, the other four peechy-wallahs and I threw our kitbags into the back of a 15-hundredweight truck and climbed in after them. As the truck drove off down the narrow road, I looked back for the last time at Kulim camp. The rows of brown squad tents, the MT park and the old planter's bungalow all quickly disappeared from view behind the trees which lined the road. It was goodbye to Kulim, which had been my happiest home during my time in Malaya and where I'd soldiered at my best.

However, feelings of sadness were rapidly superimposed by the shared excitement of five young National Servicemen who had joined the army on the same day, sailed to Malaya together 18 months previously and were now setting out on the first stage of the long voyage home.

20

Penang and HMT Empire Pride
July–August 1951

In the early afternoon of Monday, 23 July, my four companions and I arrived safely in Minden Barracks, Penang.
HQ Company personnel were all now accommodated in
tents over at the old company lines, as both the barracks
and our battalion's commitments were in the process of
being taken over by the Manchester Regiment. Our battalion, in fact, was due to sail for the UK on 7 August, only
six days after 4917 Group. I was greatly relieved that I was
escaping just in time, as I was convinced that voyaging
home with the battalion would involve a lot of bull and
generally being mucked about.

Nobody seemed interested in our arrival; even Bugle
Major Harbisher merely snarled at us and walked away. So,
eventually, we found an empty tent near the top of the
slope and moved in. We soon learned that we were the last
members of our group to arrive. Now that we were safely
in from the mainland, there was a common feeling of elation
that we'd made it. Provided that there was no mishap during
the train journey down to Singapore, we would be going
home!

That night, I went downtown with cousin John and
bought 108 dollars' worth (£13.84) of presents to take home,
consisting of a lady's gold miniature watch for my mother,
a Siamese silver cigarette case for my father and a Siamese
silver bracelet and six pairs of nylon stockings for my sister.
After completing my purchases, we partook of soft drinks
at the Green Spot before returning to barracks.

On Tuesday the 24th, our group handed in our jungle kit and webbing equipment to the stores. John had kindly provided me with a buckshee jungle hat that I was able to relinquish and thereby keep my own, of which I had grown immensely fond. The following day, we were given a medical examination and on Thursday the 26th, were interviewed for documentation. It was confirmed that on being demobbed I would be posted to the 7/9th Royal Scots for my compulsory three and a half years' reserve training with the Territorial Army.

Eric Hann and Derrick Grice, along with two platoons of 'D' Company, arrived in Minden Barracks the following day but they were all immediately quarantined, owing to a small outbreak of influenza in the company. I went downtown again with John that night. We saw a western film called *Vengeance Valley* at the Cathay, followed by a good conner and a couple of Tigers at the Broadway.

At noon on Saturday, the 28th, our group was on CO's Levee. Major Atkinson (battalion second in command) came out of his office onto the verandah where we were all lined up, and delivered a brief address.

'You can all go home feeling very proud of yourselves,' he told us. 'You've given valuable service in this troubled land, keeping it free from the Communists and at the same time helping to preserve our British way of life from those who would seek to change it.'

His words made me tingle with pride. I was delighted to think that I'd done all that! (In all seriousness though, 40 years later, I believe that the above was precisely what we had done.) Major Atkinson now walked along the line and shook each of us by the hand. He then sincerely thanked us for our contribution and wished us good luck. It was very nice and made me feel that everything had been worthwhile.

On Saturday night, I went to the NAAFI alone. Seated at a small table on the verandah, I consumed four bottles of Tiger. Then, just after 9 p.m., I wandered slowly back, meandering on the way with some wild idea that I might encounter an *Amma* (maidservant for the married quarters). Fortunately, I didn't meet one! I eventually arrived at one of the Signal Platoon tents and sat on a bed, talking to Tom Joy and Dinger Bell.

When I woke up some hours later, I was surprised to find that I was fully dressed and lying in complete darkness on what appeared to be a strange bed in an equally strange tent. Men were jumping out of other beds to put the tent walls down, as a tremendous rainstorm had begun. I looked at my luminous watch. It was 5.20 a.m. I honestly couldn't figure out where I was or how I'd got there. Then, at last, I recalled the previous night's events and presumed that I must have dropped asleep in the Signals tent. I now slept again until 8 a.m.

During that morning, our group handed in our bedding and finished off our packing, in readiness for our departure at 7 a.m. the following day. My journal entry ended with the expression most frequently uttered during our time in Malaya: 'Roll on the boat!'

On that last night in Minden Barracks, Penang – Sunday, 29 July – Eric (now released from quarantine) and I visited the NAAFI and 'hit the Tiger'. Tom Joy soon joined us, and after the NAAFI had closed, we all adjourned to the Signals Office, taking our remaining beer with us. We indulged in some rather silly fun, phoning up bints downtown whose numbers were supplied by Tom. The last one we rang up was called Pearl. Eric was speaking to her on the exchange phone and I on the office phone, both talking to her at the same time and continually cursing each other. After a while, Tom felt ill and began spewing up. So I bade Eric farewell, promising to keep in touch, and took Tom back to his tent.

Our group rose at 5.30 next morning, Monday the 30th. When we had breakfasted and were ready to go, I made a quick visit to the two Signals tents and said goodbye to all my old pals, not at all willingly.

I knew that I would never see any of them again. It just did not seem right. The Signal Platoon had been my 'family' for a year and a half.

Tom Joy shook my hand. 'Cheerio, Jock,' he said. 'I suppose the next time I see you, you'll be a sniper.' He was referring to a remark I'd made that I'd quite like to be a sniper in a conventional war situation. Then, he added: 'You'll be back, Jock. You'll never stick Civvy Street.'

'Well, I intend to give it a good try,' I said.

Tom shook his head. 'I'll give you six months,' he predicted positively.

It was time to go. Cousin John came to see me off. 'I'll see you at home in about six weeks,' he said.

'Sure,' I replied. 'I'll come down to Wallsend during your demob leave.'

Somehow it seemed unreal. Britain was still so far away. I even found myself wondering crazily whether my ship would be able to find it!

Group 4917 boarded the waiting trucks at 7.30 a.m. As our transport drove off, we gave a rousing cheer. From the back of the 3-tonner, I watched John and my Signals friends waving goodbye. I waved back, quite excited that we were at last on our way, but also feeling sad. As the rows of tents, the groves of coconut palms and the yellow-walled barrack blocks receded from my view, I pondered on the fact that I would never see this lovely place again. During my periods in Minden Barracks, I had found plenty of things to moan about – it was true – but I had known happiness here as well.

It was a long and tiring journey from Prai to Kuala Lumpur. We changed trains at KL and travelled down to Singapore on the night train. Some Marine Commandos on board were pretty drunk and noisy. One of them kept waving his unsheathed bayonet around, though he did not actually threaten anyone.

We slept rather uncomfortably on the compartment seats. Night trains were attacked fairly frequently. Our orders were that if there was any trouble, we were not to open fire unless we saw definite movement. During the night, the police Bren gunners on board the pilot locomotive fired into the customary ambush locations above the tracks, in advance of the train's passage. When we awoke in the morning, Tuesday the 31st, we were told that the train had, in fact, been fired upon at one spot. However, I certainly had not been aware of it.

From Singapore station we were transported in trucks to Nee Soon transit camp, a huge, sprawling complex of buildings and tents. There were drafts of young lads there, newly arrived from Blighty, waiting to go up-country. I couldn't believe how white their skins were. They looked really sickly. 'Don't they look awful!' I said to Johnny Ainsworth. 'Surely we didn't used to look like that?'

'Oh yes, we did!' Johnny assured me.

We were allocated to squad tents, in which we rested for the remainder of the day. That night, Hill, Hancox, Johnny and I went to the camp NAAFI. After a small supper, we found that we had enough Malayan currency left between the four of us to buy one bottle of Tiger beer. As we divided the contents between four glasses, Gordon Hill said rather solemnly: 'The last in Malaya!'

'Here's to a safe journey home!' said Johnny.

We raised our glasses. As I drank my last Tiger, I endeavoured to give maximum attention and appreciation to every mouthful.

Reveille next morning, Wednesday, 1 August, was at 5 a.m. At 7.30, we departed in trucks which took us to Singapore docks. After a long wait on the quayside, we eventually boarded HMT *Empire Pride* and were assigned to Mess 11 of Two Main Deck. On board, we soon met Geoff Clarke, now a corporal, and the others of our original draft DAFJZ who had been separated from us upon receiving orders to join the KSLI in Hong Kong. Some of them had been to Korea, after transferring to the Middlesex Regiment, but all had survived. I remembered my thoughts after we'd boarded HMT *Devonshire* 18 months before, when I'd wondered how many of us would come back. In fact, we were all going home except one – and that was poor Charlie Walker of 'B' Company, killed just two months previously.

We sailed at 12.30 p.m. Lining the ship's rails as the vessel pulled away from the docks, we watched the bustling island city of Singapore slowly growing smaller as it withdrew into the distance.

My thoughts at that time were many and rather confused. First of all, I was aware that I suddenly felt overwhelmingly safe. I was really on the boat for home and I had not been shot at the last moment. The relief that I felt was quite enormous. It was, therefore, a thankful farewell, yet it was also a sad one. I had always considered that Malaya was a beautiful country and I knew that I would treasure the memories of my experiences there for the rest of my life. I also knew, even then, that I was leaving something behind that I could never recapture – that life, for me, would never be the same again.

The song 'Malayan Rose' began to run through my mind but I inserted a slight alteration to the words at the end:

. . . From the shore the English steamboat slowly sails
    away,
Now I love Malaya, I cannot stay.

Other men around me soon began to drift away, but I remained at the rail, looking back until there was nothing to see but ocean.

The *Empire Pride* was a comparatively small transport, crammed full of troops from Hong Kong and Korea, now augmented by numerous detachments from Malaya. However, she seemed to move pretty fast. The messing system on board was identical to that of the *Devonshire* but discipline wasn't nearly as strict. I suppose that homeward-bound veterans neither needed, nor would accept, the kind of firm control required by green recruits fresh out of Blighty. As on the voyage over, we slept in hammocks.

For the first couple of days, the sea was lovely and calm, but on Thursday night, the 2nd, the wind rose and the ocean grew very rough. Consequently, most of us weren't feeling too good when we awoke next morning, and I – for one –

373

had to run up on deck in order to be sick over the ship's side. After that, however, my stomach appeared to adjust reasonably well to the ship's motion.

The ship seemed to me to be almost unbearably crowded and life aboard was awfully boring. That Friday evening, while chatting to Hill, Hancox and Emery, I asked them if they missed Malaya. They all looked at me as though I was mad and said that they definitely did not!

We sighted Ceylon at 9 a.m. on Sunday the 5th, and after following along the coast, anchored in Colombo harbour about 6 p.m. Shore leave was granted the following day, but I was unable to go ashore as I had been nominated for guard duty. There were two men on board serving long custodial sentences and five psychiatric patients – who I understood had been in Korea – all of whom had to be guarded. My initial disappointment at being denied shore leave turned to anger when it transpired that I wasn't required for guard after all. However, it was then too late to go ashore, so I did a mess orderly duty instead. We left Colombo at 5 p.m. that day.

The Indian Ocean seemed even rougher next morning, Tuesday the 7th. Even so, after being initially sick, I soon found that I didn't feel too bad. While we were seated at our mess table eating lunch, a KSLI National Service second lieutenant was doing his rounds as Orderly Officer, accompanied as always by an orderly sergeant. Johnny Ainsworth and I soon recognised this officer as being Jim Lancaster – a former companion of ours in 'X' Cadre during our basic training in Bordon. When he reached our table, he asked the prescribed question: 'Any complaints?'

We all responded in chorus: 'No, sir!' – as was mandatory in the army, no matter how bad the food was! Johnny then added: 'No complaints, Jim!'

The Orderly Sergeant looked sharply at Johnny, but Jim Lancaster merely smiled and quickly moved on to the next table.

That night, I found myself spewing up over the side for quite a prolonged period. The sea became even more turbulent during the next few days, with spray and waves washing over the decks. Strangely, I now began to feel fine all the time and others seemed well too. Perhaps we were getting used to it.

There were quite a few flying fish to be seen during this period. Frequently, I used to while away the time seated on a bollard at the rail, hoping to spot the fish skimming across the waves. Regularly played over the ship's tannoy system was a selection of tunes from the new hit show *South Pacific*. While looking out to sea, I used to find the tune 'I'm in Love with a Wonderful Guy' very uplifting. The bright and lively melody always inspired daydreams of what I imagined would be my triumphant return home. I saw myself strolling happily around the streets of Edinburgh, being greeted by old school chums, all of whom were greatly impressed by my Far East shoulder flashes and the medal ribbon on my chest. And as for the girls . . . I really enjoyed those dreams!

There were a crowd of Cameronians on our mess-deck who were the roughest, noisiest bunch imaginable. The chaps from my group really hated them and were convinced – despite my assurances to the contrary – that I was the only Scotsman in the world who was likeable! On Friday night, the 10th, I went to collect my hammock from where it was stowed at the end of the mess deck. Though I searched through the small pile of remaining hammocks several times, I just could not find mine. (At the outset, every man had written his name in ink upon the canvas of his hammock.) Eventually, I had no choice other than to comply with the recognised army maxim – of which I did not approve: 'If anyone pinches anything of yours, you pinch somebody else's!'

So I grabbed the nearest hammock, returned to my group's deck space, slung the hammock upon the ceiling-hooks and climbed in for the night. After only a short while, I became aware of a loud Scottish voice cursing and uttering threats. Peeping over the numerous rows of slung hammocks to the far end of the mess deck, I observed that two sturdy Cameronians were proceeding down the first row, reading the names on the hammocks. I instantly realised that I was in a potentially dangerous predicament but tried to remain cool while I considered my options. It seemed to me that if I suddenly got out of the hammock and hastened up on deck, it would only draw attention to myself. Anyway, I'd have to come back sometime. So I decided that all I could do was to remain where I was and let events take their course.

With mounting apprehension, I cautiously raised my head again and saw that the two beefy Scotsmen had now completed their inspection of several rows. Then I heard one of them angrily remark: 'When I get ma honds on the cunt that's taken ma hammock, I'll put the bastard oot o' the porthole!'

The sweat stood out on my brow and streamed down my face to a far greater degree than the hot, close atmosphere normally produced. The couple were now only two rows away. What am I going to do? I frantically asked myself, without reply. Then, with increasing alarm, I saw that the searchers were now checking the row of hammocks prior to mine. I glanced briefly at their hard, tough-looking faces and knew then that there was no hope. I was as good as dead! Then I could hardly believe my ears. 'Oh, bollocks tae it!' one of them exclaimed. And only half a row from their goal, the two Cameronians gave up their quest and went off – I presume – to steal someone else's hammock! I couldn't believe my luck. That was a close one!

It was with considerable relief that the following night I once more located my own hammock.

On Sunday morning, the 12th, the sea suddenly calmed, and early the following morning, we docked in Aden harbour. This time, I was not going to miss my shore leave. I purchased 10 rupees – equivalent of 15 shillings (75p) – as well as having my British money. Launches took us ashore at 8 a.m. Johnny Ainsworth, 'London' Line, Hancox and I sallied forth together. First of all, we went for a walk round the harbour and had ice cream and lime juice in an apparently French café. Then we took a taxi up the winding road

376

through the rocks and down into 'Crater' – Aden town. We strolled around for a while but found the place far from pleasant. The dirty, narrow streets were crowded with Arabs, camels and goats, and the smell was chronic. Goats seemed to run in and out of houses at will. I saw one man who had a leg twisted round with the foot somehow bent underneath, yet he could walk upon it. Another I saw was hobbling on two wooden legs and a third had no nose. The women's faces were all heavily veiled with muslin.

We were soon glad to take a taxi back to the harbour, where we returned to the French café for a meal of sausage, chips and peas, bread and butter, ice cream, coffee and cherryade, all of which we thoroughly enjoyed. About 12.30 p.m., we boarded one of the waiting launches and returned to the ship. At 2.30, we sailed off into a sea that was beautifully calm and entered the Red Sea around 9 p.m.

Those of us at my mess table were on 24-hour mental ward guard, commencing at 9 a.m. on Tuesday the 14th. The patients – unkindly referred to in my journal as 'nutters' – were allowed out of the ward, under guard, for fresh air but were confined to a small area of the deck encompassed by a rope net. The poor chaps seemed perfectly normal to me and were mostly quiet and well-behaved. Men sitting in the sun on the other side of the net tended to make fun of the situation. One 'comedian' approached the net and began counting everyone behind it, including the members of the guard, and shaking his head. It all seemed rather cruel. After all, these young men were just as much war casualties as those who had been physically wounded.

That afternoon, while standing by the ship's rail during a break, I saw a shoal of porpoises very close to the ship. They looked so graceful as they continuously rose up out of the water in an arc and then splashed back.

On Thursday night, the 16th, during our evening meal, Ginger Thompson had an argument with Ellis, who had always fancied himself as a hard case in 'D' Company. The dispute soon grew heated and the pair came to blows in an open space on the mess deck. After Ginger had thumped

Ellis onto the deck twice, the two contestants were separated by an NCO and our meal was peacefully resumed. Late that night, we stopped at Port Suez to pick up a pilot and at 7 a.m. next day commenced the journey up the Suez Canal. Consequently, we had a pleasant desert view all day. The sun was extremely hot, as it had been since we'd entered the Red Sea.

At 9.30 p.m. on Friday the 17th, we anchored in Port Said. Those of us eligible for shore leave (i.e. not on duty) were warned that the political situation was delicate and that we must ensure that we caused no trouble with the Egyptians. At 7.30 next morning, we were taken ashore in large landing craft. Johnny Ainsworth and I had one Egyptian pound between us. The buildings and shops in Port Said were quite impressive and in a pleasant setting but the pestering street vendors and beggars were a bloody menace. One Egyptian 'magician' accosted us in a pavement café where we were drinking Coca Cola. Without invitation, he took chickens from inside my shirt, made coins disappear from Johnny's hand into mine and finished up by making 25 piastres disappear from my wallet!

From there, we proceeded to the Britannia Club NAAFI, where we had a cheap snack of cakes and lemonade. When we returned to the jetty about 10 a.m., the landing craft were waiting to take us back to the ship. We sailed again at noon, and were soon heading west through the Mediterranean Sea – next stop, Liverpool! I now began to fully believe that it was really going to happen and was immensely excited at the prospect.

After entering the Med, the weather grew a little chilly and the sea became choppy at times. On Tuesday evening, the 21st, we sailed pretty close to the coast of Tunisia, and on Thursday the 23rd, we were sailing within good sight of the coast of Spain throughout most of the day. With others from my mess table, I had begun a 24-hour poop guard at 9 a.m. Our duty consisted of standing at the poop (stern) rail, watching out for anyone who might have fallen overboard. During the afternoon, I saw some porpoises swimming very

378

close to the ship; otherwise, nothing but ocean. At 5 p.m., we passed the towering Rock of Gibraltar, while Spanish Morocco was visible on the other side of the Straits. With the Atlantic wind now hitting us, it was freezing cold that night. Consequently, during our periods of stag, we stood at the poop rail with blankets wrapped around us.

On the morning of Friday the 24th, the ship's tannoy system broadcast the following announcement: 'It is known that many of you are in possession of weapons that you have taken from the enemy. You are warned that it is strictly forbidden and a punishable offence to bring illegal arms into the United Kingdom. All arms and ammunition must be handed in to the ship's orderly room by twenty-two hundred hours tonight. A kit check will be held before the ship reaches Liverpool. Anyone then found still to be in possession of arms will be charged accordingly.'

I was later told that many weapons were handed in but that many more were quietly dumped overboard during the night. In fact, the announcement was only a bluff, as no kit check for arms was ever held.

The sea grew rougher as we sailed through the Bay of Biscay on that Friday and was exceedingly stormy during the night. I found myself spewing up again with plenty of fellow sufferers. Seasickness was for me a ghastly, quite unbearable experience. It made me feel so wretchedly ill that I dreaded the thought of ever making another voyage in a troopship. However, I was greatly relieved to find that the sea had calmed down again the following morning. By this time, we had gladly packed away our tropical clothing and donned the far warmer khaki battledress.

The ship's engines stopped for a short time on Saturday afternoon, the 25th, while one of the Lascar crewmen was given a sea burial. The sea was exceptionally rough throughout Sunday the 26th and the ship was heaving like hell, yet nobody seemed to be sick. It was quite extraordinary. In the morning, those of us on deck were absolutely drenched by a huge wave which swept right over the port bow. At 2 p.m., we sighted Bishop's Rock lighthouse. Excitement was

379

high and rose even more during the night, so that sleeping wasn't easy.

On Monday morning, 27 August 1951, HMT *Empire Pride* sailed up the River Mersey and docked in Liverpool at 11 a.m. As I stood at the ship's rail, the sight of so many exclusively white faces of people waiting on the quayside below seemed very strange, and I was suddenly aware of a feeling of complete calm and peace.

At 4 p.m., our group, 4917, shouldered our kitbags and disembarked.

We were home.

21

Strensall and Edinburgh
August–September 1951

The disembarkation at Liverpool brought my Malayan journal to an end. The final entry concluded with those three words: 'We were home.'

On that evening of Monday, 27 August 1951, our group travelled by train to York. When we alighted at the station in the growing darkness, we were all shivering in what appeared to us to be incredible cold. I recall that Johnny Ainsworth and I shuddered at the sight of a woman on the platform who was selling ice cream. From York, we were conveyed in trucks to the KOYLI Depot and Light Infantry Training Centre at Strensall. On arrival at the depot, the first person we saw – to our dismay – was Corporal 'Bummer' Young, who had been well known as a 'bit of a bastard' in HQ Company. However, we had no dealings with him here and were not surprised to learn that he was awaiting a transfer to the Corps of Military Police at Colchester Military Prison!

We were accommodated in an old Nissen hut, which was to be our home for the next two days. During this short period, we were under the supervision of a small, business-like, but very civil corporal who conducted us through the various stages of final documentation and handing-in of kit; all of which took a surprising amount of time. I must say that I enjoyed those days at the depot. In the dining hall or in the NAAFI, we really stood out from all the new recruits, with our suntanned faces, General Service Medal ribbons on our chests and fancy 'KOYLI-FARELF' shoulder flashes with patches below them bearing the crossed kukris of the 17th Gurkha Division. The newly mustered-in, white-skinned conscripts always seemed respectful, even awed, in our presence, and the depot NCOs left us well alone.

All of this gave me a very satisfying, though short-lived, feeling of contentment that I was being given the kind of respect that a returned veteran (even of a small, brush-fire war) should merit. I was also very conscious at that time of a relaxed, calm certainty that my life was safe, now that I was back 'in England's green and pleasant land'. (I am, of course, speaking of the England of 1951.) I remember telling Johnny Ainsworth that I was quite happy now that we were back in the UK and felt no hurry to actually go 'home'. Johnny, however, shook his head and said that he could hardly wait to get home to Batley.

On Tuesday evening, the 28th, Johnny and I took a stroll into Strensall, which was a very pleasant little country village. Johnny would soon be resuming his theological studies, so I was not surprised when he announced that he wanted to look inside the village church. While Johnny knelt in the pews to pray, I waited at the back of the church. However, after we had returned outside, I suddenly asked Johnny to wait for a minute. I then went back into the church and said a short prayer of thanks to God for bringing me home safely from Malaya.

Our next call was to a nearby pub. Inside, we met Ginger Thompson and Derrick Snell, a short, stocky, Yorkshire lad who had been in 'B' Company. I didn't have a clue what I should drink as I had not been a drinker before going to Malaya. Ginger recommended that I should try his favourite – a pint of 'black-and-tan', so that's what I had, and very nice it was too! After one drink, Johnny decided to return to camp. I remained with Ginger and Derrick, and we had a very enjoyable drinking session. By the time we returned to camp, we had downed enough pints of black-and-tan to render us all pretty tipsy. We arrived at the NAAFI just on closing time but managed to persuade the ladies there to sell us three teas and cakes. Unfortunately, we were rather rowdy and slow to leave. While horsing around, I kicked a chair across the floor. The poor ladies were now growing rather alarmed and told us that if we didn't leave, they'd call the picket. We meant no harm and duly said goodnight and retired to our beds in the Nissen hut.

The following morning when we were nursing our hangovers, Ginger said to me: 'Thoo's interesting when thoo's pissed. Thoo talks!' – which, I suppose, more or less summed me up! That day, Wednesday the 29th, our group completed the handing in of all issued kit, other than those uniform items which would be required for our further part-time service with the Territorial Army. It was arranged that we should all meet for a farewell drink together in Strensall that night. In the event, there was a bit of a mix-up, with some of the chaps going to a different pub, and it wasn't a particularly memorable occasion.

Thursday, 30 August 1951, was my last serving day in the army. It had been scheduled that we should depart in batches, according to our destinations. As London Line and I had the greatest distances to travel, we were the first to go. I walked round the hut from bed space to bed space and shook hands with every one of these young men who, on 1 September 1949, had arrived in Bordon Camp, as I had, to commence Basic Training. One by one, I said goodbye to Bill Aisbit, Arnie Bowron, Blunsdon, Hancox, Hill, Ellis, Emery, Lake, Snell . . . and the others whose names, alas, I no longer remember. Once in Malaya we were posted to different companies and I had seen little or nothing of most of them. One or two of them I didn't particularly like. Yet, at that moment of parting, I was very conscious of the bond created by the fact that we were of the same National Service intake.

My warmest handshakes, of course, were reserved for Johnny Ainsworth and Ginger Thompson. Johnny and I had never been really close mates, but we had been good friends periodically throughout our service. Neither had Ginger ever been a mate, yet we had served a long time together in training and in 'C' Company and I'd always liked him and enjoyed his crude jesting. When I stopped at his bed and said: 'Well, cheerio, Ginger,' he gave me a broad smile and a firm handshake.

'So long, Jock,' he said. 'Take care of theeself.'

I felt sad. After shouldering my kitbag, I walked to the door, with Line close behind me. As I passed through the doorway, I called out without looking back: 'All the best, lads!' A chorus of good wishes sounded from behind me. I could hardly bear it. The final strands of the cord were being broken. The practical end of my being a soldier was only minutes away.

London Line and I now proceeded to the Depot Head-quarters offices. As we waited at a desk to collect our travel warrants, I could see an open door ahead of me, beyond which the sun was shining on the outside world. My inner voice now began to send out urgent signals.

If you walk through that door – I told myself – you'll be making the biggest mistake of your life! Apart from school, the army is the only world you've ever known. Some of it may have been hellish – some of it you've hated – but the army is the only thing that means anything to you. What the hell do you suppose you're going to find out there?

The clerk handed me my travel warrant and I walked through the open door. A waiting truck took Line and me to York Station. Before departing to our respective plat-forms, we shook hands and wished each other luck.

'Anytime you're down London way, Jock, look me up,' Line said.

'I will,' I replied, knowing that I never would. 'Cheerio, London.'

'Cheerio, Jock.'

I walked away. I was alone now. It was all over.

On the train north, I was seated in a small compartment with half a dozen civilians of both sexes. I was happily aware that one or two of my fellow passengers were glanc-ing inquisitively at my shoulder flashes and medal ribbon. To pass the time, I began to read through the various pamphlets I'd been given, containing advice about income tax, National Insurance and other matters appertaining to a soldier's return to civil life. I also glanced through my AB III Discharge Book. On the back page, beneath 'Military Conduct: Very Good', was the following testimonial:

> A good type of man who has done very well as a signaller and is a very proficient wireless operator. He is quick to learn and keen to get on. I am sure he will do well in civil life.

The army's opinion of me had apparently altered completely since Basic Training, when the report in my Skill-at-Arms Book had been so critical of my potential. Whoever had written this new testimonial may have been accurate enough about my signalling abilities but – as events were later to prove – he had little talent as a fortune-teller!

On arrival at Waverley Station, Edinburgh, in the early afternoon, I took a taxi to the TA drill hall in East Claremont Street. This was the HQ of the 7/9th Battalion, Royal Scots, and was well known by me during my army cadet days. After brief documentation, I was directed to the QM's stores, where to my dismay I was required to hand in my Light Infantry green beret and KOYLI cap badge in exchange for a khaki balmoral and Royal Scots badge. Then I lined up with about a dozen other demobbed National Servicemen to be given a welcoming address by the Battalion CO.

During this final formality, I had been required to wear my Royal Scots balmoral. However, once outside, I quickly removed it and stuffed it inside my tunic. I then travelled home by tramcar bareheaded, and fortunately didn't meet any military police on the way. Arriving at the tenement where my family resided in Morningside Road, I trudged upstairs to the top floor and let myself into the flat with my own door key. My mother instantly came out into the hall.

'Oh, hello, John,' she said brightly, as though I'd just come in after a day at school.

'Hello, Mum,' I replied calmly, as though that was exactly where I'd been.

Shortly after, my sister returned from her work with the Inland Revenue. 'He hasn't changed much, has he, Mum?' Thelma commented, sounding surprised.

'No,' my mother answered. 'He's just the same.'

The supposition that I hadn't changed seemed pleasing to my mother, but I was far from happy to think that after a year and a half of soldiering in the Far East, I created the same impression as I had as an adolescent schoolboy!

Eventually, my father also came home. Once we were all seated down to dinner, he lost no time in delivering an interminable lecture to the effect that I must find a good job as quickly as possible and start studying for some qualification which would assure me a secure and prosperous future. I listened in polite silence, while Thelma kept giving me sympathetic glances from across the table.

In truth, no form of civilian employment had ever appealed to me and I certainly had no wish to consider the matter on my first evening home, nor for the next three weeks. Although my Date Due for Discharge was the following day, 31 August, my Army Terminal Leave did not officially end until 23 September. Up to that time, I intended to take leisurely strolls around Edinburgh, go to the pictures and perhaps have a drink somewhere. Shortly, I would journey down to Wallsend-on-Tyne when cousin John arrived there on his disembarkation leave. Beyond that, I had no plans.

There was one 'stroll' that I was particularly looking forward to. Whilst in Malaya and during the voyage home, I had frequently indulged in the same daydream. The scenario envisaged that on my first Sunday night back home in Edinburgh, I would take a stroll along Princes Street wearing my uniform, displaying my fancy 'KOYLI-FAR-ELF' shoulder flashes, Gurkha divisional patches and my General Service Medal ribbon. Walking back and forward along Princes Street was a traditional Sunday night pastime for Edinburgh's young people, and the chances of meeting

386

old acquaintances amongst the regular crowds were quite high. In my daydream, I would reach 'the Mound' where public speakers used to sound off from their soapboxes, usually about politics or religion, as at Speakers' Corner in London's Hyde Park. There, I would run into two old schoolmates whom I shall call Ian and Andy.

Like me, Ian and Andy had taken their Highers in Art, but unlike me, both had been outstanding on the sports field. On occasions when observing my poor efforts at sporting activities, they were not averse to shouting 'Give the ball to Scurr!' or other such derisory comments, while dissolving into guffaws of laughter. Even so, they liked me well enough, as I did them. Both had completed their National Service prior to my doing so. Ian had served in the Royal Engineers somewhere in the Middle East, while Andy had remained in Britain with the Royal Army Education Corps. So I was confident, in my daydream, that the pair of them would be compelled to favourably reassess me in the light of my recent jungle forays as an infantryman in Malaya.

Of course, the fact that I'd been required to hand my Light Infantry beret into the TA stores had ruined my plans to wear my adorned uniform during my Terminal Leave. Nonetheless, on that first Sunday night in Edinburgh, 2 September, dressed in my civvy clothes, I took my intended stroll along Princes Street. It still seemed strange to see only white faces around me and to see so many pretty young Scottish girls; most of them made-up to the eyes and all wearing nice dresses or skirts with nylon stockings and high-heeled shoes, as was the lovely custom in those days. This sight reminded me of other daydreams that I wished to fulfil, but for the present they could wait.

When I reached the Mound, I found the open space in front of the art galleries thronged with people who were clustered around the various speakers. Almost immediately – as though they had rehearsed from the script of my daydream – my two former classmates Ian and Andy emerged from the crowds before me. Ian spotted me first and quickly nudged his companion. Confident that they would have heard that I had served in Malaya, I felt quite proud as I walked towards them and said hello.

'Have you just got back, Scurr?' Ian enquired with a grin. 'I bet you feel cold.'

'I certainly do,' I responded cheerfully.

Ian grinned again. 'I read that article about you in the paper,' he said, on the verge of laughter. He was referring to the article that had appeared in the *Edinburgh Evening Dispatch*, after I had been interviewed in Kulim by a public relations officer in October 1950.

'I didn't see the article,' Andy said, also highly amused. 'But I heard about it.'

In fact, the article had been accurate and restrained and contained nothing, in my estimation, that should inspire mirth.

Ian now leaned towards me and asked in mocking tones: 'And did you kill any bandits?'

I hesitated, feeling both embarrassed and offended by the manner in which the question was put. After all, I had been an infantry soldier on active service. It was, therefore, perfectly conceivable that I might have killed somebody, and if I had, it would be no laughing matter. Nor had toiling through the jungle been a laughing matter – with or without killing anyone.

Before I could reply, Andy scoffed: 'He never saw any bandits!'

'Oh well, I wouldn't say that,' I retorted, truthfully enough.

'Wouldn't you?' Andy exclaimed. 'I would!'

At this, they both doubled up, convulsed with laughter. I was growing increasingly irritated but was unsure how to respond to their remarks. However, at that moment, another Boroughmuir former pupil and star of the sports field approached us. Although he had known me at school, he did not say hello or even look at me but merely said to Ian and Andy: 'Come on, you chaps, let's get out of here!'

I watched the trio heading off towards the West End,

very conscious of my feelings of bitter disappointment. I hadn't expected to be welcomed home as a hero – I certainly wasn't that – but I had thought that I would at least have been greeted with respect for what I'd been through, and certainly not with ridicule.

Just then, from among the many voices sounding behind me, my ears picked up the phrase 'American and British intervention in Korea and Malaya'. I turned and made my way to the periphery of a fairly large audience that was grouped around a speaker from the British Communist Party. Over the heads of the crowd, I could distinguish a man of about 30, wearing a brown jacket and red tie, who now continued: 'It will be to the eternal shame of the Labour government, elected into office by the working-class people of this country, that they sent the British Army, first to oppress the people of Malaya and crush their gallant struggle for freedom, and secondly, to support the criminal actions of American imperialists in Korea . . .'

I turned away. I just couldn't listen to any more. Someone who espoused the cause of Communism preaching about freedom seemed to me to be a sick joke, as was describing an armed minority of terrorists as 'the people of Malaya'. I also knew that whatever the complexities of the situation in Korea, the war there had been started by Communist North Korea invading the South. It angered me to think that while British soldiers were fighting and dying in Korea and Malaya, there were people at home who were prepared to stab them in the back. I may have been naive, but while in Malaya it had never occurred to me that I might hear such things upon my return.

Welcome home, Jock Scurr! I thought to myself.

I began to walk back along Princes Street, wrestling with my deep feelings of resentment and bewilderment. Why worry about what other people think? I tried to reassure myself. You know that the cause in Malaya was just and you can be proud of the small part you played there. Let others sneer or disbelieve; you know what you did. That's all that matters.

Considering the possibility that I could eventually return to the army also helped to lift my spirits. I doubted if I would make a career out of the army but favoured the idea of enlisting again for at least three years while I was still young. Perhaps I could go to Korea with one of the Light Infantry regiments. I knew that provided I re-enlisted within a year of my discharge date, I wouldn't be required to repeat my basic training. This meant that I had plenty of time, in the meanwhile, to have a rest, take things easy and maybe get acquainted with an attractive young lady. Yes, indeed! There was plenty of time . . .

Although I had been aware of vague forebodings even when still serving in Malaya, I was quite oblivious to what fate had in store for me as I walked back along Princes Street on that Sunday night of 2 September 1951. My principal daydream of impressing former schoolmates had been shattered, but nonetheless I was home on my demob leave with no need to concern myself about work or any other problem for the present.

I began to think about my friends who were still with the battalion on its way home. By now, they should only be a couple of days away from British shores. The bright and bouncy tune of the KOYLI's regimental march, 'With Jockey to the Fair', started to run through my mind. Instinctively, my walking speed increased to Light Infantry pace.

22

'His Laurels are Green When His Locks are Grey'

On 30 July 1951, the 1st Battalion, King's Own Yorkshire Light Infantry, officially handed over operational command of the Malayan states of Kedah, Perlis and Province Wellesley to the 1st Battalion, Manchester Regiment. Consequently, on that date, Tactical HQ and the four rifle companies withdrew from their locations on the mainland to Minden Barracks, Penang Island.

Since September 1947, the battalion had lost 1 officer and 17 other ranks killed in action, while a further 1 officer and 16 other ranks had died from disease or in accidents. During this period, 39 enemy personnel were killed for certain by KOYLI patrols and possibly as many as 46. Although the 1st KOYLI's score of kills was considerably less than numbers achieved by some units operating in the more terrorist-active states in the south (the 1st Suffolks – 181; the 1st Cameronians – 125; the 2nd Scots Guards – 100), our battalion had nonetheless fought some pretty tough encounters and suffered comparatively heavy losses. Moreover, the battalion's operational area had been maintained under firm control, with the enemy kept on the run by constant patrolling of exceedingly difficult terrain. It had been a hard job, well done. Awards made to the officers and men of the battalion consisted of 1 OBE, 1 MBE, 1 MC, 1 DCM, 3 MMs, 3 BEMs, 27 Mentioned in Dispatches and 5 C.-in-C. Certificates.

On Friday, 3 August, a parade of 230 men, headed by the band and bugles, marched to St George's Church in

Georgetown to attend what proved to be a very moving memorial service in commemoration of the 2 officers and 33 other ranks of the battalion who had lost their lives during the campaign. (A memorial tablet would later be erected in this church.) Finally, on Tuesday, 7 August, the whole battalion marched proudly and smartly through Georgetown to the quayside. There, 20 officers and 690 other ranks boarded HMT *Dunera*. As the ship slipped its moorings at 4 p.m., three Vampire jet fighters from RAF Station, Butterworth, performed aerobatics overhead, the band of the Manchester Regiment played the KOYLI's regimental march 'With Jockey to the Fair' and 'Auld Lang Syne' and a large crowd of well-wishers on the quayside cheered and waved in a warm farewell.

HMT *Dunera* docked at Southampton at 10.20 p.m. on 4 September. The following morning, the battalion was officially welcomed home by the Colonel of the Regiment, Major General H. Redman, CB, CBE. After a well-deserved period of home leave, there were three other welcome-home functions. At the KOYLI Depot at Strensall on 31 October, the battalion was inspected by Her Majesty the Queen (now the Queen Mother) and then marched past in review order. The following day, 1 November, the battalion assembled at the Cavalry Barracks in York and marched from there to York Minster, where Second Lieutenants Crisp and Rowledge laid a Minden wreath in the regimental chapel in memory of the officers and men who had died in Malaya. The final parade was in Leeds, where on 2 November, the battalion marched, with colours flying, from the station to the Civic Hall for a luncheon as guests of the Lord Mayor. The officers and men who participated in these three parades considered them to be stirring occasions which fittingly commemorated the KOYLI's service in Malaya and honoured the battalion's dead.

On 10 November 1951, the battalion embarked for Dortmund, West Germany, to become part of the British Army of the Rhine. After more than two years of intensive training and tactical manoeuvres both in West Germany and Berlin, the battalion sailed for Kenya in 1954, where it once more undertook active service, this time against the Mau Mau terror gangs. Towards the close of 1955, the battalion moved to Aden, in which location it performed security duties, before flying to Cyprus the following year to participate in operations against EOKA terrorists. In 1958, the battalion returned to Germany, where it remained for three years. Then, in 1961, the battalion found itself once more in Malaya for a short spell prior to shipping out to confront the TNKU rebels in Brunei and Sarawak. In September 1964, the battalion returned home and was incorporated into the UK Strategic Reserve, from which it was dispatched to serve again in Aden during 1965. Finally, on 10 July 1968, the King's Own Yorkshire Light Infantry ceased to exist, upon being amalgamated with the Somerset and Cornwall Light Infantry, the King's Shropshire Light Infantry and the Durham Light Infantry to form a new regiment simply titled the Light Infantry.

Though it rarely made the headlines in the press and was forgotten by the British public at large, the guerrilla war in Malaya dragged on for many years. In February 1952, Lieutenant General Sir Gerald Templer was appointed High Commissioner of Malaya and Director of Operations. He co-ordinated and considerably invigorated the efforts of government officials and security forces and greatly boosted civilian morale. Consequently, the Communist terrorists were put increasingly on the defensive while their numbers gradually dwindled through eliminations and surrenders.

In July 1955, Malaya held its first general election, which resulted in a coalition government led by Tunku Abdul Rahman. The security situation continued to improve, and on 31 August 1957, Malaya achieved full independence from Britain, though remaining within the Commonwealth. British, Australian and New Zealand troops continued to assist the growing Malayan Army and police in hunting down the remaining Communist gangs. Finally, on 31 July 1960 – after 12 years of conflict – the Malayan 'Emergency' was officially declared to be over.

A gigantic victory parade was held in Kuala Lumpur on that last day of July 1960, but there were no celebrations in Britain, even though more than 100,000 British servicemen had contributed towards the victory and 446 had laid down their lives. There were to be no laurels for the veterans of Malaya other than the inner satisfaction that each man could feel, knowing that he had helped to hold a ruthless foe at bay until the people of Malaya had been sufficiently prepared both to defend and to govern themselves. Whatever may be the failings of Malaysian democracy, it has surely been preferable to the type of Communist dictatorship which the terrorists had intended to inflict upon the country.

After my discharge from National Service, I soon lost all contact with my former army comrades and never expected that I would hear anything of them again. Then, in the autumn of 1970, I read reports in the press of the sad death of Joe Costello – one of the most extraordinary characters ever to serve in the KOYLI. The reader may recall that Joe was a former tramp whom I had known briefly during my first weeks with 'C' Company. I had been greatly impressed by his vibrant personality and constant good humour and by his immense love and capacity for beer. Joe had left us late in 1950, upon volunteering for the Malayan Scouts (SAS). After Malaya, Joe had soldiered in Korea, Kenya, Aden and Cyprus and at the Joint Services Staff College. Though he had also served in other regiments, Joe had begun and ended his army career in the KOYLI.

A year after his discharge in 1962, with the rank of corporal (previously busted from serjeant), Joe returned to being a tramp, though one who bathed daily! He soon became a well-known personality, tramping the roads of Yorkshire. Tall, burly and proud, with long ginger hair, moustaches and beard, he always wore a donkey jacket festooned with his many medals and regimental badges and pushed a pram, also adorned with badges, containing his belongings. On his travels, he peddled bootlaces, razor blades, needles and cottons and sometimes worked as a nightwatchman. Always jovial and well-mannered, he was popular with local people and especially with children wherever he went.

Then, on 30 August 1970, at the age of 52, Joe was fatally injured in a road accident in South Milford, near Doncaster. Two hundred people attended his funeral at South Milford cemetery. Among former Army comrades present was 'Taggy' Bell, who had been a serjeant in 'C' Company in Malaya. Members of the SAS acted as pallbearers, and two buglers from the 2nd Battalion, Light Infantry, sounded the 'Last Post' at the graveside. A fitting send-off for a great old soldier.

Two years later, in the summer of 1972, another news headline caught my eye. This time, it was the presentation at Buckingham Palace of the George Cross to Major George Styles, Royal Army Ordnance Corps. I quickly recognised that this hero was none other than the Lieutenant Styles, RAOC, who had been in command of my draft to Malaya and had undergone jungle training with me prior to his posting to 'B' Company. The award of the George Cross was in recognition of Major Styles' gallant work with the bomb disposal teams in Northern Ireland, culminating in his dismantling of two huge bombs planted in a Belfast hotel in October 1971. The first bomb had involved seven hours of highly dangerous work and the second bomb, nine hours. In a later exchange of letters with Major Styles, I was pleased to find that he remembered me very well.

Otherwise, the only other ex-KOYLI that I had news of – and occasional contact with – over the years was, of course, my cousin, John Kitchen. John had eventually left the Civil Service and gone from success to success in the world of international banking, living in exotic locations such as Jamaica, Barbados, Bermuda and the Bahamas, where he currently resides with his wife Jean. We still keep in touch and our boyhood bond remains intact.

Then, early in 1990 while I was working upon this book, events took an unexpected and most welcome turn. Colonel John Cowley, Regimental Secretary and Curator of the

KOYLI Museum, was kindly supplying me with all manner of information in my quest for additional material and testimonies to supplement the happenings recorded in my journal. One day, he told me that two former members of the KOYLI, Tom Morgan (ex-'A' Company) and Jim Preston (ex-HQ, 'A', 'C' and 'D' Companies) were organising a first-ever KOYLI Malaya Veterans Reunion and had placed adverts to that effect in Yorkshire and Durham local newspapers. I was immensely interested and promptly contacted the two organisers.

Consequently, early in the morning of Saturday, 21 April 1990, I found myself in a car travelling north from London with two former members of 'A' Company – Corporal Tom Morgan and Private Eric Barrett, and a former lance corporal of 'C' Company, Dick Bodimeade. Dick had returned to Blighty before I joined 'C' Company and I had never previously met Tom or Eric either. During the days leading up to the reunion date, I'd been having anxious second thoughts as to the wisdom of trying to recapture something from 40 years ago by meeting up with a group of elderly men, most – perhaps all – of whom would be total strangers to me. However, once I was settled into the back seat of that car, my anxieties were swiftly dispelled. Strange as it may seem, the feeling that I was once more amongst 'family' was quite overwhelming. As Tom Morgan put it: 'Once a KOYLI, always a KOYLI!' I was back!

We arrived in Wakefield soon after 11 a.m. and shortly proceeded to the reunion, which was held in the serjeants' mess of a local TA centre. Drinking beer with the first arrivals – none of whom I knew – I remained very content as I listened to the chat about Ipoh, Klian Intan, Penang, the Broadway Café, the City Lights . . . It was great! Then, a small coachload arrived from Durham and to my joy I found myself shaking hands with Bill Aisbit and Arnie Bowron, both of whom had trained with me in Bordon and been drafted to Malaya with me. After 40 years! I could hardly believe it! Next, I was greeted by Derrick Ross, whom I remembered from 9 Platoon, 'C' Company. He expressed great delight at meeting me again and we settled down to a good chinwag over old times and current fortunes. Derrick informed me that Ginger Thompson was still going strong in Bishop Auckland but wasn't able to attend due to his wife's ill health.

Very poignant was the moment, early in the afternoon, when I was happily confronted with the man called 'Harper' in Chapter 11 of this book – the soldier who had deserted from his company with the PRI funds and whom I had escorted as a prisoner from Taiping to Penang on 5 August 1950. Still retaining a slightly roguish twinkle in his eye, he proved to be a very amicable and interesting companion.

Although no one who had been a close friend of mine was among the 45 or so men who attended the reunion, I considered all present to be old comrades and was very content that I'd made the trip. This is really magic! was the thought that came into my mind and expressed it all. As I consumed several pints of beer, chatting to those I knew and to others to whom I was introduced – Allan Trotter, the butcher from HQ Company – Jim Siddle and Jim Million of 'C' Company – Bill Carrick of 'B' Company – and periodically noting down information for my book, I suddenly felt that the 40 years since 1949–51 had been miraculously bridged. All the various disappointments and misfortunes of the years between somehow had become insignificant. I had reached back to the period of my life that really mattered to me and found that it was still there; and I knew, then, that it would always be there. The KOYLI in Malaya had happened and I had been a part of it. Nothing could ever change that.

From conversations during that memorable weekend and from subsequent correspondence, I obtained news of some of the people that I had served with in Malaya – sad news. Major F.A.S. Murray, MC – 'C' Company Commander ('the Mad Major') – had died in 1965 at the age of 46. An obituary stated: 'Tony had his wayward moments but he was a charming and cultured person. He was extremely interested in music and played the piano very well. A gallant soldier in war, we regret his early death.' Second Lieutenant David C. Wride, who had commanded 9 Platoon, had retired from the army in 1972, with the rank of major, and died in 1982, aged 53. Also dead, I learned, were Signals Serjeant Stan Haley and Corporal Bill ('Dickie') Downs, also of the Signal Platoon.

On the other hand, I was glad to be informed by Colonel John Cowley that Second Lieutenant John Crisp, 8 Platoon Commander, was living in retirement in Dorset. After serving in Germany, Cyprus and Aden, Mr Crisp had retired as a major in 1976. I promptly wrote to him and received a friendly reply. Jim Preston – one of the organisers of the reunion and a mine of information – supplied me with the address of my old friend Signals Corporal Arthur Greenacre, currently living near Melbourne, in Australia. Exchanging letters with Arthur after 40 years was a rare pleasure and seemed to me to be a veritable miracle. I was happy to learn that Arthur had become engaged to his girlfriend, Dilys, upon his return from Malaya and had married her just over a year later, receiving a wedding present – a cookery book – from Major Murray! Arthur had left the army in 1953, and he and his wife had emigrated to Australia in 1960 and have prospered there ever since. Jim also gave me the address of Corporal Frank Keenan, 8 Platoon, who had been demobbed in 1966 and had set up home with his wife, Thelma, in Ontario, Canada. Frank seemed very pleased to hear from me, as I was to hear from him.

On 27 April 1991, we held the second Malaya Veterans Reunion, with the venue in Doncaster. It was also a great success with a slightly larger attendance than the previous year. Hopefully, even more old comrades may show up on future such occasions.

Finally, on 23 August 1991 I travelled to Manchester to meet Arthur and Dilys Greenacre, who were on a short home visit from Australia. Also in the company of former members of the battalion Jim Preston and Roy Caldecott (ex-'A' Company), we had a most memorable celebration in a splendid hotel, which fittingly commemorated our return from Malaya and all that had gone before. Dilys was a lovely person and Arthur, I was pleased to find, was very much as I remembered him. It was truly wonderful!

So, that's my story – or at least the story of 'my life as a soldier'. It did not turn out as I had originally planned, of course. Life seldom does, and fate likes to play merry little tricks with us all. However, it seems to me that in our often unrewarding, industrialised world, if we can spend even a short period doing something that really matters to us, perhaps we are especially fortunate.

As I look back now over the 40 years since my discharge from the army, despite many trying times, I am grateful for my happy marriage to my wife Anne, and for some good friends and various worthwhile experiences. But I have to confess that none of the several civilian jobs that I have muddled through has meant anything to me other than a means of obtaining sufficient funds with which to pay the bills.

Yet I am both content and proud that for two years I was a soldier in a great British regiment – the King's Own Yorkshire Light Infantry – and that I played my part in a tough jungle campaign which was eventually victorious, both in vanquishing the Communist enemy and in bringing independence, with freedom, to the people of the beautiful land of Malaya.

Perhaps I can even say that to some extent and within a limited duration, my boyhood dream did come true, after all.

POSTSCRIPT TO
SECOND EDITION

In the years that have passed since I completed the first edition of this book, the KOYLI Malaya Veterans Association has steadily grown to a membership of more than 400. Consequently I have happily been enabled to renew acquaintance with numerous former members of the Signal Platoon and 'C' Company. Annual reunions and correspondence regarding my book have also produced many pleasing contacts with men who had served in other companies of the KOYLI and with sisters and widows of men who were killed in Malaya or who have unfortunately died since.

Perhaps my biggest surprise was in February 1997 when I received a letter from Mrs E.L. Johns of Helston, Cornwall, seeking a copy of the book. She turned out to be none other than Enid, who the reader may recall was the sweetheart who was constantly on the mind of my friend in 8 Platoon, 'Matt' Busby. I was delighted to hear from her but appalled by the news that she gave me.

When Matt (Don to Enid) returned from Malaya, they began building their own home in Helston – a three bed-roomed house which they called Kerana Kita, meaning 'For Two' in Malay; later renamed Kerana Tiga – 'For Three'. Enid and Matt were married in December 1953 but three months later, in March 1954, Matt was diagnosed as suffering from multiple sclerosis. His eyesight then rapidly deteriorated until he was certified blind. In March 1955, Enid gave birth to a son, Clive, who lived only nine days. Shortly after this shock, Matt was confined to a wheelchair but in

August 1958, the couple were nonetheless blessed with a second son, Graham. Matt's condition continued to deteriorate. For ten years he was unable to move any part of his body and he finally died in May 1967.

This must surely have been the saddest fate that has befallen any KOYLI Malaya veteran. Yet despite everything, so strong was the bond of love between them that Enid and Matt were grateful for every day they had together.

Malaya veterans of other regiments and corps had also managed to obtain copies of the limited first edition and wrote me some very appreciative and greatly appreciated letters. One correspondent, Michael Poole, had been a medical orderly in 7 Platoon, 'C' Company of the 1st Battalion, Somerset Light Infantry. He told me that his platoon commander had been determined that 7 Platoon would make the Somersets' first kill. This aim was achieved early in 1953, at Sungei Manggis in Selangor, when the platoon effected a night ambush in which two terrorists were killed. Much to his regret, Michael was in a position some distance from the point of action and could only listen to the heavy firing and watch the tracer bullets flying at the platoon commander's position. Some time later, while Michael happened to be on leave in Penang, 7 Platoon killed another two of the enemy. On reading this letter, I derived some perverse comfort in knowing that someone had been even more unlucky than I was!

The Somerset Light Infantry served in Malaya from November 1952 to October 1955 and very commendably eliminated a total of 61 CTs (Communist terrorists), as the 'bandits' were more aptly renamed at that time. Several former soldiers of the KOYLI undertook a second Malayan tour with the Somersets, including Arnie Bowron, Dave Sinclair and Eric Barrett, all of whom had served in 'A' Company. Also ex-KOYLI were Serjeant Jock McClung (Signals) and Serjeant Raymond Beaumont, who was posted to 'C' Company of the Somersets and killed in action when a patrol of 8 Platoon was ambushed in the South

Selangor swamps in February 1953. Serjeant Beaumont had been universally recognised as a first-class jungle soldier.

In this book I have endeavoured to portray the hard toil and regular frustration of hunting a deadly enemy in a needle-and-haystack situation with occasional, brief actions resulting in small numbers of casualties on either side. This was the general Malayan experience of the average soldier, but there were nonetheless many hard-fought encounters in this jungle war. And a 'war' it certainly was. By 1950 it was quite clear that the armed insurrection was no temporary emergency situation and that the uniformed, guerrilla army in the jungle would not be easily defeated, yet the conflict in Malaya continued to be officially described as only an 'emergency' throughout the 12 long years. The British government was apparently anxious not to provoke the new Communist regime in China by acknowledging that it was at war with 'overseas Chinese' Communists. Following his appointment as Director of Operations in March 1950, Lieutenant General Sir Harold Briggs was firmly instructed that there was to be no mention of fighting a war, only of suppressing disorder and banditry. It has also been suggested that another deciding factor in refusing to admit a state of war was to ensure that the Malayan rubber and tin industries – upon which the country's economy was dependent – would not forfeit their insurance cover for damage and loss sustained through 'riot and civil commotion'. Consequently, as it was decreed that they had not been at war, Malaya veterans only received a bar to the General Service Medal and were not awarded a campaign medal like their comrades-in-arms who fought Communist forces in Korea; nor will you find 'Malaya' emblazoned on the colours of any British regiment. Kipling's splendid poem 'Tommy' implied that Tommy Atkins is only appreciated 'when the guns begin to shoot'. Regrettably, he sometimes does not receive just recognition even then.

It would seem fitting, therefore, to end this fiftieth anniversary edition of my book about the KOYLI in Malaya by describing just a few of the outstanding actions fought by other British regiments in the Malayan campaign.

31 December 1948. Two officers and sixteen men of 4 Troop, 'A' Squadron, 4th Hussars were patrolling in two GMC personnel carriers and a 15-hundredweight truck on the Jalong road, near Sungei Siput in Perak, when they were ambushed by 70 bandits in well prepared positions on high ground overlooking a bend in the road. The truck was immediately immobilised and the men on board killed or wounded, so the other Hussars dismounted from their carriers and deployed along the road. Under fire from at least five Bren guns and with grenades exploding amongst them, the Hussars returned a determined fire. After ten minutes had passed, the troop leader, Lieutenant Questier, and six troopers were dead and all but three of the others were wounded. Nineteen-year-old Second Lieutenant Sutro, himself twice wounded, managed to get everyone back in the two carriers, with the wounded and even the dead also carried on board.

The two vehicles, one of which had flat tyres, were now driven slowly out of the ambush zone under a continuous heavy fusillade until they reached some estate buildings on a rubber plantation. Here, Second Lieutenant Sutro organised his men in defence positions. Then, with Trooper Goodier volunteering to drive, he climbed into the most serviceable of the two carriers and hastened back through the ambush zone to summon reinforcements from Sungei Siput. The relief force subsequently discovered the bodies of six of the enemy in the abandoned ambush positions.

Second Lieutenant Sutro was awarded the Military Cross and Trooper Smith, who during the ambush had crept around the terrorists' flank to open fire upon them, though himself wounded four times in the process, received the Distinguished Conduct Medal.

*

12 November 1949. A composite reconnaissance platoon of 'B' Company, 1st Battalion, Seaforth Highlanders located an enemy camp in overgrown rubber in the Segamat district of Johore and shortly found themselves in a fierce exchange of fire with 150 to 200 bandits positioned among the *bashas*. Lieutenant Hoare, MC, and Lieutenant Anderson, who had moved forward on the left flank, were both killed close together. Also killed was Lance Corporal Mackay, while Private Clarke had been wounded. After repulsing an enemy counter-attack, the badly wounded Company Commander, Major Campbell, ordered Lieutenant Brown to leave him there and withdraw the platoon to a less exposed position 50 yards to the rear. Lieutenant Brown reluctantly obeyed and Major Campbell was then killed by another burst of enemy fire.

In its new position, the platoon remained under determined attack until reinforced from the company's base camp. On once more advancing into the bandit camp as the enemy retreated, the Seaforths located the bodies of six dead bandits, to which total could be added another who had been shot dead near 'B' Company's base. Lieutenant Brown received a consequent award of the Military Cross.

22 June 1951. After a routine three-day patrol, 11 Platoon, 'D' Company, 1st Battalion, Royal West Kent Regiment was returning in motor transport through the Ulu Caledonian rubber estate, near Ulu Yam in Selangor. A sudden heavy outburst of firing from the right of the estate road instantly killed the Company Commander, Captain Deedes, and three soldiers in the leading 3-ton truck. Six men who leapt out of a 15-hundredweight truck to the rear were all killed by grenades, and as the men in the first truck scrambled out, the Platoon Commander, Second Lieutenant Gregson, was wounded twice and the Acting Platoon Sergeant, Corporal Sulley, was killed.

The survivors managed to take cover behind the left bank

of the road. Lance Corporal Martin directed his four remaining men into firing positions, and he and Private Pannell repulsed enemy attacks upon them with hand-grenades. Soon, all of the men had been hit, Pannell four times, but despite this, he killed a charging bandit with a burst from his Sten. At this point, a very brave planter and four policemen raced up the estate road in a car to reinforce the hard-pressed troops, and the terrorists were now forced to retreat into some adjacent jungle, carrying several wounded but leaving six dead behind.

The West Kents' casualties in this dreadful ambush had been one officer, ten other ranks and three Iban trackers killed, and one officer, eleven other ranks and one civil liaison officer wounded. Lance Corporal Martin was awarded the Military Medal and Private Pannell the Distinguished Conduct Medal.

6 July 1952. In South Selangor, the 1st Battalion, Suffolk Regiment had received information that the notorious Lliew Kon Kim and No.3 Platoon of the MRLA's 4th Independent Company – known as the 'Kajang gang' – were located in a camp in the Kuala Langat south swamp. After the Suffolks and two companies of the Royal West Kents had spent three days wading through the vast swamp region, 'B' Company, commanded by Major Dewar, was advancing through an indicated area in nine parallel patrols.

At 2 p.m., Second Lieutenant Hands and his two scouts, Privates Baker and Wynant – all National Servicemen – opened fire upon a fleeing terrorist, whom they then pursued along a log into a camp on a small island in the swamp. Spotting three bandits escaping, Second Lieutenant Hands killed one with a burst from his M1 carbine. He then dashed into the thigh-deep swamp after the other two, put another fatal burst into a woman armed with a shotgun, hurried on for another 150 yards, guided by the splashing sounds ahead, and shot down the third terrorist, who turned out to be the bearded Lliew Kon Kim.

Second Lieutenant Hands was subsequently awarded the Military Cross.

12 December 1955. A surrendered CT (Communist terrorist) had agreed to lead a composite company, consisting of 4 and 6 Platoons, 'B' Company and 10 Platoon, 'D' Company, 1st Battalion, Royal Hampshire Regiment to a camp within the jungle fringes, near the village of Ulu Langat, Selangor, where some high-ranking Communists were attending a course of political instruction. After much confusion as to direction on the previous day, the SEP (surrendered enemy personnel) finally guided Major Symes, MC, and a reconnaissance group to within sight of the camp by 9 a.m.

In heavy rain to begin with, the Hampshires cautiously surrounded the camp during a period of four hours. The camp stood on a steep spur between two streams. At 1.20 p.m., Major Symes led the assault group of Company HQ and half of 10 Platoon in from a slope to the north-west of the camp. After opening fire, they crossed the stream and scrambled up through the undergrowth towards the *bashas* on the crest. The occupants of the camp, after discharging just one shotgun blast, made a shambolic run for it. Eight fled southwards into the close-range firing of the Brens, automatic shotguns and FN rifles of the men of 6 Platoon, which killed at least three CTs and drove the rest of them across the stream to the east, where they were shot down in like manner by the men of 4 Platoon.

After sporadic shooting for 20 minutes, the encircling cordon of Hampshires closed in to find they had killed a total of 11 of the enemy, including the Selangor State Committee Secretary, Chan Lo, and a District Committee Member called Wahab. A female terrorist, wounded in the thigh, was taken prisoner. This was the highest total of Communist terrorists eliminated in one action by a British battalion.

*

Coming a close second to the Hampshires was the 2nd Battalion, Scots Guards, whose Right Flank Company killed 10 bandits during a well co-ordinated attack upon an enemy camp in the Slim area of Perak on Easter Monday, 1951. Laurels for the highest number killed in one action by any unit during the whole campaign go to the 1st Battalion, 2nd Gurkha Rifles. Following a running battle in the Segamat area of Johore on 22 January 1950, 22 enemy bodies were counted by 'B' Company, but the final death toll was later learned to be 35. This was achieved with only one Gurkha fatality. Runner-up would appear to be the 3rd Battalion, Malay Regiment. When a platoon of 'D' Company was ambushed on the bank of the Semur River in Kelantan on 25 March 1950, 15 Malay soldiers were killed and 3 more who were gravely wounded died later. But subsequent examination of graves at the scene indicated that at least 29 bandits had been killed in the action.

The freedom of Malaya was bought at a high price. As this book makes clear, those of us who served in the campaign had a fair amount of fun, enjoyed unforgettable comradeship and sometimes experienced moments of rare beauty. But we also endured a lot and no doubt some of us are suffering the consequences to this day. We like to reminisce about the good times, but we should not lose sight of the fact that it was the hard and unpleasant times that measured our worth as soldiers.

While we remember with deepest respect the 2,164 members of the security forces who laid down their lives for Malaya, of whom no fewer than 1,347 were personnel of the Federation of Malaya Police Force, we should not forget the 2,473 civilians who also died, mostly resulting from enemy actions but sometimes due to our own. And although we can never forget or forgive the death, destruction and human misery that the Malayan Races Liberation Army inflicted upon the people of Malaya (including the seemingly harsh but necessary government policies of resettlement, detention, deportation and food control which had to be adopted), I would like to think that – 50 years on – we can express the hope that the 6,707 Communist insurgents who died for a misguided cause may also rest in peace.